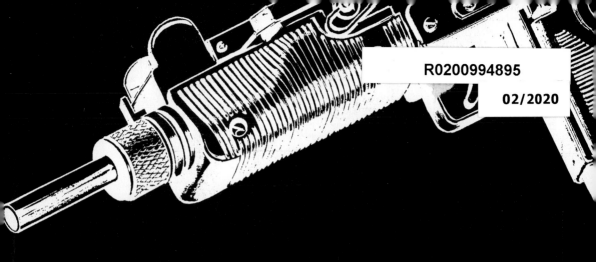

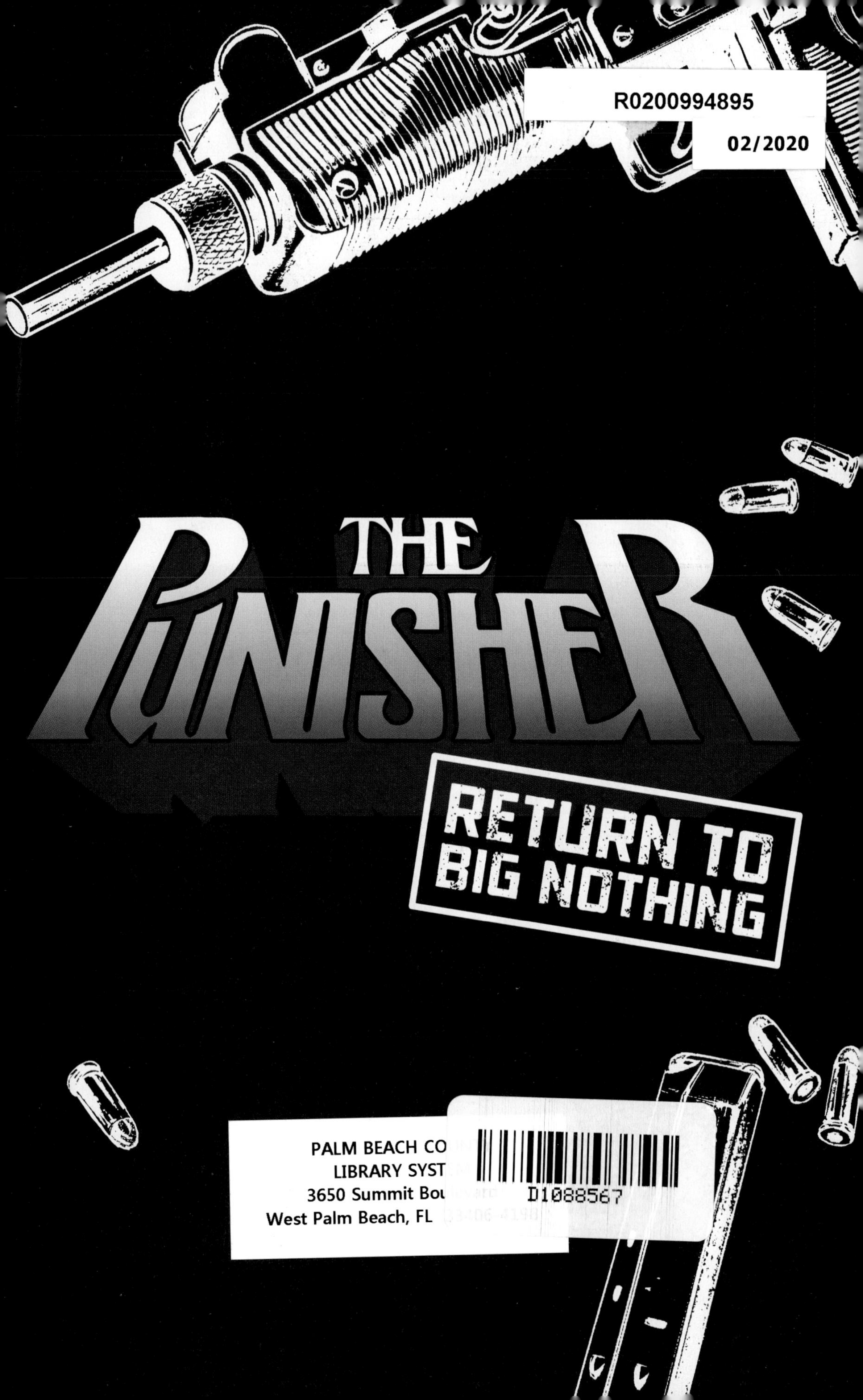

THE PUNISHER

RETURN TO BIG NOTHING

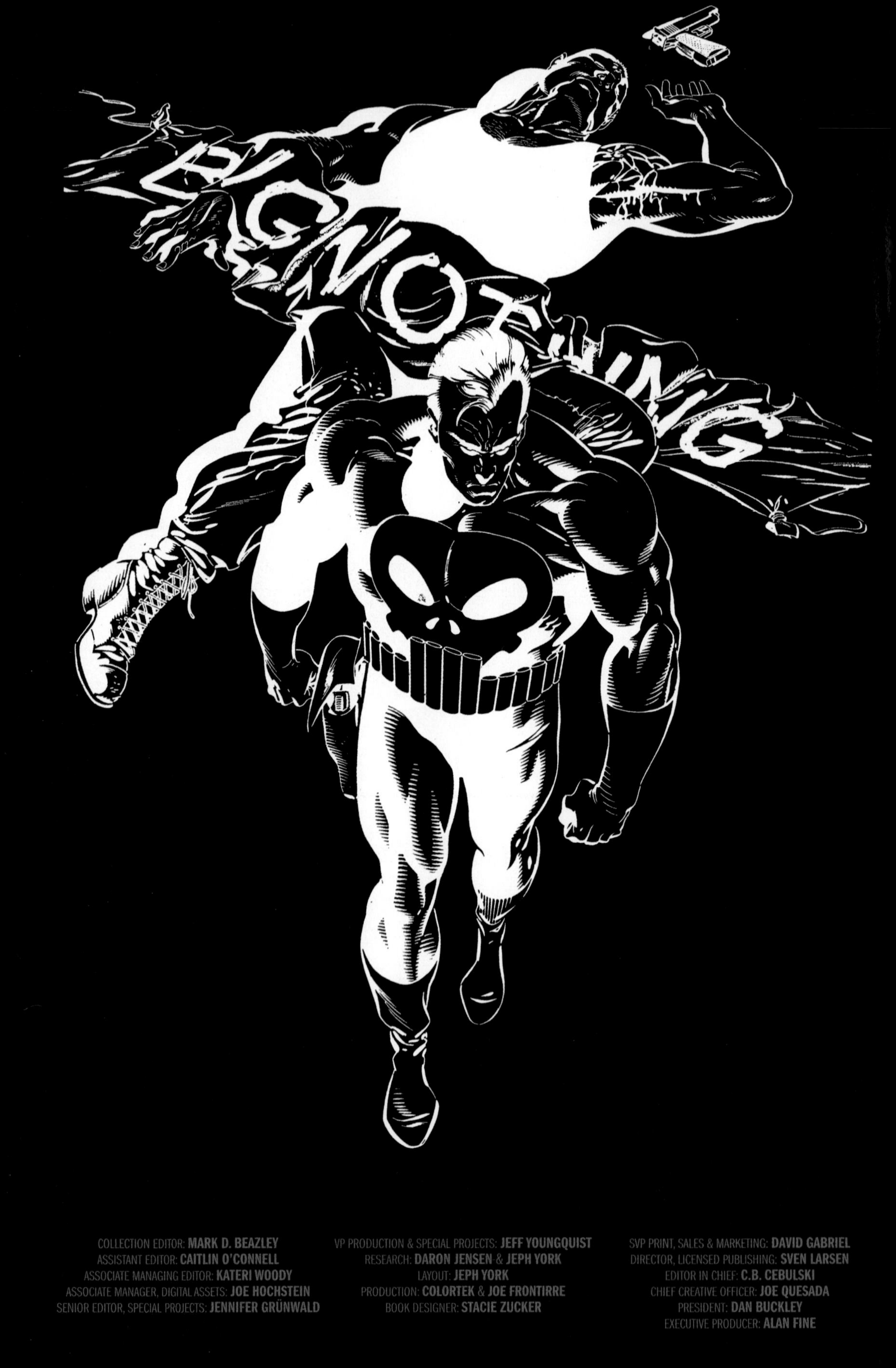

COLLECTION EDITOR: **MARK D. BEAZLEY**
ASSISTANT EDITOR: **CAITLIN O'CONNELL**
ASSOCIATE MANAGING EDITOR: **KATERI WOODY**
ASSOCIATE MANAGER, DIGITAL ASSETS: **JOE HOCHSTEIN**
SENIOR EDITOR, SPECIAL PROJECTS: **JENNIFER GRÜNWALD**

VP PRODUCTION & SPECIAL PROJECTS: **JEFF YOUNGQUIST**
RESEARCH: **DARON JENSEN & JEPH YORK**
LAYOUT: **JEPH YORK**
PRODUCTION: **COLORTEK & JOE FRONTIRRE**
BOOK DESIGNER: **STACIE ZUCKER**

SVP PRINT, SALES & MARKETING: **DAVID GABRIEL**
DIRECTOR, LICENSED PUBLISHING: **SVEN LARSEN**
EDITOR IN CHIEF: **C.B. CEBULSKI**
CHIEF CREATIVE OFFICER: **JOE QUESADA**
PRESIDENT: **DAN BUCKLEY**
EXECUTIVE PRODUCER: **ALAN FINE**

PUNISHER: RETURN TO BIG NOTHING

STEVEN GRANT
WRITER

MIKE ZECK
PENCILER

JOHN BEATTY
INKER

MIKE ZECK, IAN TETRAULT & PHIL ZIMELMAN
COLORISTS

KEN BRUZENAK
LETTERER

PUNISHER: ASSASSIN'S GUILD

JO DUFFY
WRITER

JORGE ZAFFINO
ARTIST

JULIE MICHEL
COLORIST

JIM NOVAK
LETTERER

PUNISHER: INTRUDER

MIKE BARON
WRITER

BILL REINHOLD
ARTIST

LINDA LESSMANN
COLORIST

WILLIE SCHUBERT
LETTERER

CARL POTTS
CONSULTING EDITOR

MARC McLAURIN
ASSISTANT EDITOR

MARGARET CLARK & CARL POTTS
EDITORS

MIKE ZECK & PHIL ZIMELMAN
FRONT COVER ARTISTS

BILL REINHOLD
BACK COVER ARTIST

PUNISHER: RETURN TO BIG NOTHING. Contains material originally published in magazine form as PUNISHER: RETURN TO BIG NOTHING, PUNISHER: ASSASSIN'S GUILD and PUNISHER: INTRUDER. First printing 2019. ISBN 978-1-302-91896-5. Published by MARVEL WORLDWIDE, INC., a subsidiary of MARVEL ENTERTAINMENT, LLC. OFFICE OF PUBLICATION: 135 West 50th Street, New York, NY 10020. © 2019 MARVEL. No similarity between any of the names, characters, persons, and/or institutions in this magazine with those of any living or dead person or institution is intended, and any such similarity which may exist is purely coincidental. **Printed in the U.S.A.** DAN BUCKLEY, President, Marvel Entertainment; JOHN NEE, Publisher; JOE QUESADA, Chief Creative Officer; TOM BREVOORT, SVP of Publishing; DAVID BOGART, Associate Publisher & SVP of Talent Affairs; DAVID GABRIEL, SVP of Sales & Marketing, Publishing; JEFF YOUNGQUIST, VP of Production & Special Projects; DAN CARR, Executive Director of Publishing Technology; ALEX MORALES, Director of Publishing Operations; DAN EDINGTON, Managing Editor; SUSAN CRESPI, Production Manager; STAN LEE, Chairman Emeritus. For information regarding advertising in Marvel Comics or on Marvel.com, please contact Vit DeBellis, Custom Solutions & Integrated Advertising Manager, at vdebellis@marvel.com. For Marvel subscription inquiries, please call 888-511-5480. **Manufactured between 5/31/2019 and 7/2/2019 by LSC COMMUNICATIONS INC., KENDALLVILLE, IN, USA.**

10 9 8 7 6 5 4 3 2 1

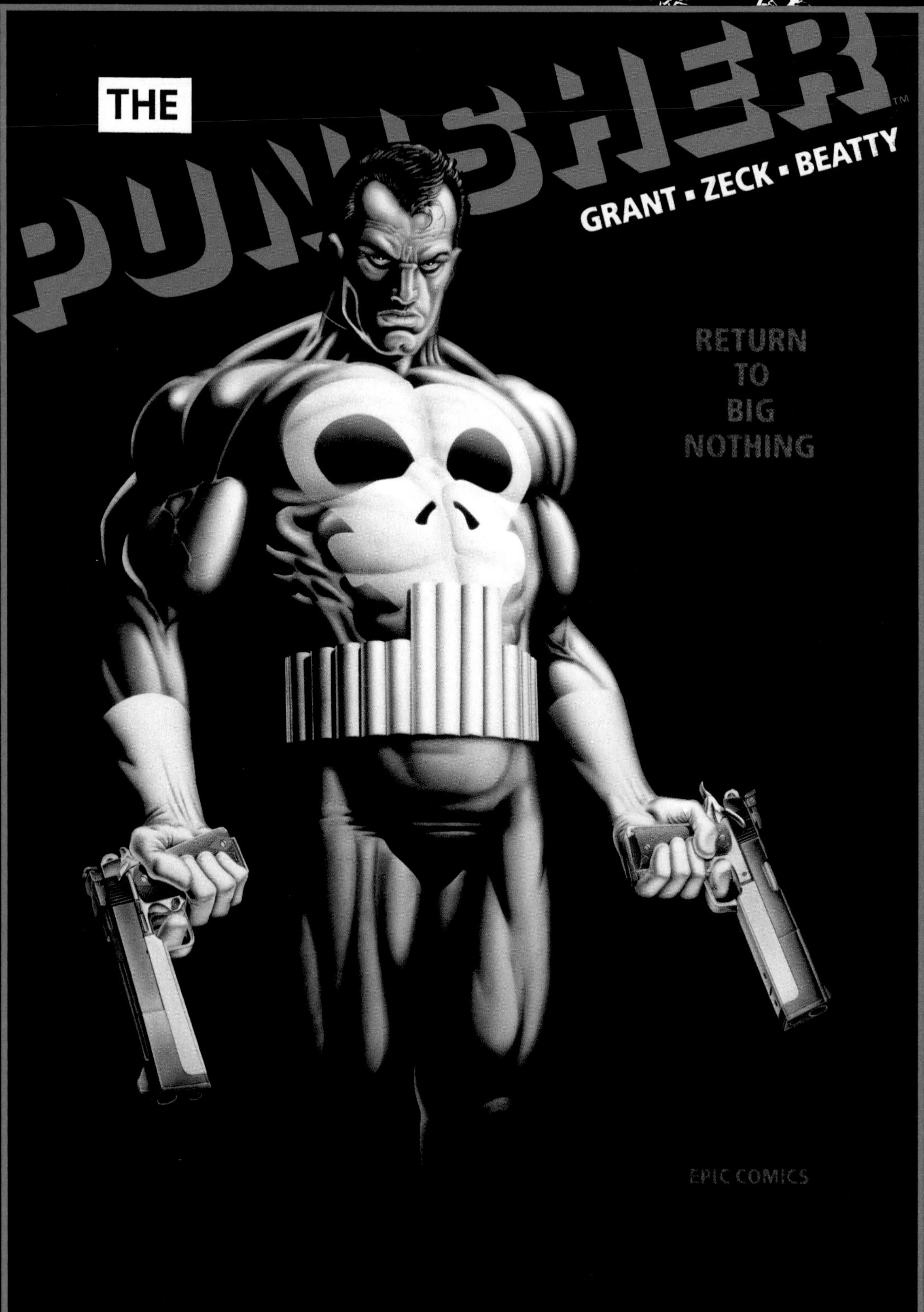
THE
PUNISHER
TM
GRANT · ZECK · BEATTY
RETURN
TO
BIG
NOTHING
EPIC COMICS

THE

PUNISHER

RETURN TO BIG NOTHING

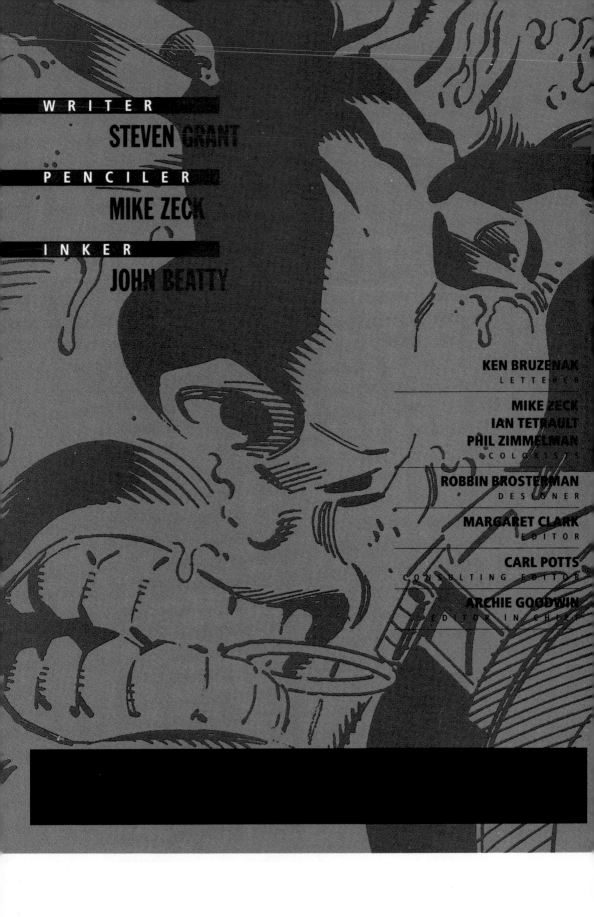

WRITER
STEVEN GRANT

PENCILER
MIKE ZECK

INKER
JOHN BEATTY

KEN BRUZENAK
LETTERER

MIKE ZECK
IAN TETRAULT
PHIL ZIMMELMAN
COLORISTS

ROBBIN BROSTERMAN
DESIGNER

MARGARET CLARK
EDITOR

CARL POTTS
CONSULTING EDITOR

ARCHIE GOODWIN
EDITOR IN CHIEF

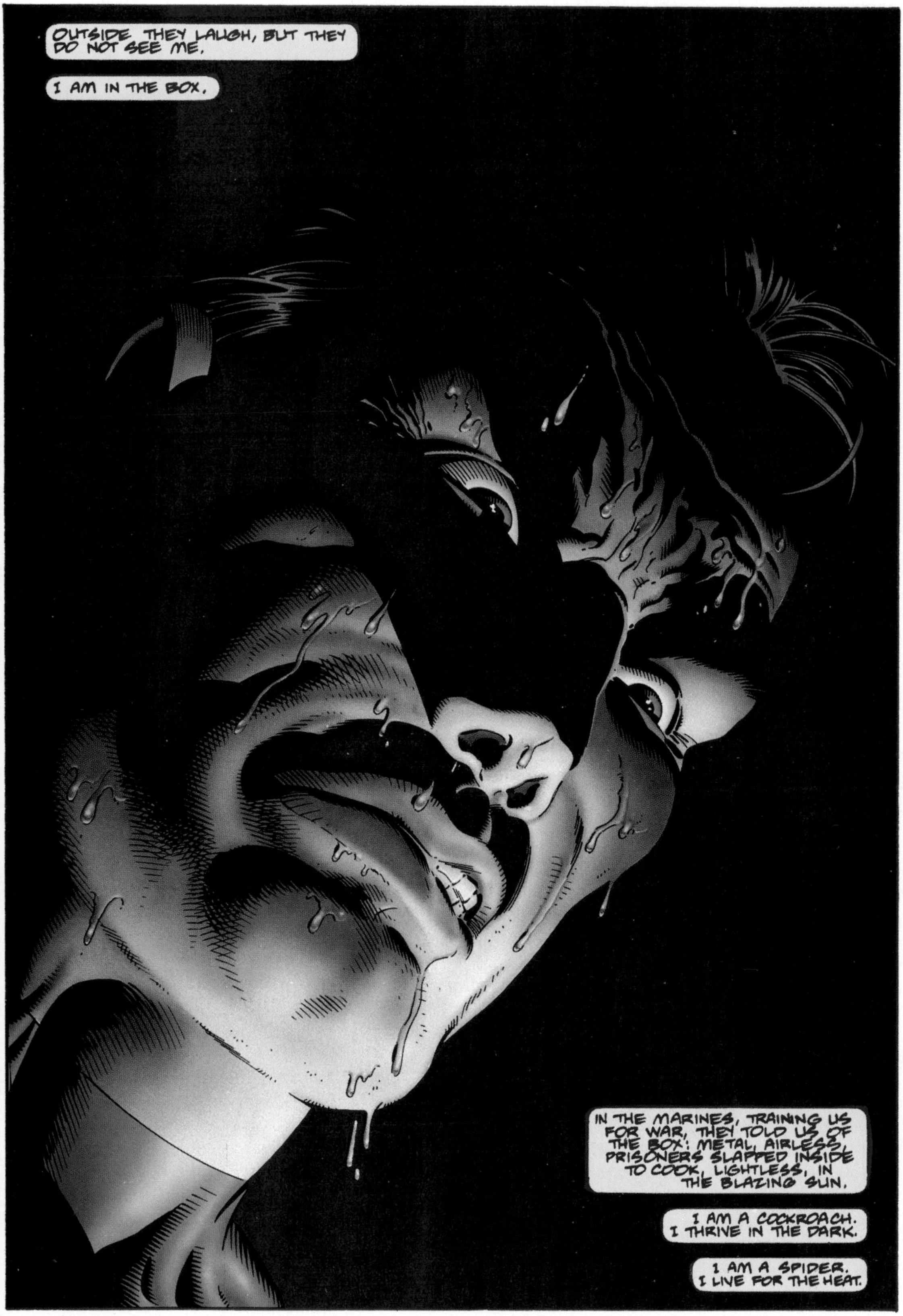
OUTSIDE THEY LAUGH, BUT THEY DO NOT SEE ME.
I AM IN THE BOX.
IN THE MARINES, TRAINING US FOR WAR, THEY TOLD US OF THE BOX: METAL, AIRLESS, PRISONERS SLAPPED INSIDE TO COOK, LIGHTLESS, IN THE BLAZING SUN.
I AM A COCKROACH. I THRIVE IN THE DARK.
I AM A SPIDER. I LIVE FOR THE HEAT.

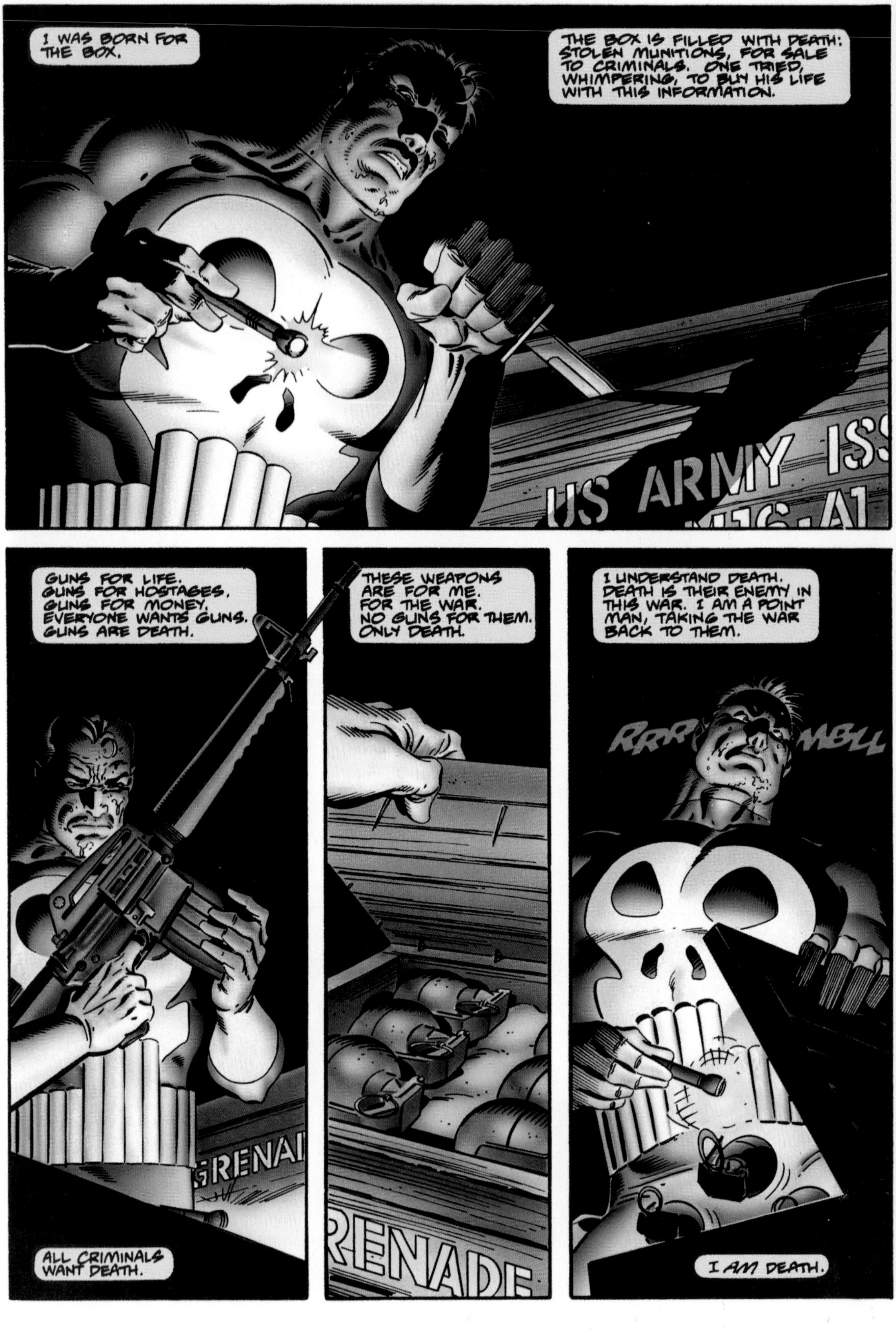
I WAS BORN FOR THE BOX.
THE BOX IS FILLED WITH DEATH: STOLEN MUNITIONS, FOR SALE TO CRIMINALS. ONE TRIED, WHIMPERING, TO BUY HIS LIFE WITH THIS INFORMATION.
US ARMY ISS
GUNS FOR LIFE. GUNS FOR HOSTAGES. GUNS FOR MONEY. EVERYONE WANTS GUNS. GUNS ARE DEATH.
GRENAI
ALL CRIMINALS WANT DEATH.
THESE WEAPONS ARE FOR ME. FOR THE WAR. NO GUNS FOR THEM. ONLY DEATH.
RENADE
I UNDERSTAND DEATH. DEATH IS THEIR ENEMY IN THIS WAR. I AM A POINT MAN, TAKING THE WAR BACK TO THEM.
RRRUMBLL
I AM DEATH.

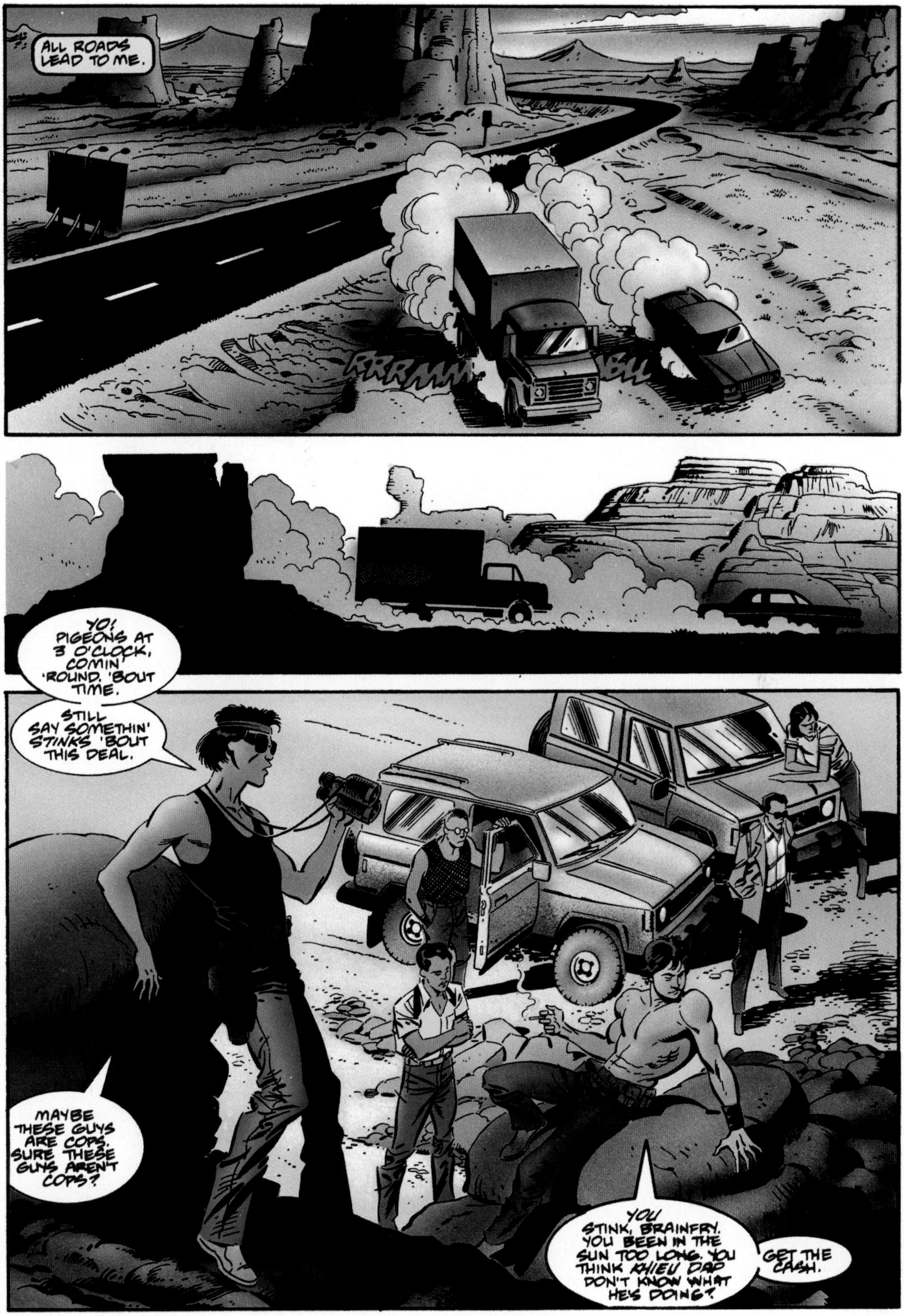
ALL ROADS LEAD TO ME.
RRRMMM
BU
YO! PIGEONS AT 3 O'CLOCK, COMIN' 'ROUND. 'BOUT TIME.
STILL SAY SOMETHIN' STINKS 'BOUT THIS DEAL.
MAYBE THESE GUYS ARE COPS. SURE THESE GUYS AREN'T COPS?
YOU STINK, BRAINFRY. YOU BEEN IN THE SUN TOO LONG. YOU THINK KHIEU DAP DON'T KNOW WHAT HE'S DOING?
GET THE CASH.

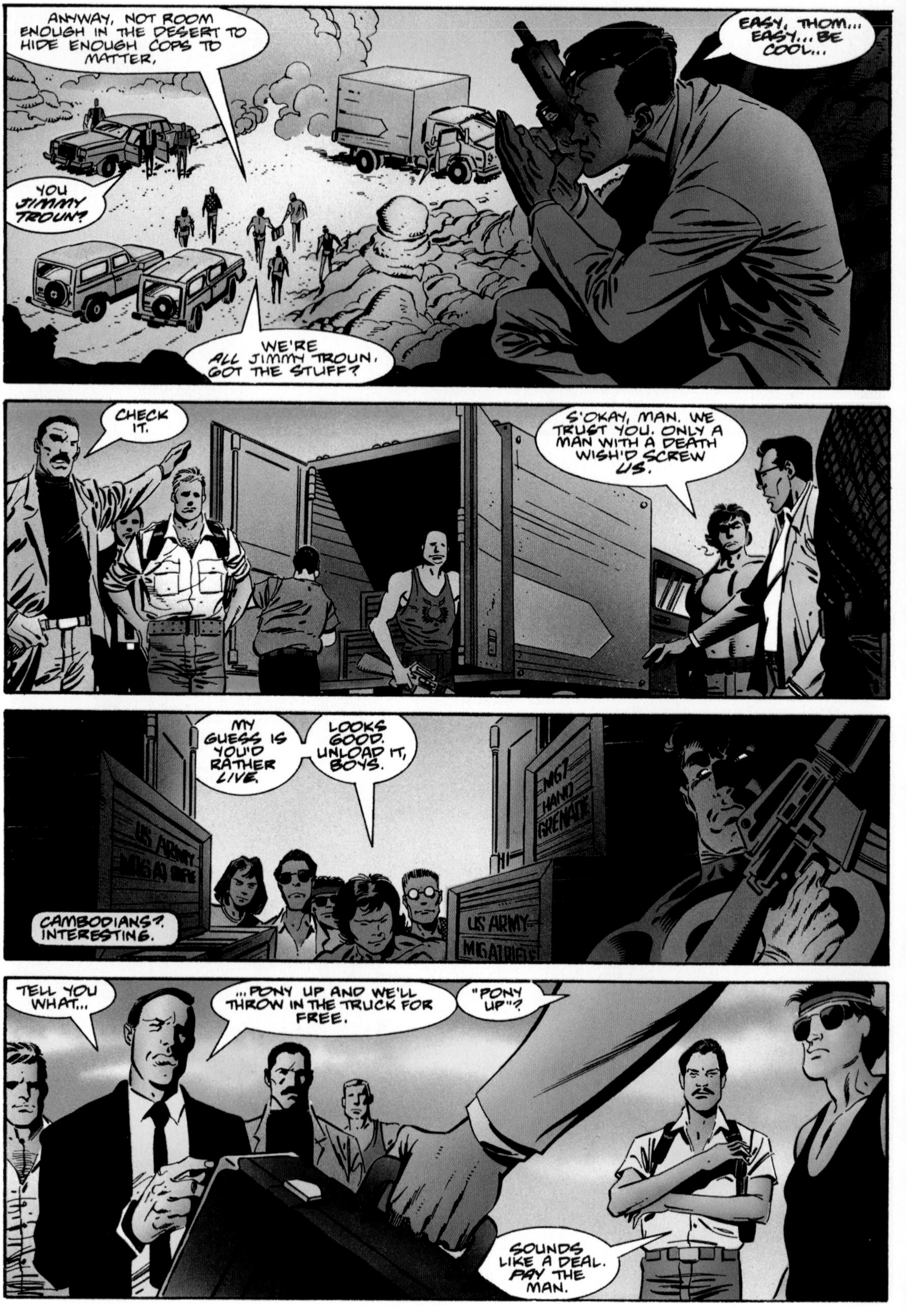
ANYWAY, NOT ROOM ENOUGH IN THE DESERT TO HIDE ENOUGH COPS TO MATTER.
EASY, THOM... EASY... BE COOL...
YOU JIMMY TROUN?
WE'RE ALL JIMMY TROUN. GOT THE STUFF?
CHECK IT.
S'OKAY, MAN. WE TRUST YOU. ONLY A MAN WITH A DEATH WISH'D SCREW US.
MY GUESS IS YOU'D RATHER LIVE.
LOOKS GOOD. UNLOAD IT, BOYS.
US ARMY
CAMBODIANS? INTERESTING.
US ARMY
TELL YOU WHAT...
...PONY UP AND WE'LL THROW IN THE TRUCK FOR FREE.
"PONY UP"?
SOUNDS LIKE A DEAL. PAY THE MAN.

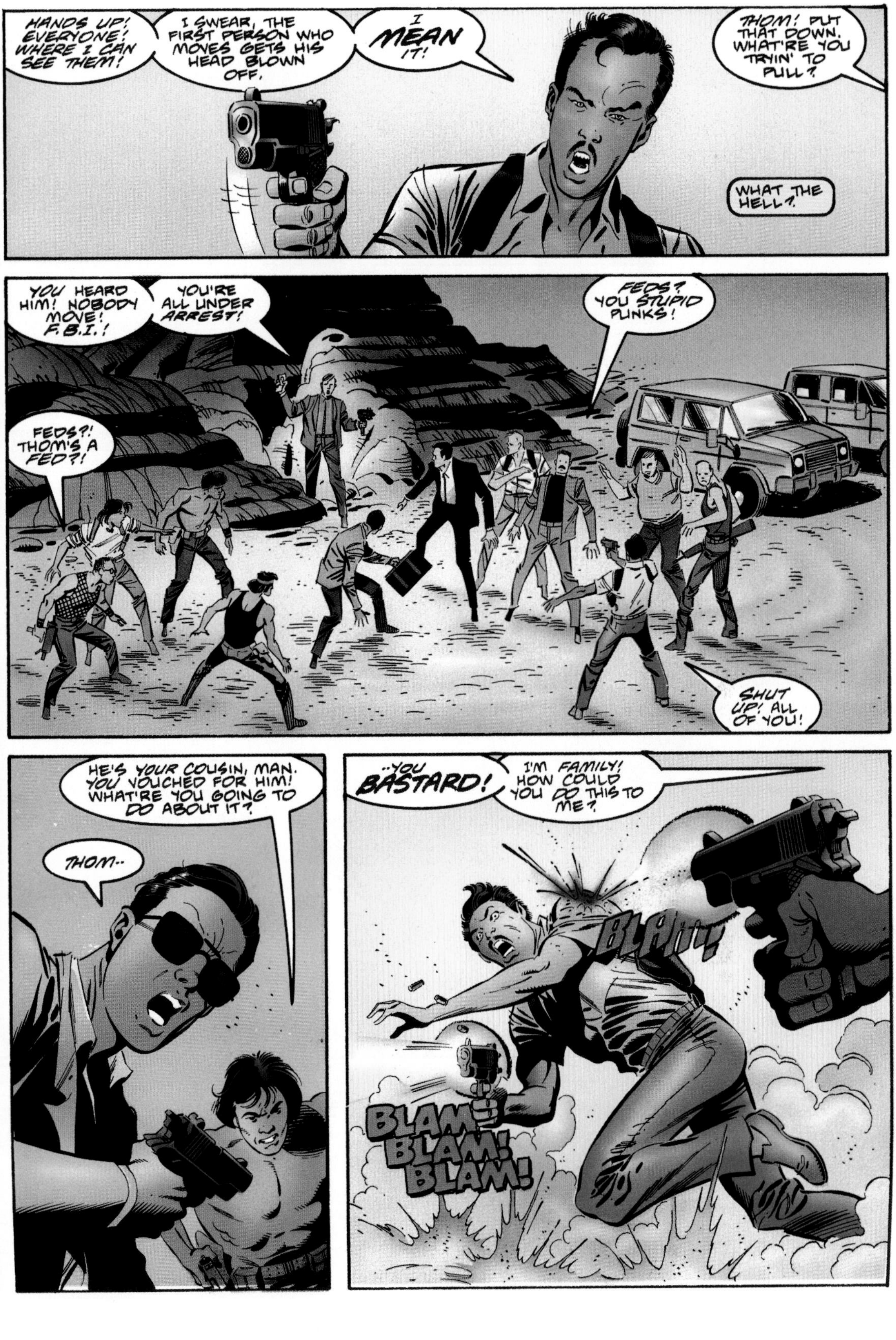
HANDS UP! EVERYONE! WHERE I CAN SEE THEM!
I SWEAR, THE FIRST PERSON WHO MOVES GETS HIS HEAD BLOWN OFF.
I MEAN IT!
THOM! PUT THAT DOWN. WHAT'RE YOU TRYIN' TO PULL?
WHAT THE HELL?
YOU HEARD HIM! NOBODY MOVE! F.B.I.!
YOU'RE ALL UNDER ARREST!
FEDS? YOU STUPID PUNKS!
FEDS?! THOM'S A FED?!
SHUT UP! ALL OF YOU!
HE'S YOUR COUSIN, MAN. YOU VOUCHED FOR HIM! WHAT'RE YOU GOING TO DO ABOUT IT?
THOM..
..YOU BASTARD!
I'M FAMILY! HOW COULD YOU DO THIS TO ME?
BLAM
BLAM! BLAM! BLAM!

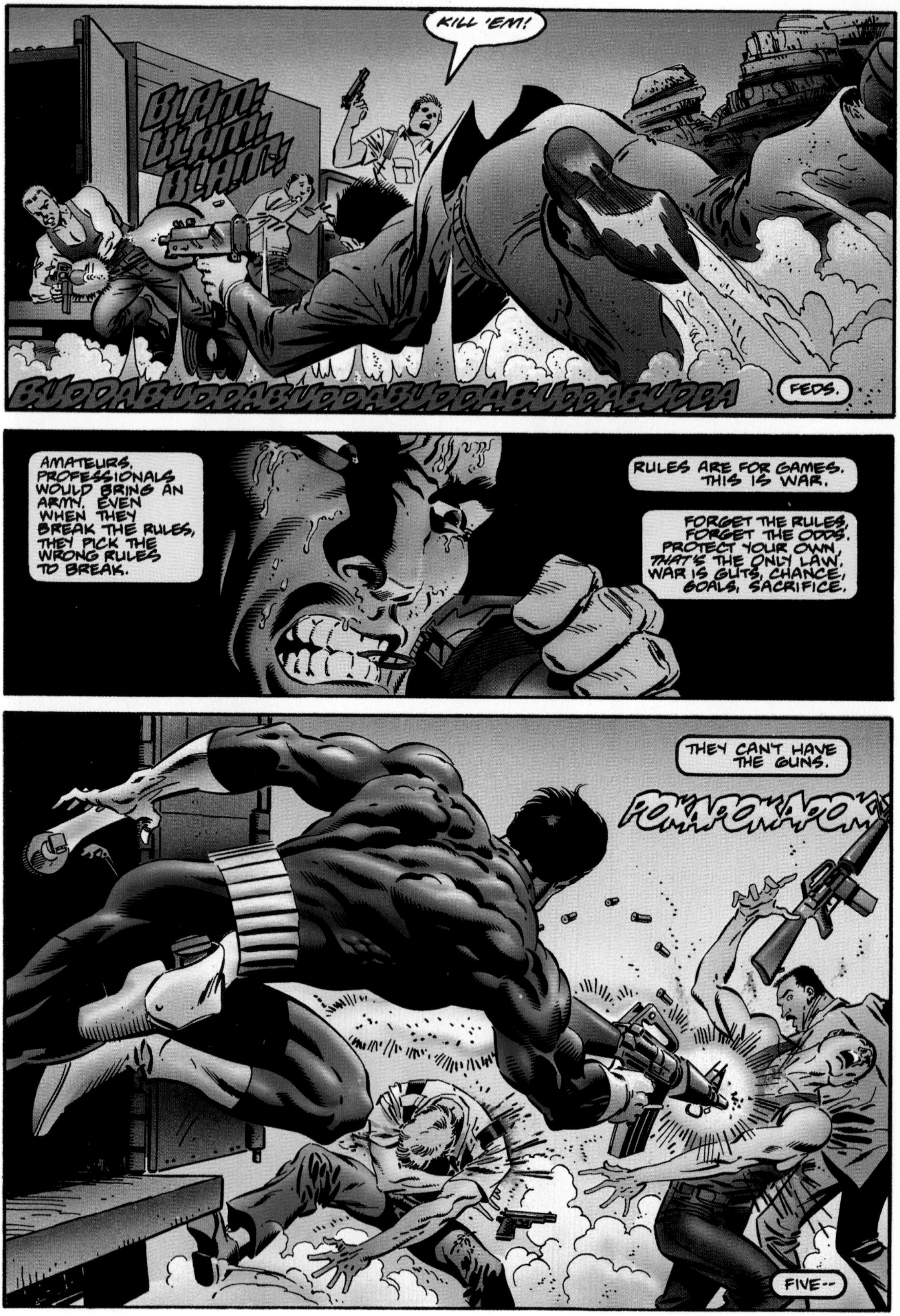
KILL 'EM!
BLAM! BLAM! BLAM!
BUDDABUDDABUDDABUDDABUDDABUDDA
FEDS.
AMATEURS. PROFESSIONALS WOULD BRING AN ARMY. EVEN WHEN THEY BREAK THE RULES, THEY PICK THE WRONG RULES TO BREAK.
RULES ARE FOR GAMES. THIS IS WAR.
FORGET THE RULES, FORGET THE ODDS. PROTECT YOUR OWN. THAT'S THE ONLY LAW. WAR IS GUTS, CHANCE, GOALS, SACRIFICE.
THEY CAN'T HAVE THE GUNS.
POKAPOKAPOK
FIVE--

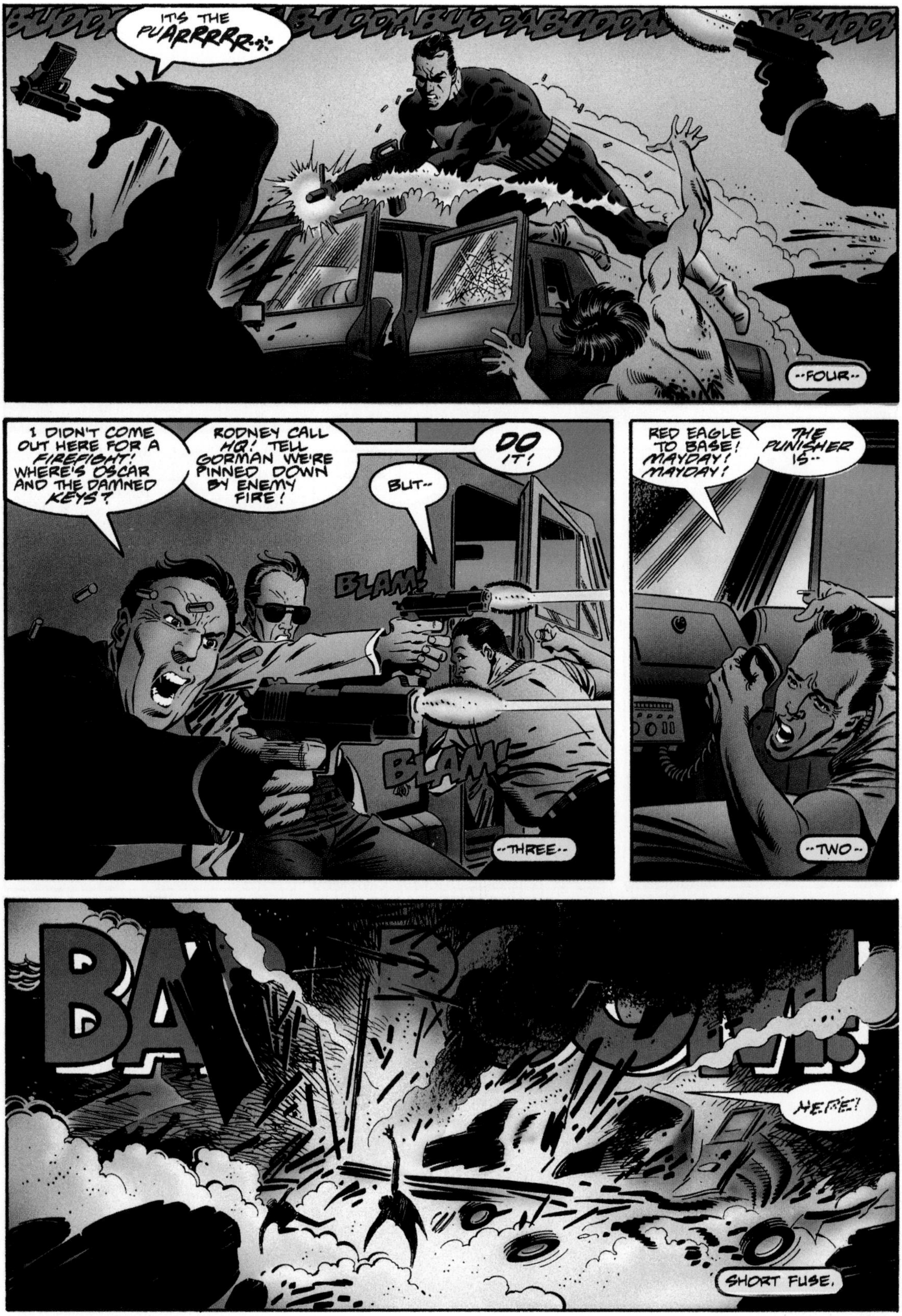

IT'S THE PUARRRRR-
--FOUR--
I DIDN'T COME OUT HERE FOR A FIREFIGHT! WHERE'S OSCAR AND THE DAMNED KEYS?
RODNEY CALL HQ! TELL GORMAN WE'RE PINNED DOWN BY ENEMY FIRE!
BUT--
DO IT!
BLAM!
BLAM!
--THREE--
RED EAGLE TO BASE! MAYDAY! MAYDAY!
THE PUNISHER IS--
--TWO--
HERE!
SHORT FUSE.

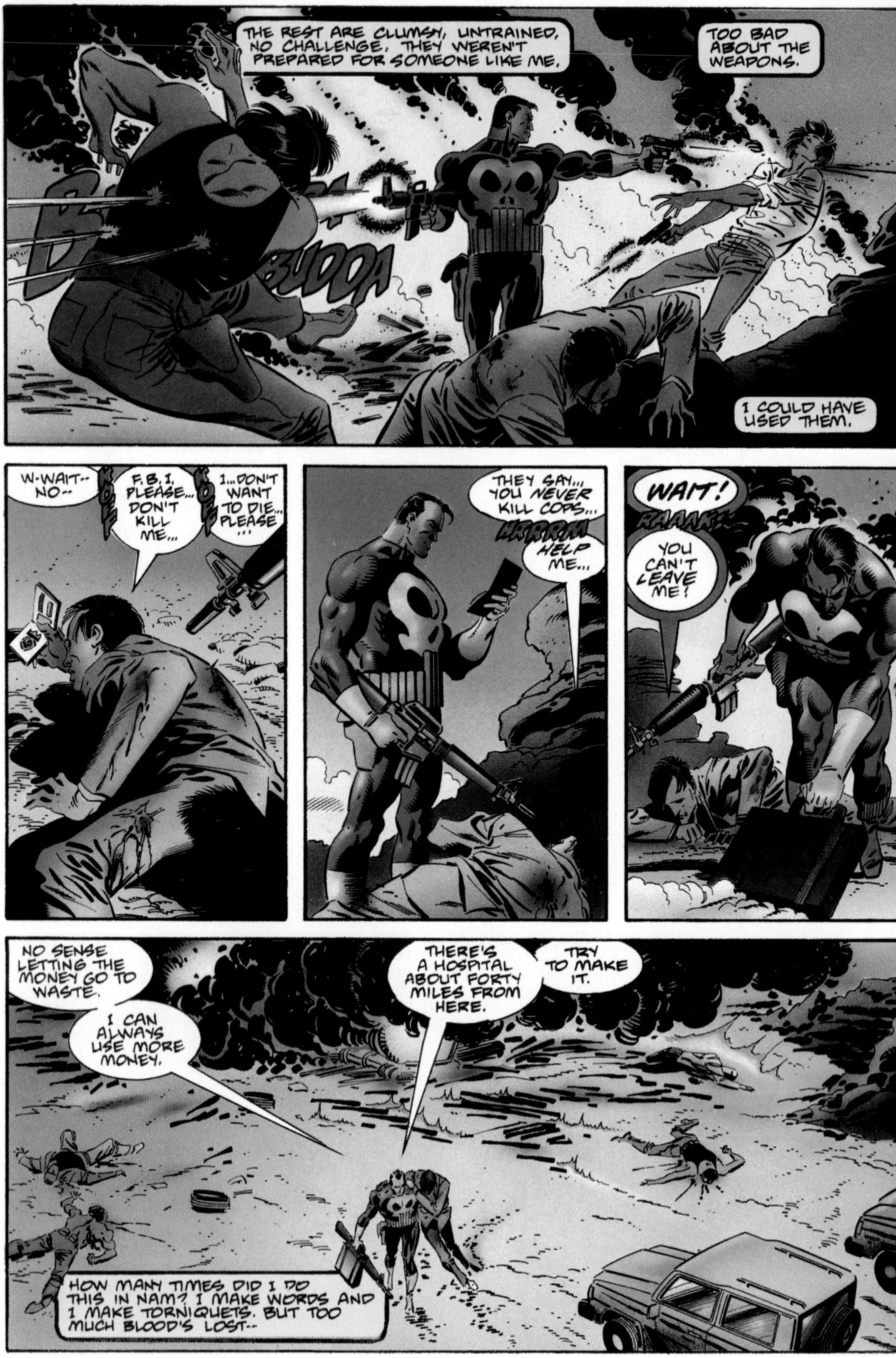
THE REST ARE CLUMSY, UNTRAINED, NO CHALLENGE. THEY WEREN'T PREPARED FOR SOMEONE LIKE ME.
TOO BAD ABOUT THE WEAPONS.
BUDDA
I COULD HAVE USED THEM.
W-WAIT-- NO--
F.B.I. PLEASE... DON'T KILL ME...
I...DON'T WANT TO DIE... PLEASE ...
THEY SAY... YOU NEVER KILL COPS...
HELP ME...
WAIT!
YOU CAN'T LEAVE ME!
NO SENSE LETTING THE MONEY GO TO WASTE.
I CAN ALWAYS USE MORE MONEY.
THERE'S A HOSPITAL ABOUT FORTY MILES FROM HERE.
TRY TO MAKE IT.
HOW MANY TIMES DID I DO THIS IN NAM? I MAKE WORDS AND I MAKE TORNIQUETS. BUT TOO MUCH BLOOD'S LOST--

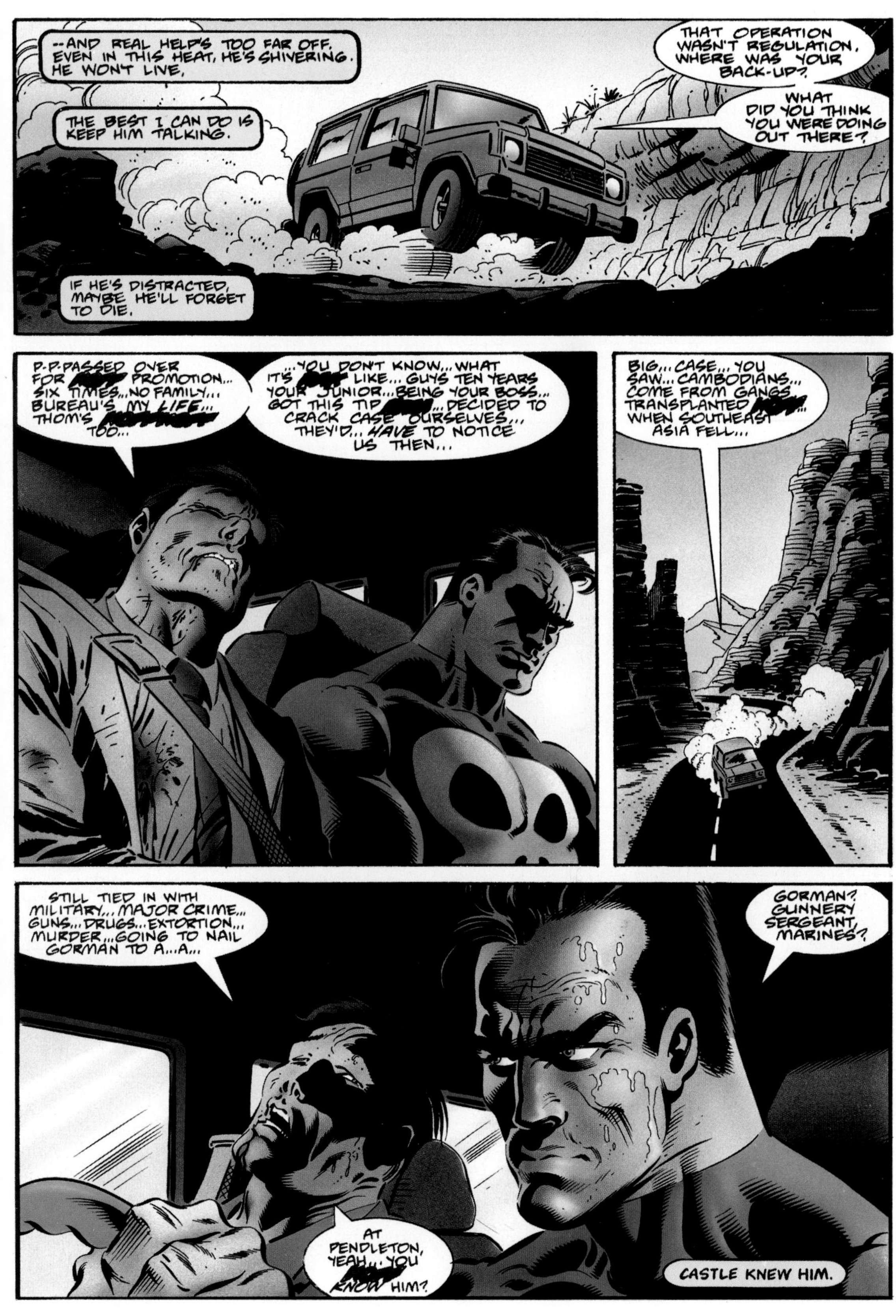

--AND REAL HELP'S TOO FAR OFF. EVEN IN THIS HEAT, HE'S SHIVERING. HE WON'T LIVE.
THAT OPERATION WASN'T REGULATION. WHERE WAS YOUR BACK-UP?
WHAT DID YOU THINK YOU WERE DOING OUT THERE?
THE BEST I CAN DO IS KEEP HIM TALKING.
IF HE'S DISTRACTED, MAYBE HE'LL FORGET TO DIE.
P-P-PASSED OVER FOR [redacted] PROMOTION... SIX TIMES... NO FAMILY... BUREAU'S MY LIFE... THOM'S [redacted] TOO...
...YOU DON'T KNOW... WHAT IT'S [redacted] LIKE... GUYS TEN YEARS YOUR JUNIOR... BEING YOUR BOSS... GOT THIS TIP [redacted]... DECIDED TO CRACK CASE OURSELVES... THEY'D... HAVE TO NOTICE US THEN...
BIG... CASE... YOU SAW... CAMBODIANS... COME FROM GANGS TRANSPLANTED [redacted] WHEN SOUTHEAST ASIA FELL...
STILL TIED IN WITH MILITARY... MAJOR CRIME... GUNS... DRUGS... EXTORTION... MURDER... GOING TO NAIL GORMAN TO A...A...
GORMAN? GUNNERY SERGEANT, MARINES?
AT PENDLETON, YEAH... YOU [redacted] KNOW HIM?
CASTLE KNEW HIM.

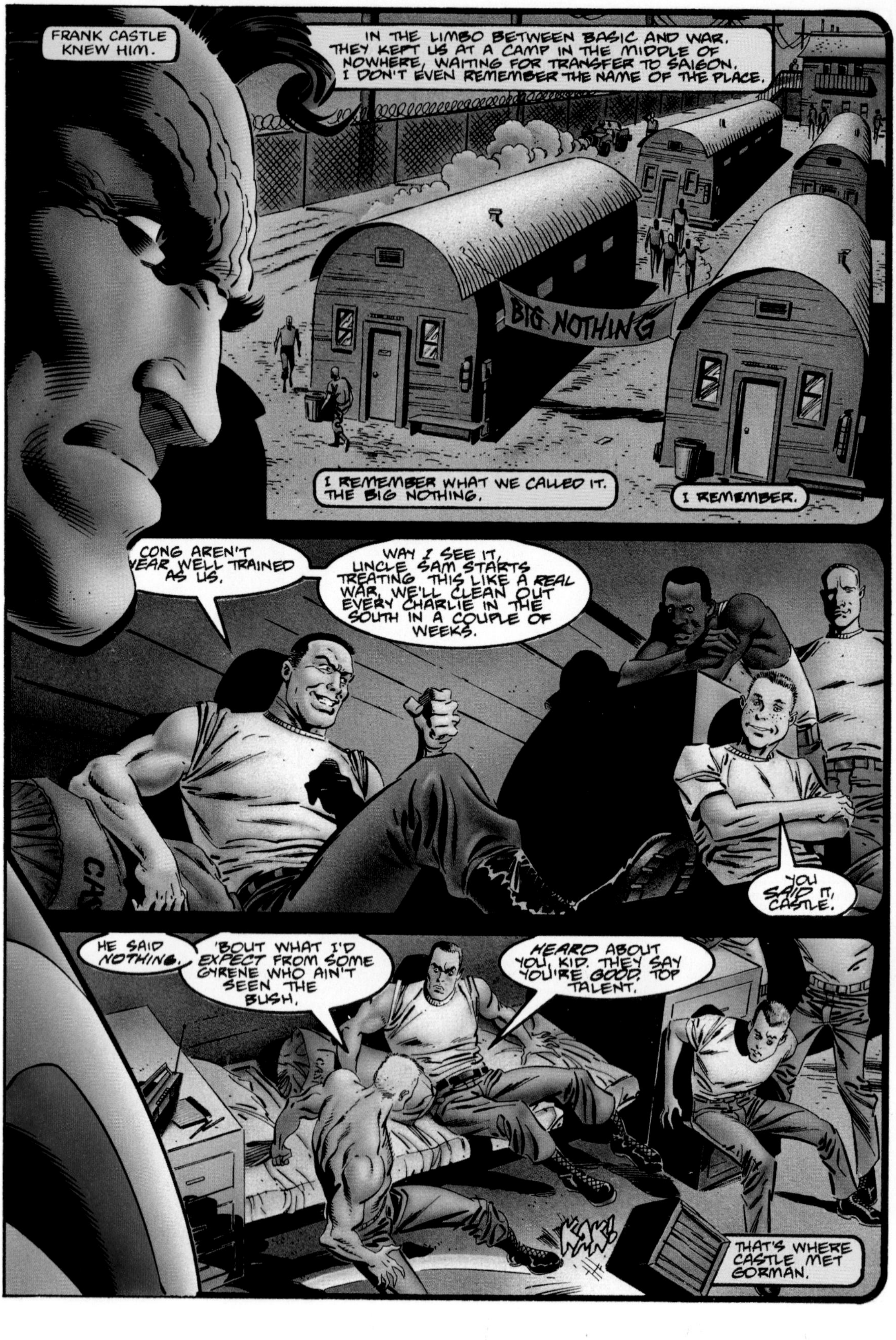
FRANK CASTLE KNEW HIM.
IN THE LIMBO BETWEEN BASIC AND WAR. THEY KEPT US AT A CAMP IN THE MIDDLE OF NOWHERE, WAITING FOR TRANSFER TO SAIGON. I DON'T EVEN REMEMBER THE NAME OF THE PLACE.
BIG NOTHING
I REMEMBER WHAT WE CALLED IT. THE BIG NOTHING.
I REMEMBER.
CONG AREN'T NEAR WELL TRAINED AS US.
WAY I SEE IT, UNCLE SAM STARTS TREATING THIS LIKE A REAL WAR, WE'LL CLEAN OUT EVERY CHARLIE IN THE SOUTH IN A COUPLE OF WEEKS.
YOU SAID IT, CASTLE.
HE SAID NOTHING.
'BOUT WHAT I'D EXPECT FROM SOME GYRENE WHO AIN'T SEEN THE BUSH.
HEARD ABOUT YOU, KID. THEY SAY YOU'RE GOOD. TOP TALENT.
THAT'S WHERE CASTLE MET GORMAN.

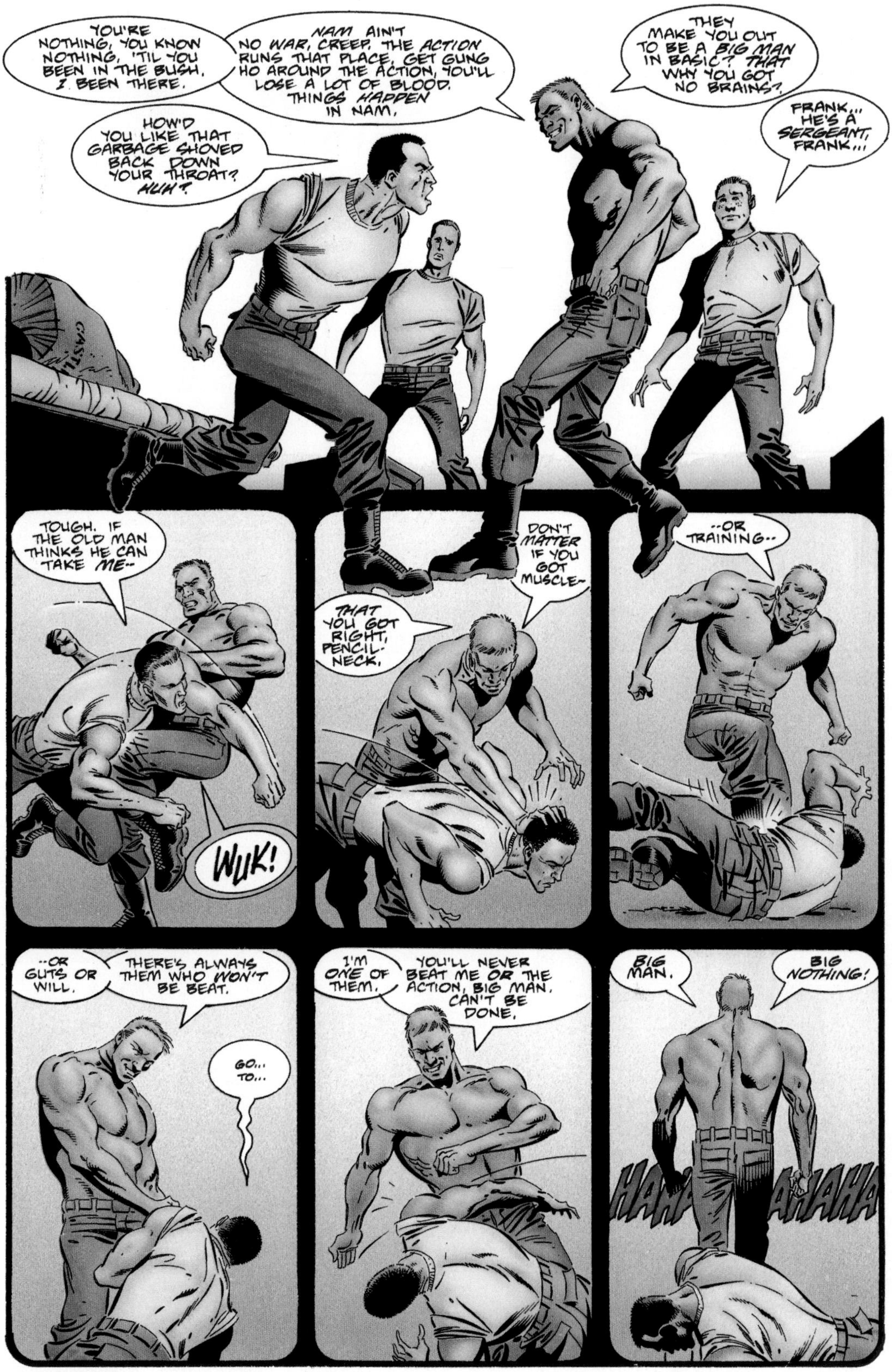
YOU'RE NOTHING, YOU KNOW NOTHING, 'TIL YOU BEEN IN THE BUSH. I BEEN THERE.
NAM AIN'T NO WAR, CREEP. THE ACTION RUNS THAT PLACE. GET GUNG HO AROUND THE ACTION, YOU'LL LOSE A LOT OF BLOOD. THINGS HAPPEN IN NAM.
HOW'D YOU LIKE THAT GARBAGE SHOVED BACK DOWN YOUR THROAT? HUH?
THEY MAKE YOU OUT TO BE A BIG MAN IN BASIC? THAT WHY YOU GOT NO BRAINS?
FRANK... HE'S A SERGEANT, FRANK...
TOUGH. IF THE OLD MAN THINKS HE CAN TAKE ME--
WUK!
DON'T MATTER IF YOU GOT MUSCLE--
THAT YOU GOT RIGHT, PENCIL NECK.
--OR TRAINING--
--OR GUTS OR WILL.
THERE'S ALWAYS THEM WHO WON'T BE BEAT.
GO... TO...
I'M ONE OF THEM.
YOU'LL NEVER BEAT ME OR THE ACTION, BIG MAN. CAN'T BE DONE.
BIG MAN.
BIG NOTHING!
HAHA
AHAHA

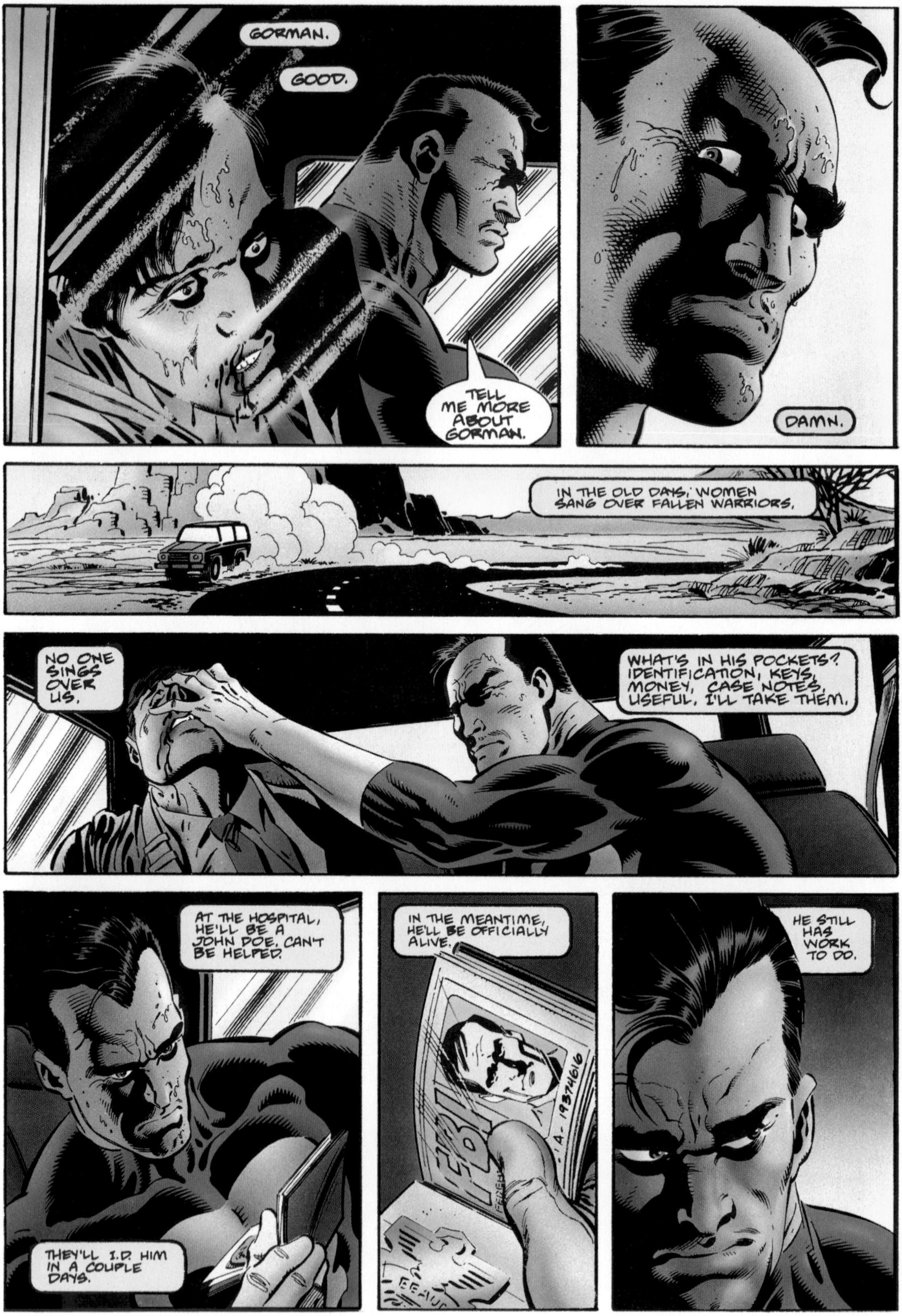
GORMAN.
GOOD.
TELL ME MORE ABOUT GORMAN.
DAMN.
IN THE OLD DAYS, WOMEN SANG OVER FALLEN WARRIORS.
NO ONE SINGS OVER US.
WHAT'S IN HIS POCKETS? IDENTIFICATION, KEYS, MONEY, CASE NOTES. USEFUL. I'LL TAKE THEM.
AT THE HOSPITAL, HE'LL BE A JOHN DOE. CAN'T BE HELPED.
THEY'LL I.D. HIM IN A COUPLE DAYS.
IN THE MEANTIME, HE'LL BE OFFICIALLY ALIVE.
FBI
HE STILL HAS WORK TO DO.

WHEN WE GET TO PENDLETON.

HERE'S THE TAPE YOU ASKED FOR, CLEVE.

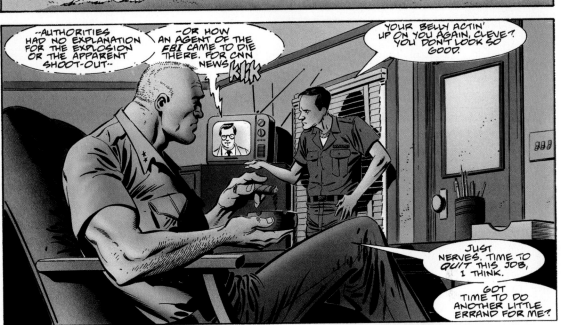

--AUTHORITIES HAD NO EXPLANATION FOR THE EXPLOSION OR THE APPARENT SHOOT-OUT--

--OR HOW AN AGENT OF THE FBI CAME TO DIE THERE. FOR CNN NEWS

YOUR BELLY ACTIN' UP ON YOU AGAIN, CLEVE? YOU DON'T LOOK SO GOOD.

JUST NERVES. TIME TO QUIT THIS JOB, I THINK.

GOT TIME TO DO ANOTHER LITTLE ERRAND FOR ME?

GOT WORD WE SHOULD BE ON THE LOOKOUT FOR SOME CHARACTER CALLED THE PUNISHER.

SEE WHAT KIND OF FILES WE'VE GOT ON HIM, OKAY?

WILL DO.

WHY ME?

TWELVE YEARS WITHOUT A SCREWUP. TWELVE YEARS. AND NOW THIS...

SNOW AND HIS DAMNED SO-CALLED PROFESSIONALS.

beep beep beep beep

WHAT I GET FOR BEING A NICE GUY...PHASING HIM IN EARLY...

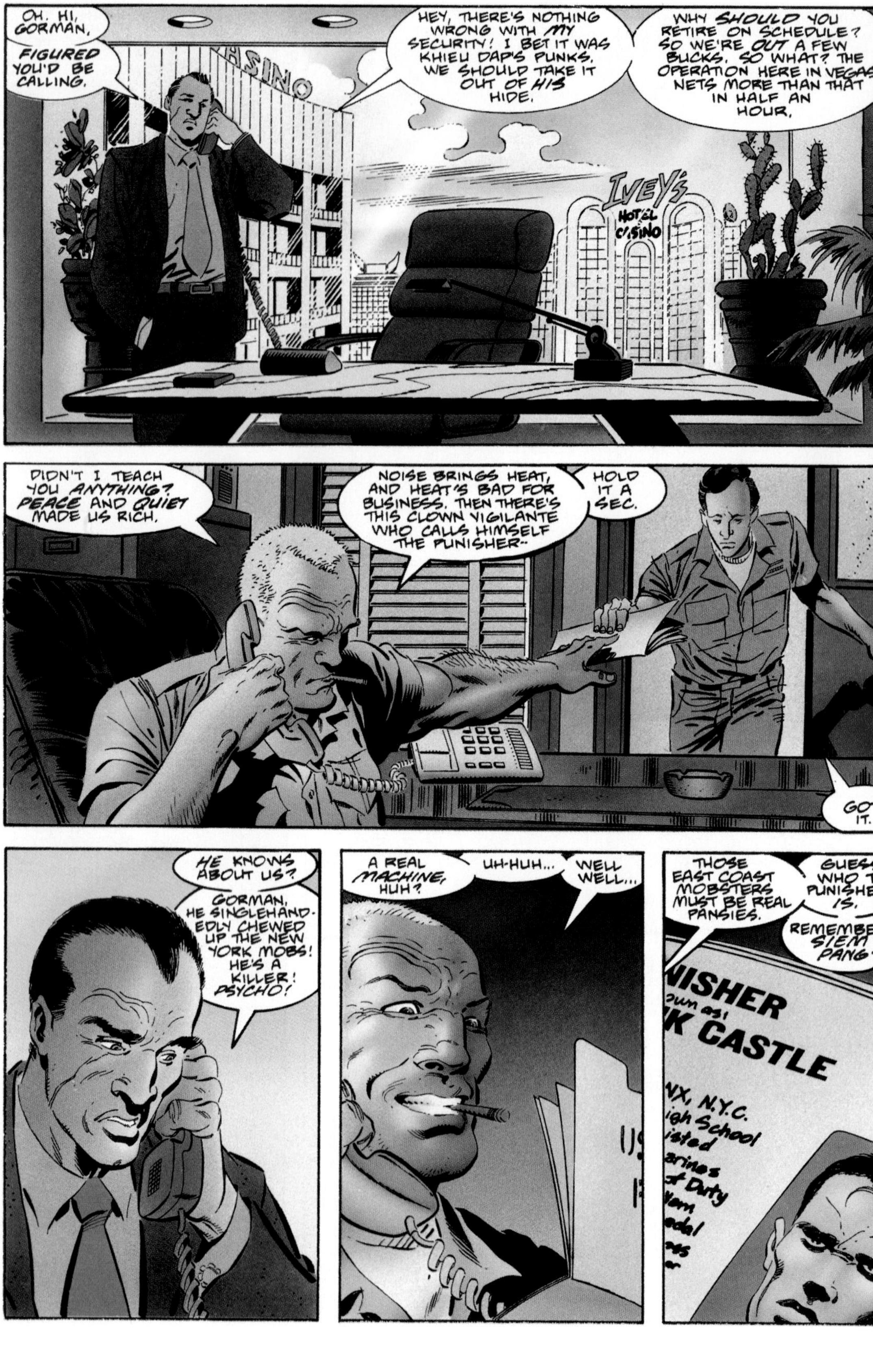
OH. HI, GORMAN. FIGURED YOU'D BE CALLING.
HEY, THERE'S NOTHING WRONG WITH MY SECURITY! I BET IT WAS KHIEU DAP'S PUNKS. WE SHOULD TAKE IT OUT OF HIS HIDE.
WHY SHOULD YOU RETIRE ON SCHEDULE? SO WE'RE OUT A FEW BUCKS. SO WHAT? THE OPERATION HERE IN VEGAS NETS MORE THAN THAT IN HALF AN HOUR.
IVEY'S HOTEL CASINO
DIDN'T I TEACH YOU ANYTHING? PEACE AND QUIET MADE US RICH.
NOISE BRINGS HEAT, AND HEAT'S BAD FOR BUSINESS. THEN THERE'S THIS CLOWN VIGILANTE WHO CALLS HIMSELF THE PUNISHER--
HOLD IT A SEC.
GOT IT.
HE KNOWS ABOUT US?
GORMAN, HE SINGLEHANDEDLY CHEWED UP THE NEW YORK MOBS! HE'S A KILLER! PSYCHO!
A REAL MACHINE, HUH?
UH-HUH...
WELL WELL...
THOSE EAST COAST MOBSTERS MUST BE REAL PANSIES.
GUESS WHO THE PUNISHER IS.
REMEMBER SIEM PANG?
NISHER
K CASTLE
NX, N.Y.C.
igh School
isted
arines
of Duty
dal

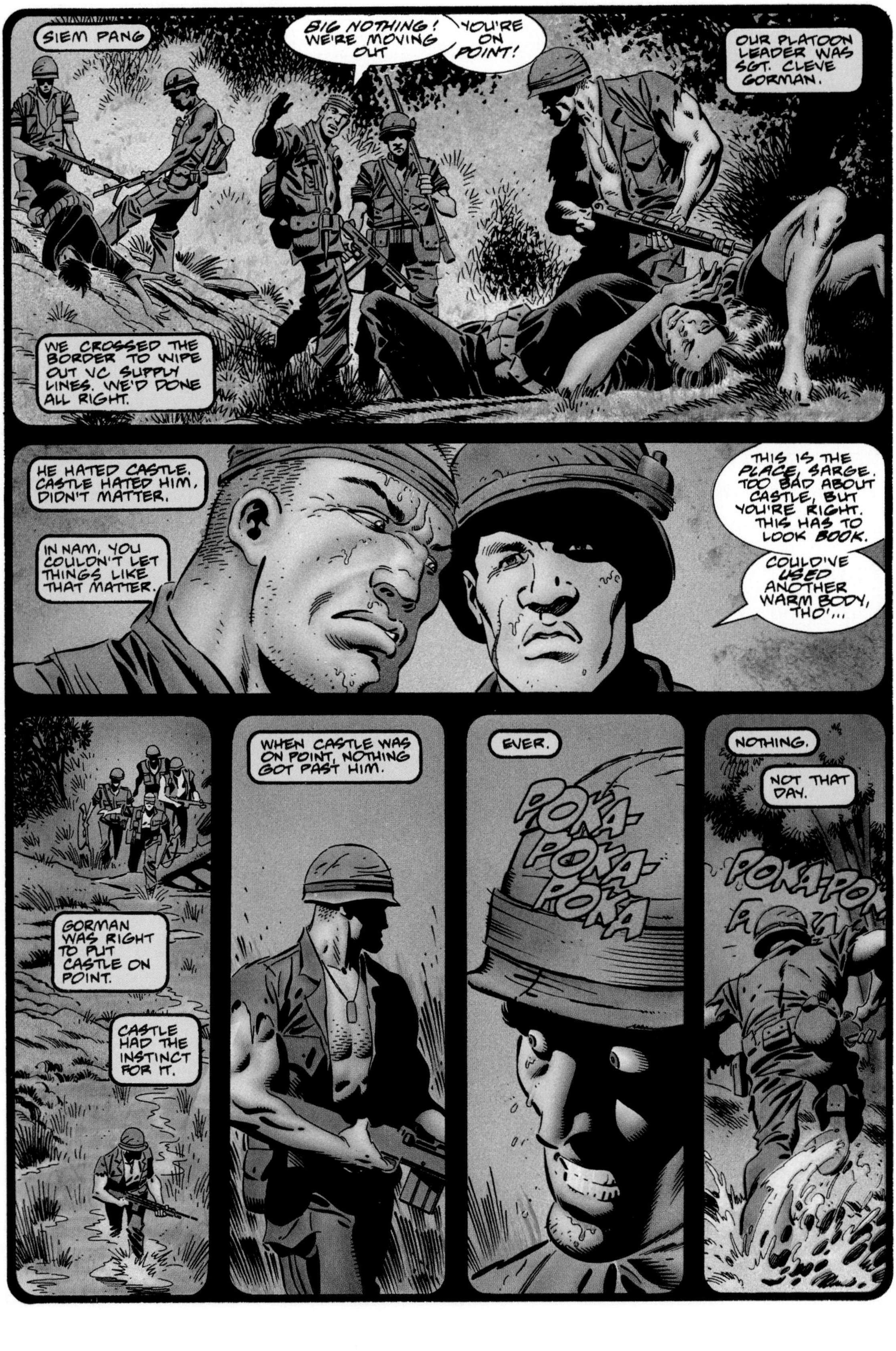
SIEM PANG
BIG NOTHING! WE'RE MOVING OUT
YOU'RE ON POINT!
OUR PLATOON LEADER WAS SGT. CLEVE GORMAN.
WE CROSSED THE BORDER TO WIPE OUT VC SUPPLY LINES. WE'D DONE ALL RIGHT.
HE HATED CASTLE. CASTLE HATED HIM. DIDN'T MATTER.
IN NAM, YOU COULDN'T LET THINGS LIKE THAT MATTER.
THIS IS THE PLACE, SARGE. TOO BAD ABOUT CASTLE, BUT YOU'RE RIGHT. THIS HAS TO LOOK BOOK.
COULD'VE USED ANOTHER WARM BODY, THO'...
GORMAN WAS RIGHT TO PUT CASTLE ON POINT.
CASTLE HAD THE INSTINCT FOR IT.
WHEN CASTLE WAS ON POINT, NOTHING GOT PAST HIM.
EVER.
POKA-POKA-POKA
NOTHING.
NOT THAT DAY.
POKA-POK

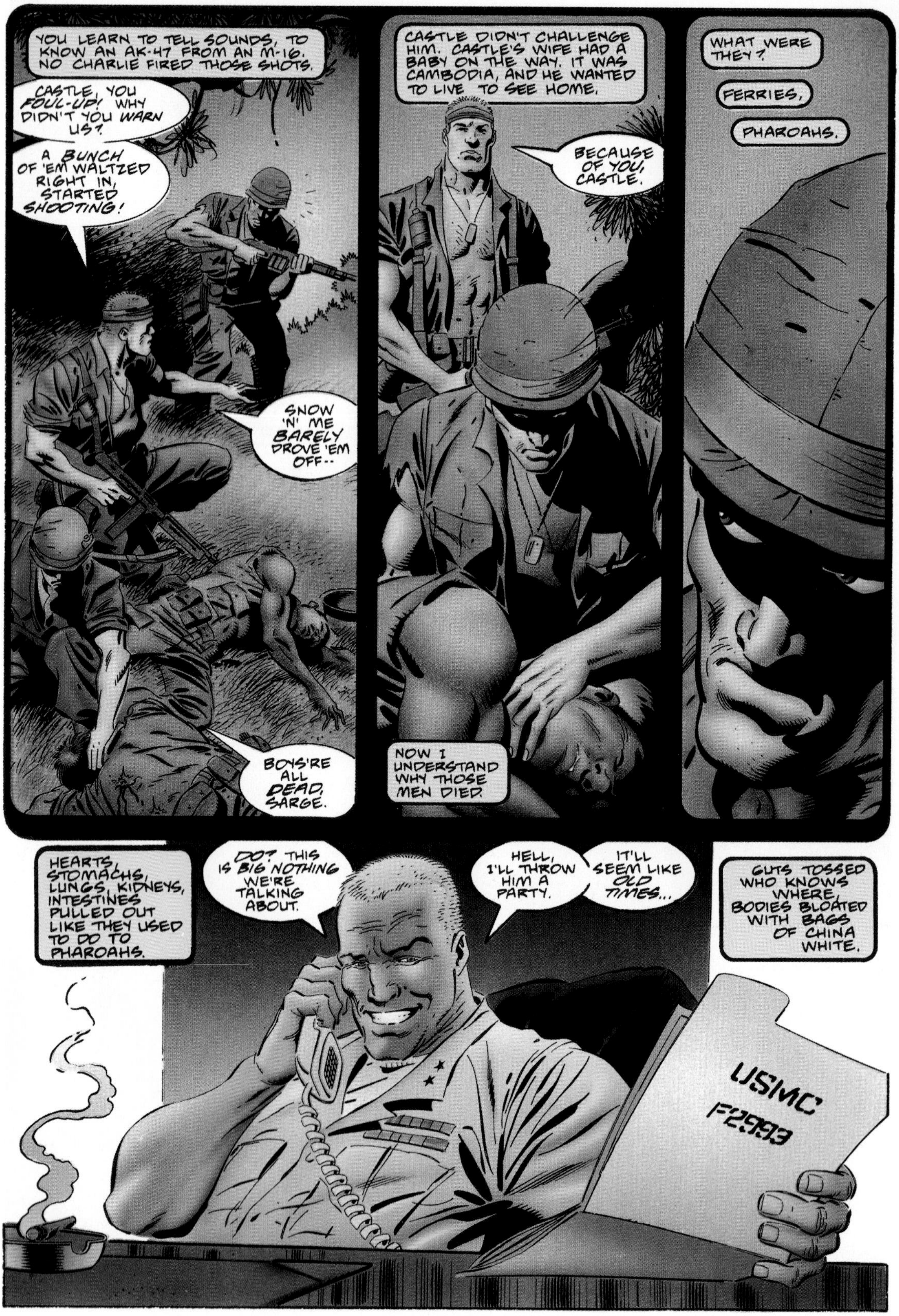

YOU LEARN TO TELL SOUNDS, TO KNOW AN AK-47 FROM AN M-16. NO CHARLIE FIRED THOSE SHOTS.
CASTLE, YOU FOUL-UP! WHY DIDN'T YOU WARN US?
A BUNCH OF 'EM WALTZED RIGHT IN, STARTED SHOOTING!
SNOW 'N' ME BARELY DROVE 'EM OFF--
BOYS'RE ALL DEAD, SARGE.
CASTLE DIDN'T CHALLENGE HIM. CASTLE'S WIFE HAD A BABY ON THE WAY. IT WAS CAMBODIA, AND HE WANTED TO LIVE TO SEE HOME.
BECAUSE OF YOU, CASTLE.
NOW I UNDERSTAND WHY THOSE MEN DIED.
WHAT WERE THEY?
FERRIES.
PHAROAHS.
HEARTS, STOMACHS, LUNGS, KIDNEYS, INTESTINES PULLED OUT LIKE THEY USED TO DO TO PHAROAHS.
DO? THIS IS BIG NOTHING WE'RE TALKING ABOUT.
HELL, I'LL THROW HIM A PARTY.
IT'LL SEEM LIKE OLD TIMES...
GUTS TOSSED WHO KNOWS WHERE, BODIES BLOATED WITH BAGS OF CHINA WHITE.
USMC
F2993

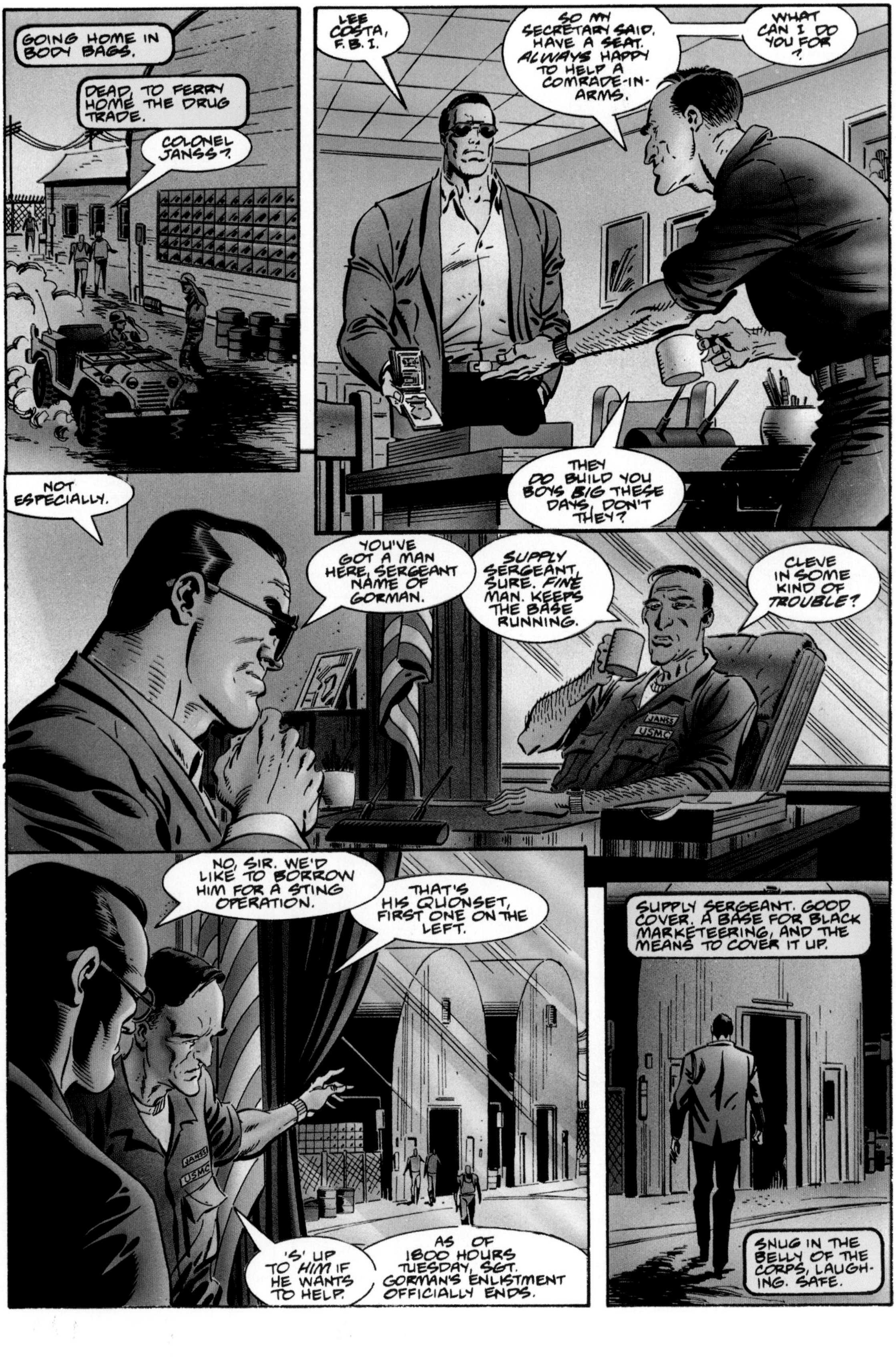
GOING HOME IN BODY BAGS.
DEAD, TO FERRY HOME THE DRUG TRADE.
COLONEL JANSS?
LEE COSTA, F.B.I.
SO MY SECRETARY SAID. HAVE A SEAT. ALWAYS HAPPY TO HELP A COMRADE-IN-ARMS.
WHAT CAN I DO YOU FOR?
THEY DO BUILD YOU BOYS BIG THESE DAYS, DON'T THEY?
NOT ESPECIALLY.
YOU'VE GOT A MAN HERE, SERGEANT NAME OF GORMAN.
SUPPLY SERGEANT, SURE. FINE MAN. KEEPS THE BASE RUNNING.
CLEVE IN SOME KIND OF TROUBLE?
JANSS
USMC
NO, SIR. WE'D LIKE TO BORROW HIM FOR A STING OPERATION.
THAT'S HIS QUONSET, FIRST ONE ON THE LEFT.
'S' UP TO HIM IF HE WANTS TO HELP.
AS OF 1800 HOURS TUESDAY, SGT. GORMAN'S ENLISTMENT OFFICIALLY ENDS.
SUPPLY SERGEANT. GOOD COVER. A BASE FOR BLACK MARKETEERING, AND THE MEANS TO COVER IT UP.
SNUG IN THE BELLY OF THE CORPS, LAUGHING. SAFE.

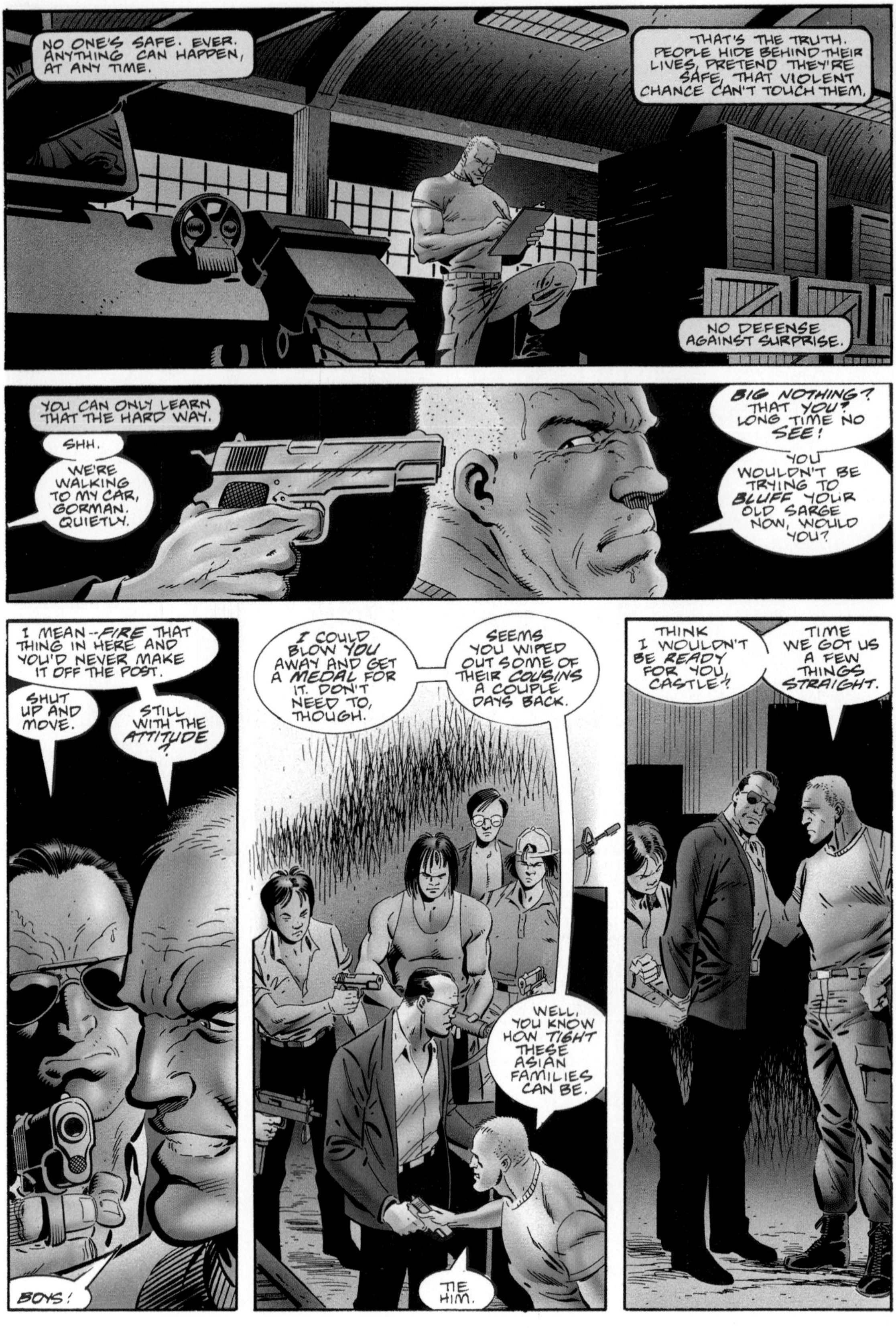
NO ONE'S SAFE. EVER. ANYTHING CAN HAPPEN, AT ANY TIME.
THAT'S THE TRUTH. PEOPLE HIDE BEHIND THEIR LIVES, PRETEND THEY'RE SAFE, THAT VIOLENT CHANCE CAN'T TOUCH THEM.
NO DEFENSE AGAINST SURPRISE.
YOU CAN ONLY LEARN THAT THE HARD WAY.
SHH.
WE'RE WALKING TO MY CAR, GORMAN. QUIETLY.
BIG NOTHING? THAT YOU? LONG TIME NO SEE!
YOU WOULDN'T BE TRYING TO BLUFF YOUR OLD SARGE NOW, WOULD YOU?
I MEAN--FIRE THAT THING IN HERE AND YOU'D NEVER MAKE IT OFF THE POST.
SHUT UP AND MOVE.
STILL WITH THE ATTITUDE?
BOYS!
I COULD BLOW YOU AWAY AND GET A MEDAL FOR IT. DON'T NEED TO, THOUGH.
SEEMS YOU WIPED OUT SOME OF THEIR COUSINS A COUPLE DAYS BACK.
WELL, YOU KNOW HOW TIGHT THESE ASIAN FAMILIES CAN BE.
TIE HIM.
THINK I WOULDN'T BE READY FOR YOU, CASTLE?
TIME WE GOT US A FEW THINGS STRAIGHT.

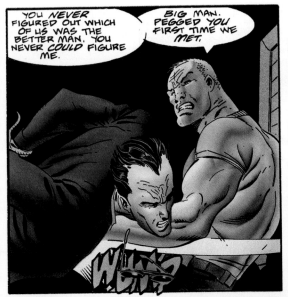

YOU *NEVER* FIGURED OUT WHICH OF US WAS THE *BETTER MAN.* YOU NEVER *COULD* FIGURE ME.

BIG MAN. PEGGED YOU *FIRST TIME* WE *MET.*

WHAT'S YOUR *NAME*, *SOLDIER*? WHAT'D I *NAME* YOU?

LET'S HEAR IT FROM *YOUR LIPS.*

SAY IT!

NO.

SAY IT!

NO.

I *REFUSE* TO LOSE.

I REFUSE TO *FALL.*

I REFUSE.

WAK!

NO! NOT HERE! I DON'T WANT A *MESS* TO EXPLAIN.

DON'T EVER BUTT INTO MY *FIGHTS* AGAIN.

DO HIM LIKE YOU DID THE *GERMAN.* MAKE SURE IT'S IN THE *DESERT* WHERE YOU WON'T BE *SEEN*..AND *BURN* HIM.

25

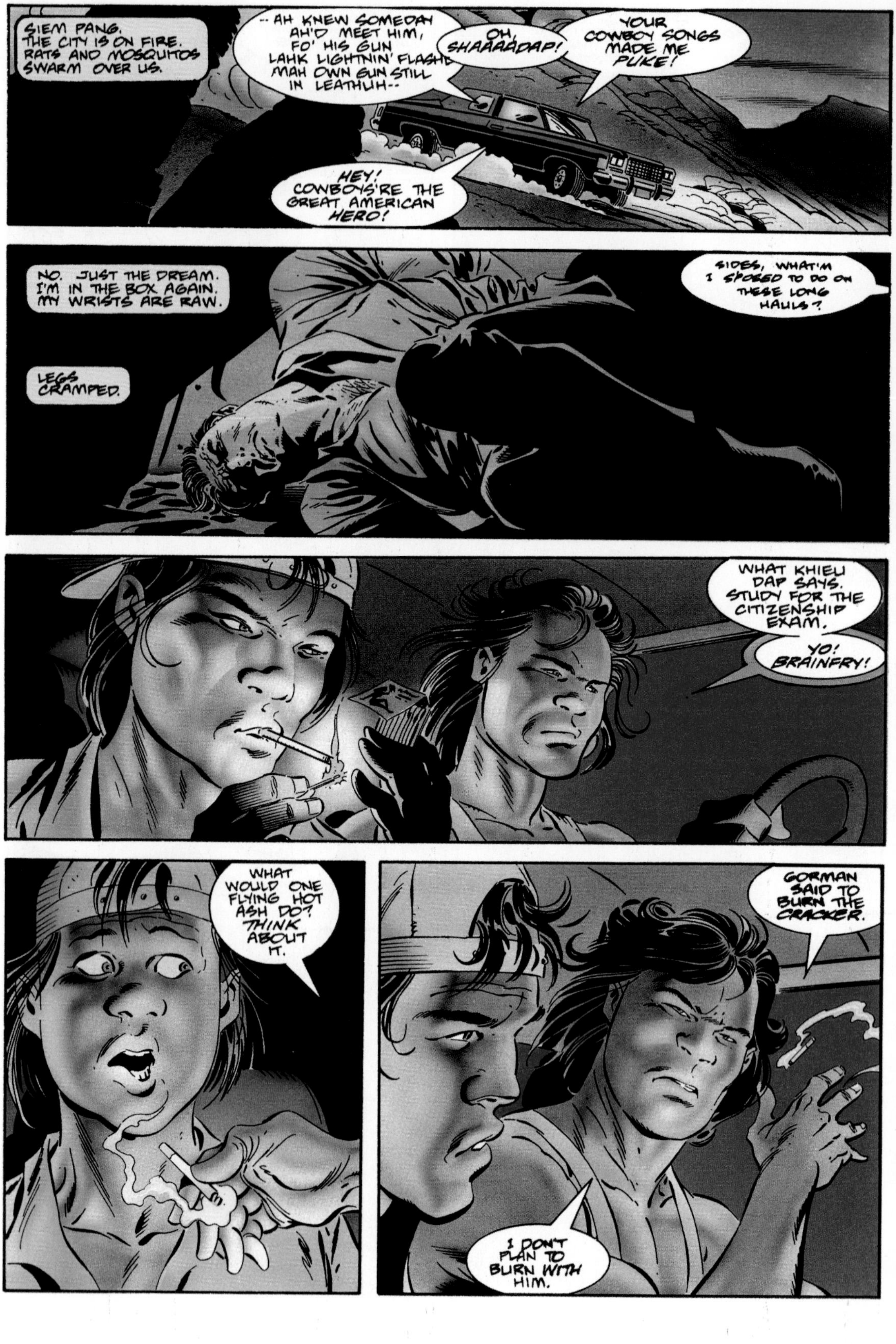
SIEM PANG. THE CITY IS ON FIRE. RATS AND MOSQUITOS SWARM OVER US.
--AH KNEW SOMEDAY AH'D MEET HIM, FO' HIS GUN LAHK LIGHTNIN' FLASHED MAH OWN GUN STILL IN LEATHUH--
OH, SHAAAADAP!
YOUR COWBOY SONGS MADE ME PUKE!
HEY! COWBOYS'RE THE GREAT AMERICAN HERO!
NO. JUST THE DREAM. I'M IN THE BOX AGAIN. MY WRISTS ARE RAW.
LEGS CRAMPED.
SIDES, WHAT'M I S'POSED TO DO ON THESE LONG HAULS?
WHAT KHIEU DAP SAYS. STUDY FOR THE CITIZENSHIP EXAM.
YO! BRAINFRY!
WHAT WOULD ONE FLYING HOT ASH DO? THINK ABOUT IT.
GORMAN SAID TO BURN THE CRACKER.
I DON'T PLAN TO BURN WITH HIM.

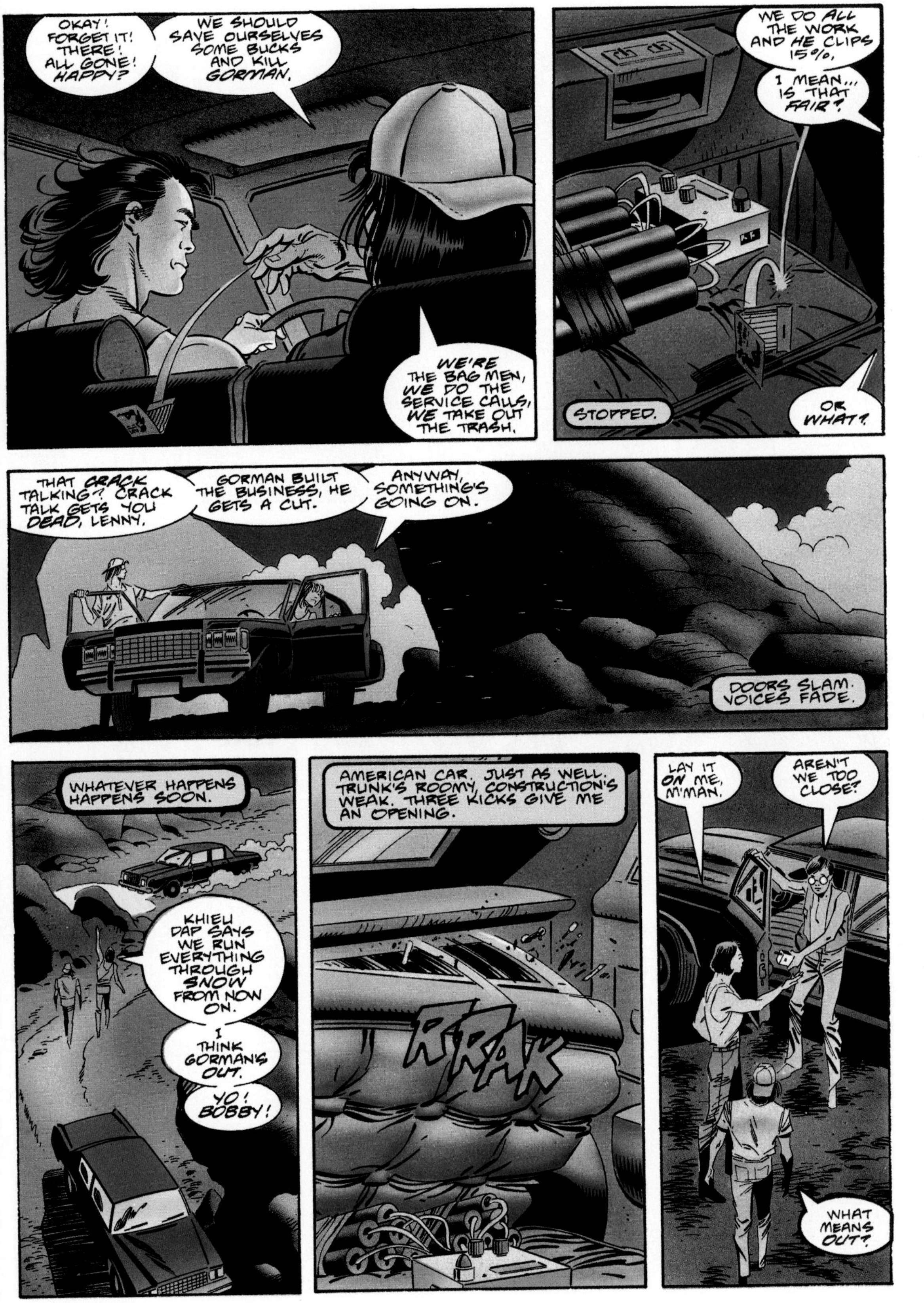
OKAY! FORGET IT! THERE! ALL GONE! HAPPY?
WE SHOULD SAVE OURSELVES SOME BUCKS AND KILL GORMAN.
WE'RE THE BAG MEN, WE DO THE SERVICE CALLS, WE TAKE OUT THE TRASH.
WE DO ALL THE WORK AND HE CLIPS 15%.
I MEAN... IS THAT FAIR?
STOPPED.
OR WHAT?
THAT CRACK TALKING? CRACK TALK GETS YOU DEAD, LENNY.
GORMAN BUILT THE BUSINESS, HE GETS A CUT.
ANYWAY, SOMETHING'S GOING ON.
DOORS SLAM. VOICES FADE.
WHATEVER HAPPENS HAPPENS SOON.
KHIEU DAP SAYS WE RUN EVERYTHING THROUGH SNOW FROM NOW ON.
I THINK GORMAN'S OUT.
YO! BOBBY!
AMERICAN CAR. JUST AS WELL. TRUNK'S ROOMY, CONSTRUCTION'S WEAK. THREE KICKS GIVE ME AN OPENING.
RRAK
LAY IT ON ME, M'MAN.
AREN'T WE TOO CLOSE?
WHAT MEANS OUT?

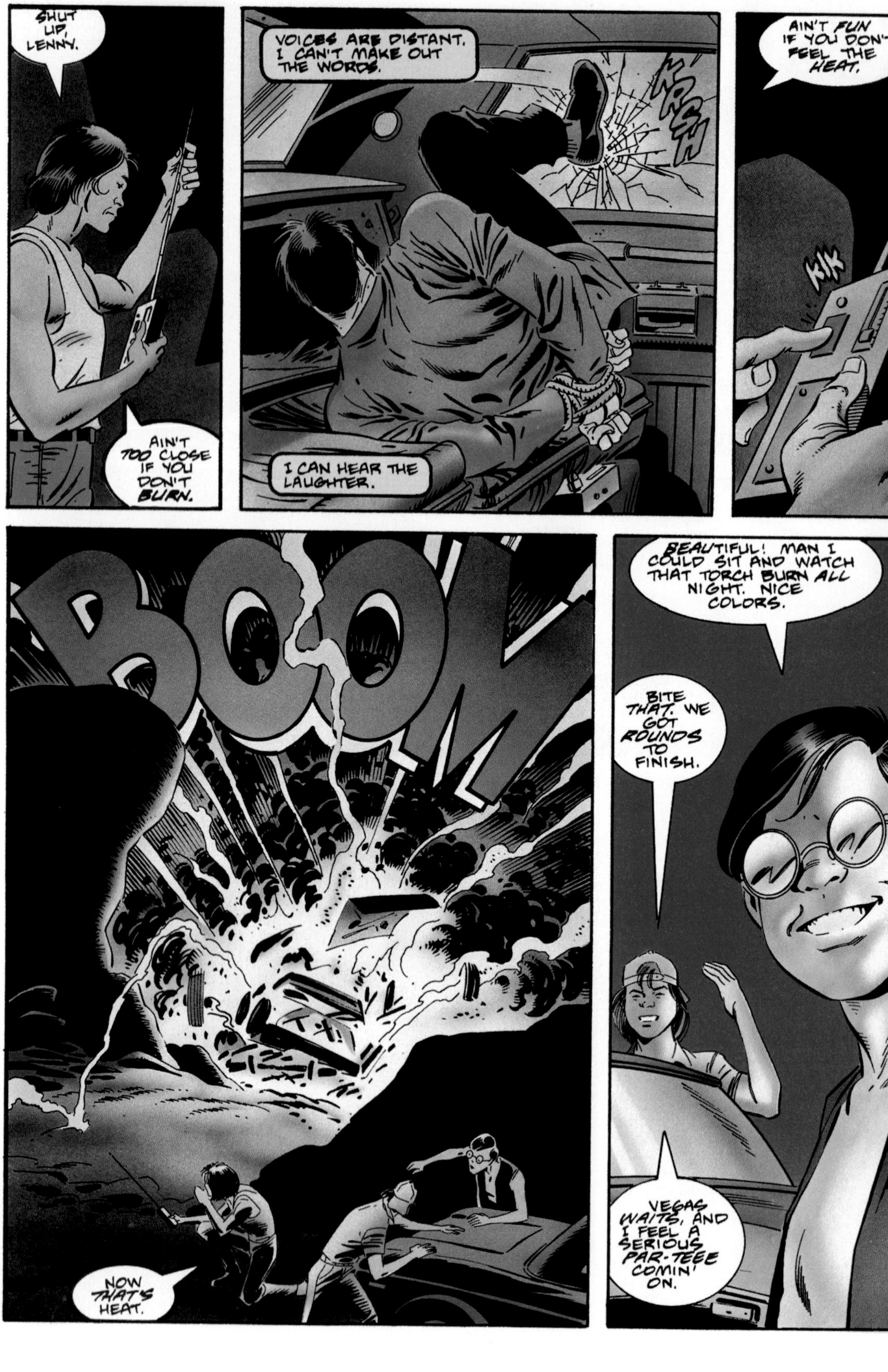

SHUT UP, LENNY.
AIN'T TOO CLOSE IF YOU DON'T BURN.
VOICES ARE DISTANT. I CAN'T MAKE OUT THE WORDS.
KRSH
I CAN HEAR THE LAUGHTER.
AIN'T FUN IF YOU DON'T FEEL THE HEAT.
KIK
BOOM
NOW THAT'S HEAT.
BEAUTIFUL! MAN I COULD SIT AND WATCH THAT TORCH BURN ALL NIGHT. NICE COLORS.
BITE THAT. WE GOT ROUNDS TO FINISH.
VEGAS WAITS, AND I FEEL A SERIOUS PAR-TEEE COMIN' ON.

THE VOICES ARE GONE, THE CAR IS GONE. HOW LONG DID I LIE HERE?

MORE AMATEURS.

NO CHECKING TO SEE THE JOB'S DONE, NO QUALITY CONTROL. THOSE CONCEPTS MAKE THEM LAUGH.

THEIR KIND IS EASY.

WRECKED METAL GOUGES MY WRISTS, FLESH SEARS. I FEEL NO PAIN.

NO PAIN.

NO PAIN.

CONCEN-TRATE ON OTHER THINGS. ON THEM.

NO NEED TO CHASE THEM.

I KNOW WHERE THEY'LL BE.

Verta "Hows" GOODSPRING NEVADA

LET THEM RUN.

I'LL BE WAITING.

29

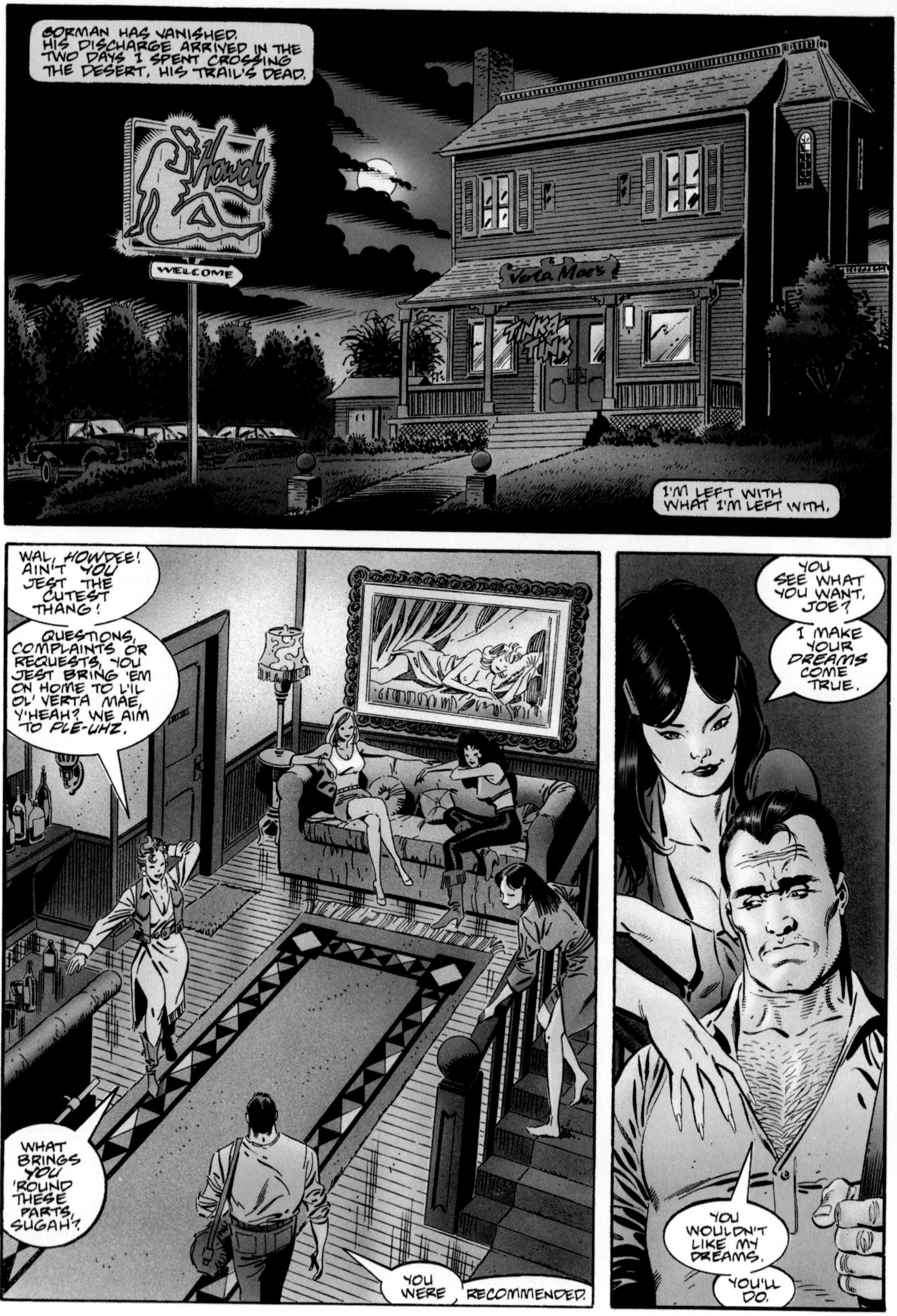
GORMAN HAS VANISHED. HIS DISCHARGE ARRIVED IN THE TWO DAYS I SPENT CROSSING THE DESERT. HIS TRAIL'S DEAD.
Howdy
WELCOME
Verta Mae's
TINKA TINK
I'M LEFT WITH WHAT I'M LEFT WITH.
WAL, HOWDEE! AIN'T YOU JEST THE CUTEST THANG!
QUESTIONS, COMPLAINTS OR REQUESTS, YOU JEST BRING 'EM ON HOME TO L'IL OL' VERTA MAE, Y'HEAH? WE AIM TO PLE-UHZ.
WHAT BRINGS YOU 'ROUND THESE PARTS, SUGAH?
YOU WERE RECOMMENDED.
YOU SEE WHAT YOU WANT, JOE?
I MAKE YOUR DREAMS COME TRUE.
YOU WOULDN'T LIKE MY DREAMS.
YOU'LL DO.

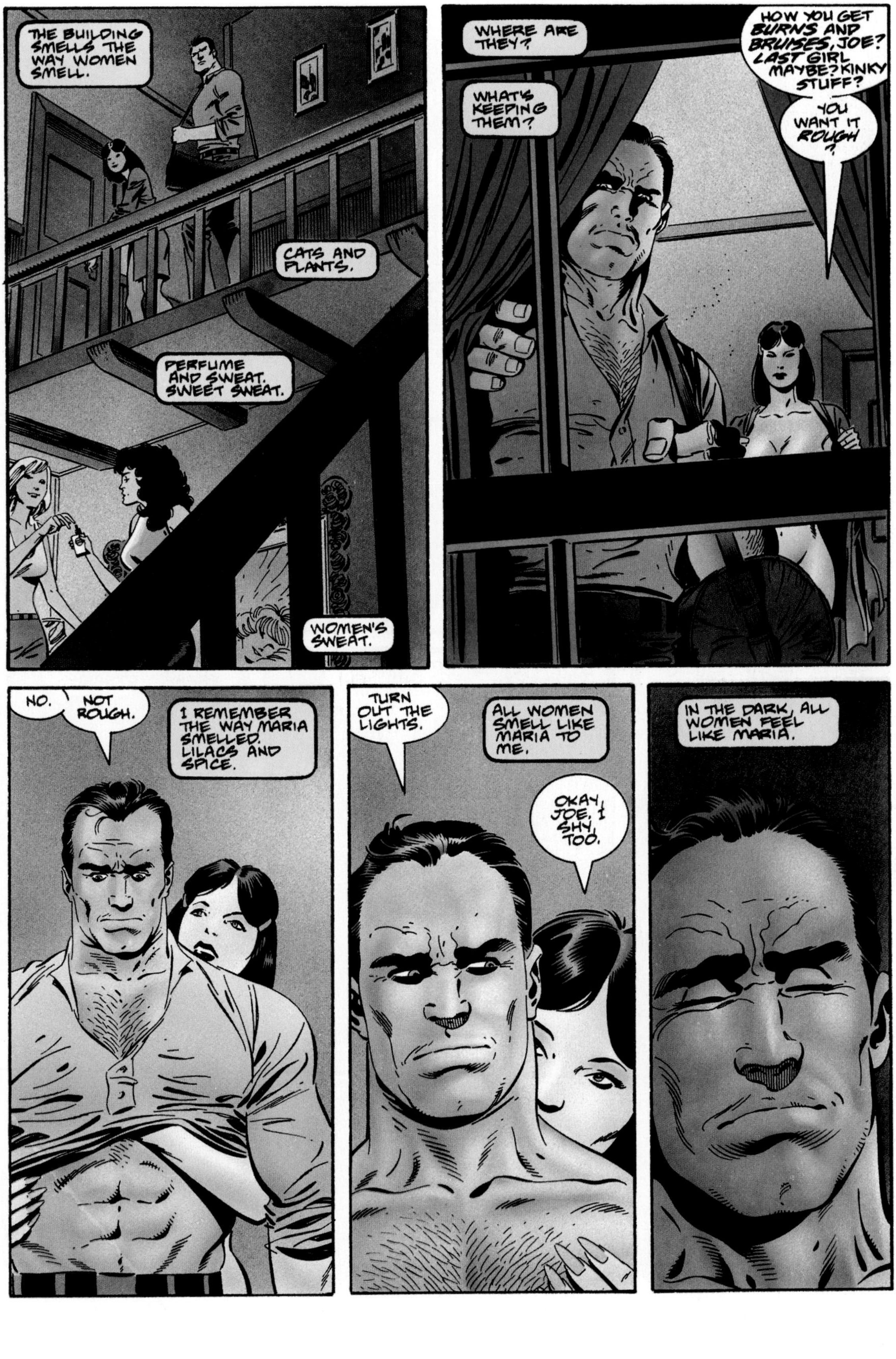
THE BUILDING SMELLS THE WAY WOMEN SMELL.
CATS AND PLANTS.
PERFUME AND SWEAT. SWEET SWEAT.
WOMEN'S SWEAT.
WHERE ARE THEY?
WHAT'S KEEPING THEM?
HOW YOU GET BURNS AND BRUISES, JOE? LAST GIRL MAYBE? KINKY STUFF?
YOU WANT IT ROUGH?
NO.
NOT ROUGH.
I REMEMBER THE WAY MARIA SMELLED. LILACS AND SPICE.
TURN OUT THE LIGHTS.
ALL WOMEN SMELL LIKE MARIA TO ME.
OKAY, JOE, I SHY, TOO.
IN THE DARK, ALL WOMEN FEEL LIKE MARIA.

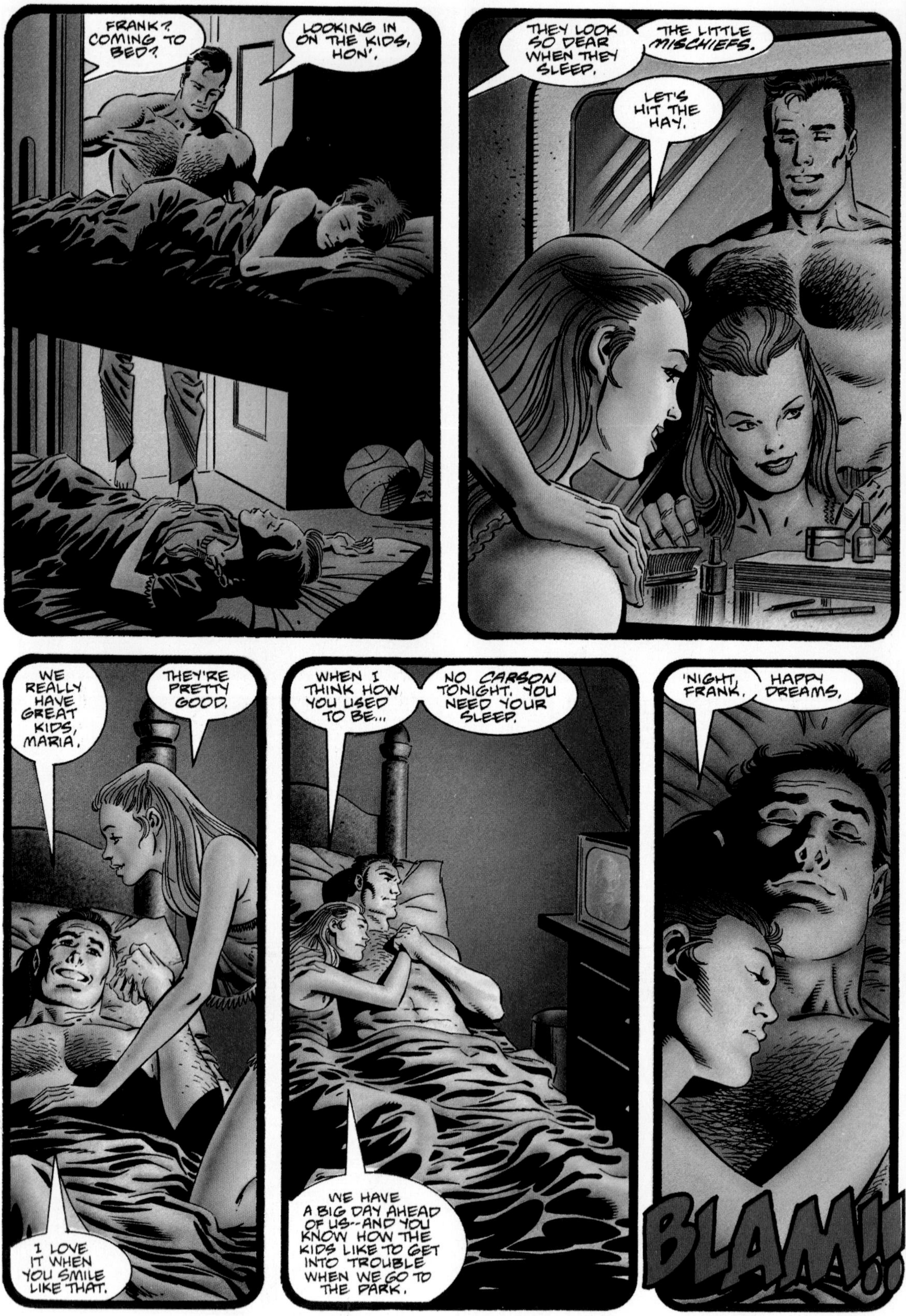

FRANK? COMING TO BED?
LOOKING IN ON THE KIDS, HON'.
THEY LOOK SO DEAR WHEN THEY SLEEP.
THE LITTLE MISCHIEFS.
LET'S HIT THE HAY.
WE REALLY HAVE GREAT KIDS, MARIA.
THEY'RE PRETTY GOOD.
I LOVE IT WHEN YOU SMILE LIKE THAT.
WHEN I THINK HOW YOU USED TO BE...
NO CARSON TONIGHT. YOU NEED YOUR SLEEP.
WE HAVE A BIG DAY AHEAD OF US--AND YOU KNOW HOW THE KIDS LIKE TO GET INTO TROUBLE WHEN WE GO TO THE PARK.
'NIGHT, FRANK.
HAPPY DREAMS.
BLAM!!

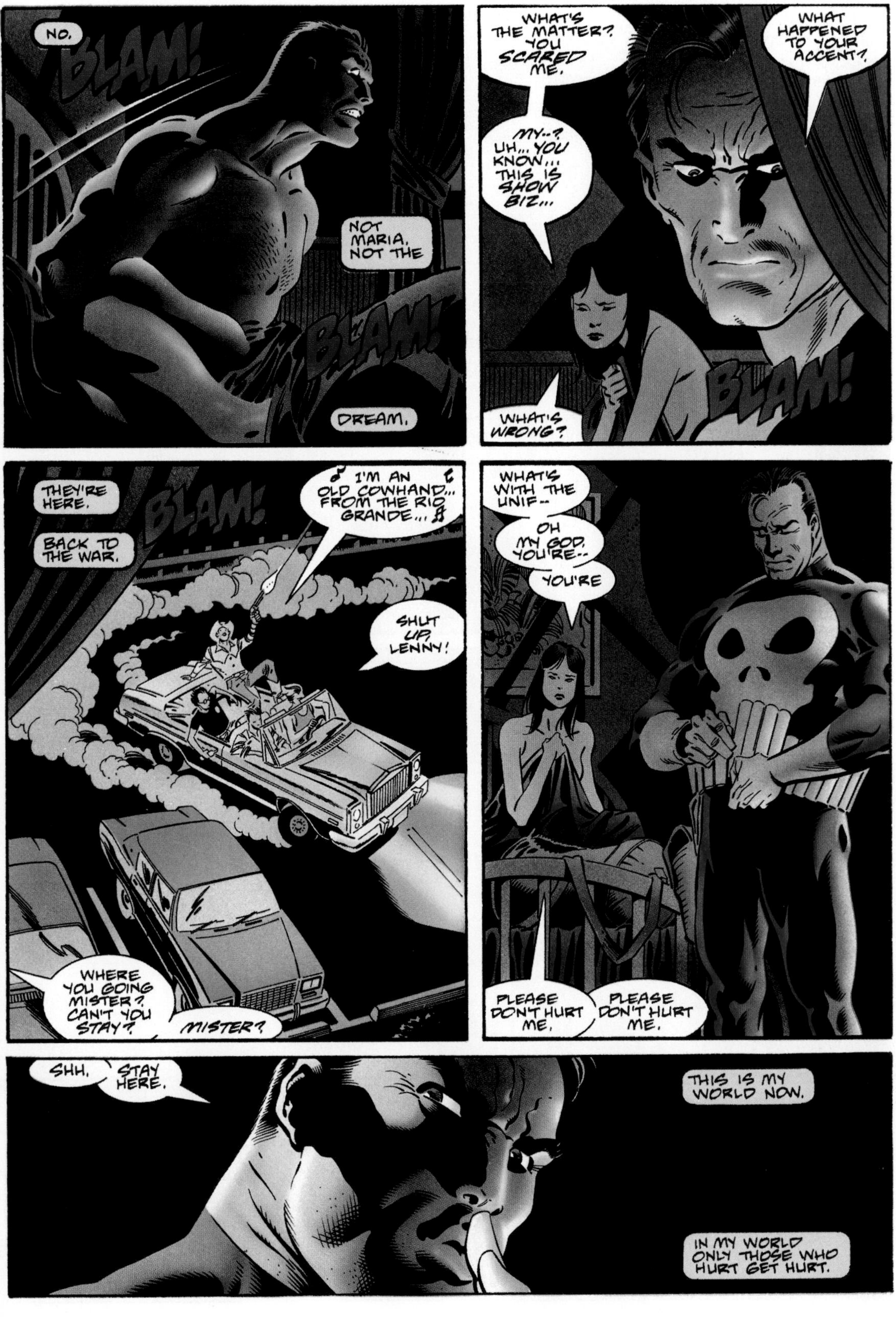
NO.
BLAM!
NOT MARIA, NOT THE
BLAM!
DREAM.
WHAT'S THE MATTER? YOU SCARED ME.
WHAT HAPPENED TO YOUR ACCENT?
MY..? UH... YOU KNOW... THIS IS SHOW BIZ...
WHAT'S WRONG?
BLAM!
THEY'RE HERE.
BLAM!
BACK TO THE WAR.
I'M AN OLD COWHAND... FROM THE RIO GRANDE...
SHUT UP, LENNY!
WHERE YOU GOING MISTER? CAN'T YOU STAY?
MISTER?
WHAT'S WITH THE UNIF--
OH MY GOD. YOU'RE--
YOU'RE
PLEASE DON'T HURT ME.
PLEASE DON'T HURT ME.
SHH.
STAY HERE.
THIS IS MY WORLD NOW.
IN MY WORLD ONLY THOSE WHO HURT GET HURT.

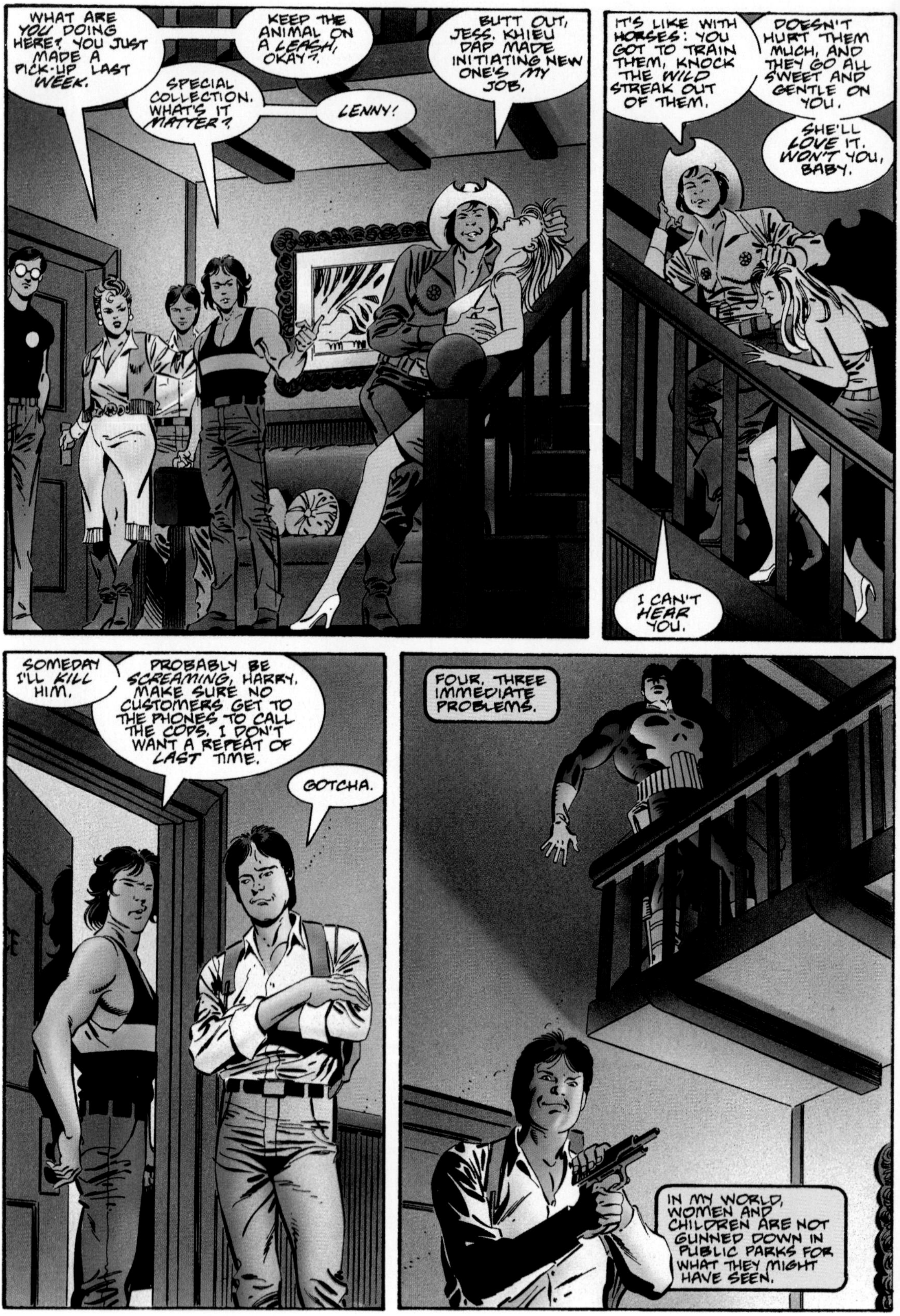

WHAT ARE YOU DOING HERE? YOU JUST MADE A PICK-UP LAST WEEK.
KEEP THE ANIMAL ON A LEASH, OKAY?
SPECIAL COLLECTION. WHAT'S IT MATTER?
LENNY!
BUTT OUT, JESS. KHIEU DAP MADE INITIATING NEW ONE'S MY JOB.
IT'S LIKE WITH HORSES: YOU GOT TO TRAIN THEM, KNOCK THE WILD STREAK OUT OF THEM.
DOESN'T HURT THEM MUCH, AND THEY GO ALL SWEET AND GENTLE ON YOU.
SHE'LL LOVE IT. WON'T YOU, BABY.
I CAN'T HEAR YOU.
SOMEDAY I'LL KILL HIM.
PROBABLY BE SCREAMING, HARRY. MAKE SURE NO CUSTOMERS GET TO THE PHONES TO CALL THE COPS. I DON'T WANT A REPEAT OF LAST TIME.
GOTCHA.
FOUR. THREE IMMEDIATE PROBLEMS.
IN MY WORLD, WOMEN AND CHILDREN ARE NOT GUNNED DOWN IN PUBLIC PARKS FOR WHAT THEY MIGHT HAVE SEEN.

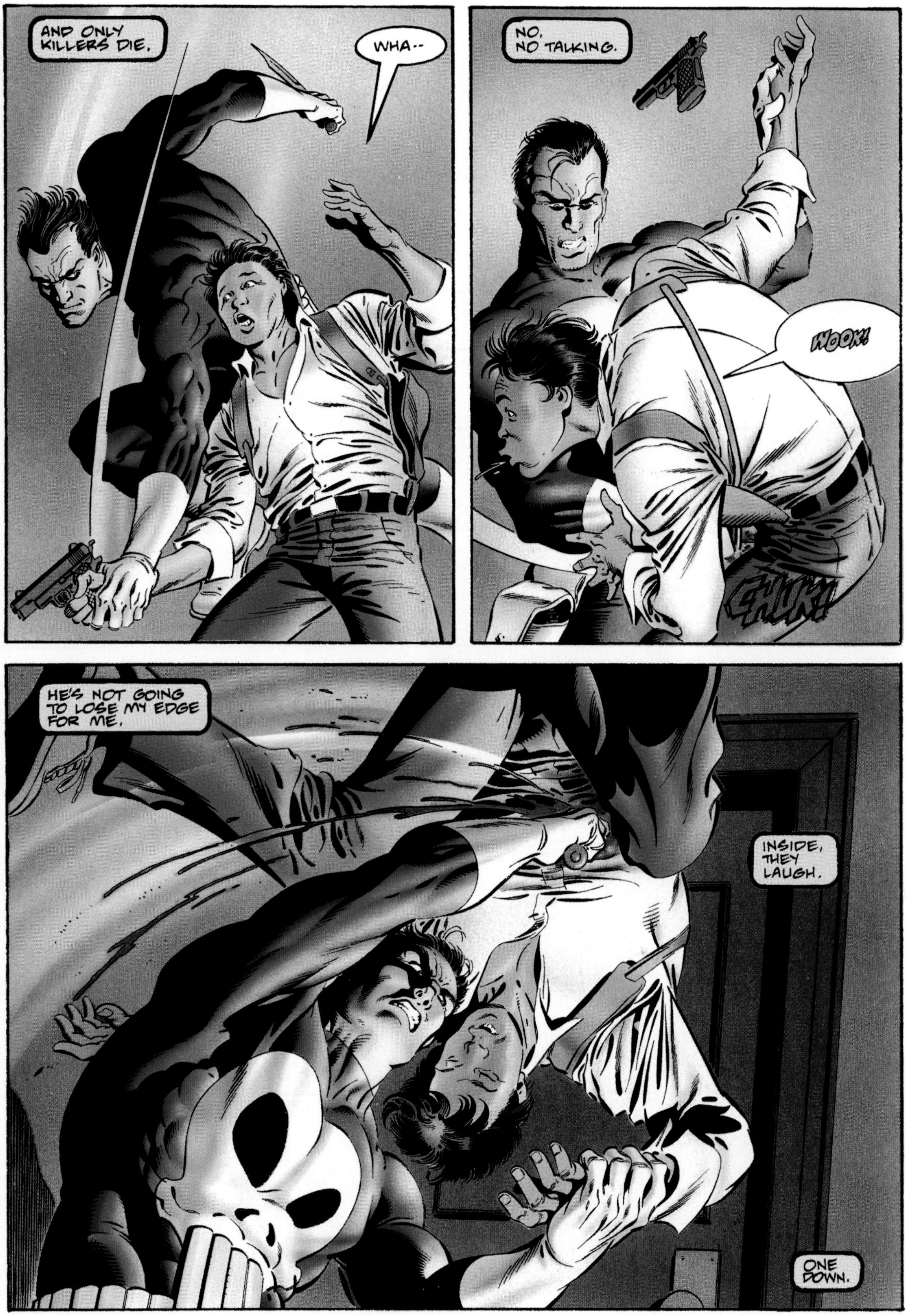
AND ONLY KILLERS DIE.
WHA--
NO. NO TALKING.
WOOK!
CHUK!
HE'S NOT GOING TO LOSE MY EDGE FOR ME.
INSIDE, THEY LAUGH.
ONE DOWN.

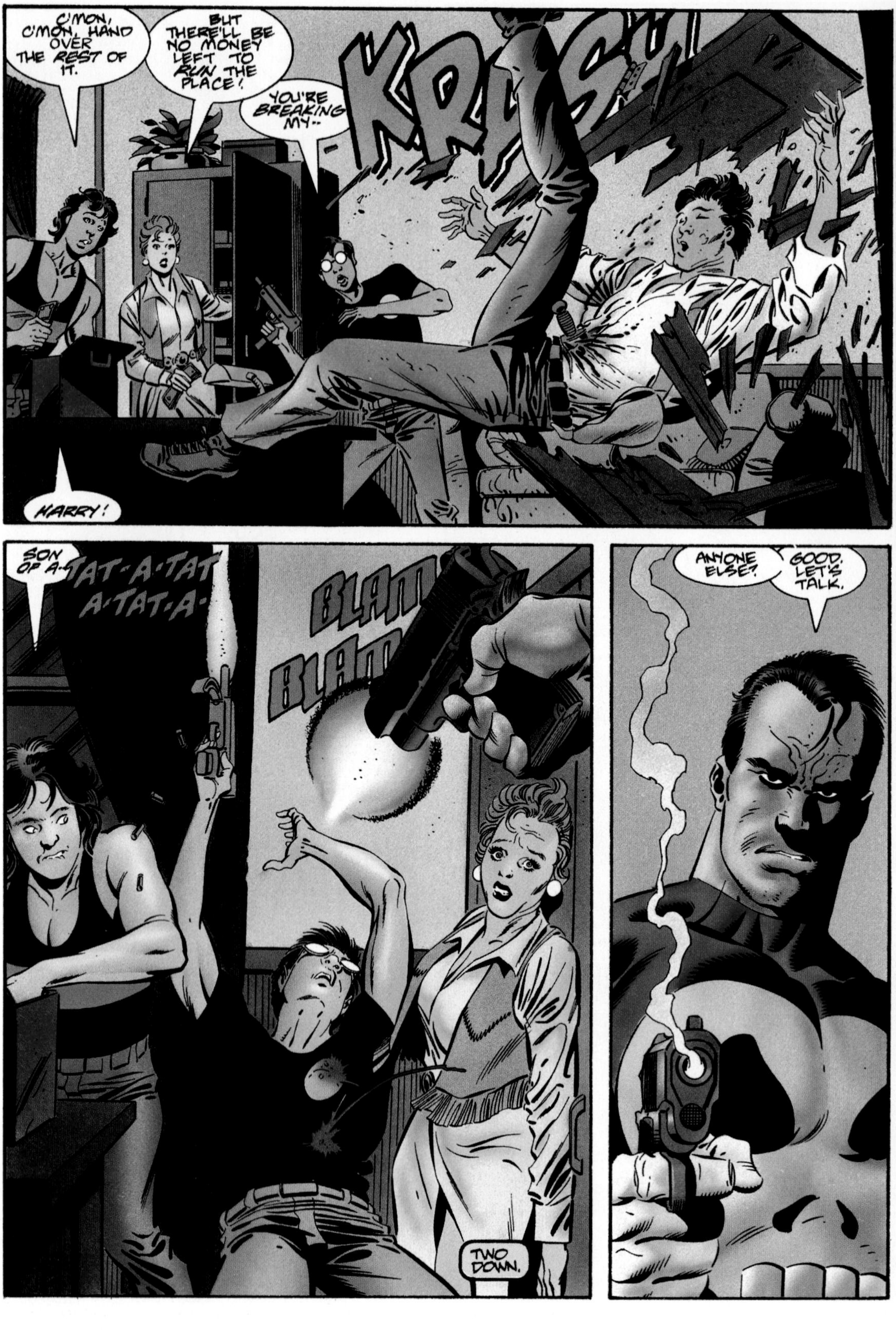
C'MON, C'MON, HAND OVER THE REST OF IT.
BUT THERE'LL BE NO MONEY LEFT TO RUN THE PLACE!
YOU'RE BREAKING MY--
KRASH!
HARRY!
SON OF A--
TAT-A-TAT A-TAT-A-
BLAM BLAM
TWO DOWN.
ANYONE ELSE?
GOOD. LET'S TALK.

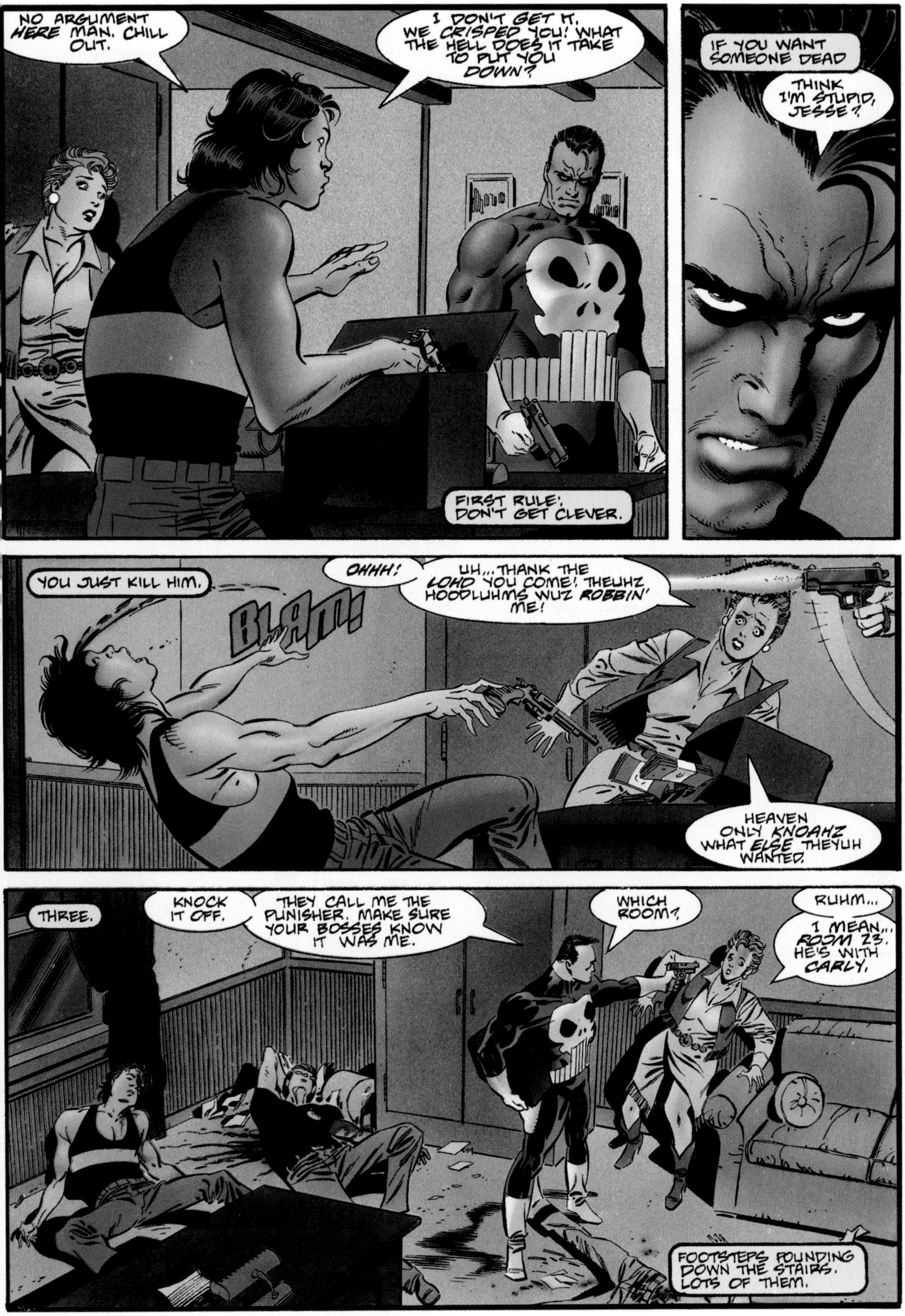
NO ARGUMENT HERE MAN. CHILL OUT.
I DON'T GET IT. WE CRISPED YOU! WHAT THE HELL DOES IT TAKE TO PUT YOU DOWN?
FIRST RULE: DON'T GET CLEVER.
IF YOU WANT SOMEONE DEAD
THINK I'M STUPID, JESSE?
YOU JUST KILL HIM.
BLAM!
OHHH!
UH,.. THANK THE LOHD YOU COME! THEUHZ HOODLUHMS WUZ ROBBIN' ME!
HEAVEN ONLY KNOAHZ WHAT ELSE THEYUH WANTED.
THREE.
KNOCK IT OFF.
THEY CALL ME THE PUNISHER. MAKE SURE YOUR BOSSES KNOW IT WAS ME.
WHICH ROOM?
RUHM...
I MEAN... ROOM 23. HE'S WITH CARLY.
FOOTSTEPS POUNDING DOWN THE STAIRS. LOTS OF THEM.

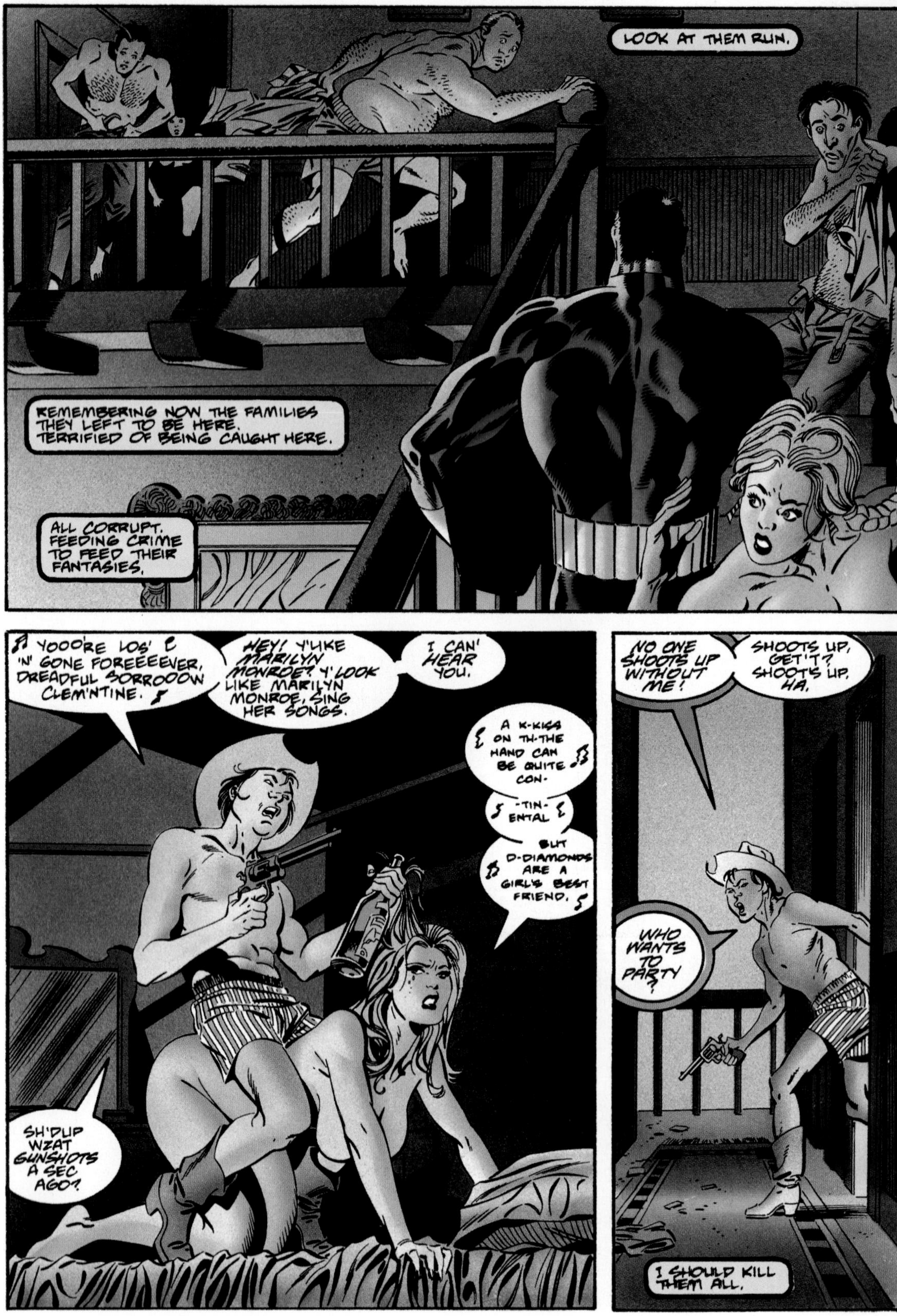
LOOK AT THEM RUN.
REMEMBERING NOW THE FAMILIES THEY LEFT TO BE HERE. TERRIFIED OF BEING CAUGHT HERE.
ALL CORRUPT. FEEDING CRIME TO FEED THEIR FANTASIES.
YOOO'RE LOS' 'N' GONE FOREEEEVER, DREADFUL SORROOOW CLEM'NTINE.
HEY! Y'LIKE MARILYN MONROE? Y' LOOK LIKE MARILYN MONROE, SING HER SONGS.
I CAN' HEAR YOU.
A K-KISS ON TH-THE HAND CAN BE QUITE CON-
-TIN-ENTAL
BUT D-DIAMONDS ARE A GIRL'S BEST FRIEND.
SH'DUP WZAT GUNSHOTS A SEC AGO?
NO ONE SHOOTS UP WITHOUT ME!
SHOOTS UP, GET'T? SHOOT'S UP, HA.
WHO WANTS TO PARTY?
I SHOULD KILL THEM ALL.

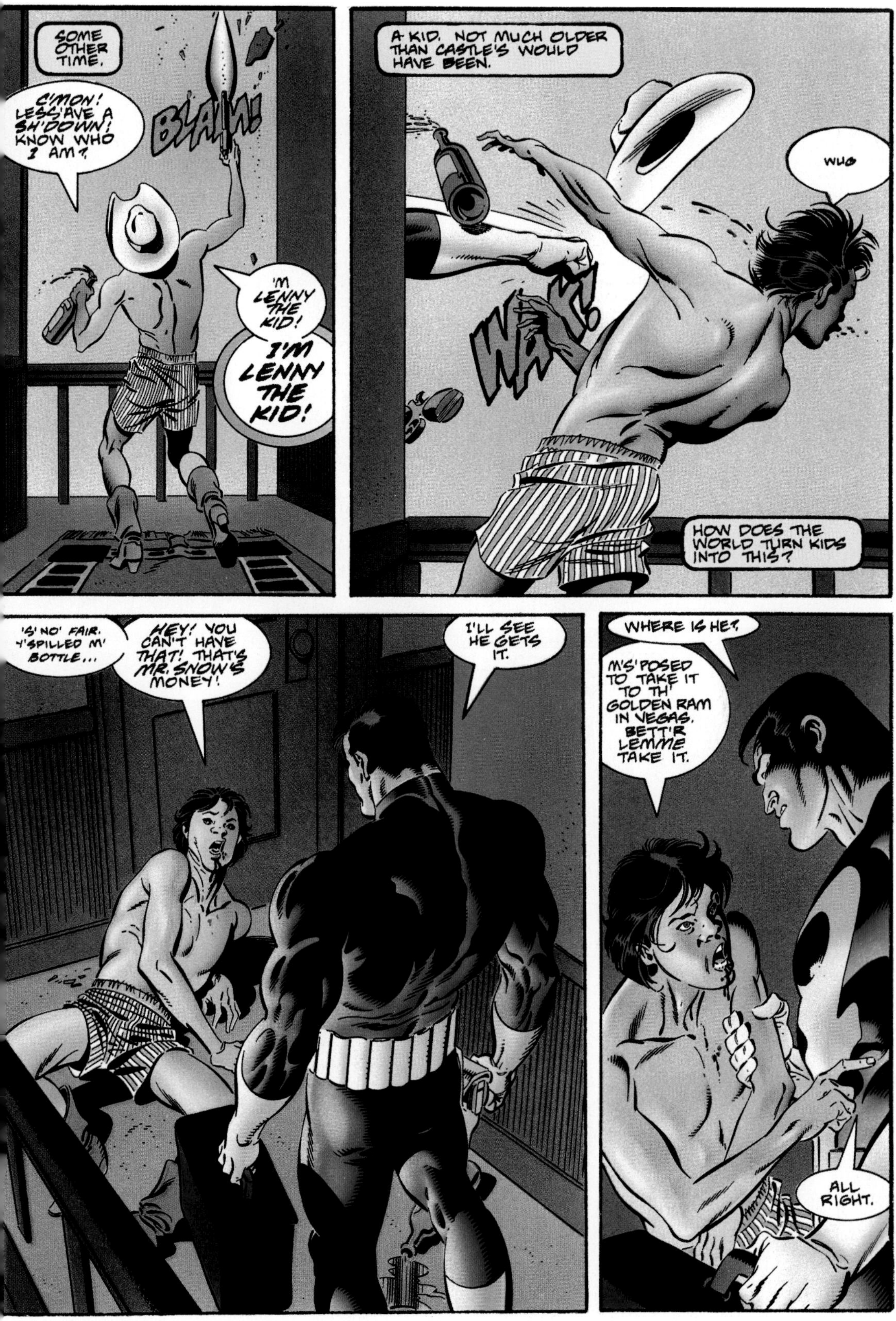
SOME OTHER TIME.
C'MON! LESS'AVE A SH'DOWN! KNOW WHO I AM?
BLAM!
'M LENNY THE KID!
I'M LENNY THE KID!
A KID. NOT MUCH OLDER THAN CASTLE'S WOULD HAVE BEEN.
WUG
HOW DOES THE WORLD TURN KIDS INTO THIS?
'S NO' FAIR. Y'SPILLED M' BOTTLE...
HEY! YOU CAN'T HAVE THAT! THAT'S MR. SNOW'S MONEY!
I'LL SEE HE GETS IT.
WHERE IS HE?
M'S'POSED TO TAKE IT TO TH' GOLDEN RAM IN VEGAS. BETT'R LEMME TAKE IT.
ALL RIGHT.

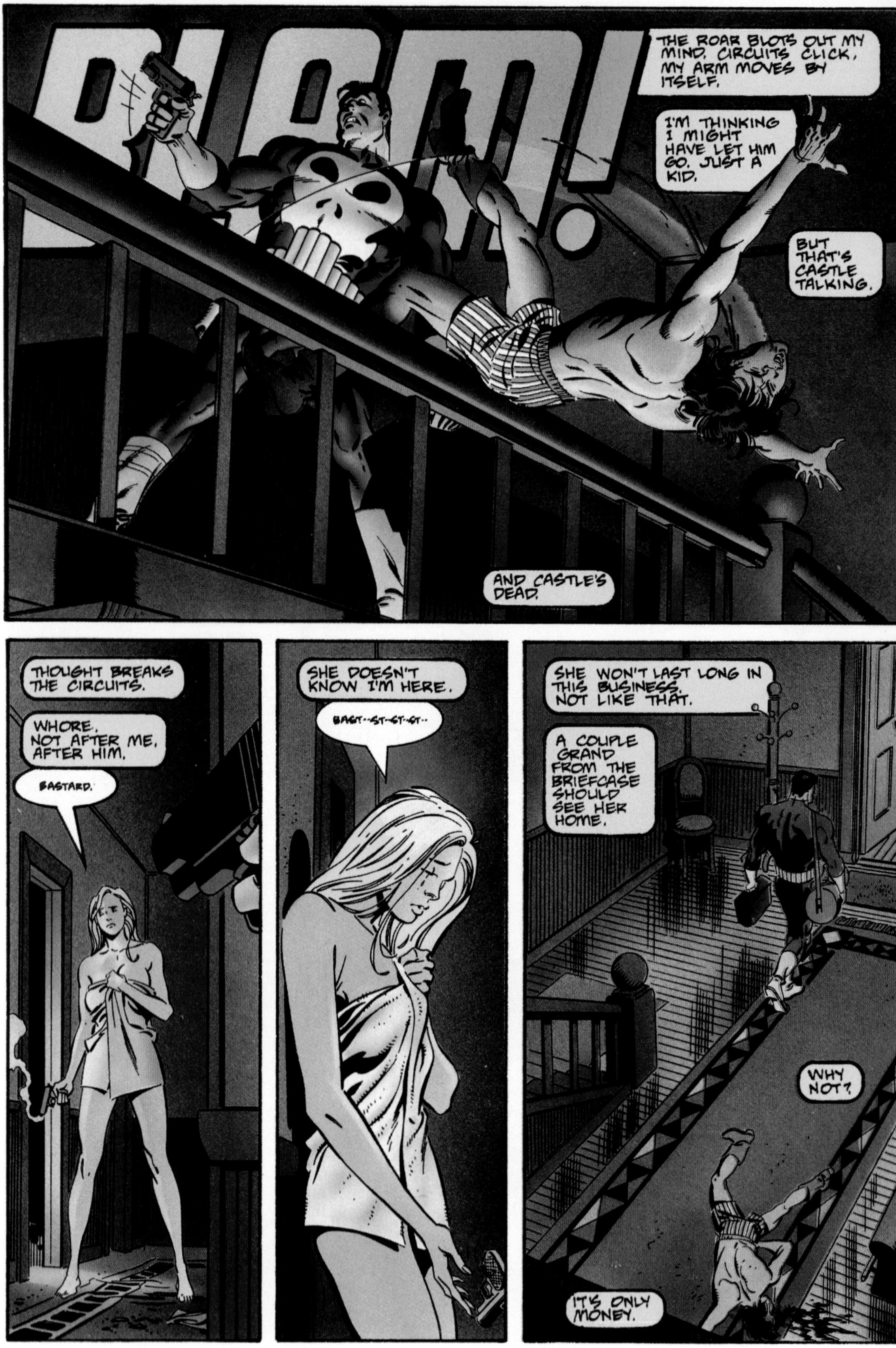
THE ROAR BLOTS OUT MY MIND. CIRCUITS CLICK. MY ARM MOVES BY ITSELF.
I'M THINKING I MIGHT HAVE LET HIM GO. JUST A KID.
BUT THAT'S CASTLE TALKING.
AND CASTLE'S DEAD.
THOUGHT BREAKS THE CIRCUITS.
WHORE. NOT AFTER ME. AFTER HIM.
BASTARD.
SHE DOESN'T KNOW I'M HERE.
SHE WON'T LAST LONG IN THIS BUSINESS. NOT LIKE THAT.
A COUPLE GRAND FROM THE BRIEFCASE SHOULD SEE HER HOME.
WHY NOT?
IT'S ONLY MONEY.

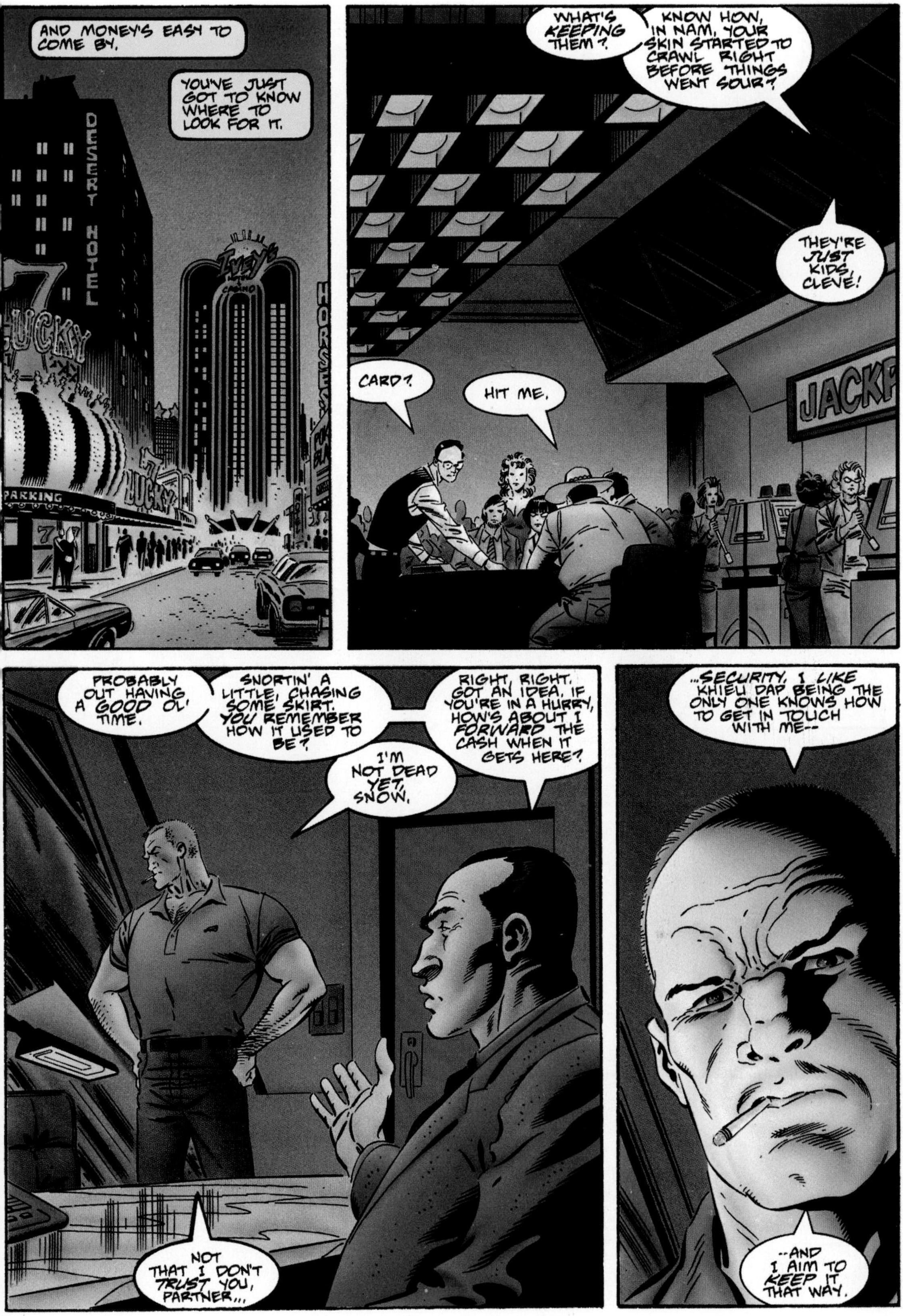
AND MONEY'S EASY TO COME BY.
YOU'VE JUST GOT TO KNOW WHERE TO LOOK FOR IT.
DESERT HOTEL
LUCKY
PARKING
HORSES
WHAT'S KEEPING THEM?
KNOW HOW, IN NAM, YOUR SKIN STARTED TO CRAWL RIGHT BEFORE THINGS WENT SOUR?
THEY'RE JUST KIDS, CLEVE!
CARD?
HIT ME.
PROBABLY OUT HAVING A GOOD OL' TIME.
SNORTIN' A LITTLE, CHASING SOME SKIRT. YOU REMEMBER HOW IT USED TO BE?
RIGHT, RIGHT. GOT AN IDEA. IF YOU'RE IN A HURRY, HOW'S ABOUT I FORWARD THE CASH WHEN IT GETS HERE?
I'M NOT DEAD YET, SNOW.
NOT THAT I DON'T TRUST YOU, PARTNER...
...SECURITY. I LIKE KHIEU DAP BEING THE ONLY ONE KNOWS HOW TO GET IN TOUCH WITH ME--
--AND I AIM TO KEEP IT THAT WAY.

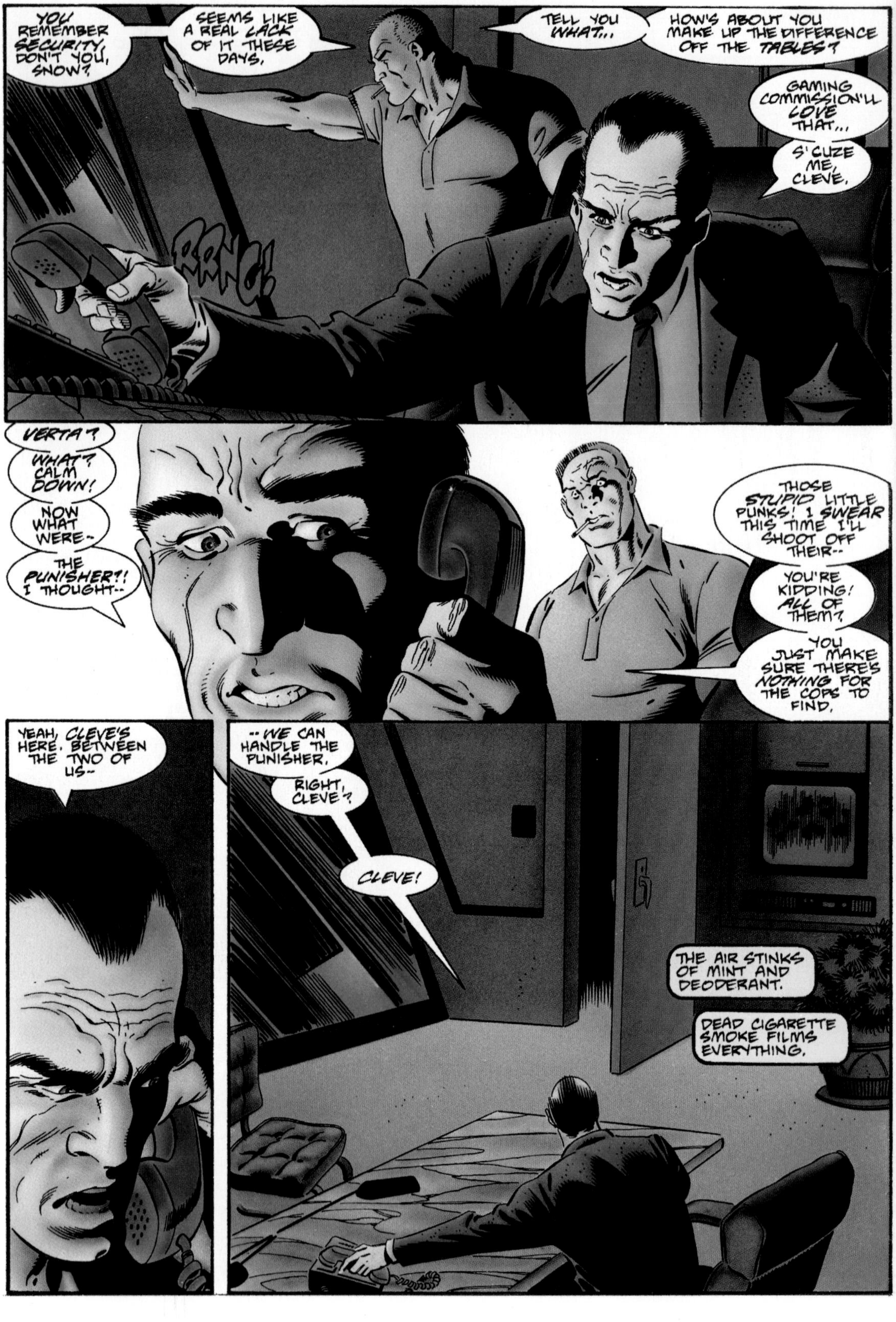
YOU REMEMBER SECURITY, DON'T YOU, SNOW?
SEEMS LIKE A REAL LACK OF IT THESE DAYS.
TELL YOU WHAT...
HOW'S ABOUT YOU MAKE UP THE DIFFERENCE OFF THE TABLES?
GAMING COMMISSION'LL LOVE THAT...
S'CUZE ME, CLEVE.
BRRNG!
VERTA?
WHAT? CALM DOWN!
NOW WHAT WERE--
THE PUNISHER?! I THOUGHT--
THOSE STUPID LITTLE PUNKS! I SWEAR THIS TIME I'LL SHOOT OFF THEIR--
YOU'RE KIDDING! ALL OF THEM?
YOU JUST MAKE SURE THERE'S NOTHING FOR THE COPS TO FIND.
YEAH, CLEVE'S HERE. BETWEEN THE TWO OF US--
--WE CAN HANDLE THE PUNISHER.
RIGHT, CLEVE?
CLEVE!
THE AIR STINKS OF MINT AND DEODERANT.
DEAD CIGARETTE SMOKE FILMS EVERYTHING.

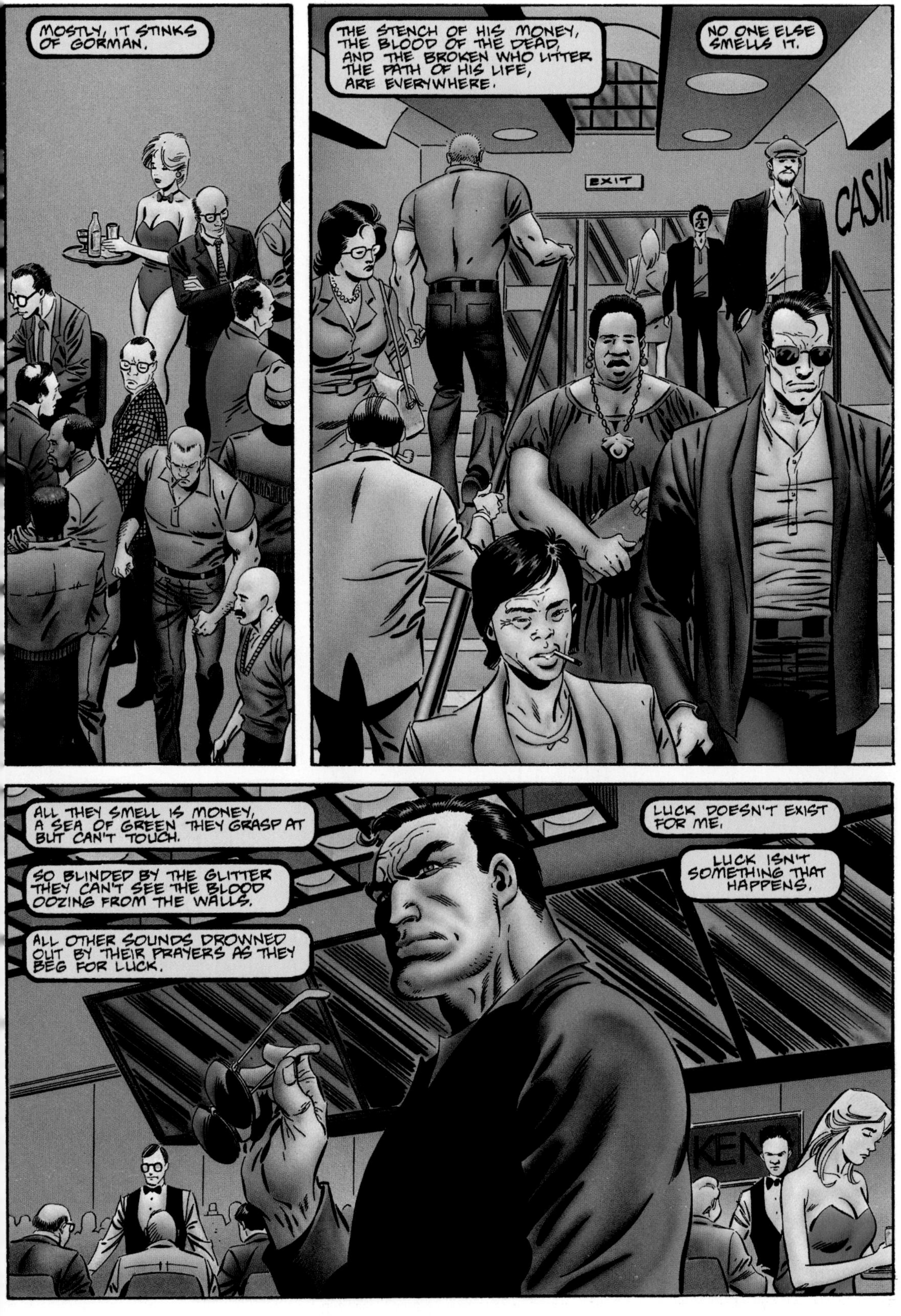
MOSTLY, IT STINKS OF GORMAN.
THE STENCH OF HIS MONEY, THE BLOOD OF THE DEAD, AND THE BROKEN WHO LITTER THE PATH OF HIS LIFE, ARE EVERYWHERE.
NO ONE ELSE SMELLS IT.
EXIT
CASIN
ALL THEY SMELL IS MONEY, A SEA OF GREEN THEY GRASP AT BUT CAN'T TOUCH.
SO BLINDED BY THE GLITTER THEY CAN'T SEE THE BLOOD OOZING FROM THE WALLS.
ALL OTHER SOUNDS DROWNED OUT BY THEIR PRAYERS AS THEY BEG FOR LUCK.
LUCK DOESN'T EXIST FOR ME.
LUCK ISN'T SOMETHING THAT HAPPENS.
KEN

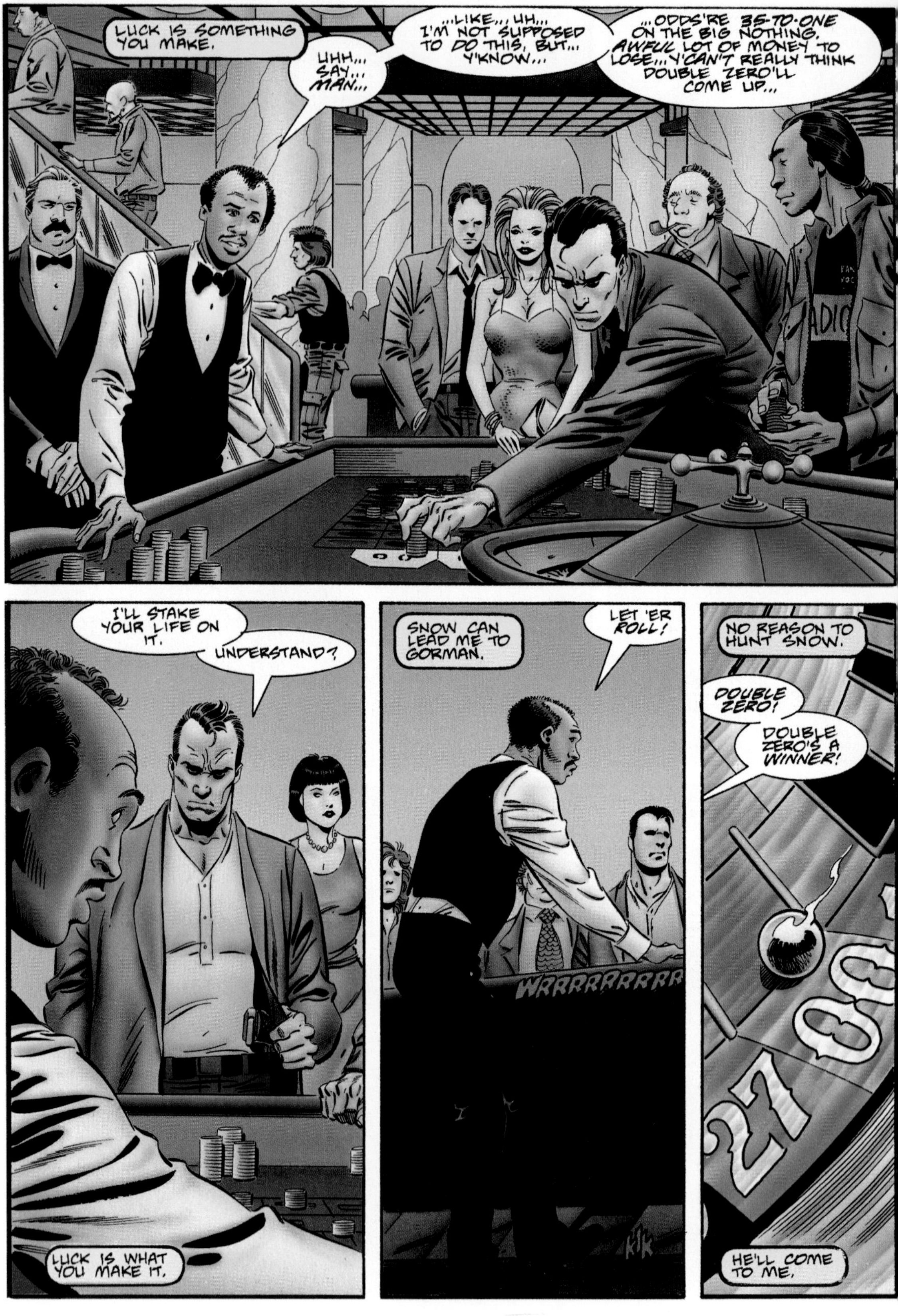

LUCK IS SOMETHING YOU MAKE.
UHH... SAY... MAN...
...LIKE... UH... I'M NOT SUPPOSED TO DO THIS, BUT... Y'KNOW...
...ODDS'RE 35-TO-ONE ON THE BIG NOTHING. AWFUL LOT OF MONEY TO LOSE... Y'CAN'T REALLY THINK DOUBLE ZERO'LL COME UP...
I'LL STAKE YOUR LIFE ON IT.
UNDERSTAND?
LUCK IS WHAT YOU MAKE IT.
SNOW CAN LEAD ME TO GORMAN.
LET 'ER ROLL!
WRRRRRRRRR
NO REASON TO HUNT SNOW.
DOUBLE ZERO!
DOUBLE ZERO'S A WINNER!
HE'LL COME TO ME.

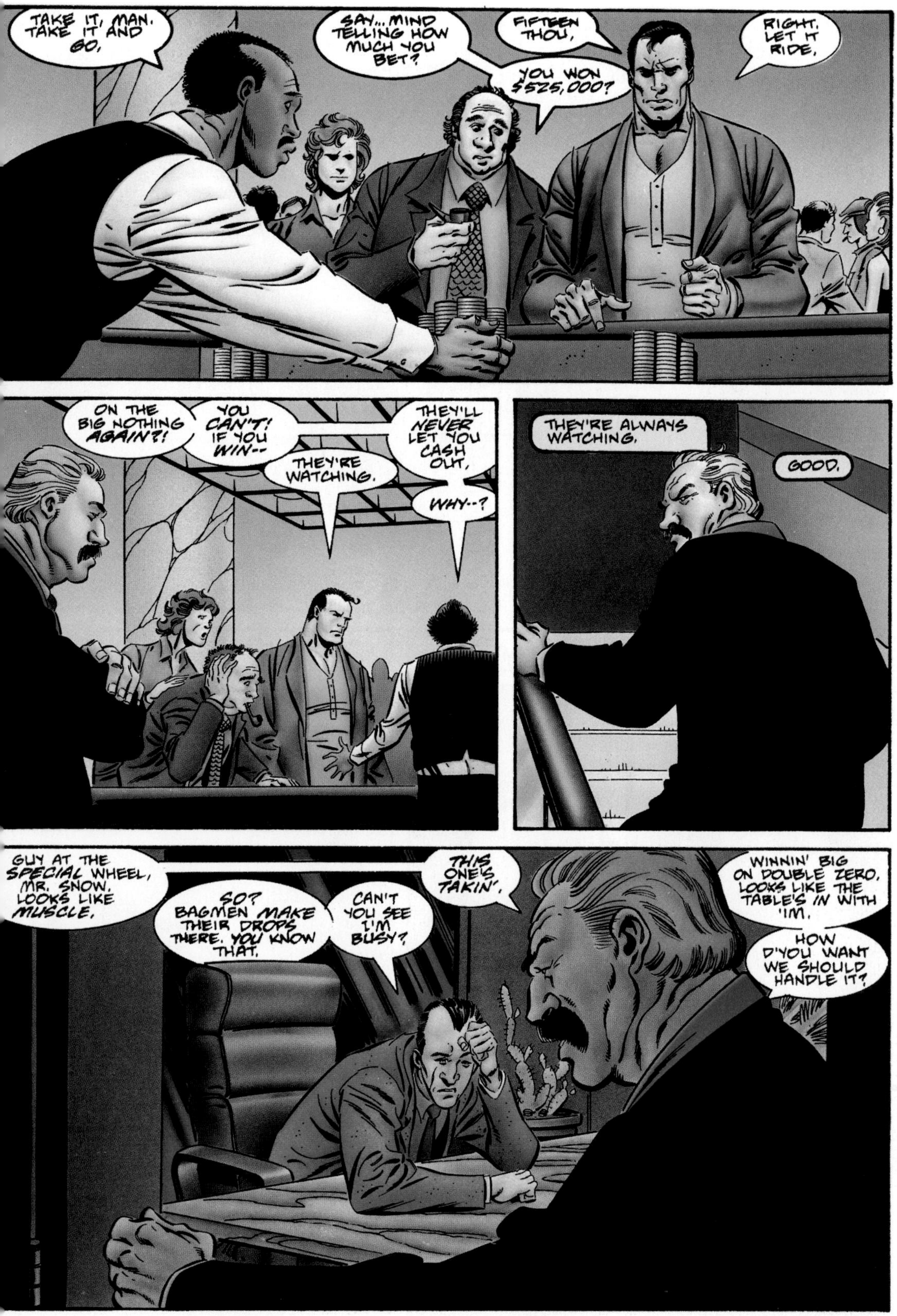
TAKE IT, MAN. TAKE IT AND GO.
SAY... MIND TELLING HOW MUCH YOU BET?
FIFTEEN THOU.
YOU WON $525,000?
RIGHT. LET IT RIDE.
ON THE BIG NOTHING AGAIN?!
YOU CAN'T! IF YOU WIN--
THEY'RE WATCHING.
THEY'LL NEVER LET YOU CASH OUT.
WHY--?
THEY'RE ALWAYS WATCHING.
GOOD.
GUY AT THE SPECIAL WHEEL, MR. SNOW. LOOKS LIKE MUSCLE.
SO? BAGMEN MAKE THEIR DROPS THERE. YOU KNOW THAT.
CAN'T YOU SEE I'M BUSY?
THIS ONE'S TAKIN'.
WINNIN' BIG ON DOUBLE ZERO. LOOKS LIKE THE TABLE'S IN WITH 'IM.
HOW D'YOU WANT WE SHOULD HANDLE IT?

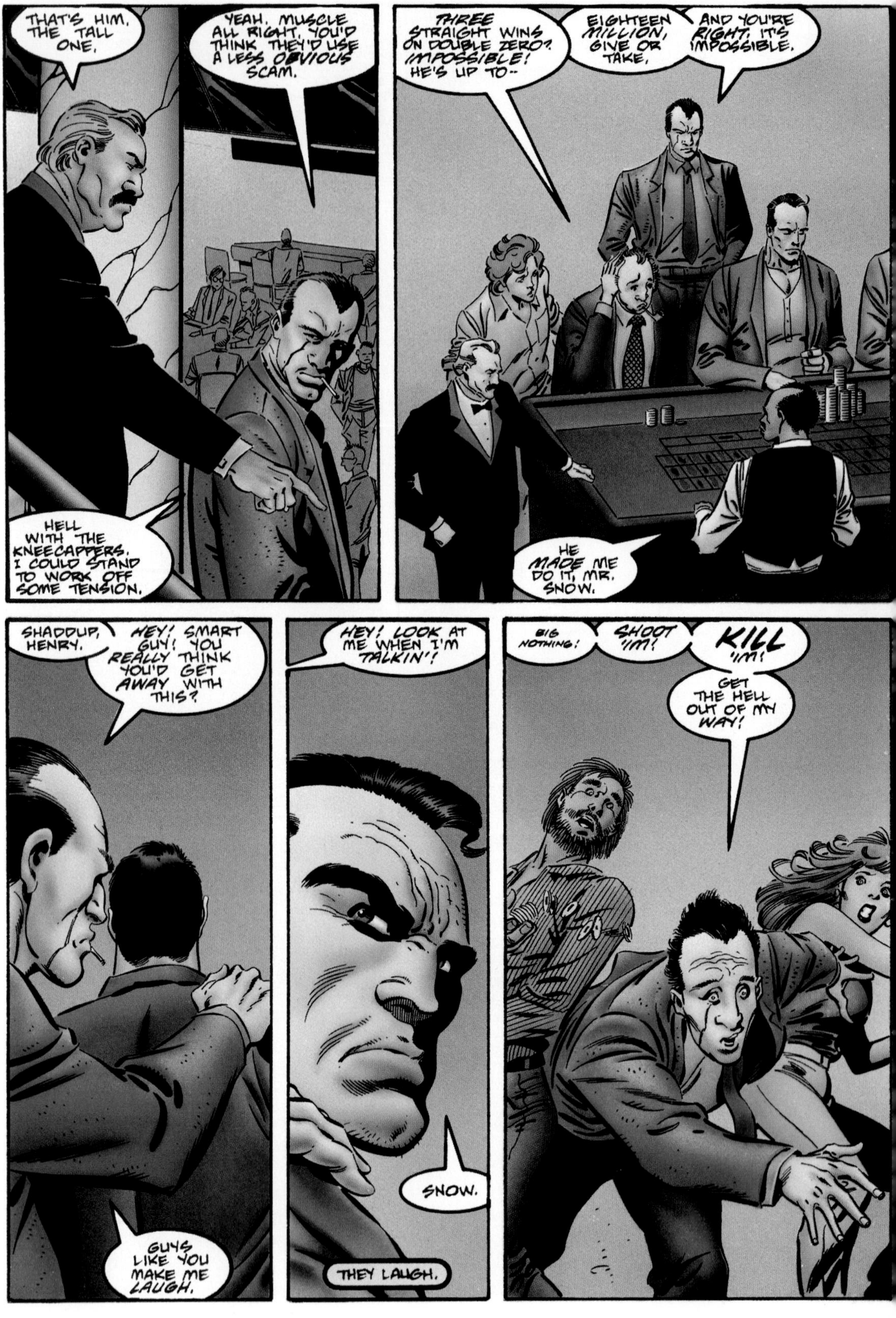
THAT'S HIM, THE TALL ONE.
YEAH. MUSCLE ALL RIGHT. YOU'D THINK THEY'D USE A LESS OBVIOUS SCAM.
HELL WITH THE KNEECAPPERS. I COULD STAND TO WORK OFF SOME TENSION.
THREE STRAIGHT WINS ON DOUBLE ZERO? IMPOSSIBLE! HE'S UP TO--
EIGHTEEN MILLION, GIVE OR TAKE.
AND YOU'RE RIGHT. IT'S IMPOSSIBLE.
HE MADE ME DO IT, MR. SNOW.
SHADDUP, HENRY.
HEY! SMART GUY! YOU REALLY THINK YOU'D GET AWAY WITH THIS?
GUYS LIKE YOU MAKE ME LAUGH.
HEY! LOOK AT ME WHEN I'M TALKIN'!
SNOW.
THEY LAUGH.
BIG NOTHING!
SHOOT 'IM!
KILL 'IM!
GET THE HELL OUT OF MY WAY!

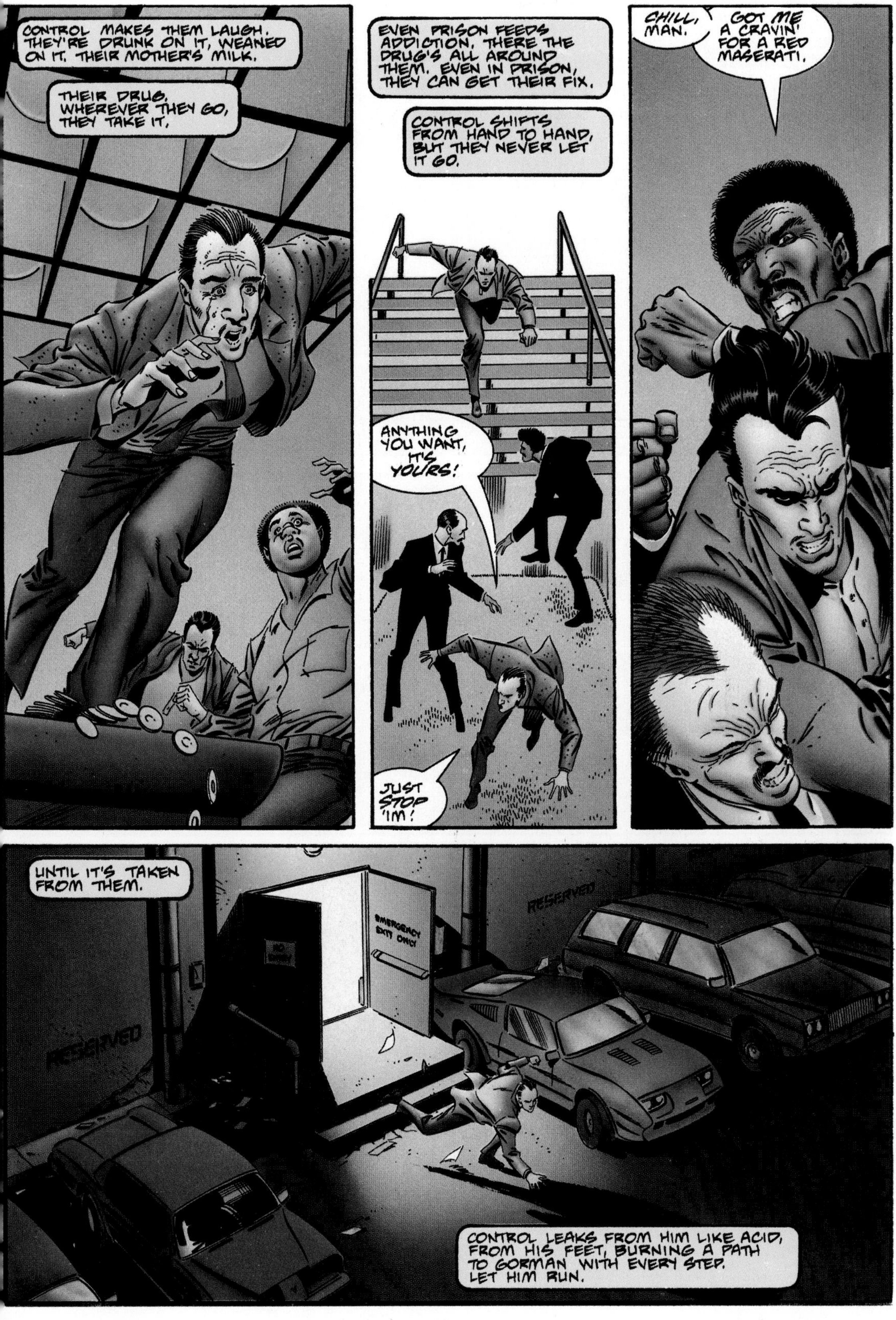
CONTROL MAKES THEM LAUGH. THEY'RE DRUNK ON IT, WEANED ON IT. THEIR MOTHER'S MILK.
THEIR DRUG. WHEREVER THEY GO, THEY TAKE IT.
EVEN PRISON FEEDS ADDICTION. THERE THE DRUG'S ALL AROUND THEM. EVEN IN PRISON, THEY CAN GET THEIR FIX.
CONTROL SHIFTS FROM HAND TO HAND, BUT THEY NEVER LET IT GO.
ANYTHING YOU WANT, IT'S YOURS!
JUST STOP 'IM!
CHILL, MAN.
GOT ME A CRAVIN' FOR A RED MASERATI.
UNTIL IT'S TAKEN FROM THEM.
RESERVED
EMERGENCY EXIT ONLY
RESERVED
CONTROL LEAKS FROM HIM LIKE ACID, FROM HIS FEET, BURNING A PATH TO GORMAN WITH EVERY STEP. LET HIM RUN.

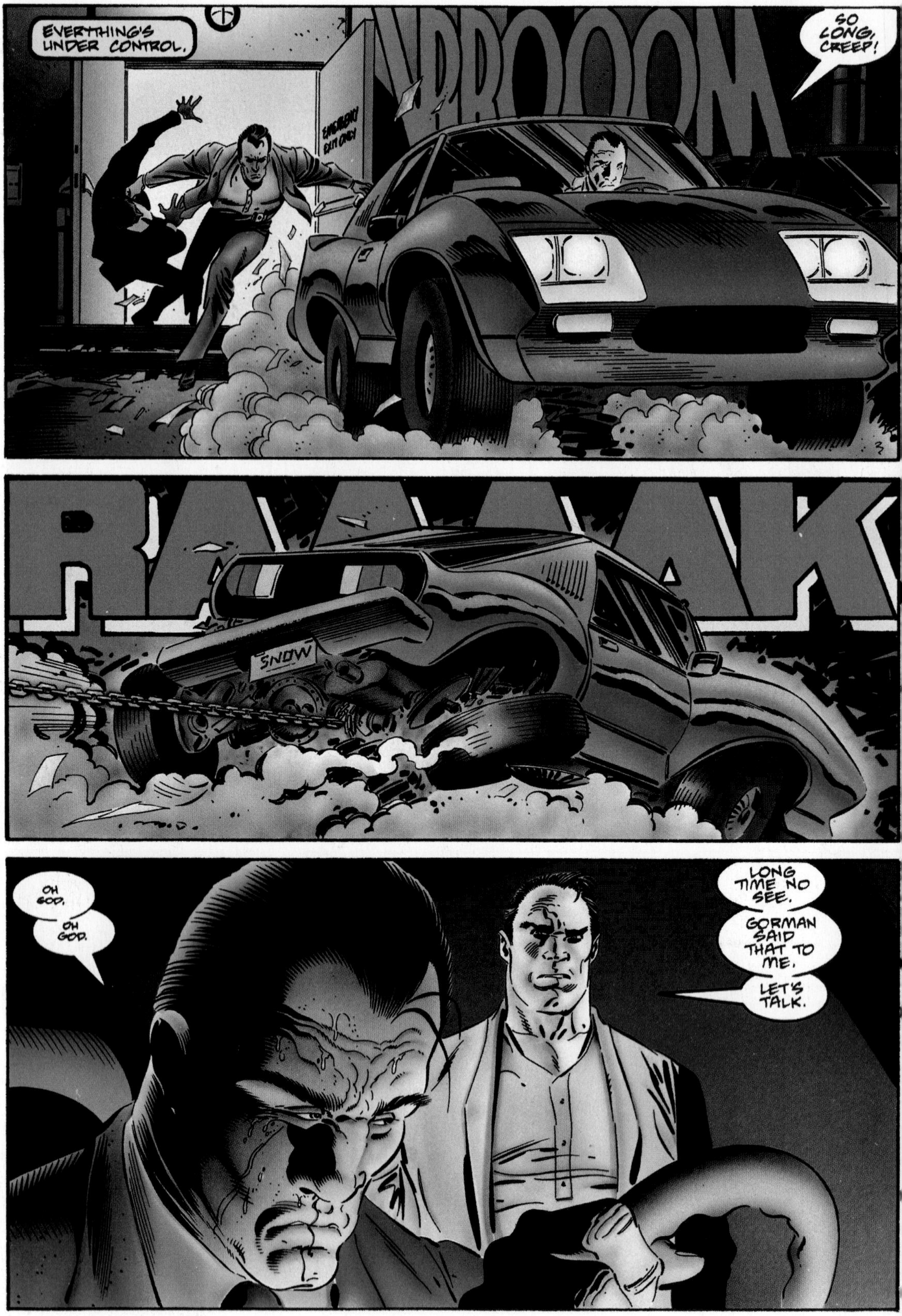
EVERYTHING'S UNDER CONTROL.
VRROOOM
SO LONG, CREEP!
RAAAK
SNOW
OH GOD.
OH GOD.
LONG TIME NO SEE.
GORMAN SAID THAT TO ME.
LET'S TALK.

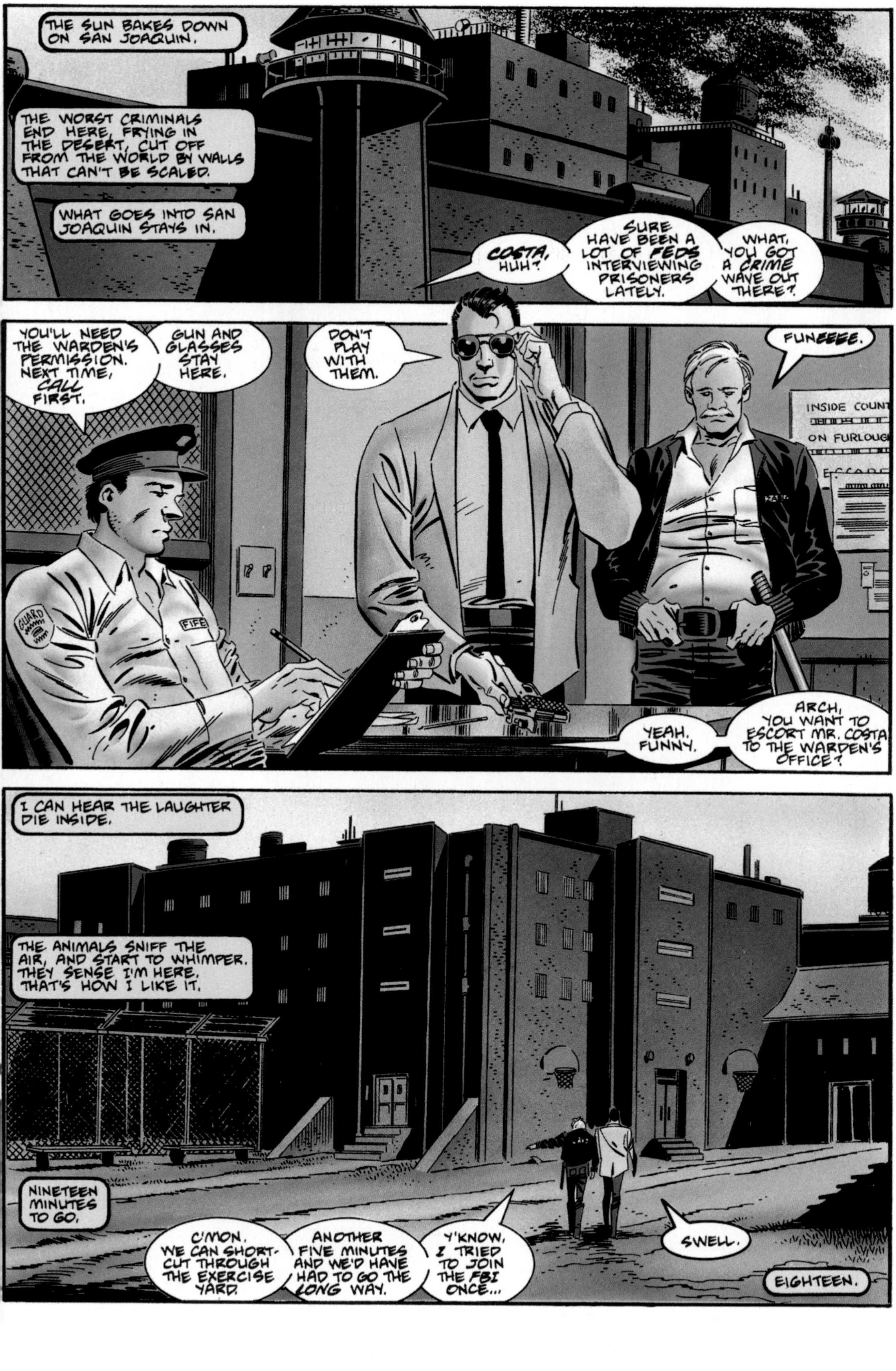
THE SUN BAKES DOWN ON SAN JOAQUIN.
THE WORST CRIMINALS END HERE, FRYING IN THE DESERT, CUT OFF FROM THE WORLD BY WALLS THAT CAN'T BE SCALED.
WHAT GOES INTO SAN JOAQUIN STAYS IN.
COSTA, HUH?
SURE HAVE BEEN A LOT OF FEDS INTERVIEWING PRISONERS LATELY.
WHAT, YOU GOT A CRIME WAVE OUT THERE?
YOU'LL NEED THE WARDEN'S PERMISSION. NEXT TIME, CALL FIRST.
GUN AND GLASSES STAY HERE.
DON'T PLAY WITH THEM.
FUNEEEE.
INSIDE COUNT
ON FURLOUGH
GUARD
FIFE
YEAH. FUNNY.
ARCH, YOU WANT TO ESCORT MR. COSTA TO THE WARDEN'S OFFICE?
I CAN HEAR THE LAUGHTER DIE INSIDE.
THE ANIMALS SNIFF THE AIR, AND START TO WHIMPER. THEY SENSE I'M HERE. THAT'S HOW I LIKE IT.
NINETEEN MINUTES TO GO.
C'MON. WE CAN SHORT-CUT THROUGH THE EXERCISE YARD.
ANOTHER FIVE MINUTES AND WE'D HAVE HAD TO GO THE LONG WAY.
Y'KNOW, I TRIED TO JOIN THE FBI ONCE...
SWELL.
EIGHTEEN.

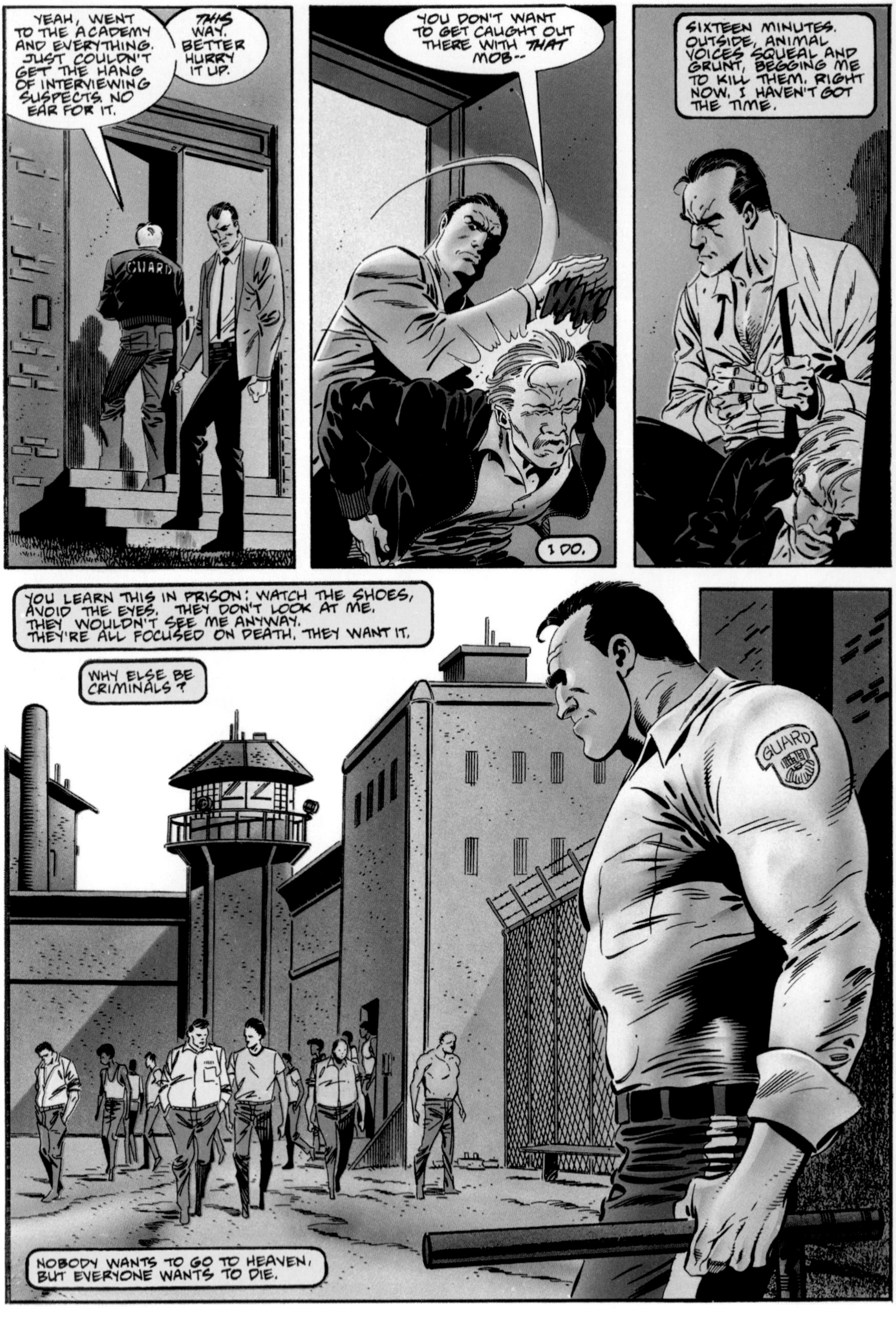
YEAH, WENT TO THE ACADEMY AND EVERYTHING. JUST COULDN'T GET THE HANG OF INTERVIEWING SUSPECTS. NO EAR FOR IT.
THIS WAY. BETTER HURRY IT UP.
GUARD
YOU DON'T WANT TO GET CAUGHT OUT THERE WITH THAT MOB--
WAK!
I DO.
SIXTEEN MINUTES. OUTSIDE, ANIMAL VOICES SQUEAL AND GRUNT, BEGGING ME TO KILL THEM. RIGHT NOW, I HAVEN'T GOT THE TIME.
YOU LEARN THIS IN PRISON: WATCH THE SHOES, AVOID THE EYES. THEY DON'T LOOK AT ME. THEY WOULDN'T SEE ME ANYWAY. THEY'RE ALL FOCUSED ON DEATH. THEY WANT IT.
WHY ELSE BE CRIMINALS?
GUARD
NOBODY WANTS TO GO TO HEAVEN, BUT EVERYONE WANTS TO DIE.

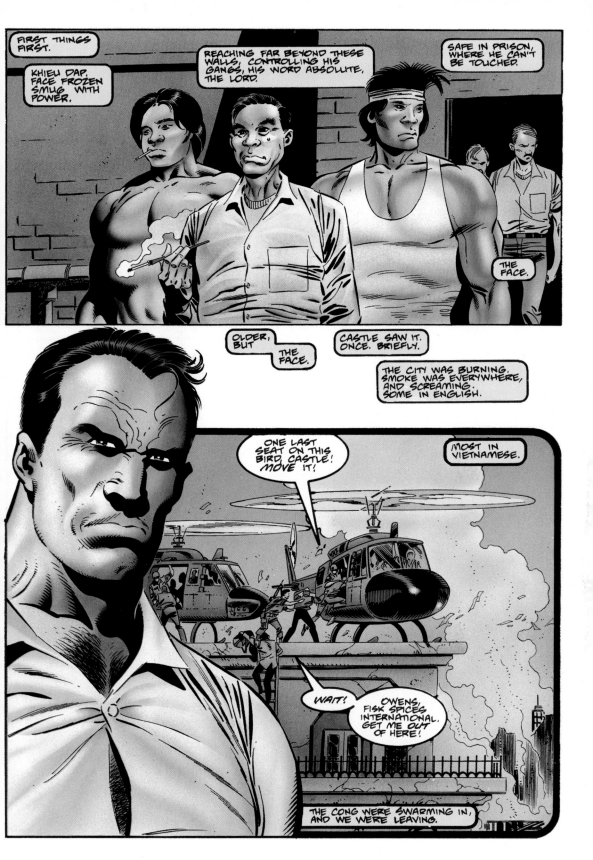

FIRST THINGS FIRST.

KHIEU DAP, FACE FROZEN SMUG WITH POWER.

REACHING FAR BEYOND THESE WALLS, CONTROLLING HIS GANGS, HIS WORD ABSOLUTE, THE LORD.

SAFE IN PRISON, WHERE HE CAN'T BE TOUCHED.

THE FACE.

OLDER, BUT THE FACE.

CASTLE SAW IT. ONCE. BRIEFLY.

THE CITY WAS BURNING. SMOKE WAS EVERYWHERE, AND SCREAMING. SOME IN ENGLISH.

ONE LAST SEAT ON THIS BIRD, CASTLE! MOVE IT!

MOST IN VIETNAMESE.

WAIT!

OWENS, FISK SPICES INTERNATIONAL, GET ME OUT OF HERE!

THE CONG WERE SWARMING IN, AND WE WERE LEAVING.

51

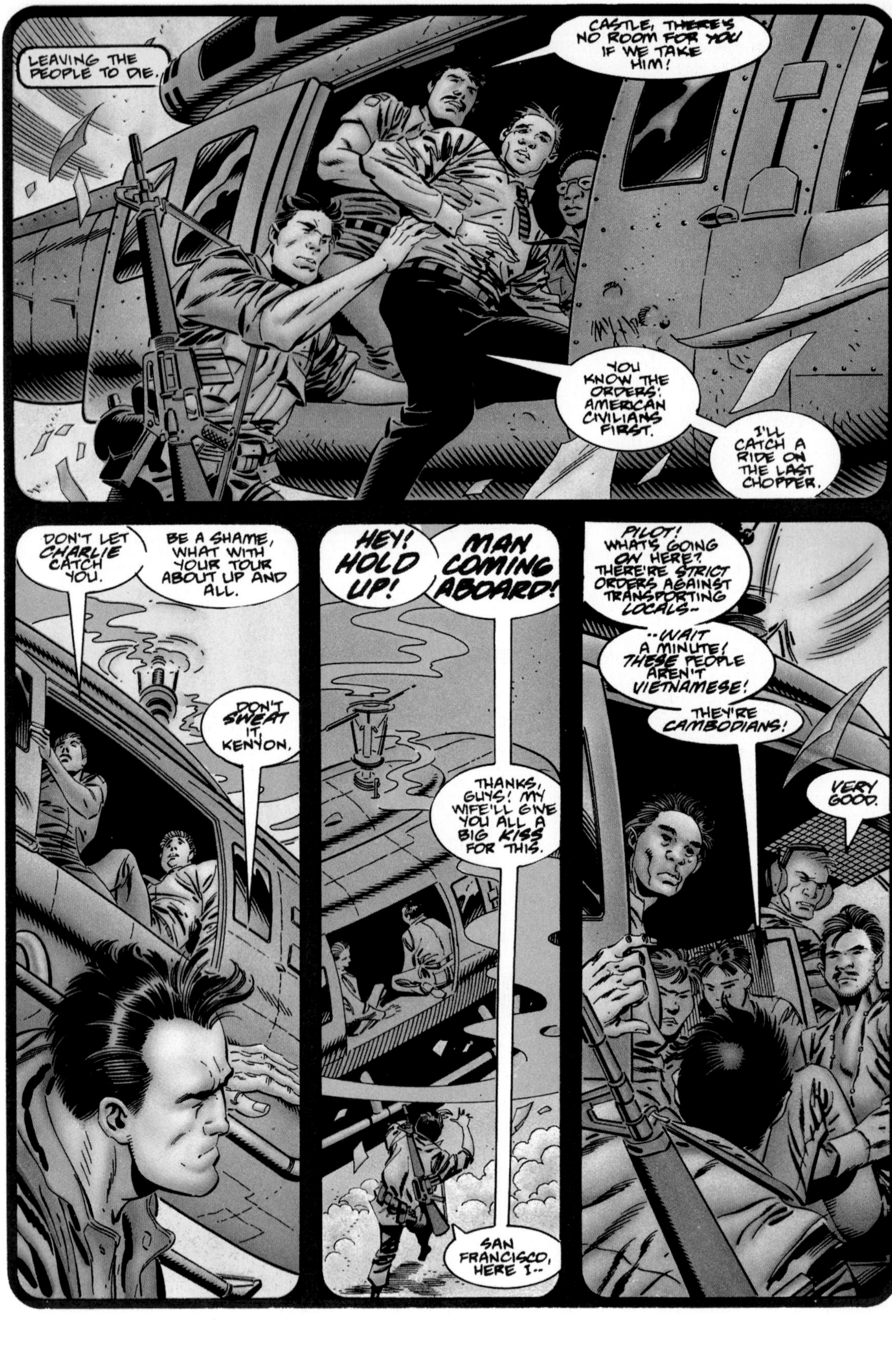

LEAVING THE PEOPLE TO DIE.
CASTLE, THERE'S NO ROOM FOR YOU IF WE TAKE HIM!
YOU KNOW THE ORDERS: AMERICAN CIVILIANS FIRST.
I'LL CATCH A RIDE ON THE LAST CHOPPER.
DON'T LET CHARLIE CATCH YOU.
BE A SHAME, WHAT WITH YOUR TOUR ABOUT UP AND ALL.
DON'T SWEAT IT, KENYON.
HEY! HOLD UP!
MAN COMING ABOARD!
THANKS, GUYS! MY WIFE'LL GIVE YOU ALL A BIG KISS FOR THIS.
SAN FRANCISCO, HERE I--
PILOT! WHAT'S GOING ON HERE? THERE'RE STRICT ORDERS AGAINST TRANSPORTING LOCALS--
--WAIT A MINUTE! THESE PEOPLE AREN'T VIETNAMESE!
THEY'RE CAMBODIANS!
VERY GOOD.

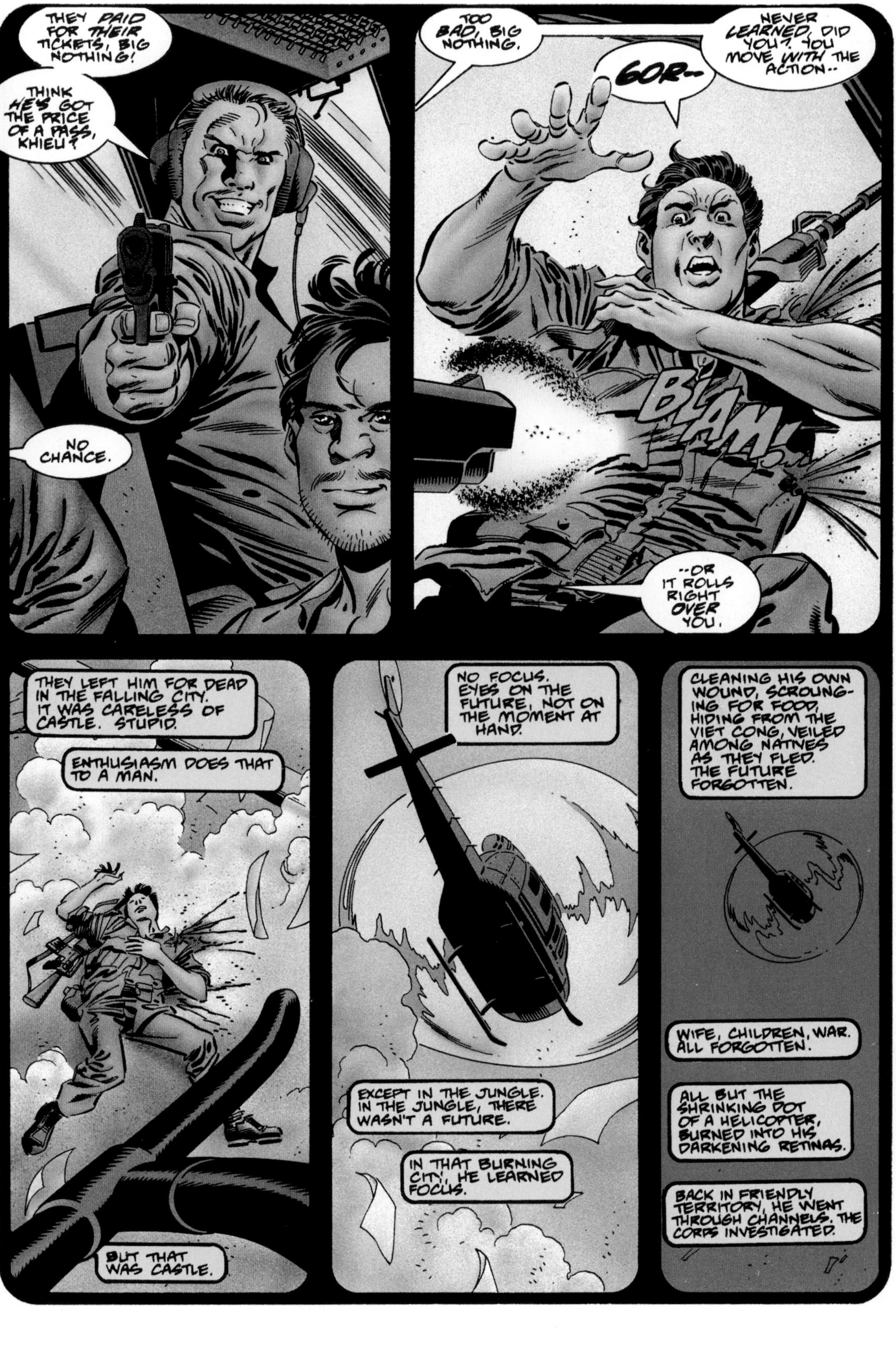
THEY PAID FOR THEIR TICKETS, BIG NOTHING!
THINK HE'S GOT THE PRICE OF A PASS, KHIEU?
NO CHANCE.
TOO BAD, BIG NOTHING.
NEVER LEARNED, DID YOU? YOU MOVE WITH THE ACTION..
GOR--
BLAM!
--OR IT ROLLS RIGHT OVER YOU.
THEY LEFT HIM FOR DEAD IN THE FALLING CITY. IT WAS CARELESS OF CASTLE. STUPID.
ENTHUSIASM DOES THAT TO A MAN.
BUT THAT WAS CASTLE.
NO FOCUS. EYES ON THE FUTURE, NOT ON THE MOMENT AT HAND.
EXCEPT IN THE JUNGLE. IN THE JUNGLE, THERE WASN'T A FUTURE.
IN THAT BURNING CITY, HE LEARNED FOCUS.
CLEANING HIS OWN WOUND, SCROUNGING FOR FOOD, HIDING FROM THE VIET CONG, VEILED AMONG NATIVES AS THEY FLED. THE FUTURE FORGOTTEN.
WIFE, CHILDREN, WAR. ALL FORGOTTEN.
ALL BUT THE SHRINKING DOT OF A HELICOPTER, BURNED INTO HIS DARKENING RETINAS.
BACK IN FRIENDLY TERRITORY, HE WENT THROUGH CHANNELS. THE CORPS INVESTIGATED.

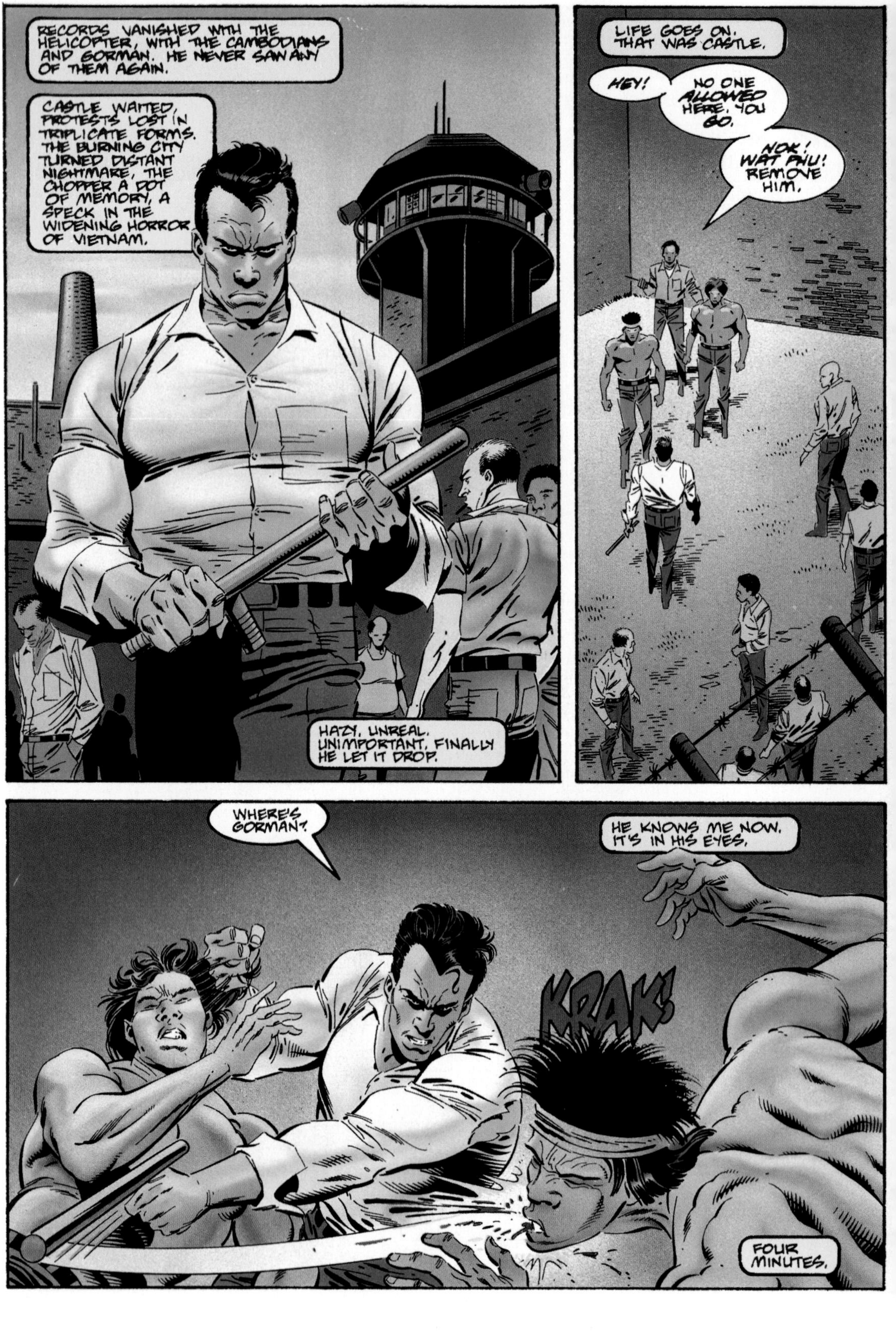
RECORDS VANISHED WITH THE HELICOPTER, WITH THE CAMBODIANS AND GORMAN. HE NEVER SAW ANY OF THEM AGAIN.
CASTLE WAITED, PROTESTS LOST IN TRIPLICATE FORMS. THE BURNING CITY TURNED DISTANT NIGHTMARE, THE CHOPPER A DOT OF MEMORY, A SPECK IN THE WIDENING HORROR OF VIETNAM.
HAZY, UNREAL, UNIMPORTANT. FINALLY HE LET IT DROP.
LIFE GOES ON. THAT WAS CASTLE.
HEY!
NO ONE ALLOWED HERE. YOU GO.
NOK! WAT PHU! REMOVE HIM.
WHERE'S GORMAN?
HE KNOWS ME NOW. IT'S IN HIS EYES.
KRAK!
FOUR MINUTES.

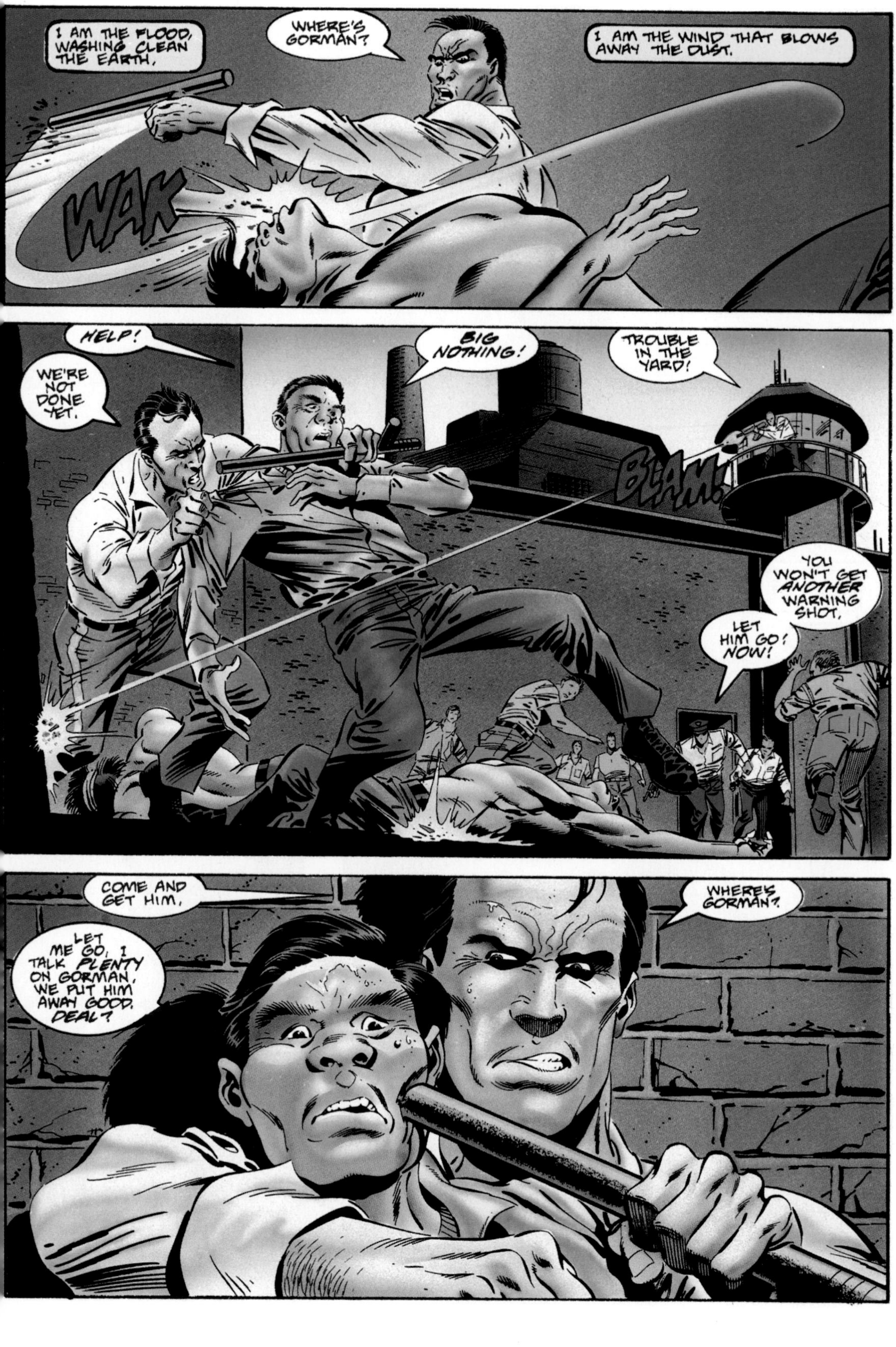
I AM THE FLOOD, WASHING CLEAN THE EARTH,
WHERE'S GORMAN?
I AM THE WIND THAT BLOWS AWAY THE DUST.
WAK
HELP!
WE'RE NOT DONE YET.
BIG NOTHING!
TROUBLE IN THE YARD!
BLAM!
YOU WON'T GET ANOTHER WARNING SHOT,
LET HIM GO! NOW!
COME AND GET HIM,
WHERE'S GORMAN?
LET ME GO, I TALK PLENTY ON GORMAN, WE PUT HIM AWAY GOOD. DEAL?

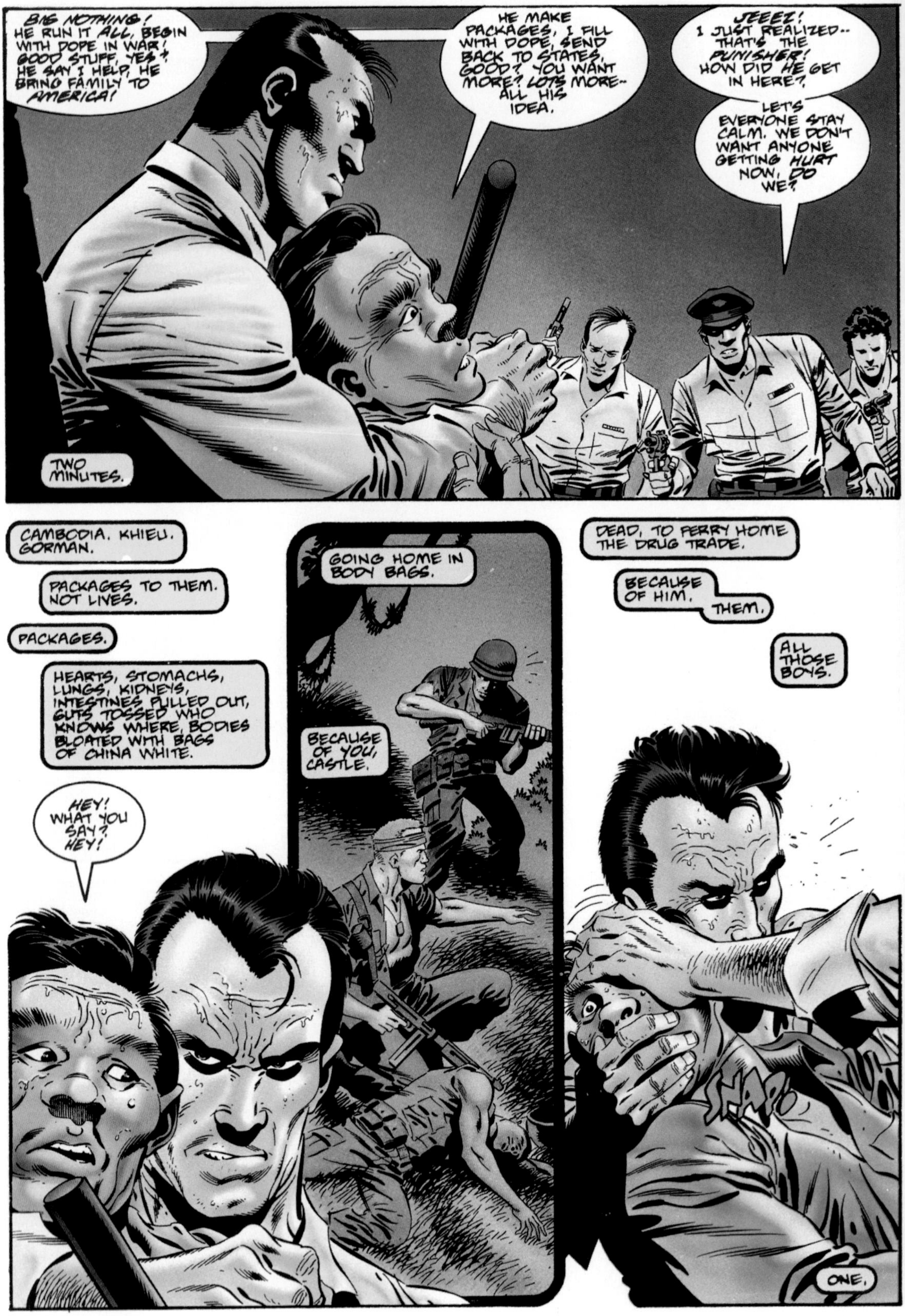
BIG NOTHING! HE RUN IT ALL, BEGIN WITH DOPE IN WAR! GOOD STUFF, YES? HE SAY I HELP, HE BRING FAMILY TO AMERICA!
HE MAKE PACKAGES, I FILL WITH DOPE, SEND BACK TO STATES, GOOD? YOU WANT MORE? LOTS MORE-- ALL HIS IDEA.
JEEEZ! I JUST REALIZED.. THAT'S THE PUNISHER! HOW DID HE GET IN HERE?
LET'S EVERYONE STAY CALM. WE DON'T WANT ANYONE GETTING HURT NOW, DO WE?
TWO MINUTES.
CAMBODIA. KHIEU. GORMAN.
PACKAGES TO THEM. NOT LIVES.
PACKAGES.
HEARTS, STOMACHS, LUNGS, KIDNEYS, INTESTINES PULLED OUT, GUTS TOSSED WHO KNOWS WHERE, BODIES BLOATED WITH BAGS OF CHINA WHITE.
HEY! WHAT YOU SAY? HEY!
GOING HOME IN BODY BAGS.
BECAUSE OF YOU, CASTLE.
DEAD, TO FERRY HOME THE DRUG TRADE.
BECAUSE OF HIM.
THEM.
ALL THOSE BOYS.
ONE.

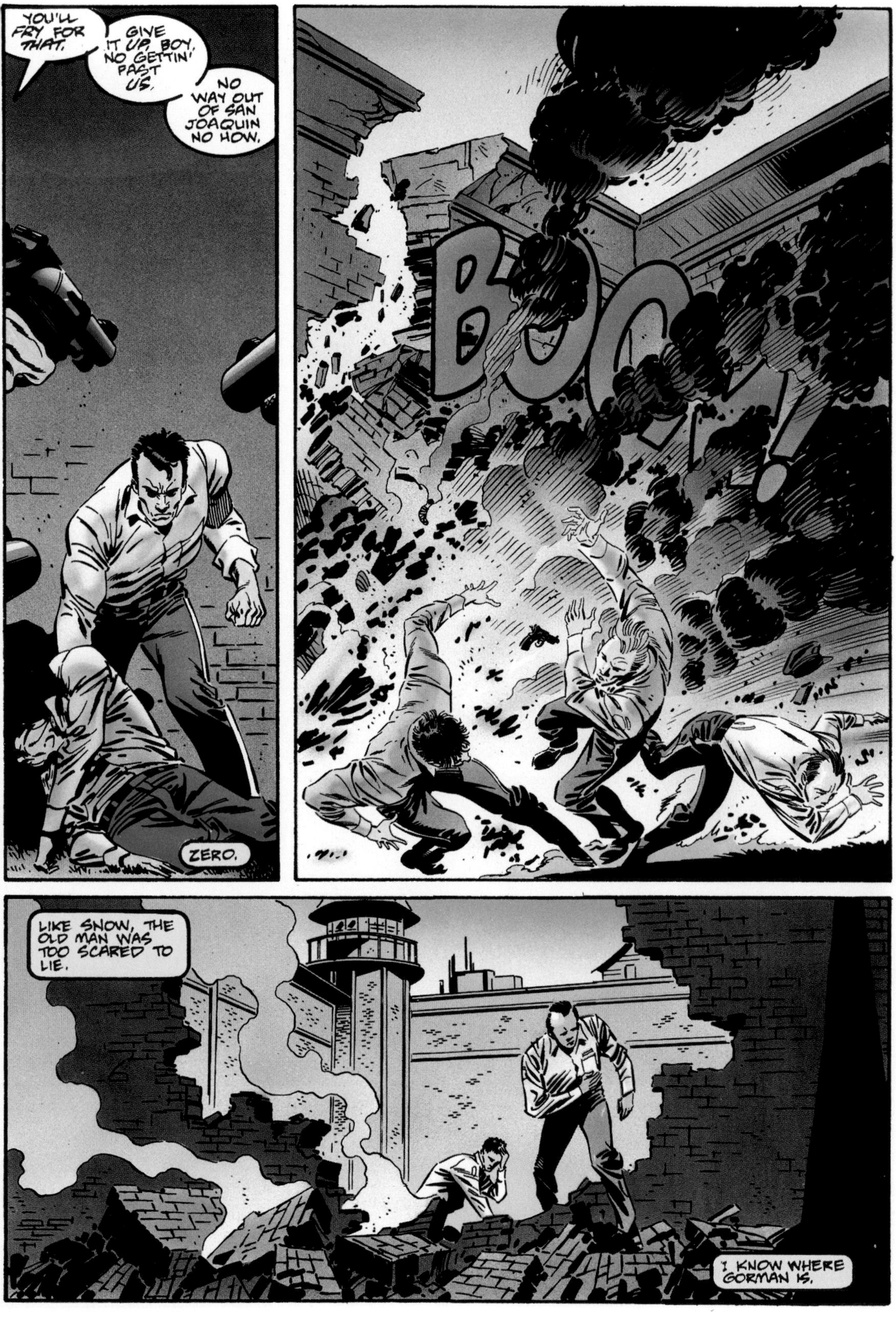
YOU'LL FRY FOR THAT.
GIVE IT UP, BOY. NO GETTIN' PAST US.
NO WAY OUT OF SAN JOAQUIN NO HOW.
ZERO.
BOOM!
LIKE SNOW, THE OLD MAN WAS TOO SCARED TO LIE.
I KNOW WHERE GORMAN IS.

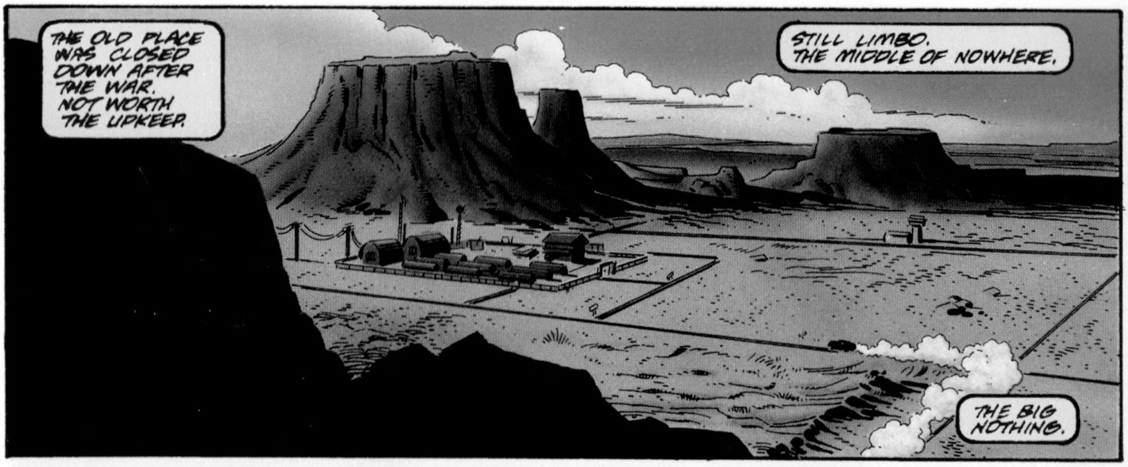
THE OLD PLACE WAS CLOSED DOWN AFTER THE WAR. NOT WORTH THE UPKEEP.
STILL LIMBO. THE MIDDLE OF NOWHERE.
THE BIG NOTHING.

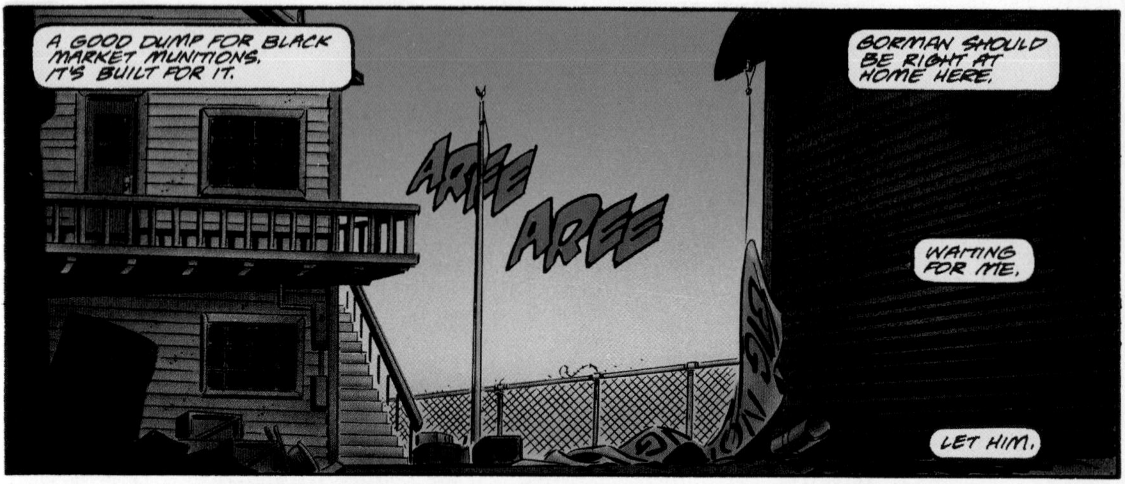
A GOOD DUMP FOR BLACK MARKET MUNITIONS. IT'S BUILT FOR IT.
AREE
AREE
BORMAN SHOULD BE RIGHT AT HOME HERE.
WAITING FOR ME.
LET HIM.

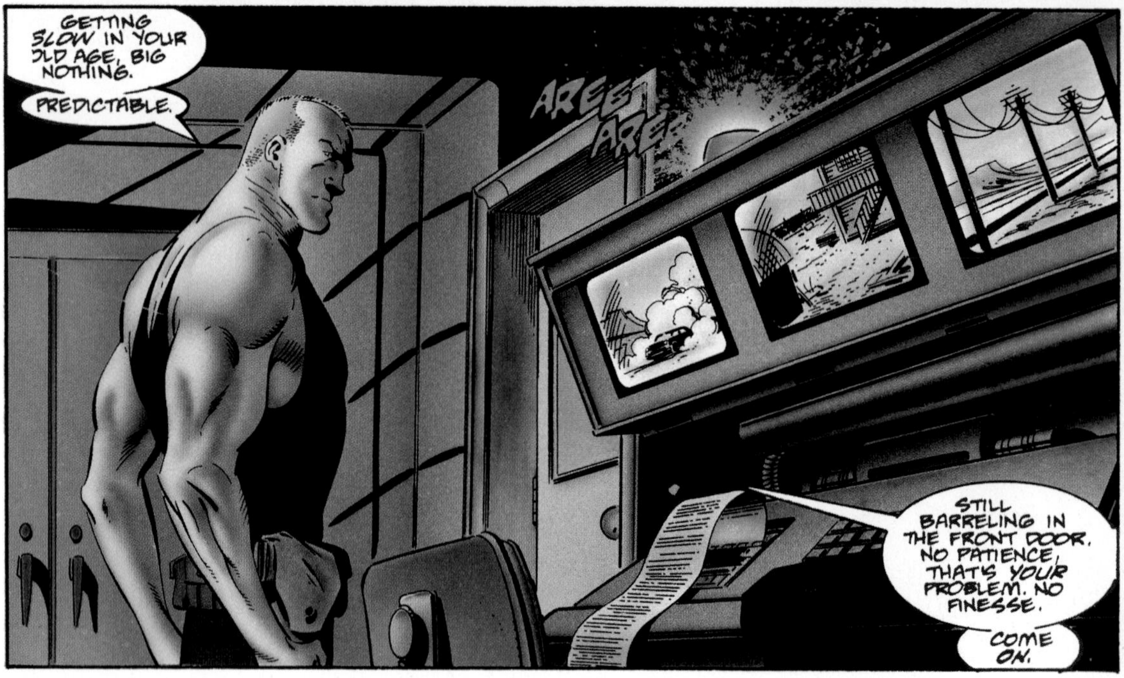
GETTING SLOW IN YOUR OLD AGE, BIG NOTHING.
PREDICTABLE.
AREE
STILL BARRELING IN THE FRONT DOOR. NO PATIENCE, THAT'S YOUR PROBLEM. NO FINESSE.
COME ON.

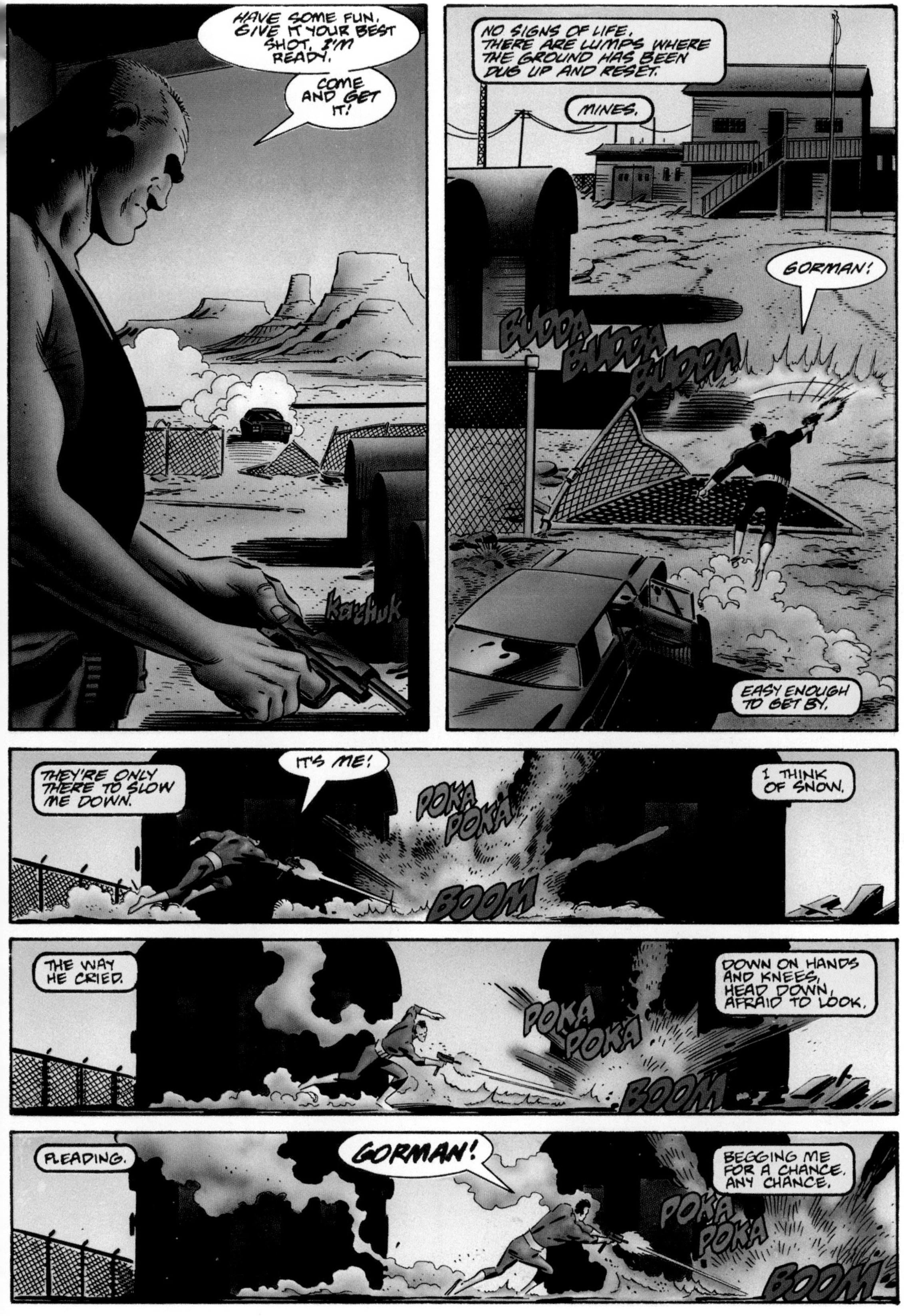
HAVE SOME FUN, GIVE IT YOUR BEST SHOT. I'M READY.
COME AND GET IT!
KaChuk
NO SIGNS OF LIFE. THERE ARE LUMPS WHERE THE GROUND HAS BEEN DUG UP AND RESET.
MINES.
GORMAN!
BUDDA BUDDA BUDDA
EASY ENOUGH TO GET BY.
THEY'RE ONLY THERE TO SLOW ME DOWN.
IT'S ME!
POKA POKA
BOOM
I THINK OF SNOW.
THE WAY HE CRIED.
DOWN ON HANDS AND KNEES, HEAD DOWN, AFRAID TO LOOK.
POKA POKA
BOOM
PLEADING.
GORMAN!
BEGGING ME FOR A CHANCE. ANY CHANCE.
POKA POKA
BOOM

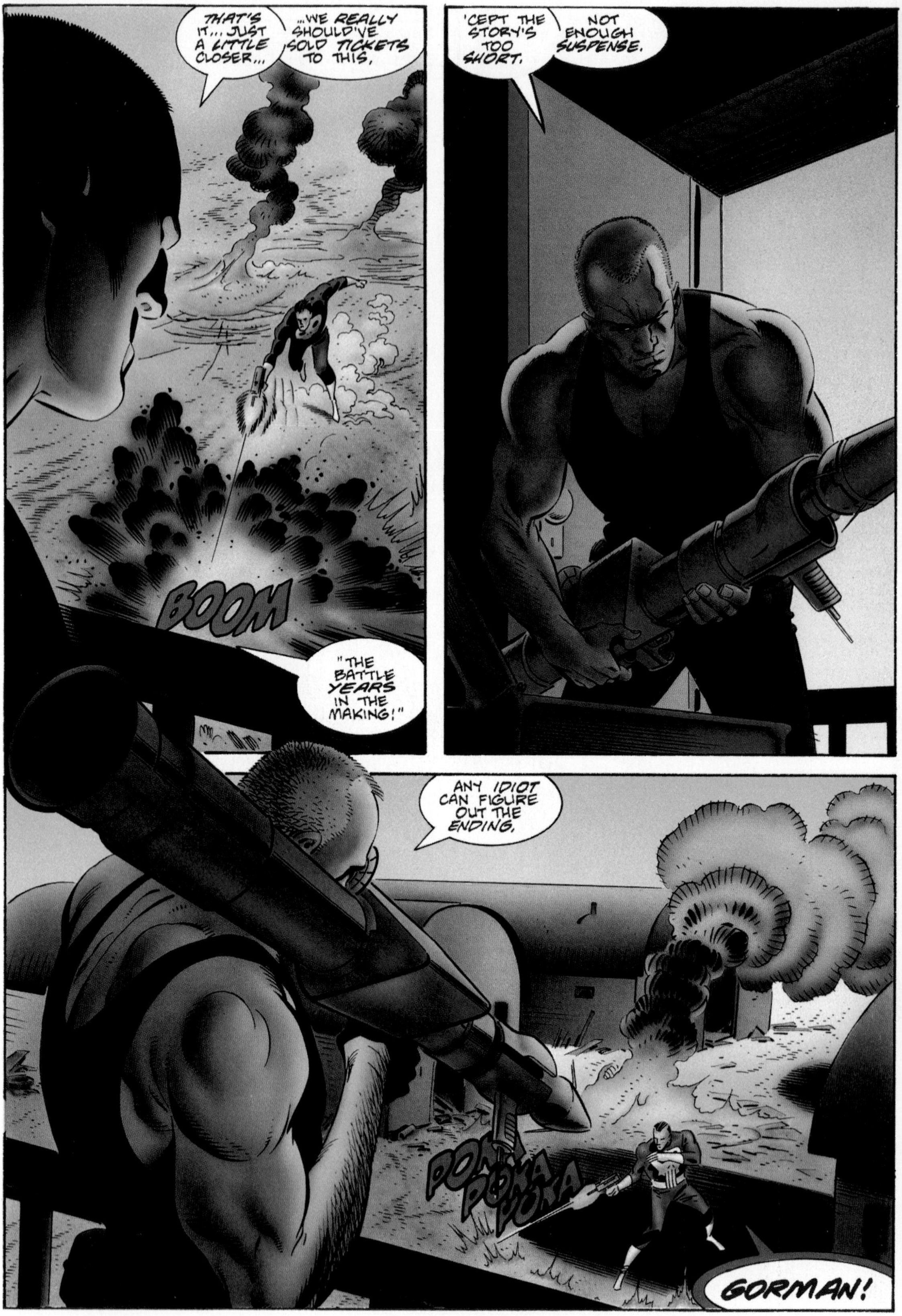
THAT'S IT... JUST A LITTLE CLOSER...
...WE REALLY SHOULD'VE SOLD TICKETS TO THIS,
BOOM
"THE BATTLE YEARS IN THE MAKING!"
'CEPT THE STORY'S TOO SHORT.
NOT ENOUGH SUSPENSE.
ANY IDIOT CAN FIGURE OUT THE ENDING,
GORMAN!

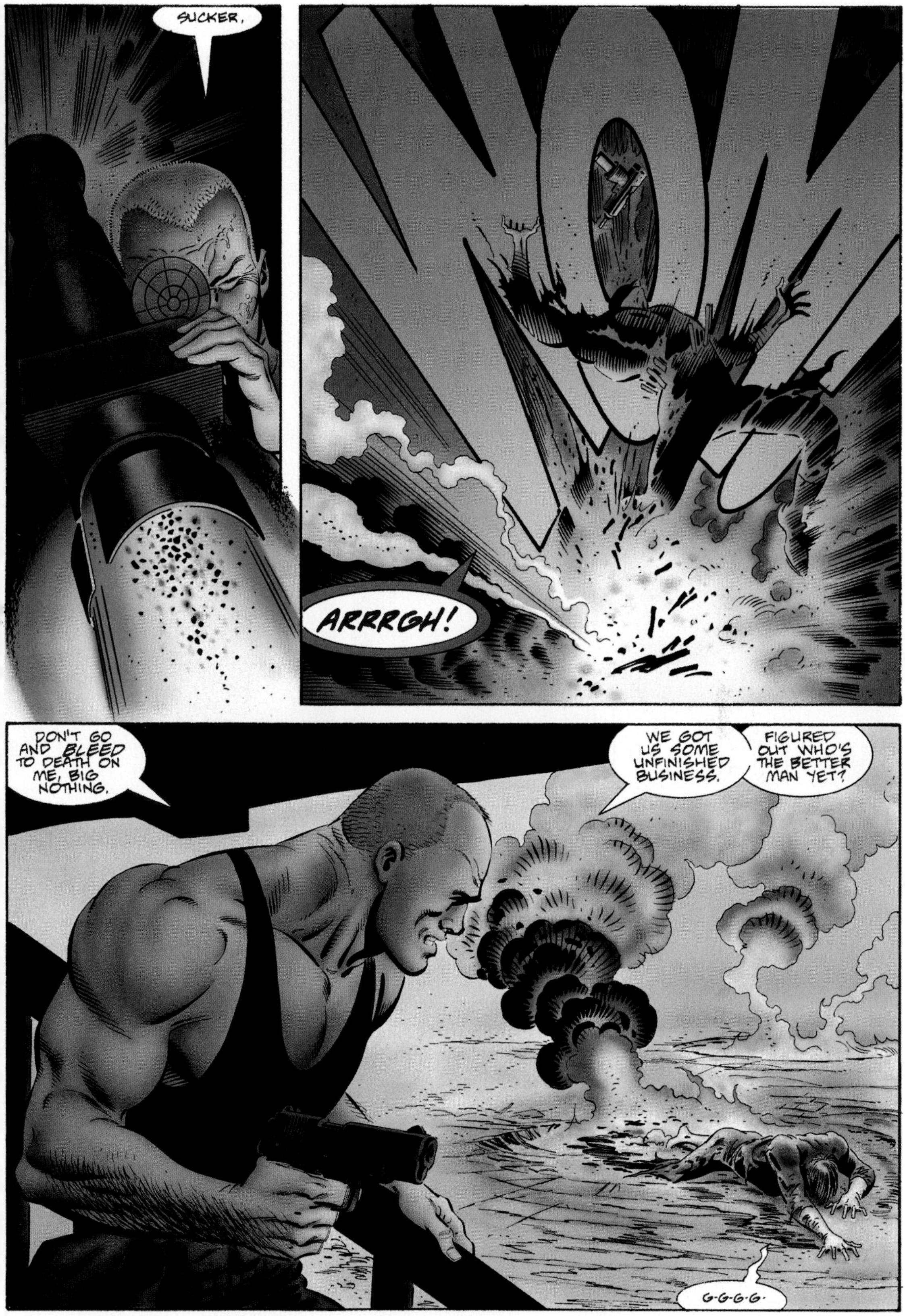
SUCKER.
ARRRGH!
DON'T GO AND BLEED TO DEATH ON ME, BIG NOTHING.
WE GOT US SOME UNFINISHED BUSINESS.
FIGURED OUT WHO'S THE BETTER MAN YET?
G-G-G-G.

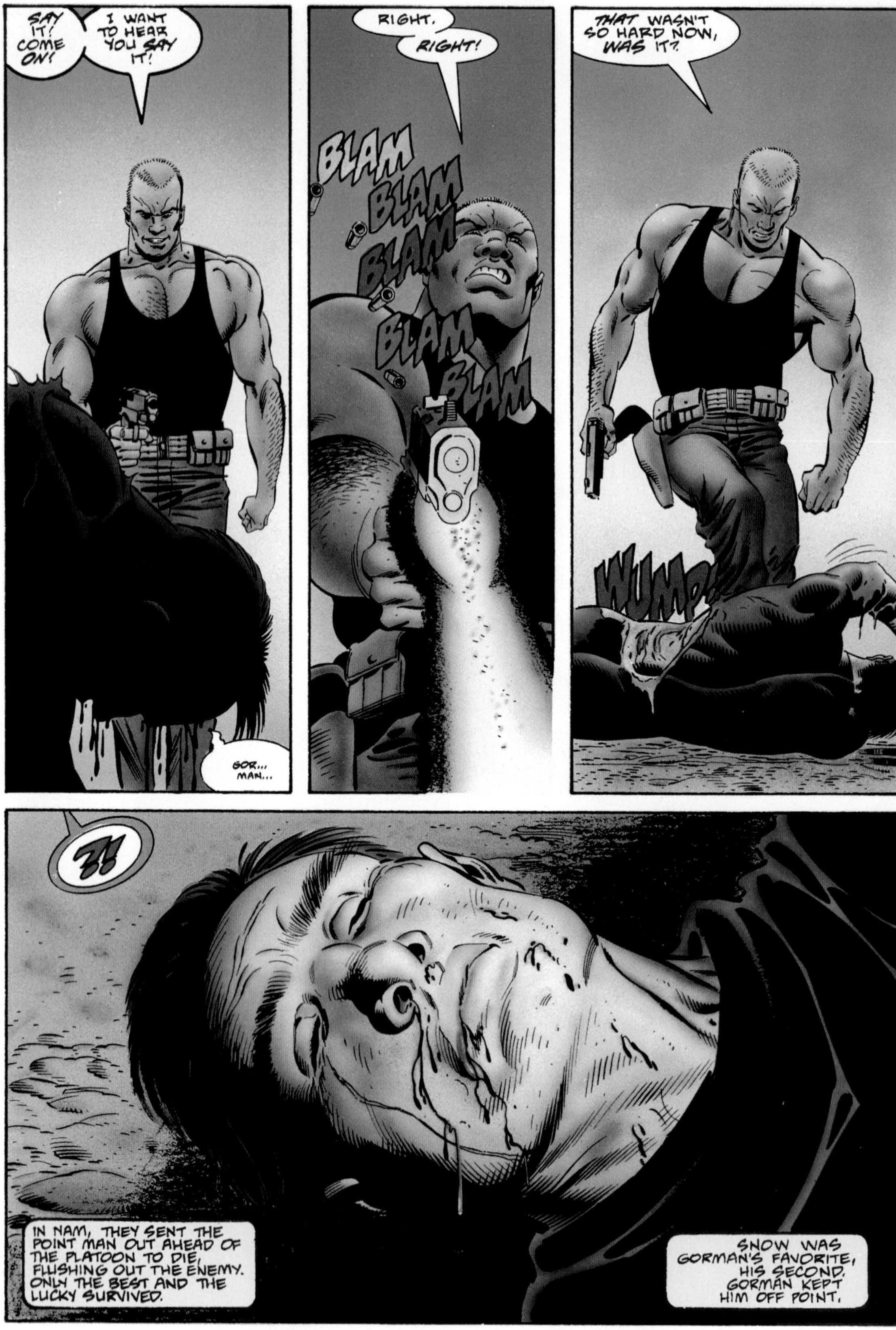
SAY IT! COME ON!
I WANT TO HEAR YOU SAY IT!
GOR... MAN...
RIGHT.
RIGHT!
BLAM
BLAM
BLAM
BLAM
BLAM
BLAM
THAT WASN'T SO HARD NOW, WAS IT?
WUMP
IN NAM, THEY SENT THE POINT MAN OUT AHEAD OF THE PLATOON TO DIE, FLUSHING OUT THE ENEMY. ONLY THE BEST AND THE LUCKY SURVIVED.
SNOW WAS GORMAN'S FAVORITE, HIS SECOND. GORMAN KEPT HIM OFF POINT.

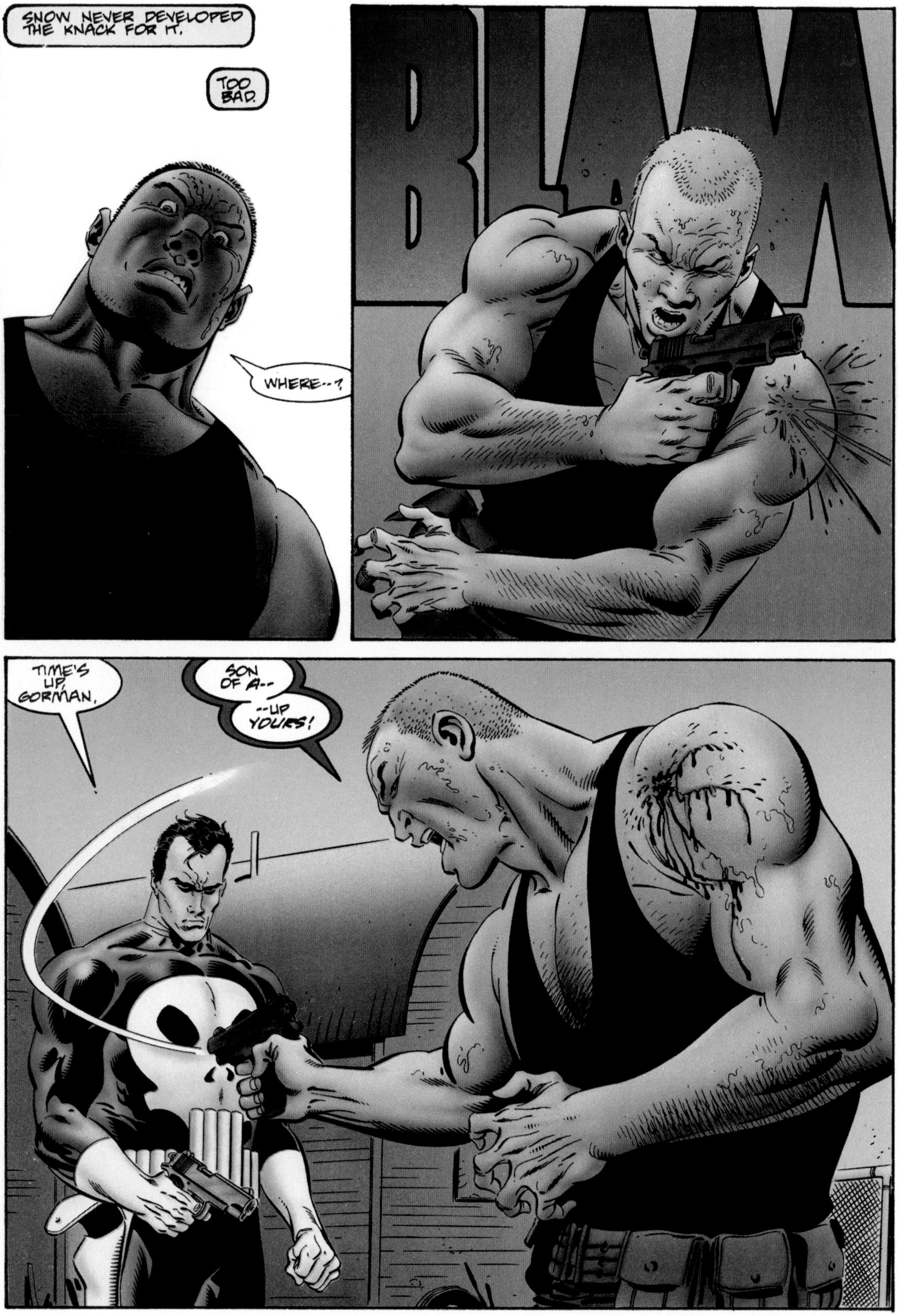
SNOW NEVER DEVELOPED THE KNACK FOR IT.
TOO BAD.
WHERE--?
BLAM
TIME'S UP, GORMAN.
SON OF A--
--UP YOURS!

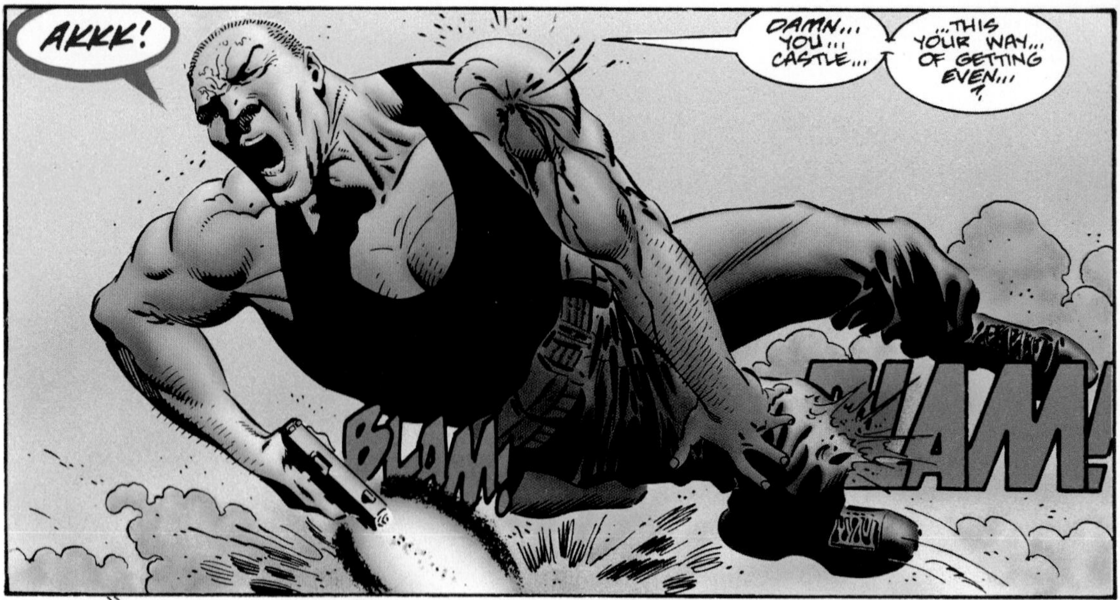
AKKK!
DAMN... YOU... CASTLE...
...THIS YOUR WAY... OF GETTING EVEN...?
BLAM!
BLAM!

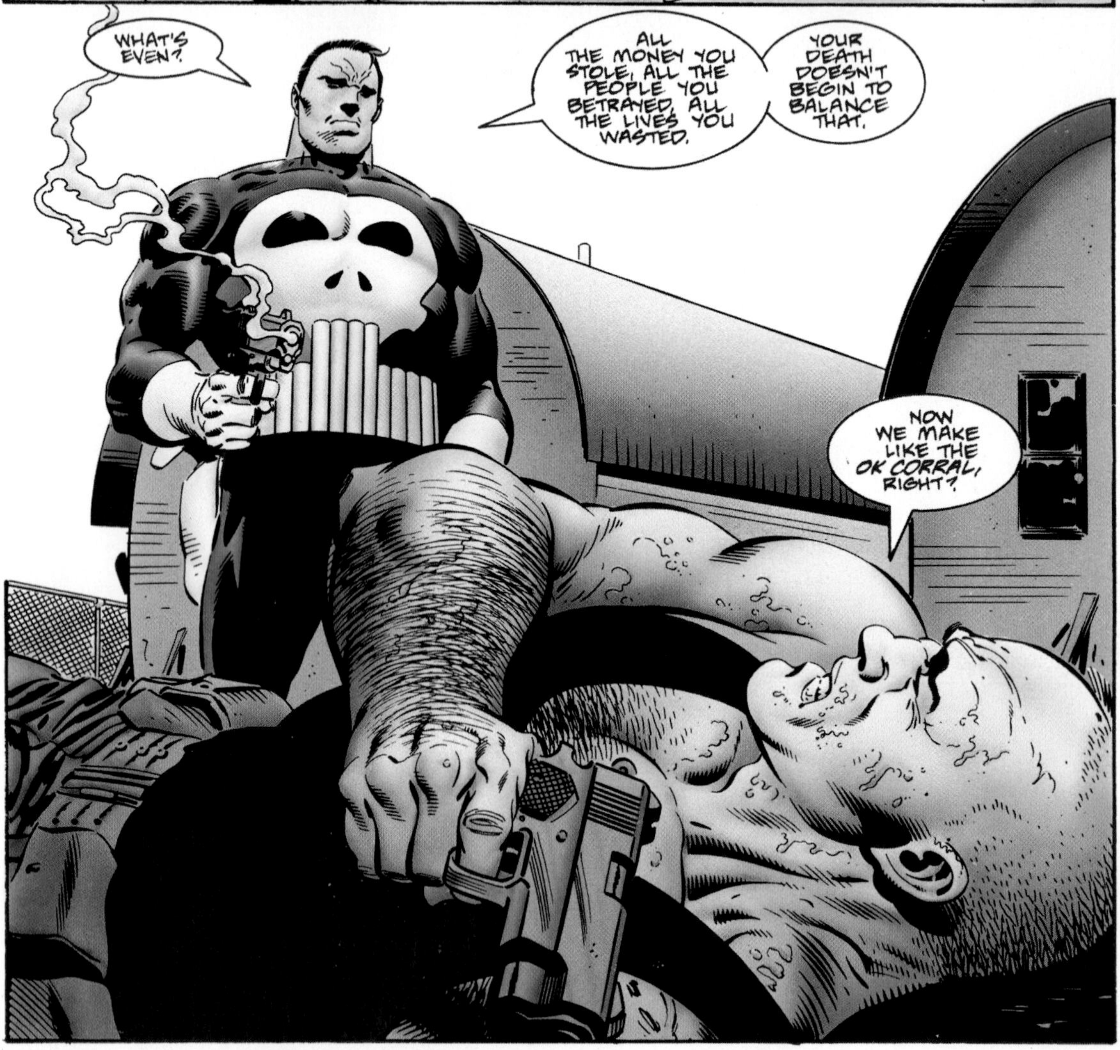
WHAT'S EVEN?
ALL THE MONEY YOU STOLE, ALL THE PEOPLE YOU BETRAYED, ALL THE LIVES YOU WASTED.
YOUR DEATH DOESN'T BEGIN TO BALANCE THAT.
NOW WE MAKE LIKE THE OK CORRAL, RIGHT?

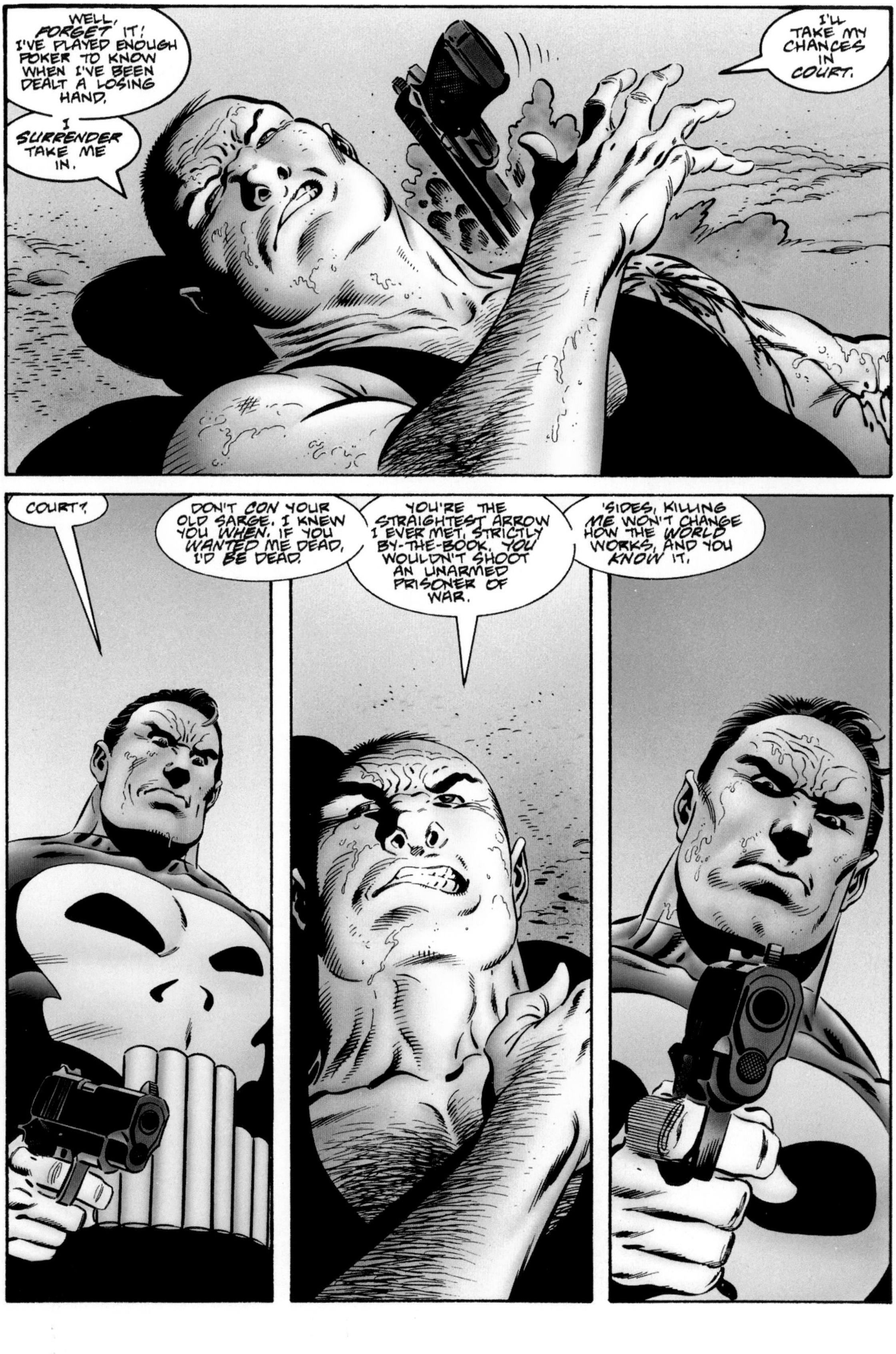
WELL, FORGET IT! I'VE PLAYED ENOUGH POKER TO KNOW WHEN I'VE BEEN DEALT A LOSING HAND.
I SURRENDER TAKE ME IN.
I'LL TAKE MY CHANCES IN COURT.
COURT?
DON'T CON YOUR OLD SARGE. I KNEW YOU WHEN. IF YOU WANTED ME DEAD, I'D BE DEAD.
YOU'RE THE STRAIGHTEST ARROW I EVER MET, STRICTLY BY-THE-BOOK. YOU WOULDN'T SHOOT AN UNARMED PRISONER OF WAR.
'SIDES, KILLING ME WON'T CHANGE HOW THE WORLD WORKS, AND YOU KNOW IT.

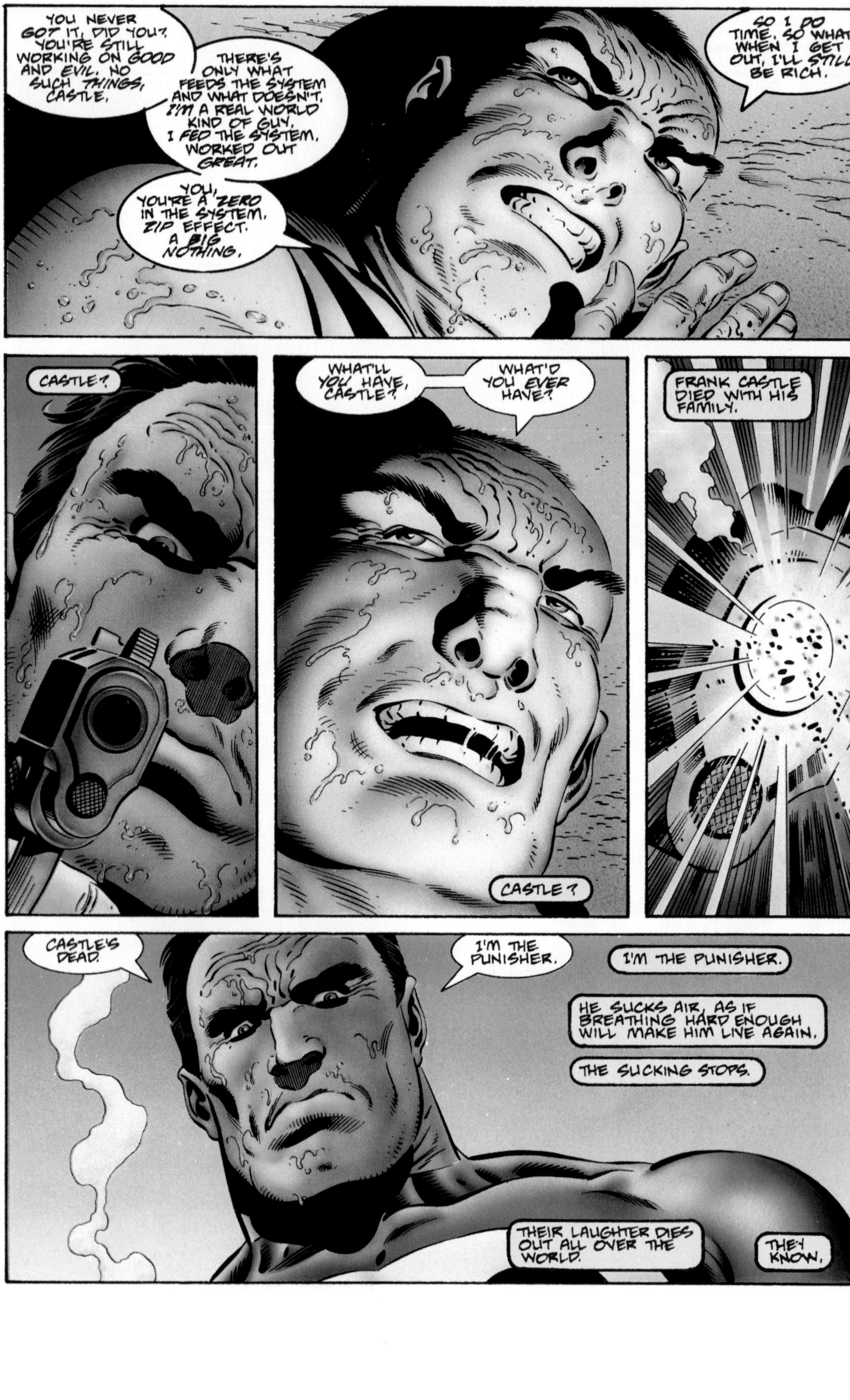
YOU NEVER GOT IT, DID YOU? YOU'RE STILL WORKING ON GOOD AND EVIL. NO SUCH THINGS, CASTLE.
THERE'S ONLY WHAT FEEDS THE SYSTEM AND WHAT DOESN'T. I'M A REAL WORLD KIND OF GUY. I FED THE SYSTEM. WORKED OUT GREAT.
YOU, YOU'RE A ZERO IN THE SYSTEM. ZIP EFFECT. A BIG NOTHING.
SO I DO TIME. SO WHAT? WHEN I GET OUT, I'LL STILL BE RICH.
CASTLE?
WHAT'LL YOU HAVE, CASTLE?
WHAT'D YOU EVER HAVE?
CASTLE?
FRANK CASTLE DIED WITH HIS FAMILY.
CASTLE'S DEAD.
I'M THE PUNISHER.
I'M THE PUNISHER.
HE SUCKS AIR, AS IF BREATHING HARD ENOUGH WILL MAKE HIM LIVE AGAIN.
THE SUCKING STOPS.
THEIR LAUGHTER DIES OUT ALL OVER THE WORLD.
THEY KNOW.

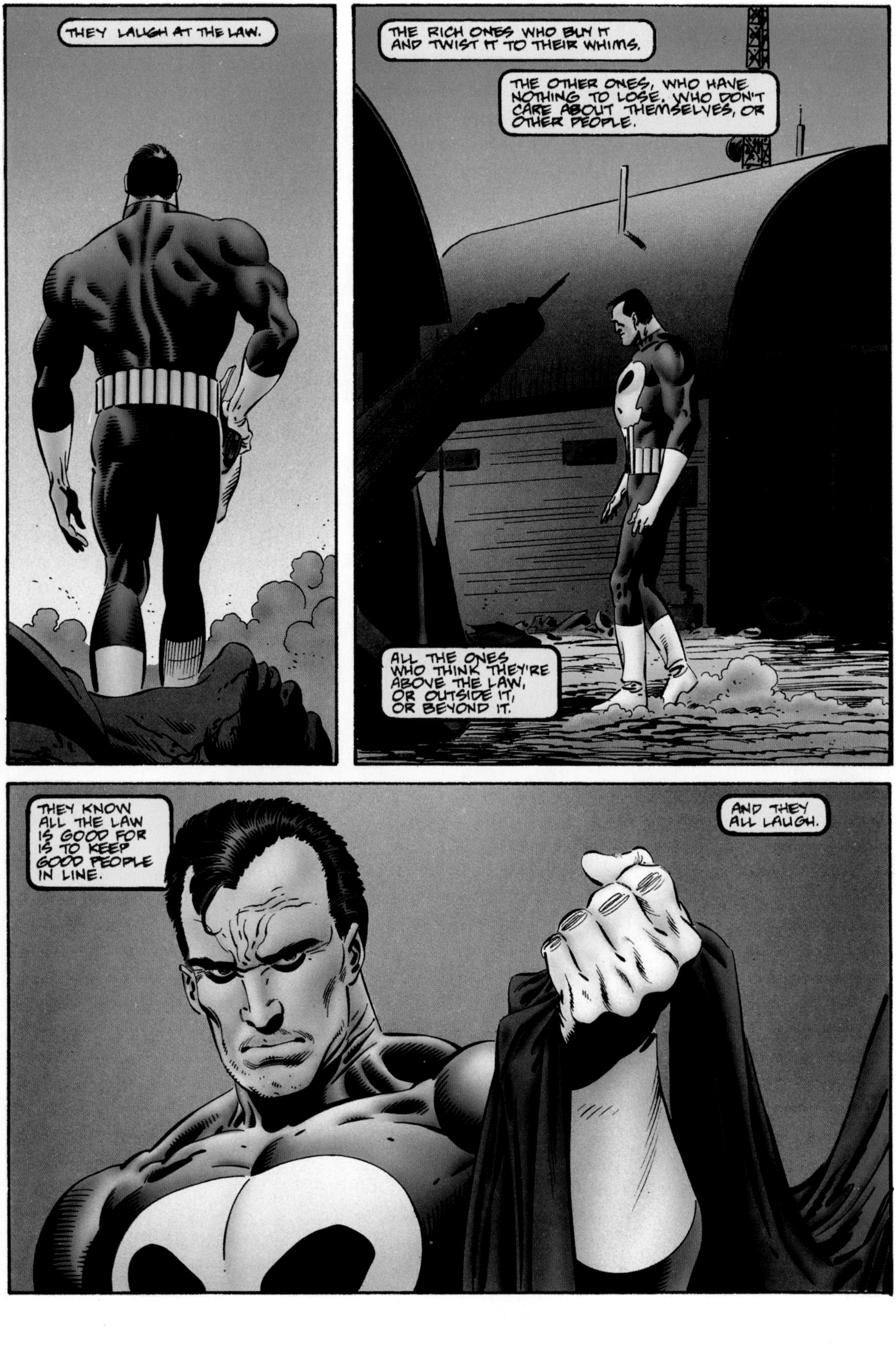
THEY LAUGH AT THE LAW.
THE RICH ONES WHO BUY IT AND TWIST IT TO THEIR WHIMS.
THE OTHER ONES, WHO HAVE NOTHING TO LOSE, WHO DON'T CARE ABOUT THEMSELVES, OR OTHER PEOPLE.
ALL THE ONES WHO THINK THEY'RE ABOVE THE LAW, OR OUTSIDE IT, OR BEYOND IT.
THEY KNOW ALL THE LAW IS GOOD FOR IS TO KEEP GOOD PEOPLE IN LINE.
AND THEY ALL LAUGH.

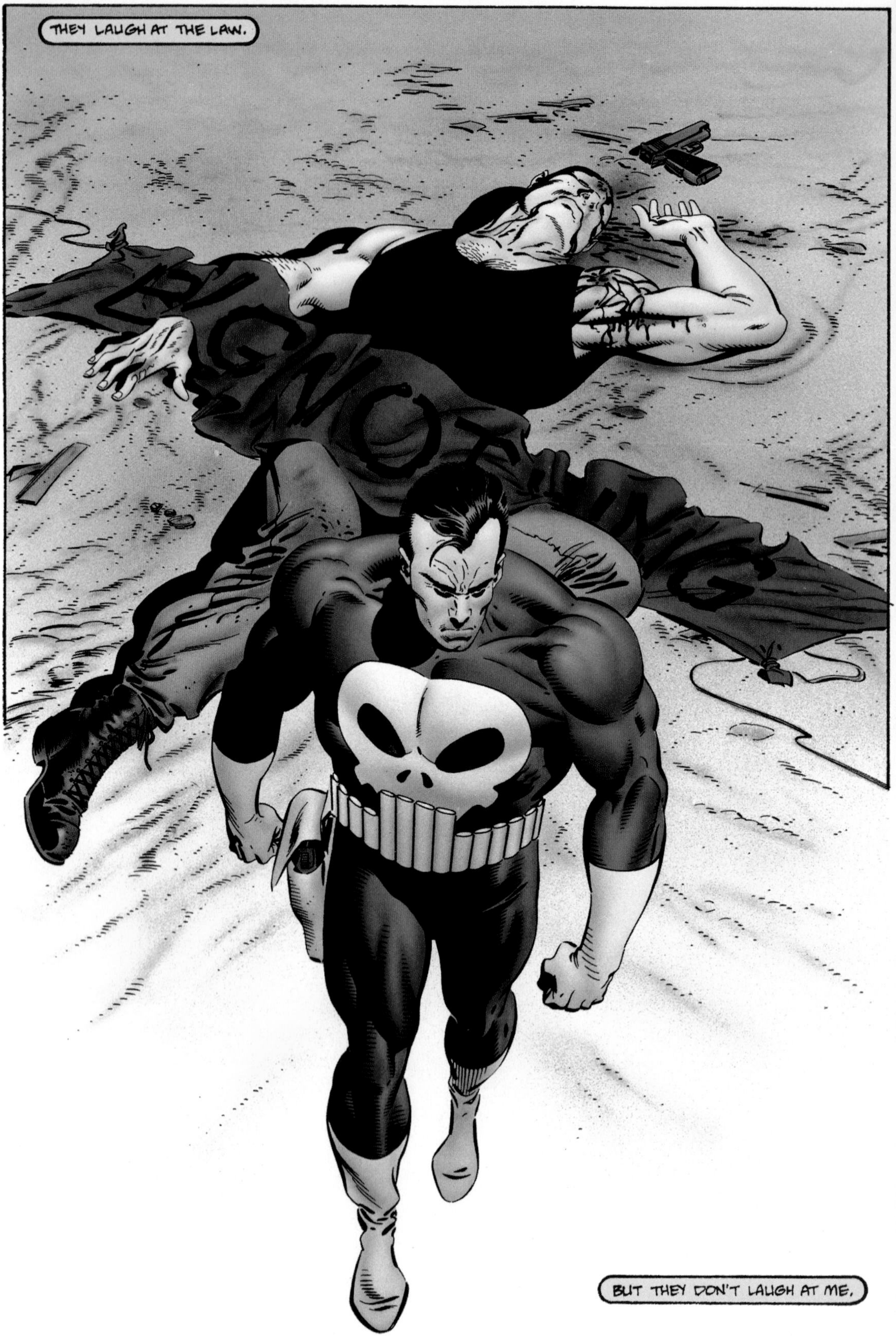
THEY LAUGH AT THE LAW.
BUT THEY DON'T LAUGH AT ME.

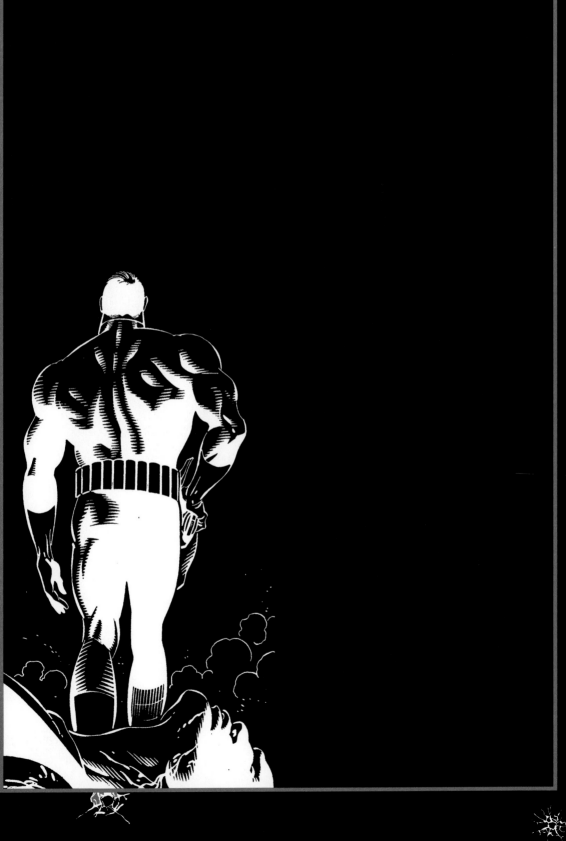

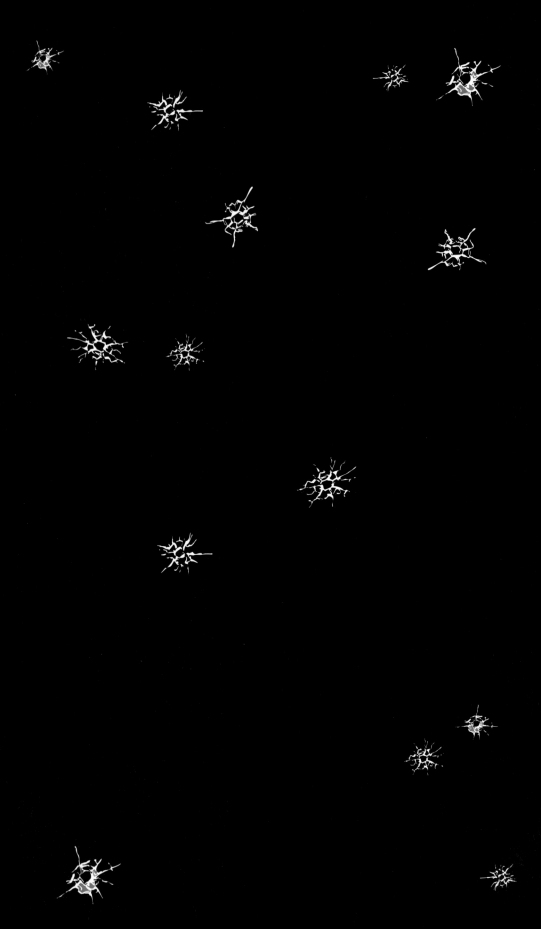

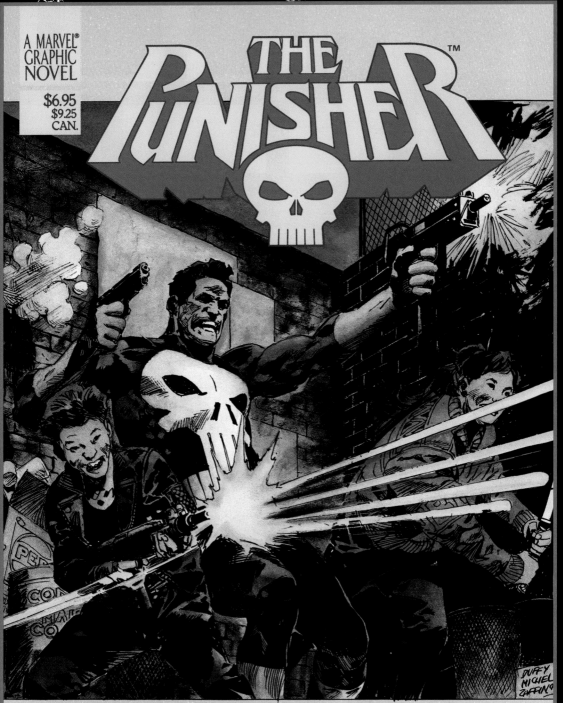

A MARVEL®
GRAPHIC
NOVEL

$6.95
$9.25
CAN.

THE PUNISHER™

ASSASSIN'S GUILD™

JO DUFFY

by JORGE ZAFFINO

JULIE MICHEL

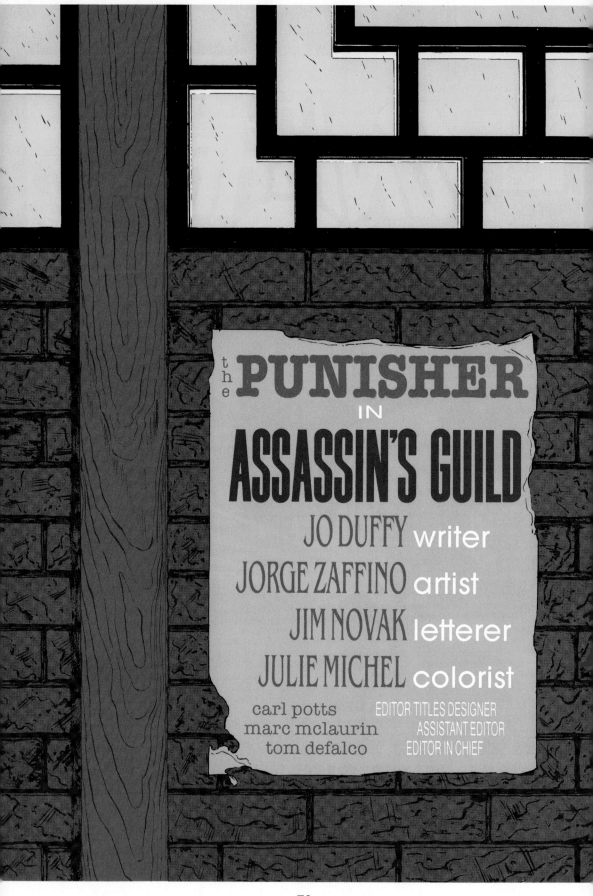

the **PUNISHER** IN
ASSASSIN'S GUILD

JO DUFFY writer
JORGE ZAFFINO artist
JIM NOVAK letterer
JULIE MICHEL colorist

carl potts EDITOR TITLES DESIGNER
marc mclaurin ASSISTANT EDITOR
tom defalco EDITOR IN CHIEF

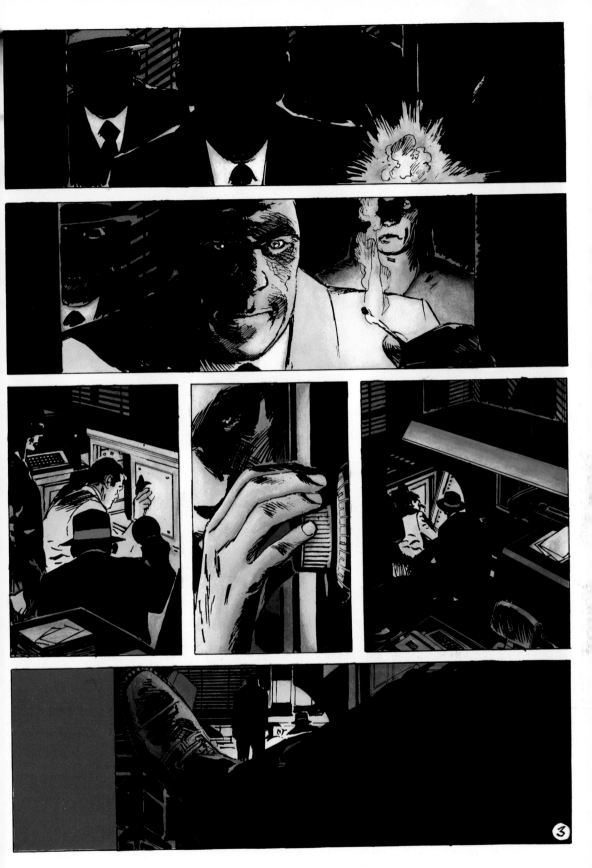

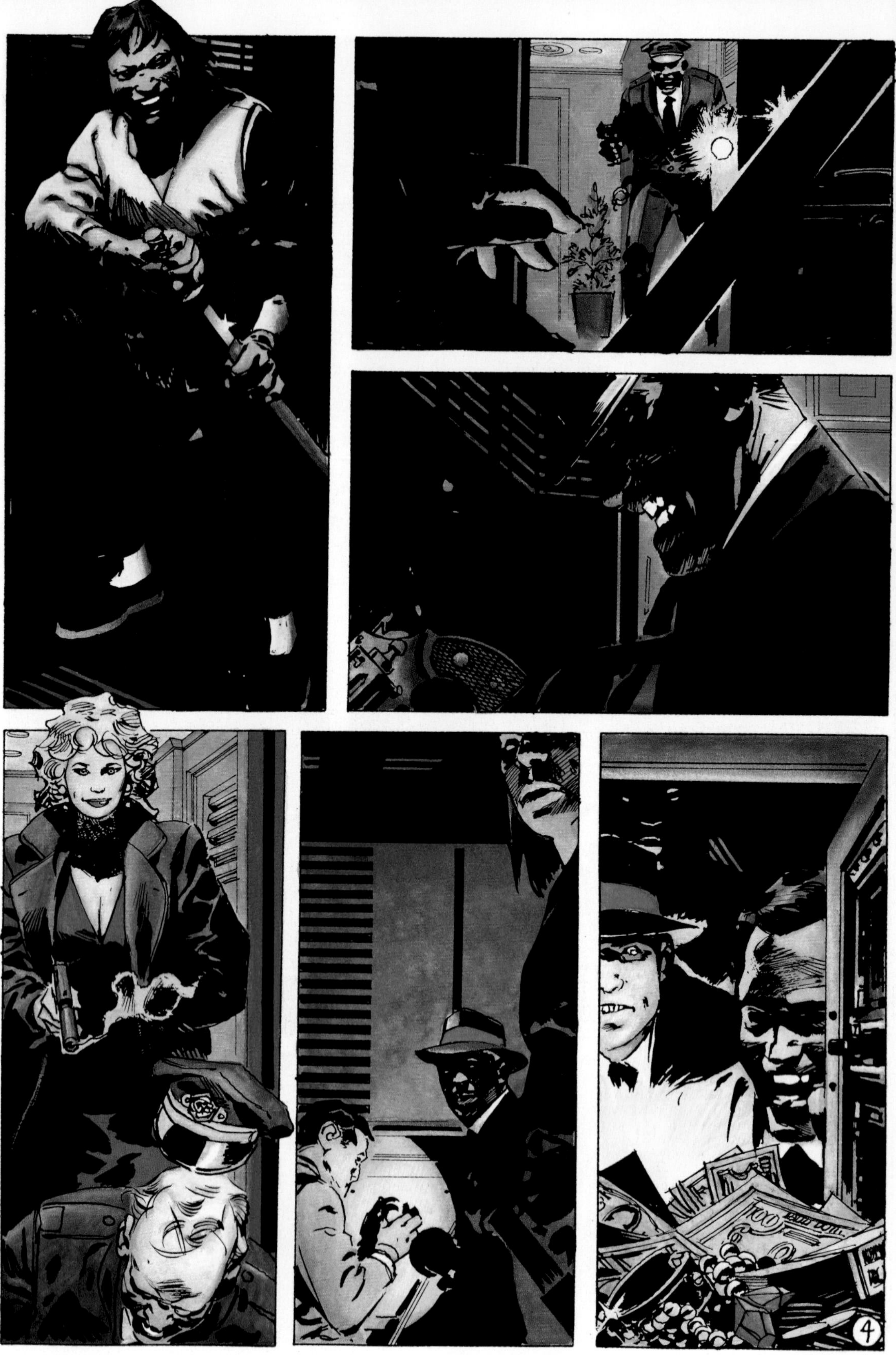
4

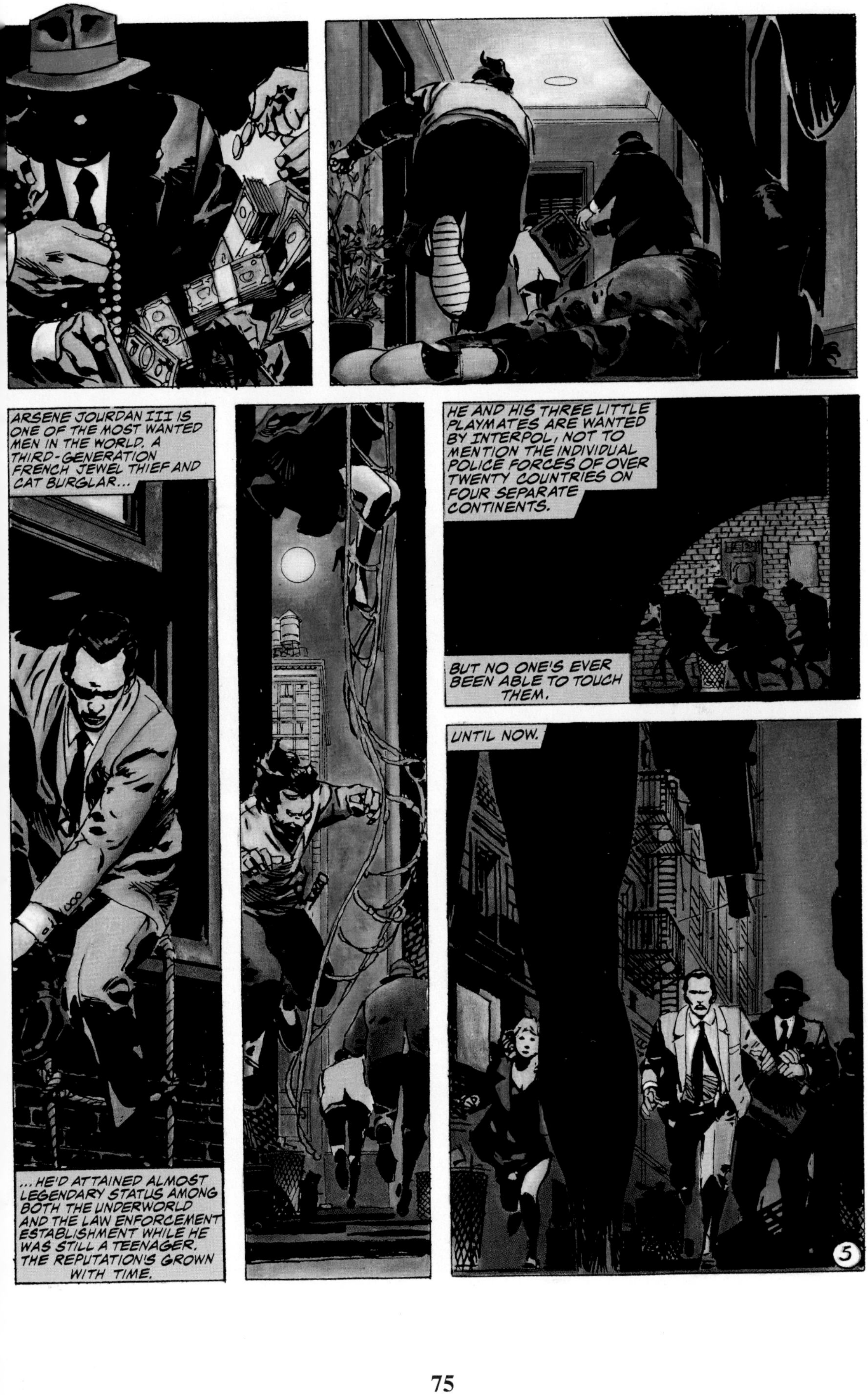
ARSENE JOURDAN III IS ONE OF THE MOST WANTED MEN IN THE WORLD. A THIRD-GENERATION FRENCH JEWEL THIEF AND CAT BURGLAR...
...HE'D ATTAINED ALMOST LEGENDARY STATUS AMONG BOTH THE UNDERWORLD AND THE LAW ENFORCEMENT ESTABLISHMENT WHILE HE WAS STILL A TEENAGER. THE REPUTATION'S GROWN WITH TIME.
HE AND HIS THREE LITTLE PLAYMATES ARE WANTED BY INTERPOL, NOT TO MENTION THE INDIVIDUAL POLICE FORCES OF OVER TWENTY COUNTRIES ON FOUR SEPARATE CONTINENTS.
BUT NO ONE'S EVER BEEN ABLE TO TOUCH THEM.
UNTIL NOW.
5

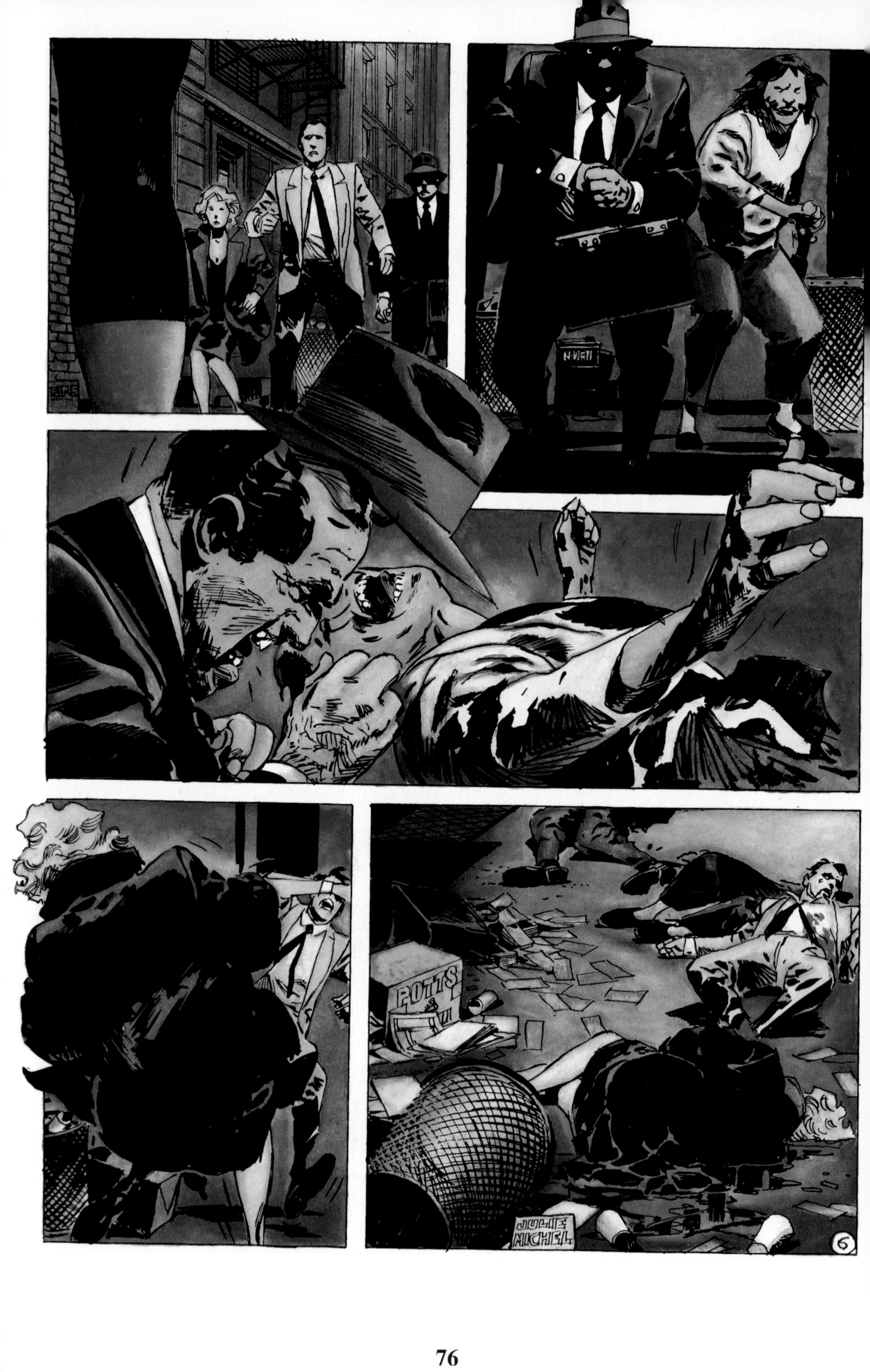
POTTS
JULIE MICHEL

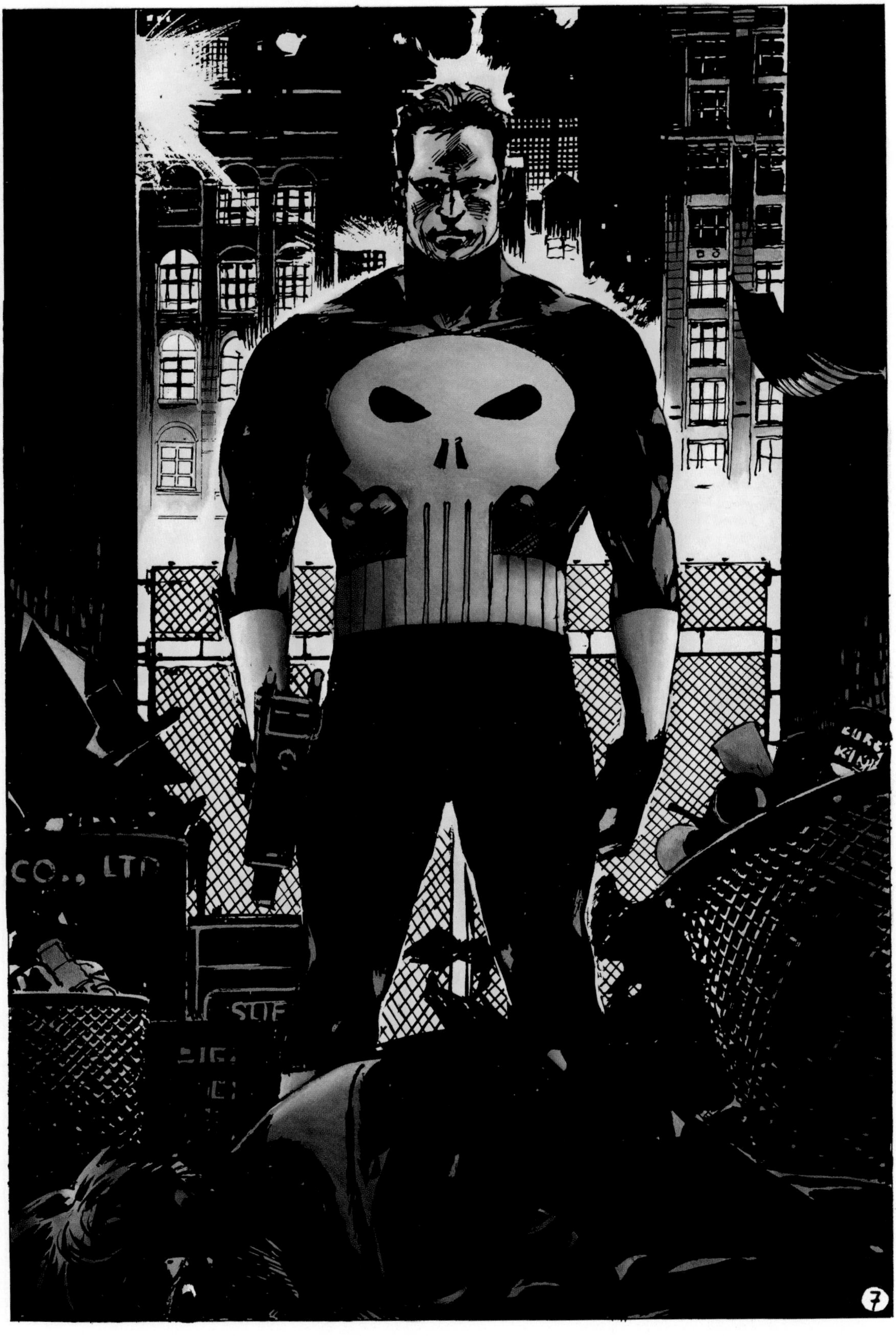

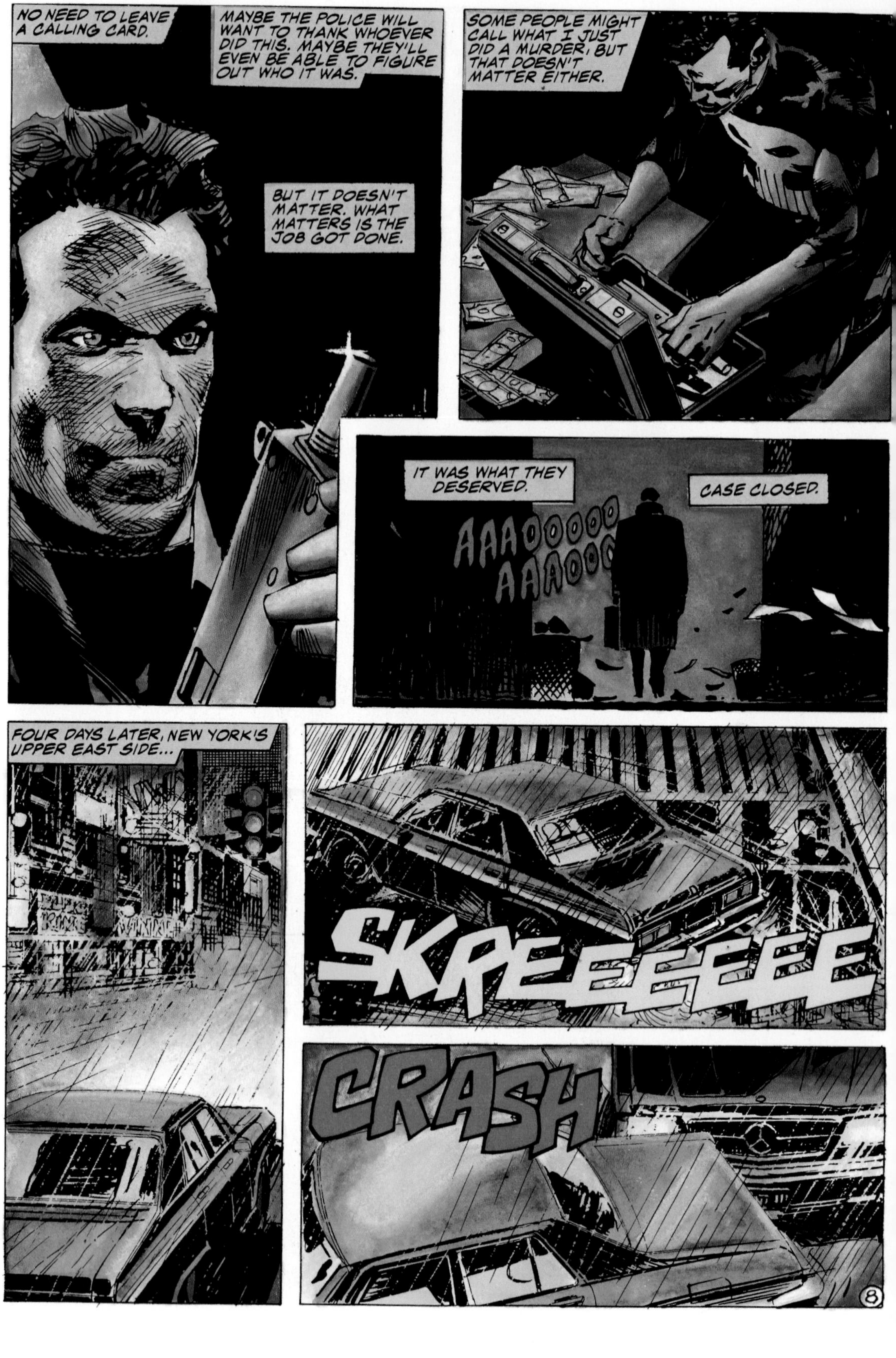
NO NEED TO LEAVE A CALLING CARD.
MAYBE THE POLICE WILL WANT TO THANK WHOEVER DID THIS. MAYBE THEY'LL EVEN BE ABLE TO FIGURE OUT WHO IT WAS.
BUT IT DOESN'T MATTER. WHAT MATTERS IS THE JOB GOT DONE.
SOME PEOPLE MIGHT CALL WHAT I JUST DID A MURDER, BUT THAT DOESN'T MATTER EITHER.
IT WAS WHAT THEY DESERVED.
AAAOOOOO
AAAOOO
CASE CLOSED.
FOUR DAYS LATER, NEW YORK'S UPPER EAST SIDE...
SKREEEEEEE
CRASH
8

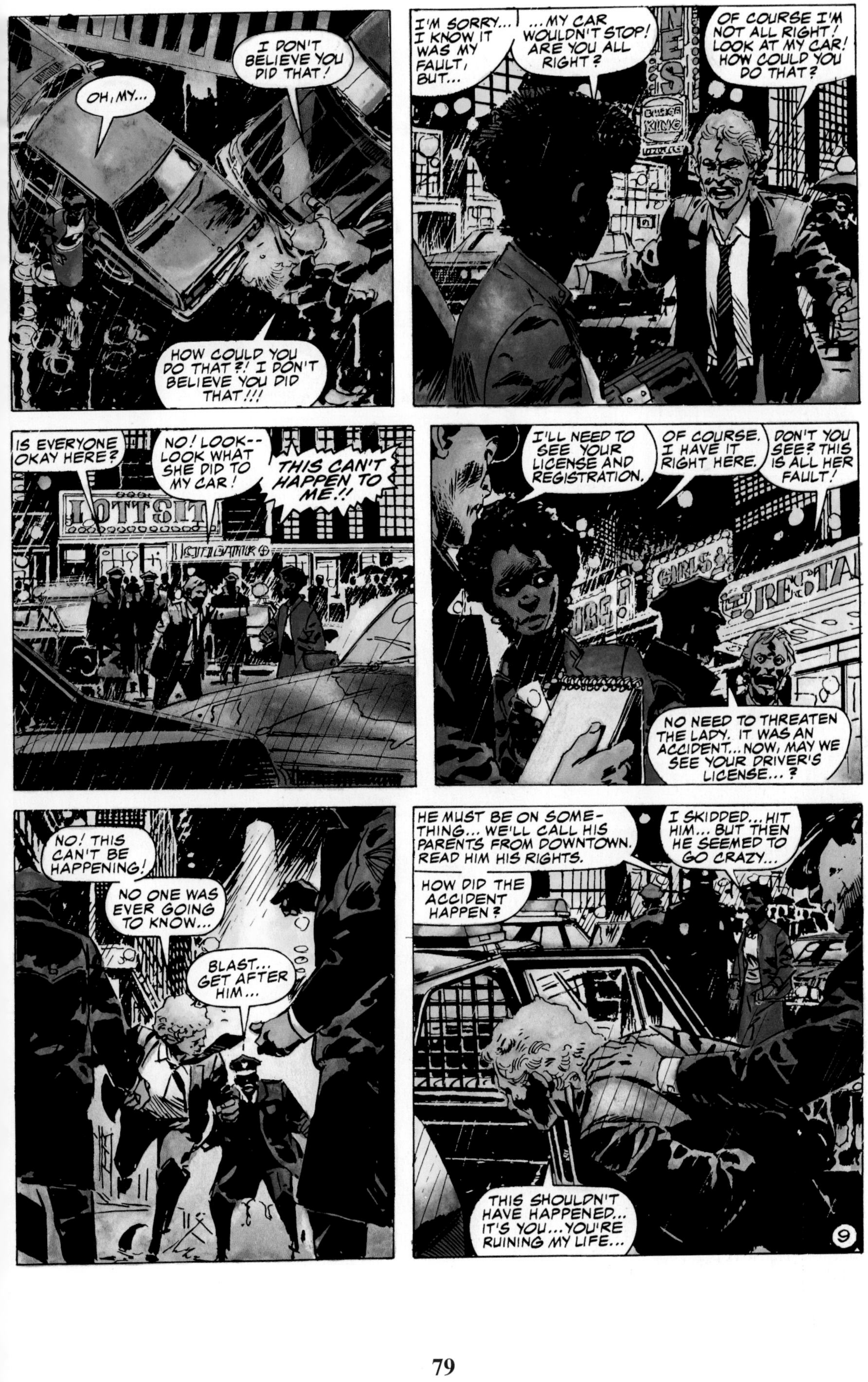
OH, MY...
I DON'T BELIEVE YOU DID THAT!
HOW COULD YOU DO THAT?! I DON'T BELIEVE YOU DID THAT!!!
I'M SORRY... I KNOW IT WAS MY FAULT, BUT...
...MY CAR WOULDN'T STOP! ARE YOU ALL RIGHT?
OF COURSE I'M NOT ALL RIGHT! LOOK AT MY CAR! HOW COULD YOU DO THAT?
IS EVERYONE OKAY HERE?
NO! LOOK-- LOOK WHAT SHE DID TO MY CAR!
THIS CAN'T HAPPEN TO ME!!
I'LL NEED TO SEE YOUR LICENSE AND REGISTRATION.
OF COURSE. I HAVE IT RIGHT HERE.
DON'T YOU SEE? THIS IS ALL HER FAULT!
NO NEED TO THREATEN THE LADY. IT WAS AN ACCIDENT... NOW, MAY WE SEE YOUR DRIVER'S LICENSE...?
NO! THIS CAN'T BE HAPPENING!
NO ONE WAS EVER GOING TO KNOW...
BLAST... GET AFTER HIM...
HE MUST BE ON SOMETHING... WE'LL CALL HIS PARENTS FROM DOWNTOWN. READ HIM HIS RIGHTS.
I SKIDDED... HIT HIM... BUT THEN HE SEEMED TO GO CRAZY...
HOW DID THE ACCIDENT HAPPEN?
THIS SHOULDN'T HAVE HAPPENED... IT'S YOU... YOU'RE RUINING MY LIFE...
9

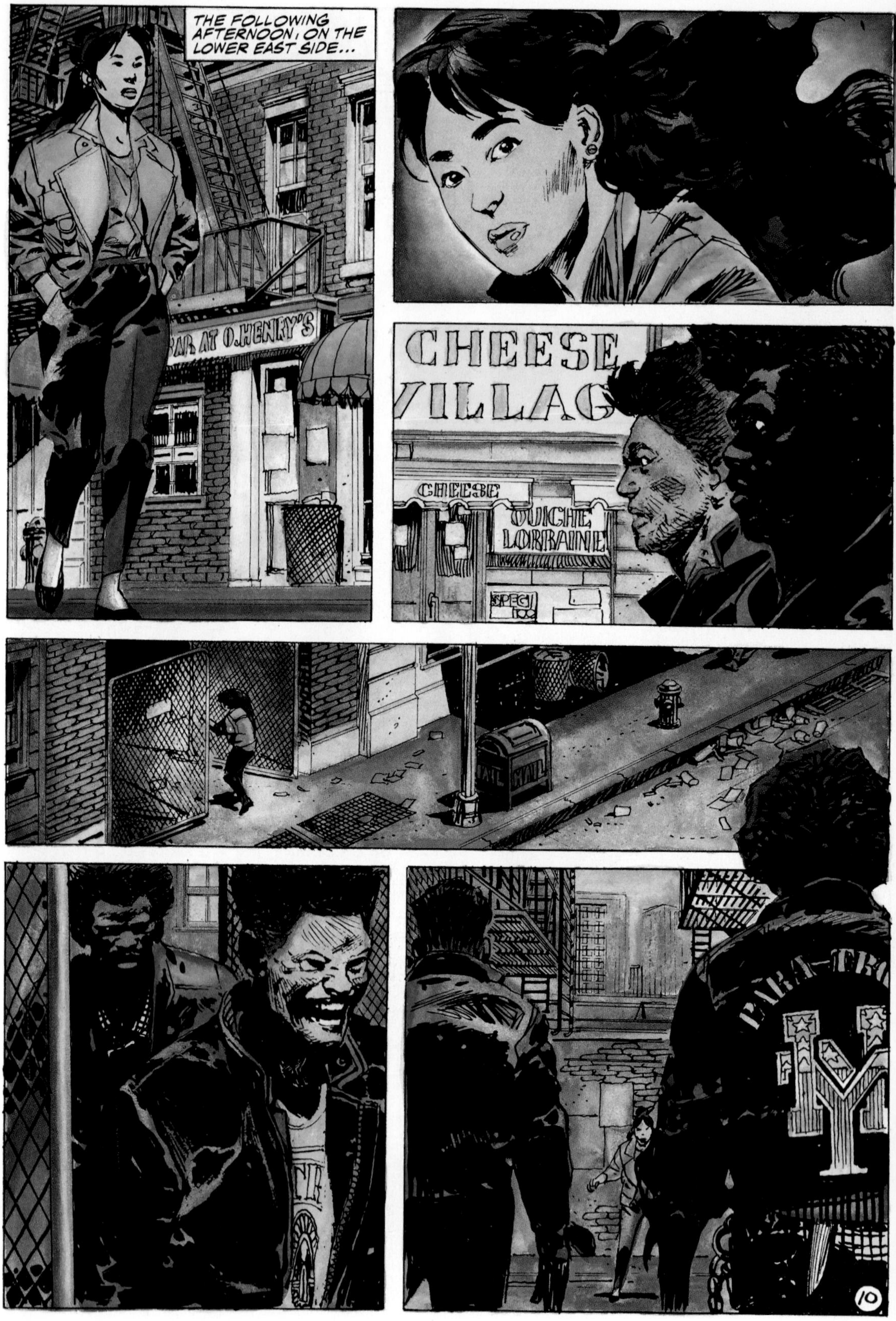
THE FOLLOWING AFTERNOON, ON THE LOWER EAST SIDE...
BAR AT O.HENRY'S
CHEESE
VILLAG
CHEESE
QUICHE LORRAINE
PARA-TRO
10

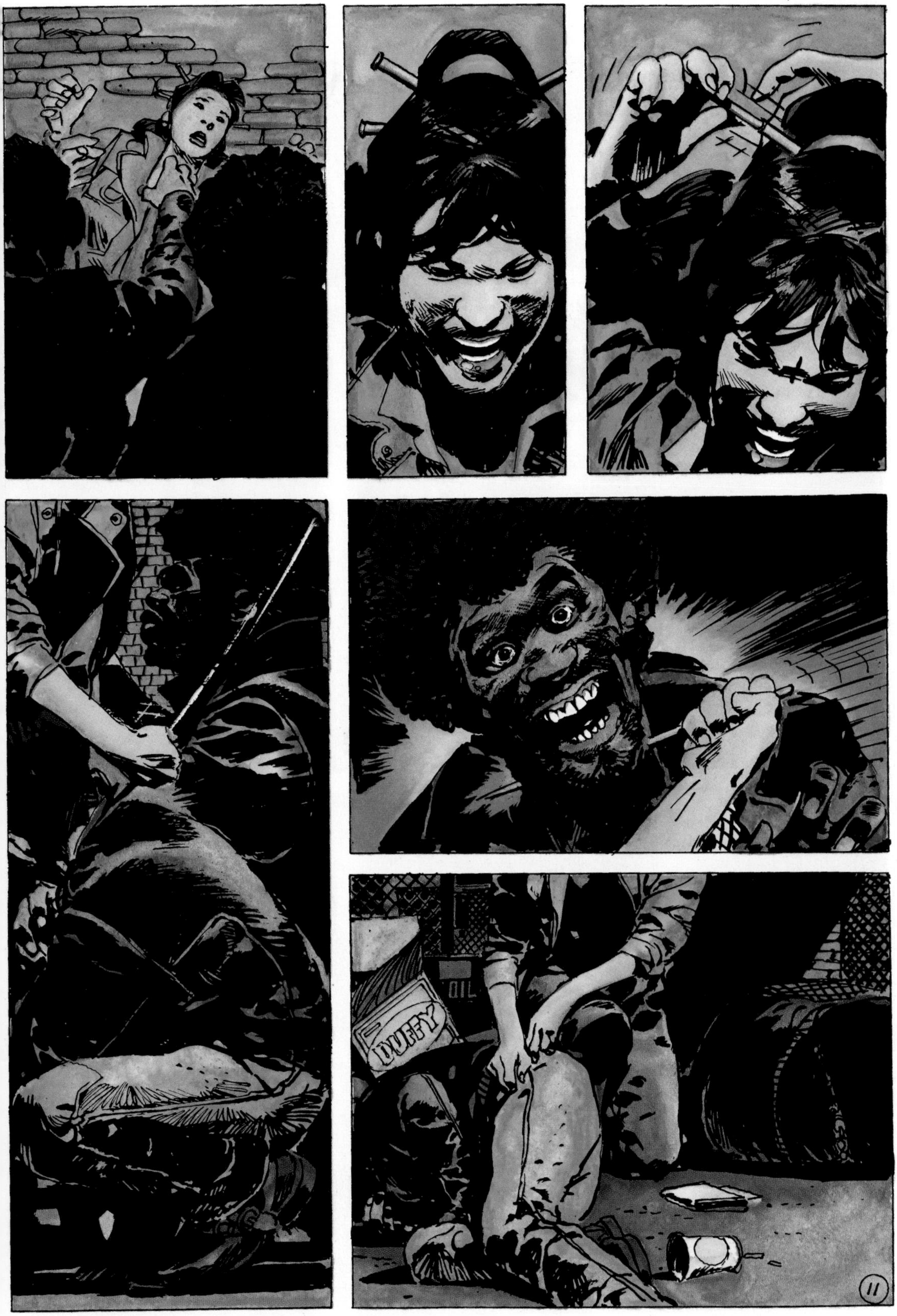
OIL
DUFFY
11

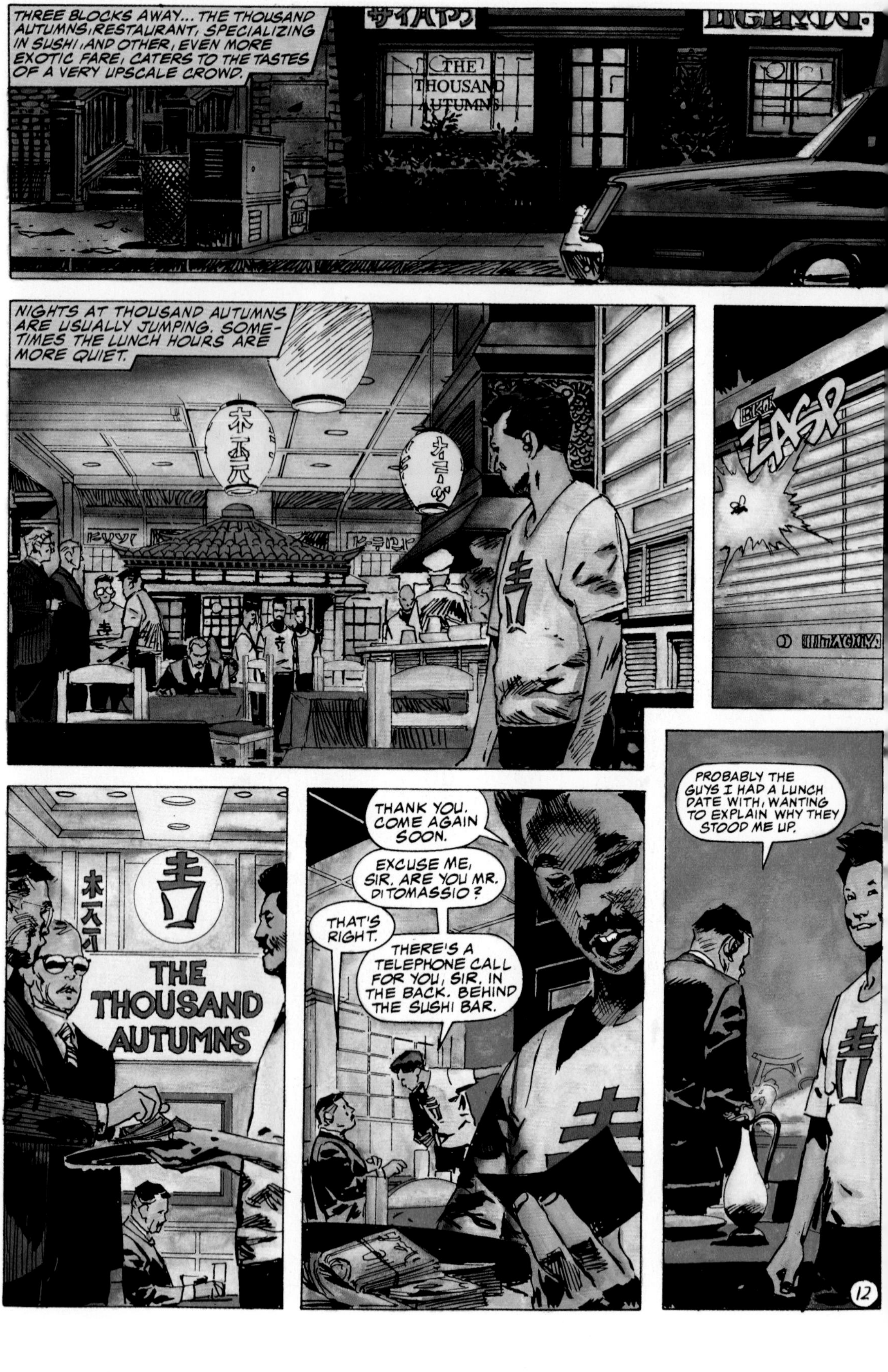
THREE BLOCKS AWAY... THE THOUSAND AUTUMNS RESTAURANT, SPECIALIZING IN SUSHI AND OTHER, EVEN MORE EXOTIC FARE, CATERS TO THE TASTES OF A VERY UPSCALE CROWD.
THE THOUSAND AUTUMNS
NIGHTS AT THOUSAND AUTUMNS ARE USUALLY JUMPING. SOMETIMES THE LUNCH HOURS ARE MORE QUIET.
ZASP
THE THOUSAND AUTUMNS
THANK YOU. COME AGAIN SOON.
EXCUSE ME, SIR. ARE YOU MR. DITOMASSIO?
THAT'S RIGHT.
THERE'S A TELEPHONE CALL FOR YOU, SIR. IN THE BACK. BEHIND THE SUSHI BAR.
PROBABLY THE GUYS I HAD A LUNCH DATE WITH, WANTING TO EXPLAIN WHY THEY STOOD ME UP.
12

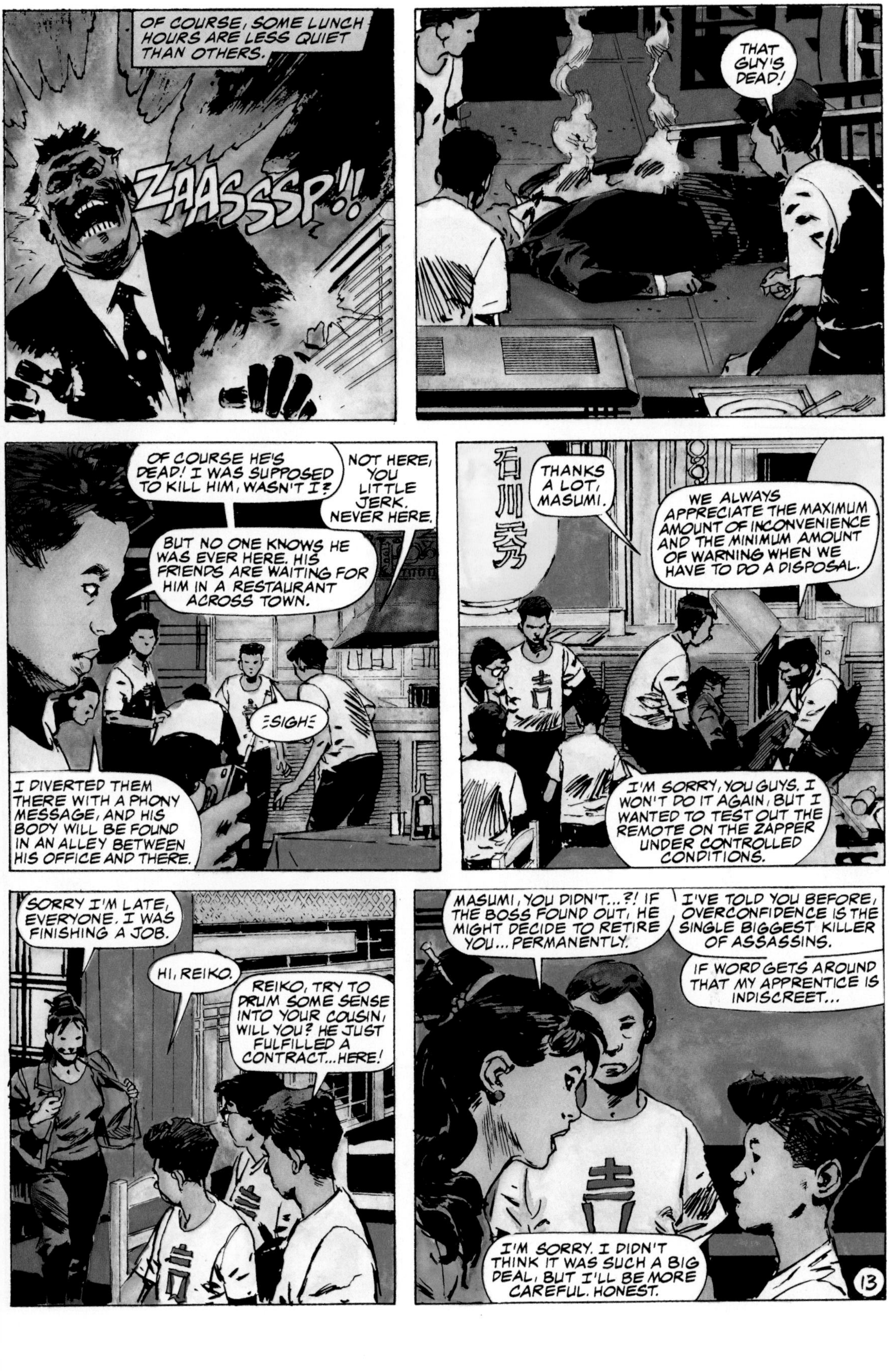
OF COURSE, SOME LUNCH HOURS ARE LESS QUIET THAN OTHERS.
ZAASSSSP!!
THAT GUY'S DEAD!
OF COURSE HE'S DEAD! I WAS SUPPOSED TO KILL HIM, WASN'T I?
NOT HERE, YOU LITTLE JERK. NEVER HERE.
BUT NO ONE KNOWS HE WAS EVER HERE. HIS FRIENDS ARE WAITING FOR HIM IN A RESTAURANT ACROSS TOWN.
SIGH
I DIVERTED THEM THERE WITH A PHONY MESSAGE, AND HIS BODY WILL BE FOUND IN AN ALLEY BETWEEN HIS OFFICE AND THERE.
石川秀
THANKS A LOT, MASUMI.
WE ALWAYS APPRECIATE THE MAXIMUM AMOUNT OF INCONVENIENCE AND THE MINIMUM AMOUNT OF WARNING WHEN WE HAVE TO DO A DISPOSAL.
I'M SORRY, YOU GUYS. I WON'T DO IT AGAIN, BUT I WANTED TO TEST OUT THE REMOTE ON THE ZAPPER UNDER CONTROLLED CONDITIONS.
SORRY I'M LATE, EVERYONE. I WAS FINISHING A JOB.
HI, REIKO.
REIKO, TRY TO DRUM SOME SENSE INTO YOUR COUSIN, WILL YOU? HE JUST FULFILLED A CONTRACT...HERE!
MASUMI, YOU DIDN'T...?! IF THE BOSS FOUND OUT, HE MIGHT DECIDE TO RETIRE YOU... PERMANENTLY.
I'VE TOLD YOU BEFORE, OVERCONFIDENCE IS THE SINGLE BIGGEST KILLER OF ASSASSINS.
IF WORD GETS AROUND THAT MY APPRENTICE IS INDISCREET...
I'M SORRY. I DIDN'T THINK IT WAS SUCH A BIG DEAL, BUT I'LL BE MORE CAREFUL. HONEST.
13

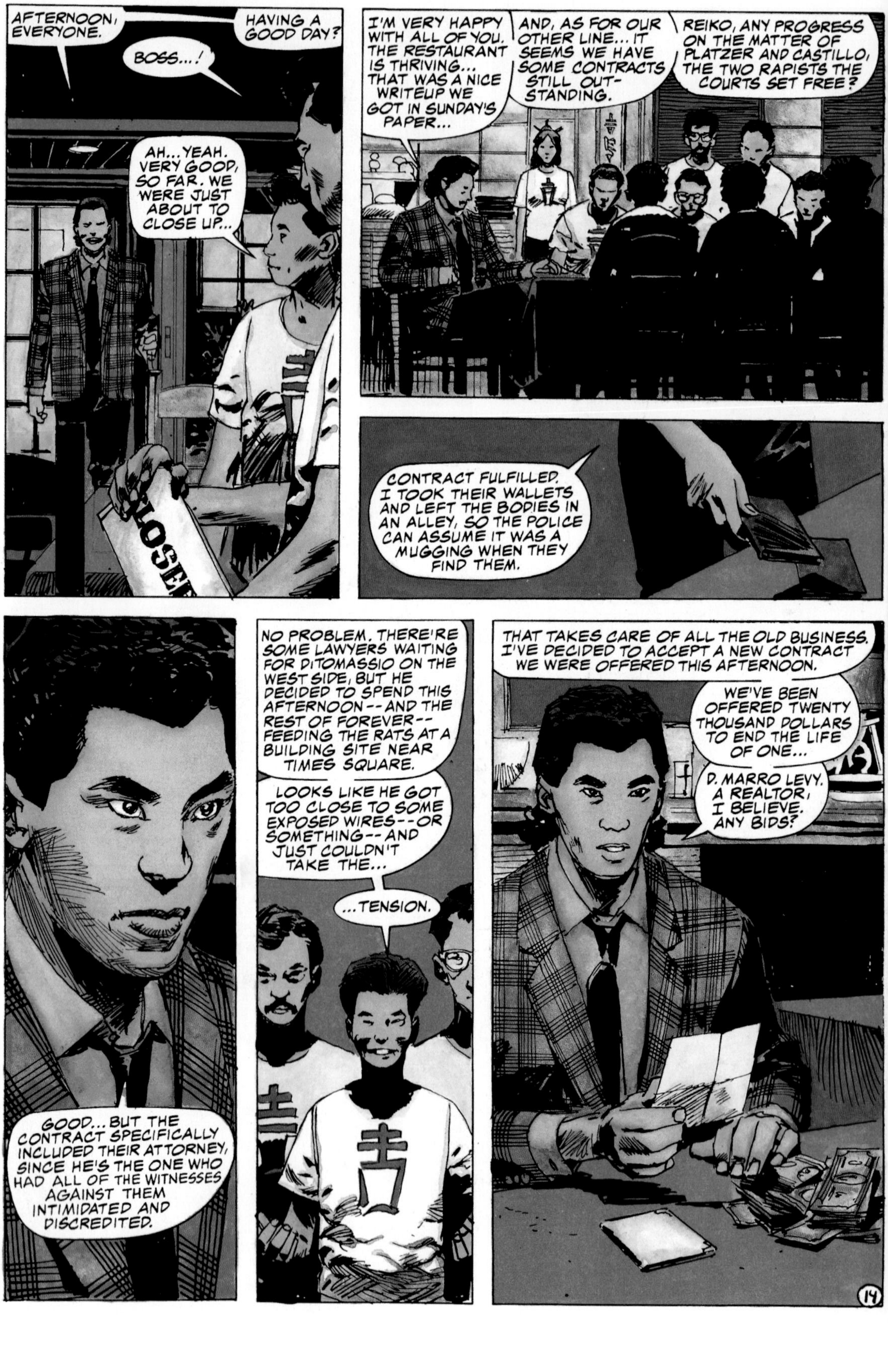
AFTERNOON, EVERYONE.
HAVING A GOOD DAY?
BOSS...!
AH... YEAH. VERY GOOD, SO FAR. WE WERE JUST ABOUT TO CLOSE UP...
I'M VERY HAPPY WITH ALL OF YOU. THE RESTAURANT IS THRIVING... THAT WAS A NICE WRITEUP WE GOT IN SUNDAY'S PAPER...
AND, AS FOR OUR OTHER LINE... IT SEEMS WE HAVE SOME CONTRACTS STILL OUT-STANDING.
REIKO, ANY PROGRESS ON THE MATTER OF PLATZER AND CASTILLO, THE TWO RAPISTS THE COURTS SET FREE?
CONTRACT FULFILLED. I TOOK THEIR WALLETS AND LEFT THE BODIES IN AN ALLEY, SO THE POLICE CAN ASSUME IT WAS A MUGGING WHEN THEY FIND THEM.
GOOD... BUT THE CONTRACT SPECIFICALLY INCLUDED THEIR ATTORNEY, SINCE HE'S THE ONE WHO HAD ALL OF THE WITNESSES AGAINST THEM INTIMIDATED AND DISCREDITED.
NO PROBLEM. THERE'RE SOME LAWYERS WAITING FOR DITOMASSIO ON THE WEST SIDE, BUT HE DECIDED TO SPEND THIS AFTERNOON--AND THE REST OF FOREVER--FEEDING THE RATS AT A BUILDING SITE NEAR TIMES SQUARE.
LOOKS LIKE HE GOT TOO CLOSE TO SOME EXPOSED WIRES--OR SOMETHING--AND JUST COULDN'T TAKE THE...
...TENSION.
THAT TAKES CARE OF ALL THE OLD BUSINESS. I'VE DECIDED TO ACCEPT A NEW CONTRACT WE WERE OFFERED THIS AFTERNOON.
WE'VE BEEN OFFERED TWENTY THOUSAND DOLLARS TO END THE LIFE OF ONE...
D. MARRO LEVY. A REALTOR, I BELIEVE. ANY BIDS?
14

NINETEEN THOUSAND, FIVE HUNDRED DOLLARS.

NINETEEN THOUSAND.

EIGHTEEN.

FIFTEEN THOUSAND DOLLARS.

FOURTEEN THOUSAND, FIVE HUNDRED.

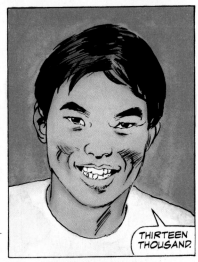

THIRTEEN THOUSAND.

ANY OF THE REST OF YOU WHO'D LIKE TO ENTER THE GUILD, CONCENTRATE ON YOUR TRAINING. AND REMEMBER, IF YOU'RE IMMIGRANTS, NO ONE JOINS UNTIL HE'S FLUENT IN ENGLISH. IN AMERICA, BE AMERICANS.

RIGHT, BOSS.

NO OTHER BIDS? THEN THE JOB IS DARYL'S, FOR THIRTEEN THOUSAND. THE GUILD'S PROFIT, WHEN THE CONTRACT IS FULFILLED, WILL BE SEVEN THOUSAND DOLLARS.

TAKE THE REST OF THE AFTERNOON OFF. HAVE LUNCH. I'LL SEE YOU BACK AT DINNER TIME. REIKO, YOU AND MASUMI WILL FIND THE FEE FOR THIS LAST JOB IN YOUR NEXT PAYCHECKS. IN CASH.

MIDTOWN, THE PLACE I'M CURRENTLY CALLING HOME.

IN MOST THINGS, IT PAYS TO ADVERTISE.

THE FLASHY COSTUME, THE REPUTATION I'VE BUILT FOR MYSELF, THE WHOLE MYSTIQUE THAT GETS CONJURED UP BY CALLING MYSELF THE PUNISHER...

ALL OF THOSE HAVE HELPED ME DO THE JOB I SET OUT TO DO WHEN I STARTED MY WAR ON CRIME...

BUT SOMETIMES, IT ALSO PAYS TO BE CAREFUL...

THAT'S WHY I HAVE PLACES LIKE THIS ONE-- RENTED IN THE NAME OF JAMES MAXWELL, A WELL-TO-DO AND ENTIRELY FICTIONAL IDENTITY I CREATED FOR MYSELF...

WITH GENUINE BUSINESS INTERESTS AND A GENUINE HOME...

...WHERE THE PUNISHER'S ENEMIES ARE NOT LIKELY TO GO LOOKING FOR HIM.

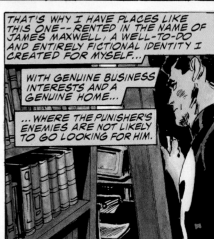

IF THEY EVER DO, MAXWELL WILL HAVE OUTLIVED HIS USEFUL-NESS, AND IT WILL BE TIME FOR ME TO STEP INTO ONE OF THE OTHER DUMMY CHARACTERS I'VE CREATED TO HIDE OUT IN.

BUT MAXWELL IS NOT AT HOME TONIGHT. TONIGHT THE PUNISHER IS HOME...

AND HE WANTS TO KNOW IF THERE'S ANYTHING GOING ON OUT THERE THAT COULD USE HIS ATTENTION.

16

MR. MULVEY?

AH...AH... YEAH.

MR. ABBEY WILL SEE YOU NOW.

SO, MR. MULVEY...OR-- IT'S TIMMY, ISN'T IT? I CAN CALL YOU TIMMY, CAN'T I?

SO, TIMMY...I UNDERSTAND YOU'RE IN SOME KIND OF TROUBLE...

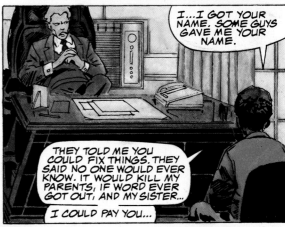

I...I GOT YOUR NAME. SOME GUYS GAVE ME YOUR NAME.

THEY TOLD ME YOU COULD FIX THINGS. THEY SAID NO ONE WOULD EVER KNOW. IT WOULD KILL MY PARENTS, IF WORD EVER GOT OUT, AND MY SISTER...

I COULD PAY YOU...

NOW, TIMMY... YOU'RE BEING A LITTLE PREMATURE, AREN'T YOU?

I'D HAVE TO EXAMINE YOUR PROBLEM FROM EVERY ANGLE, CONSIDER THINGS, BEFORE I DECIDE ...AND AS TO WHAT THE CHARGE WILL BE...

BUT I...

NO...

DON'T BE AFRAID. I KNOW YOU'RE A DESPERATE YOUNG MAN. AND I PROMISE YOU...

I WON'T KEEP YOU IN SUSPENSE FOR LONG.

NO...G'BYE...

THAT WILL BE ALL, TIMMY. YOU WOULDN'T WANT TO MAKE ME ANGRY, NOW, WOULD YOU?

KAY, I WANT YOU TO RUN A FULL CHECK ON TIM MULVEY'S FAMILY. SEE WHETHER IT MIGHT BE WORTH OUR WHILE TO LET THEIR SON BECOME DEPENDENT ON US...

ALREADY BEGUN, SIR.

THAT'S MY GIRL. AND RING RICHARD FLETCHER FOR ME. HE'LL BE PLEASED TO KNOW THAT WE MAY HAVE A NEW CLIENT ON THE LINE.

17

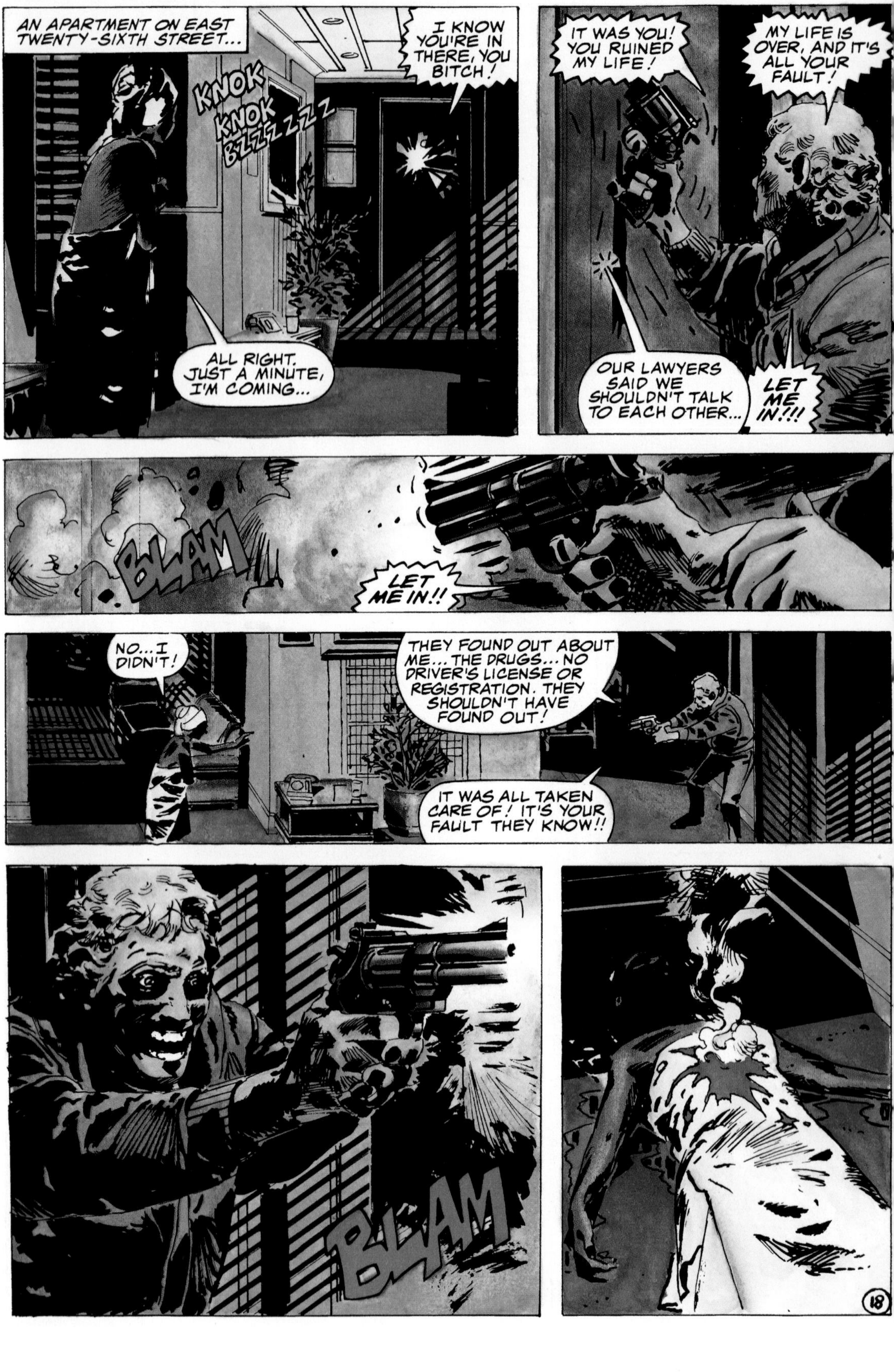
AN APARTMENT ON EAST TWENTY-SIXTH STREET...
KNOK KNOK BZZZZZZZ
I KNOW YOU'RE IN THERE, YOU BITCH!
ALL RIGHT. JUST A MINUTE, I'M COMING...
IT WAS YOU! YOU RUINED MY LIFE!
MY LIFE IS OVER, AND IT'S ALL YOUR FAULT!
OUR LAWYERS SAID WE SHOULDN'T TALK TO EACH OTHER...
LET ME IN!!!
BLAM
LET ME IN!!
NO... I DIDN'T!
THEY FOUND OUT ABOUT ME... THE DRUGS... NO DRIVER'S LICENSE OR REGISTRATION. THEY SHOULDN'T HAVE FOUND OUT!
IT WAS ALL TAKEN CARE OF! IT'S YOUR FAULT THEY KNOW!!
BLAM
18

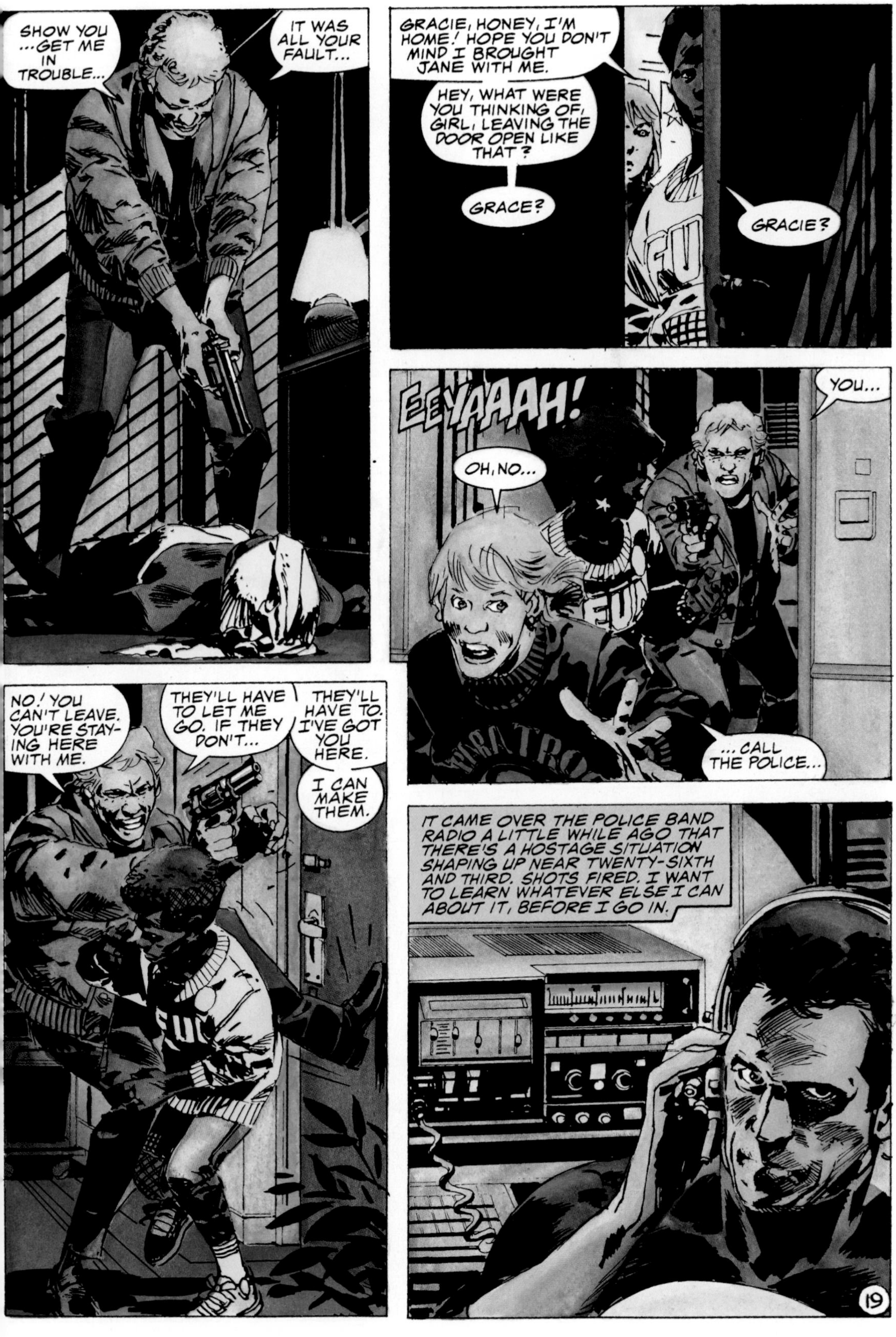
SHOW YOU ...GET ME IN TROUBLE...
IT WAS ALL YOUR FAULT...
GRACIE, HONEY, I'M HOME! HOPE YOU DON'T MIND I BROUGHT JANE WITH ME.
HEY, WHAT WERE YOU THINKING OF, GIRL, LEAVING THE DOOR OPEN LIKE THAT?
GRACE?
GRACIE?
EEYAAAH!
YOU...
OH, NO...
...CALL THE POLICE...
NO! YOU CAN'T LEAVE. YOU'RE STAYING HERE WITH ME.
THEY'LL HAVE TO LET ME GO. IF THEY DON'T...
THEY'LL HAVE TO. I'VE GOT YOU HERE.
I CAN MAKE THEM.
IT CAME OVER THE POLICE BAND RADIO A LITTLE WHILE AGO THAT THERE'S A HOSTAGE SITUATION SHAPING UP NEAR TWENTY-SIXTH AND THIRD. SHOTS FIRED. I WANT TO LEARN WHATEVER ELSE I CAN ABOUT IT, BEFORE I GO IN.
19

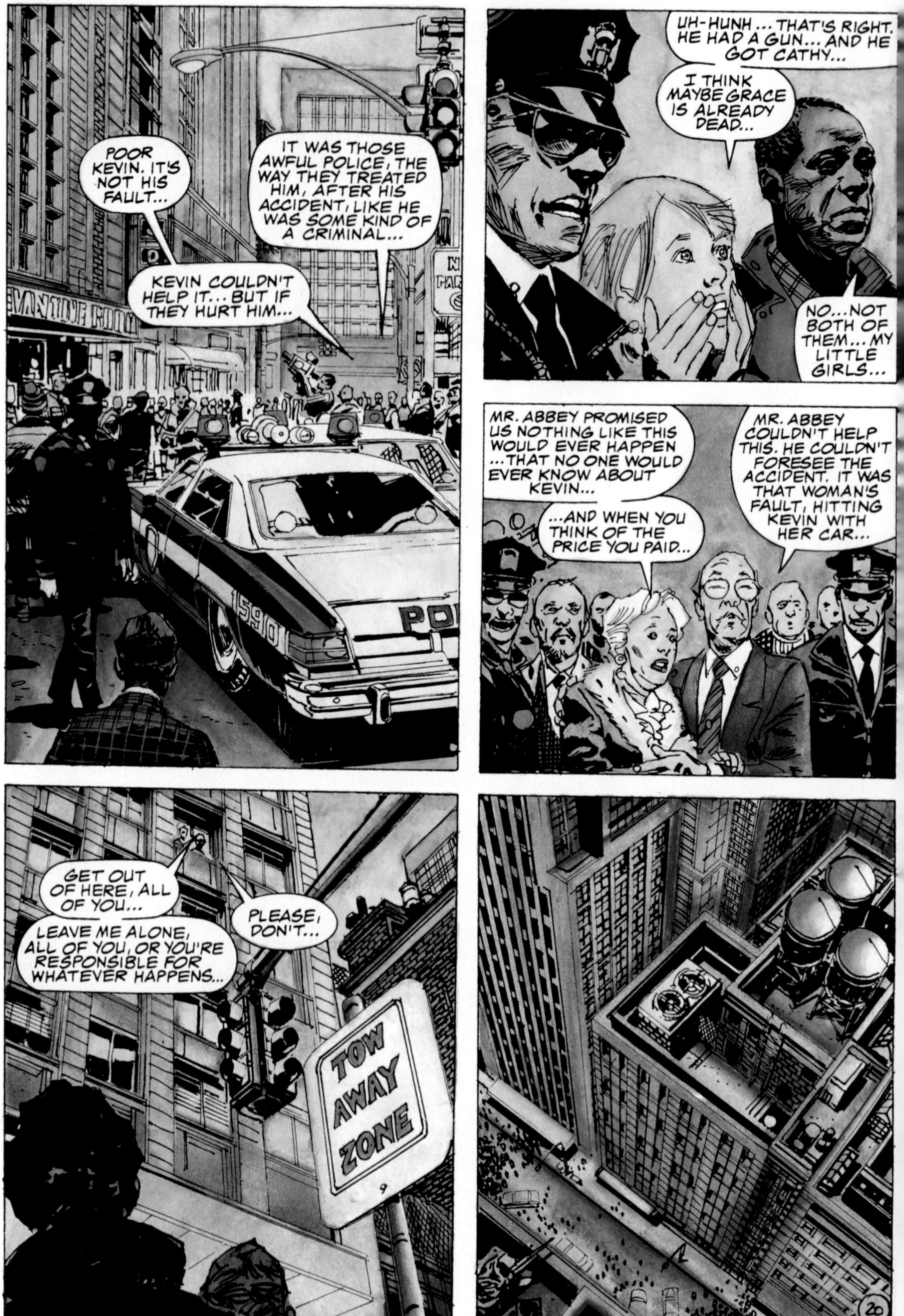
POOR KEVIN. IT'S NOT HIS FAULT...
IT WAS THOSE AWFUL POLICE, THE WAY THEY TREATED HIM, AFTER HIS ACCIDENT, LIKE HE WAS SOME KIND OF A CRIMINAL...
KEVIN COULDN'T HELP IT... BUT IF THEY HURT HIM...
POL
UH-HUNH... THAT'S RIGHT. HE HAD A GUN... AND HE GOT CATHY...
I THINK MAYBE GRACE IS ALREADY DEAD...
NO...NOT BOTH OF THEM... MY LITTLE GIRLS...
MR. ABBEY PROMISED US NOTHING LIKE THIS WOULD EVER HAPPEN ...THAT NO ONE WOULD EVER KNOW ABOUT KEVIN...
...AND WHEN YOU THINK OF THE PRICE YOU PAID...
MR. ABBEY COULDN'T HELP THIS. HE COULDN'T FORESEE THE ACCIDENT. IT WAS THAT WOMAN'S FAULT, HITTING KEVIN WITH HER CAR...
GET OUT OF HERE, ALL OF YOU...
LEAVE ME ALONE, ALL OF YOU, OR YOU'RE RESPONSIBLE FOR WHATEVER HAPPENS...
PLEASE, DON'T...
TOW AWAY ZONE
20

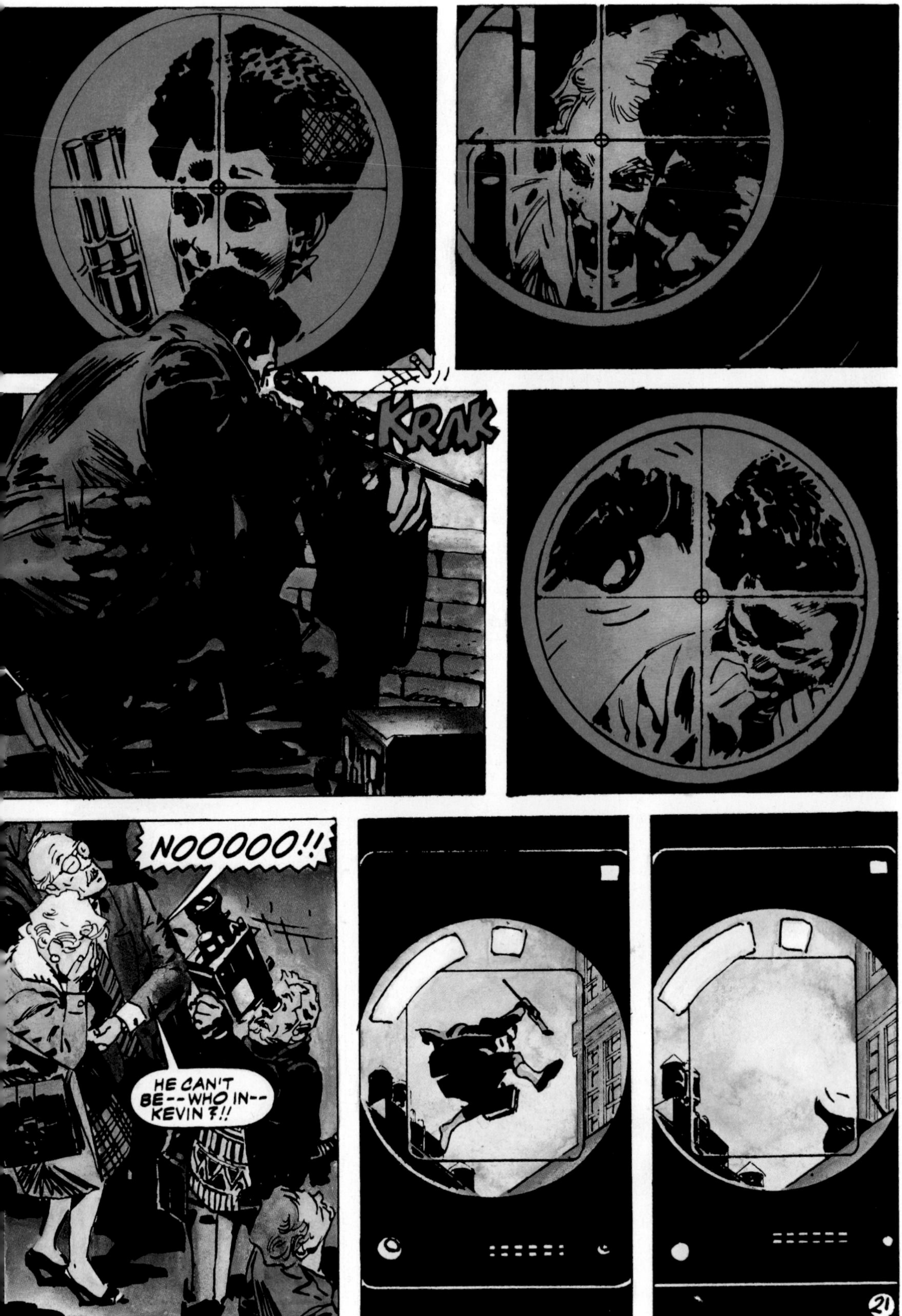
KRAK
NOOOOO!!
HE CAN'T BE--WHO IN-- KEVIN ?!!
21

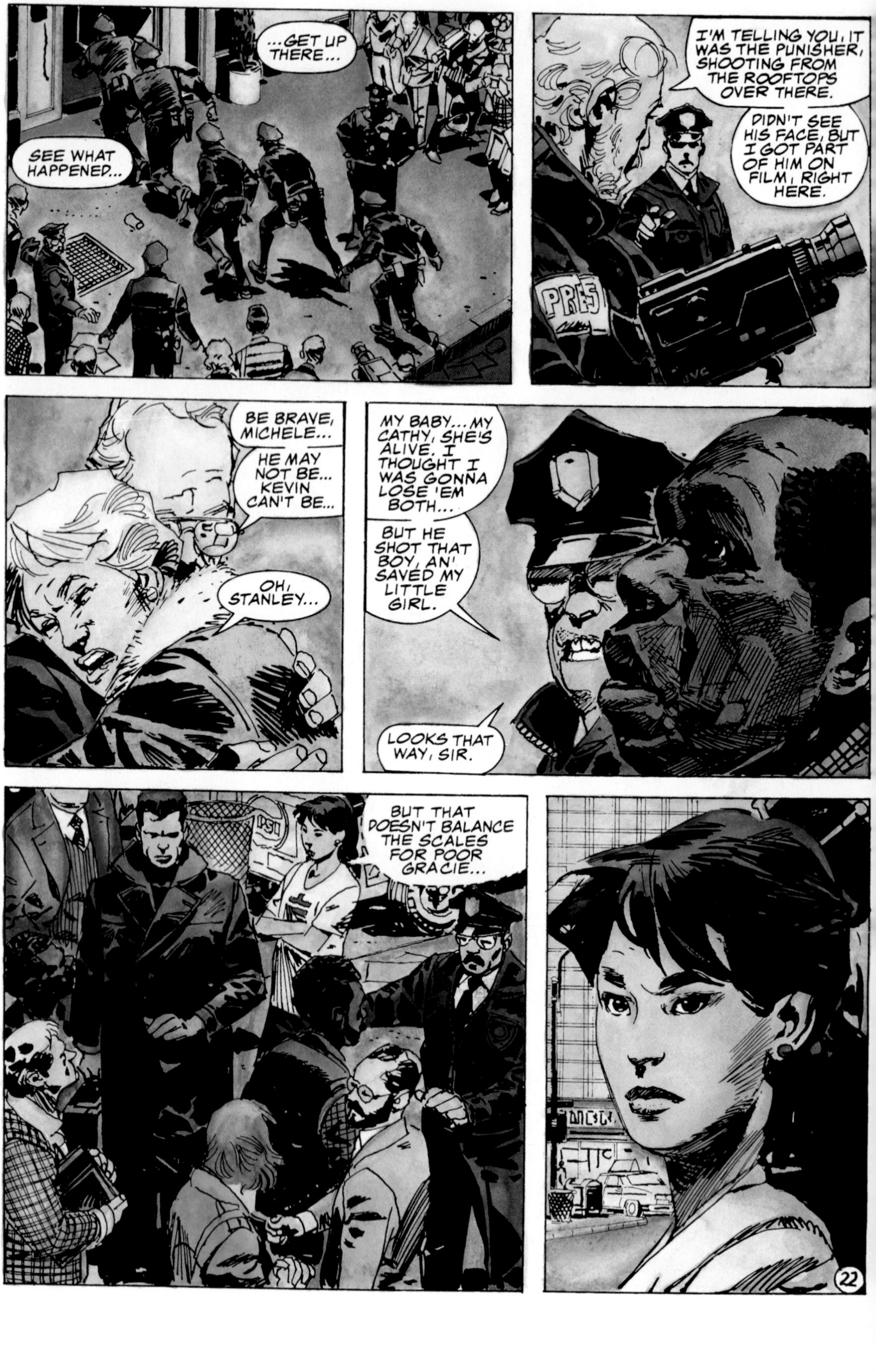
...GET UP THERE...
SEE WHAT HAPPENED...
I'M TELLING YOU, IT WAS THE PUNISHER, SHOOTING FROM THE ROOFTOPS OVER THERE.
DIDN'T SEE HIS FACE, BUT I GOT PART OF HIM ON FILM, RIGHT HERE.
PRESS
BE BRAVE, MICHELE...
HE MAY NOT BE... KEVIN CAN'T BE...
OH, STANLEY...
MY BABY... MY CATHY, SHE'S ALIVE. I THOUGHT I WAS GONNA LOSE 'EM BOTH...
BUT HE SHOT THAT BOY, AN' SAVED MY LITTLE GIRL.
LOOKS THAT WAY, SIR.
BUT THAT DOESN'T BALANCE THE SCALES FOR POOR GRACIE...
22

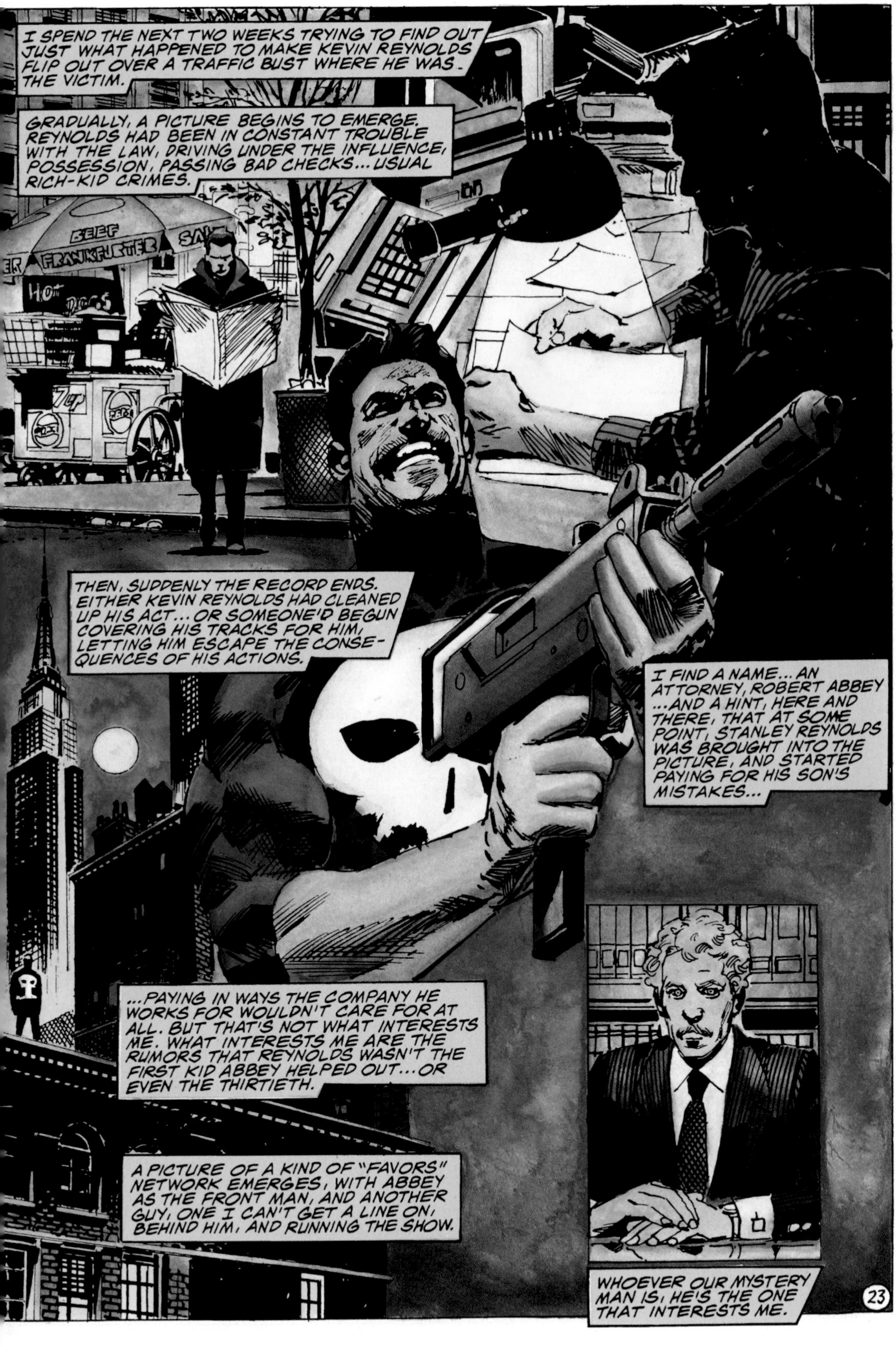
I SPEND THE NEXT TWO WEEKS TRYING TO FIND OUT JUST WHAT HAPPENED TO MAKE KEVIN REYNOLDS FLIP OUT OVER A TRAFFIC BUST WHERE HE WAS THE VICTIM.
GRADUALLY, A PICTURE BEGINS TO EMERGE. REYNOLDS HAD BEEN IN CONSTANT TROUBLE WITH THE LAW, DRIVING UNDER THE INFLUENCE, POSSESSION, PASSING BAD CHECKS... USUAL RICH-KID CRIMES.
BEEF FRANKFURTER
HOT DOGS
THEN, SUDDENLY THE RECORD ENDS. EITHER KEVIN REYNOLDS HAD CLEANED UP HIS ACT... OR SOMEONE'D BEGUN COVERING HIS TRACKS FOR HIM, LETTING HIM ESCAPE THE CONSEQUENCES OF HIS ACTIONS.
I FIND A NAME... AN ATTORNEY, ROBERT ABBEY ...AND A HINT, HERE AND THERE, THAT AT SOME POINT, STANLEY REYNOLDS WAS BROUGHT INTO THE PICTURE, AND STARTED PAYING FOR HIS SON'S MISTAKES...
...PAYING IN WAYS THE COMPANY HE WORKS FOR WOULDN'T CARE FOR AT ALL. BUT THAT'S NOT WHAT INTERESTS ME. WHAT INTERESTS ME ARE THE RUMORS THAT REYNOLDS WASN'T THE FIRST KID ABBEY HELPED OUT... OR EVEN THE THIRTIETH.
A PICTURE OF A KIND OF "FAVORS" NETWORK EMERGES, WITH ABBEY AS THE FRONT MAN, AND ANOTHER GUY, ONE I CAN'T GET A LINE ON, BEHIND HIM, AND RUNNING THE SHOW.
WHOEVER OUR MYSTERY MAN IS, HE'S THE ONE THAT INTERESTS ME.
23

MR. WILLIAMS... WE'RE GLAD TO SEE YOU AGAIN... EVERYONE WAS SO SORRY...

THANK YOU... THE FLOWERS YOU SENT FOR GRACIE... THEY WERE...

YOU KNOW, THAT BOY, THE ONE WHO KILLED HER, HE WASN'T EVEN SUPPOSED TO BE WALKIN' AROUND. SUPPOSED TO BE IN JAIL.

I HEARD WHAT HIS FOLKS SAID THAT DAY... HOW THERE WAS A MAN WHO GOT HIM OFF. SUCH A DAMNED SHAME...

WELL, IF THERE'S ANYTHING ANYONE HERE CAN DO...

I'LL LET YOU KNOW.

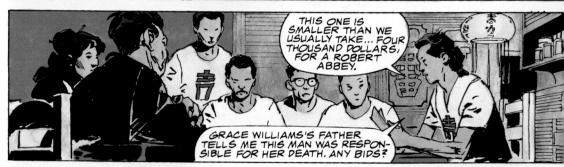

THIS ONE IS SMALLER THAN WE USUALLY TAKE... FOUR THOUSAND DOLLARS, FOR A ROBERT ABBEY.

GRACE WILLIAMS'S FATHER TELLS ME THIS MAN WAS RESPONSIBLE FOR HER DEATH. ANY BIDS?

THREE THOUSAND, EIGHT HUNDRED.

THREE THOUSAND EVEN.

THREE HUNDRED DOLLARS.

SHE WAS A FRIEND OF YOURS, WASN'T SHE, REIKO? ANY OTHER BIDS?

THEN, THE GUILD'S TAKE IS THIRTY-SEVEN HUNDRED DOLLARS, AND THE JOB IS REIKO'S FOR THREE.

REIKO'S AND MINE.

24

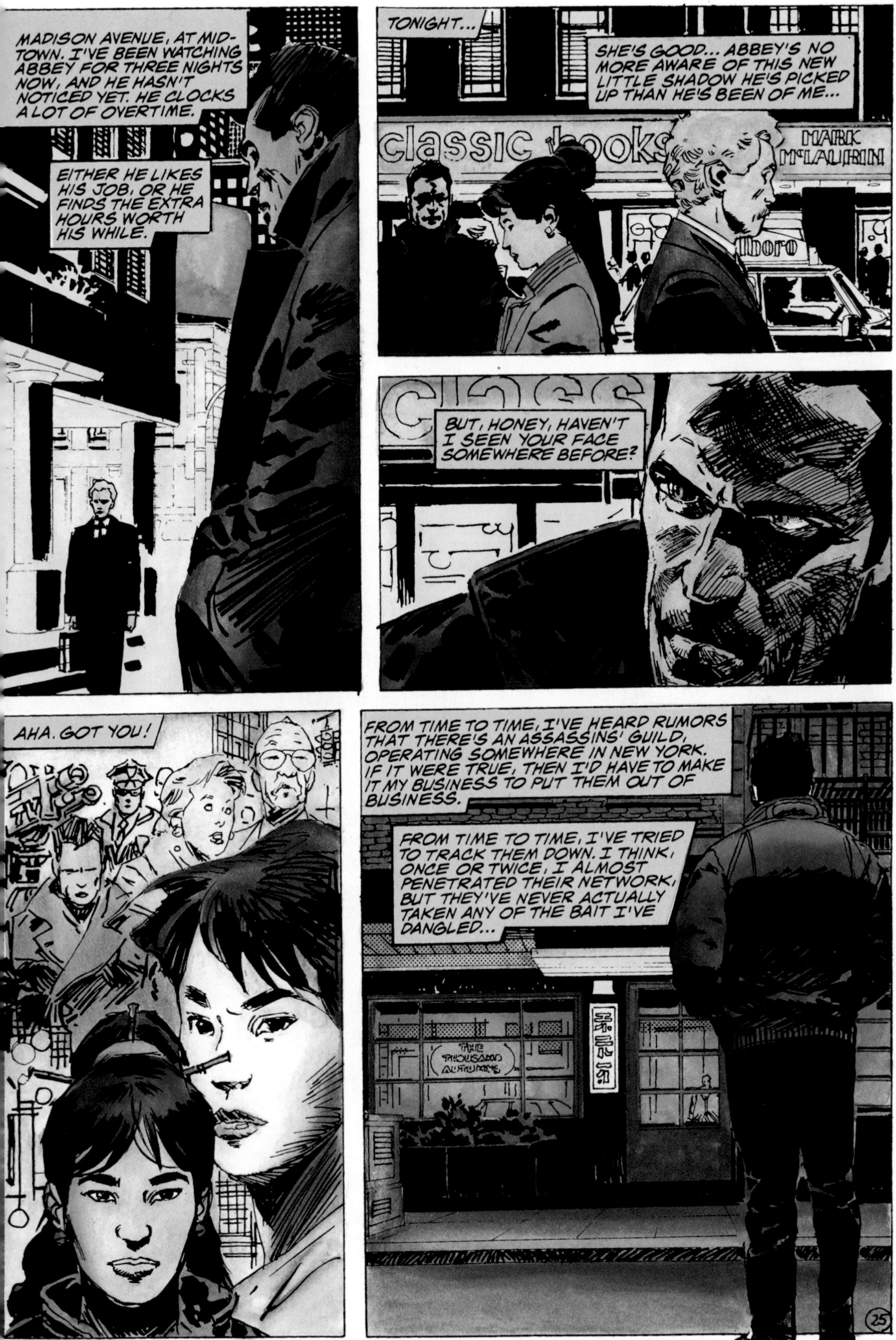
MADISON AVENUE, AT MID-TOWN. I'VE BEEN WATCHING ABBEY FOR THREE NIGHTS NOW, AND HE HASN'T NOTICED YET. HE CLOCKS A LOT OF OVERTIME.
EITHER HE LIKES HIS JOB, OR HE FINDS THE EXTRA HOURS WORTH HIS WHILE.
TONIGHT...
SHE'S GOOD... ABBEY'S NO MORE AWARE OF THIS NEW LITTLE SHADOW HE'S PICKED UP THAN HE'S BEEN OF ME...
classic books
MARK McLAURIN
BUT, HONEY, HAVEN'T I SEEN YOUR FACE SOMEWHERE BEFORE?
AHA. GOT YOU!
FROM TIME TO TIME, I'VE HEARD RUMORS THAT THERE'S AN ASSASSINS' GUILD, OPERATING SOMEWHERE IN NEW YORK. IF IT WERE TRUE, THEN I'D HAVE TO MAKE IT MY BUSINESS TO PUT THEM OUT OF BUSINESS.
FROM TIME TO TIME, I'VE TRIED TO TRACK THEM DOWN. I THINK, ONCE OR TWICE, I ALMOST PENETRATED THEIR NETWORK, BUT THEY'VE NEVER ACTUALLY TAKEN ANY OF THE BAIT I'VE DANGLED...
THE THOUSAND AUTUMNS
25

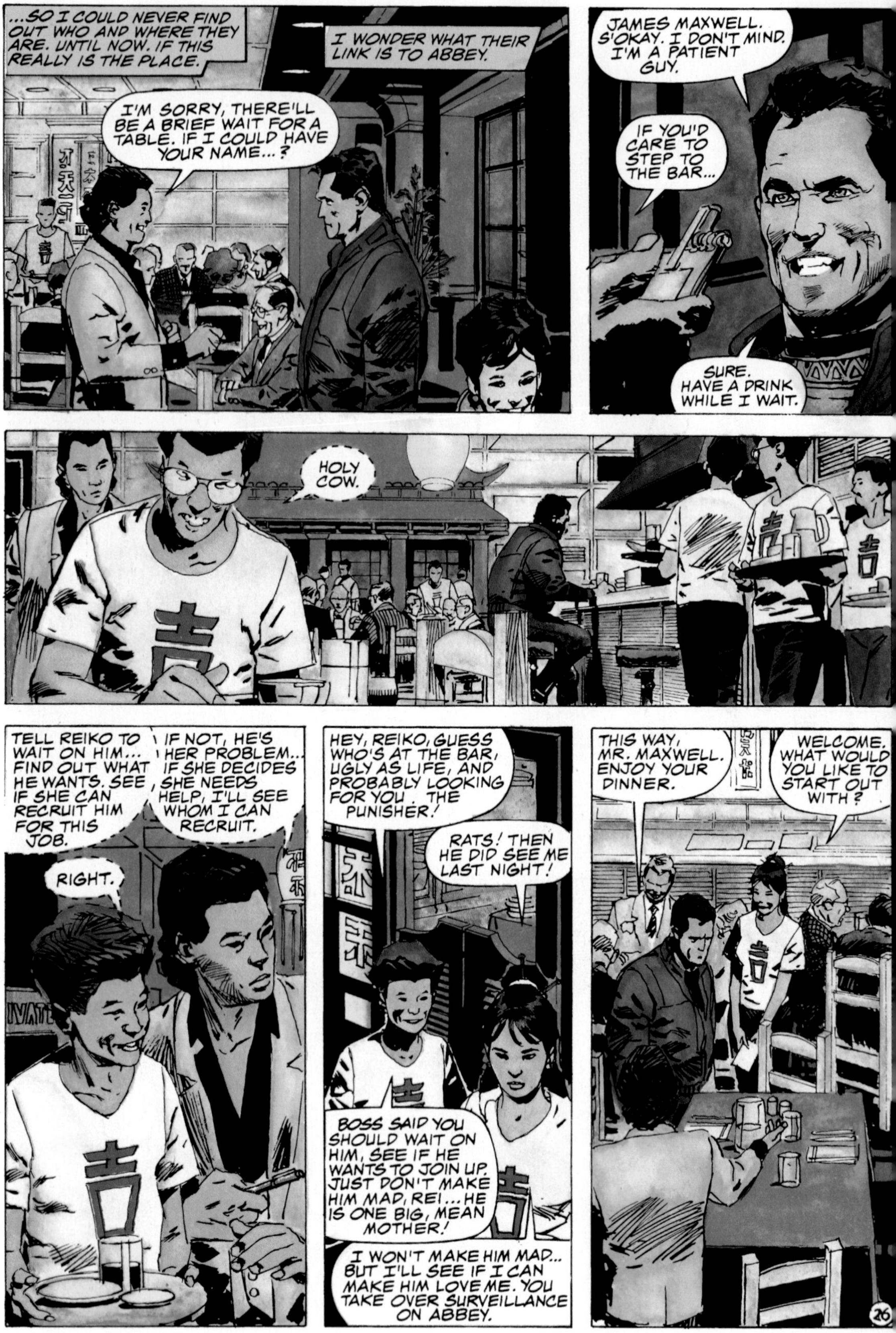
...SO I COULD NEVER FIND OUT WHO AND WHERE THEY ARE. UNTIL NOW. IF THIS REALLY IS THE PLACE.
I WONDER WHAT THEIR LINK IS TO ABBEY.
I'M SORRY, THERE'LL BE A BRIEF WAIT FOR A TABLE. IF I COULD HAVE YOUR NAME...?
JAMES MAXWELL. S'OKAY. I DON'T MIND. I'M A PATIENT GUY.
IF YOU'D CARE TO STEP TO THE BAR...
SURE. HAVE A DRINK WHILE I WAIT.
HOLY COW.
TELL REIKO TO WAIT ON HIM... FIND OUT WHAT HE WANTS. SEE IF SHE CAN RECRUIT HIM FOR THIS JOB.
IF NOT, HE'S HER PROBLEM... IF SHE DECIDES SHE NEEDS HELP, I'LL SEE WHOM I CAN RECRUIT.
RIGHT.
HEY, REIKO, GUESS WHO'S AT THE BAR, UGLY AS LIFE, AND PROBABLY LOOKING FOR YOU. THE PUNISHER!
RATS! THEN HE DID SEE ME LAST NIGHT!
BOSS SAID YOU SHOULD WAIT ON HIM, SEE IF HE WANTS TO JOIN UP. JUST DON'T MAKE HIM MAD, REI... HE IS ONE BIG, MEAN MOTHER!
I WON'T MAKE HIM MAD... BUT I'LL SEE IF I CAN MAKE HIM LOVE ME. YOU TAKE OVER SURVEILLANCE ON ABBEY.
THIS WAY, MR. MAXWELL. ENJOY YOUR DINNER.
WELCOME. WHAT WOULD YOU LIKE TO START OUT WITH?
26

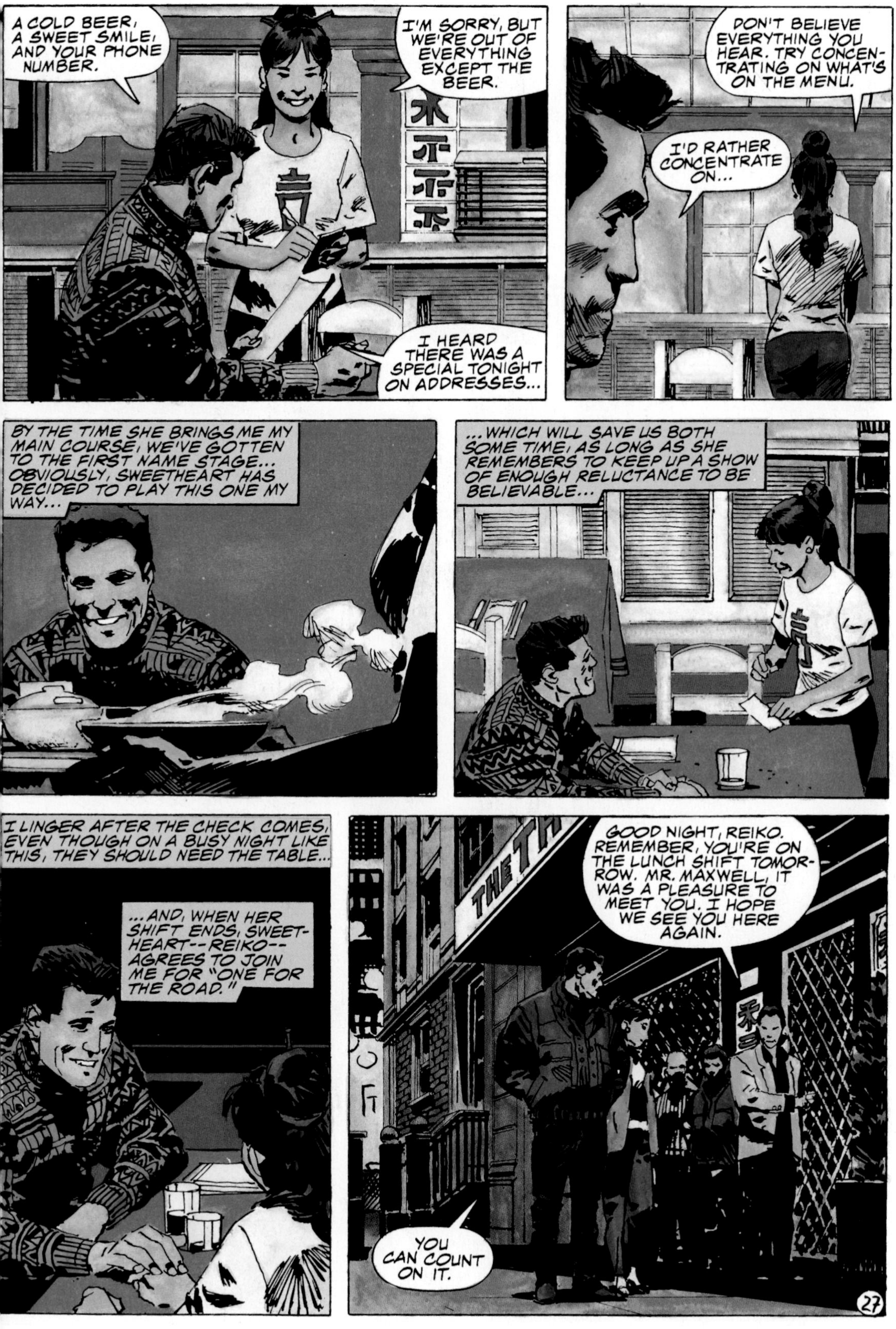
A COLD BEER, A SWEET SMILE, AND YOUR PHONE NUMBER.
I'M SORRY, BUT WE'RE OUT OF EVERYTHING EXCEPT THE BEER.
I HEARD THERE WAS A SPECIAL TONIGHT ON ADDRESSES...
DON'T BELIEVE EVERYTHING YOU HEAR. TRY CONCENTRATING ON WHAT'S ON THE MENU.
I'D RATHER CONCENTRATE ON...
BY THE TIME SHE BRINGS ME MY MAIN COURSE, WE'VE GOTTEN TO THE FIRST NAME STAGE... OBVIOUSLY, SWEETHEART HAS DECIDED TO PLAY THIS ONE MY WAY...
...WHICH WILL SAVE US BOTH SOME TIME, AS LONG AS SHE REMEMBERS TO KEEP UP A SHOW OF ENOUGH RELUCTANCE TO BE BELIEVABLE...
I LINGER AFTER THE CHECK COMES, EVEN THOUGH ON A BUSY NIGHT LIKE THIS, THEY SHOULD NEED THE TABLE...
...AND, WHEN HER SHIFT ENDS, SWEETHEART--REIKO--AGREES TO JOIN ME FOR "ONE FOR THE ROAD."
GOOD NIGHT, REIKO. REMEMBER, YOU'RE ON THE LUNCH SHIFT TOMORROW. MR. MAXWELL, IT WAS A PLEASURE TO MEET YOU. I HOPE WE SEE YOU HERE AGAIN.
YOU CAN COUNT ON IT.
27

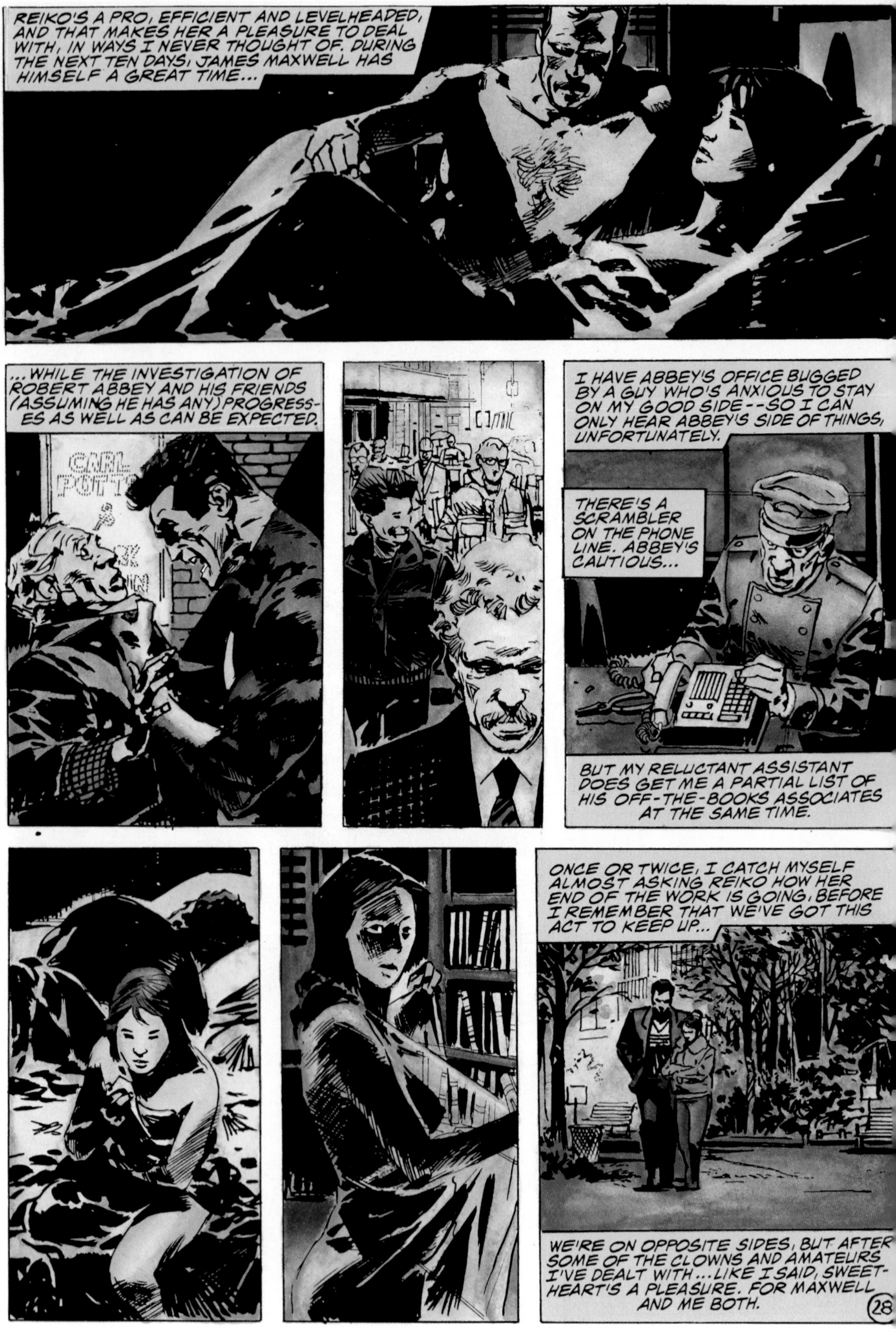
REIKO'S A PRO, EFFICIENT AND LEVELHEADED, AND THAT MAKES HER A PLEASURE TO DEAL WITH, IN WAYS I NEVER THOUGHT OF. DURING THE NEXT TEN DAYS, JAMES MAXWELL HAS HIMSELF A GREAT TIME...
...WHILE THE INVESTIGATION OF ROBERT ABBEY AND HIS FRIENDS (ASSUMING HE HAS ANY) PROGRESSES AS WELL AS CAN BE EXPECTED.
I HAVE ABBEY'S OFFICE BUGGED BY A GUY WHO'S ANXIOUS TO STAY ON MY GOOD SIDE--SO I CAN ONLY HEAR ABBEY'S SIDE OF THINGS, UNFORTUNATELY.
THERE'S A SCRAMBLER ON THE PHONE LINE. ABBEY'S CAUTIOUS...
BUT MY RELUCTANT ASSISTANT DOES GET ME A PARTIAL LIST OF HIS OFF-THE-BOOKS ASSOCIATES AT THE SAME TIME.
ONCE OR TWICE, I CATCH MYSELF ALMOST ASKING REIKO HOW HER END OF THE WORK IS GOING, BEFORE I REMEMBER THAT WE'VE GOT THIS ACT TO KEEP UP...
WE'RE ON OPPOSITE SIDES, BUT AFTER SOME OF THE CLOWNS AND AMATEURS I'VE DEALT WITH... LIKE I SAID, SWEETHEART'S A PLEASURE. FOR MAXWELL AND ME BOTH.
28

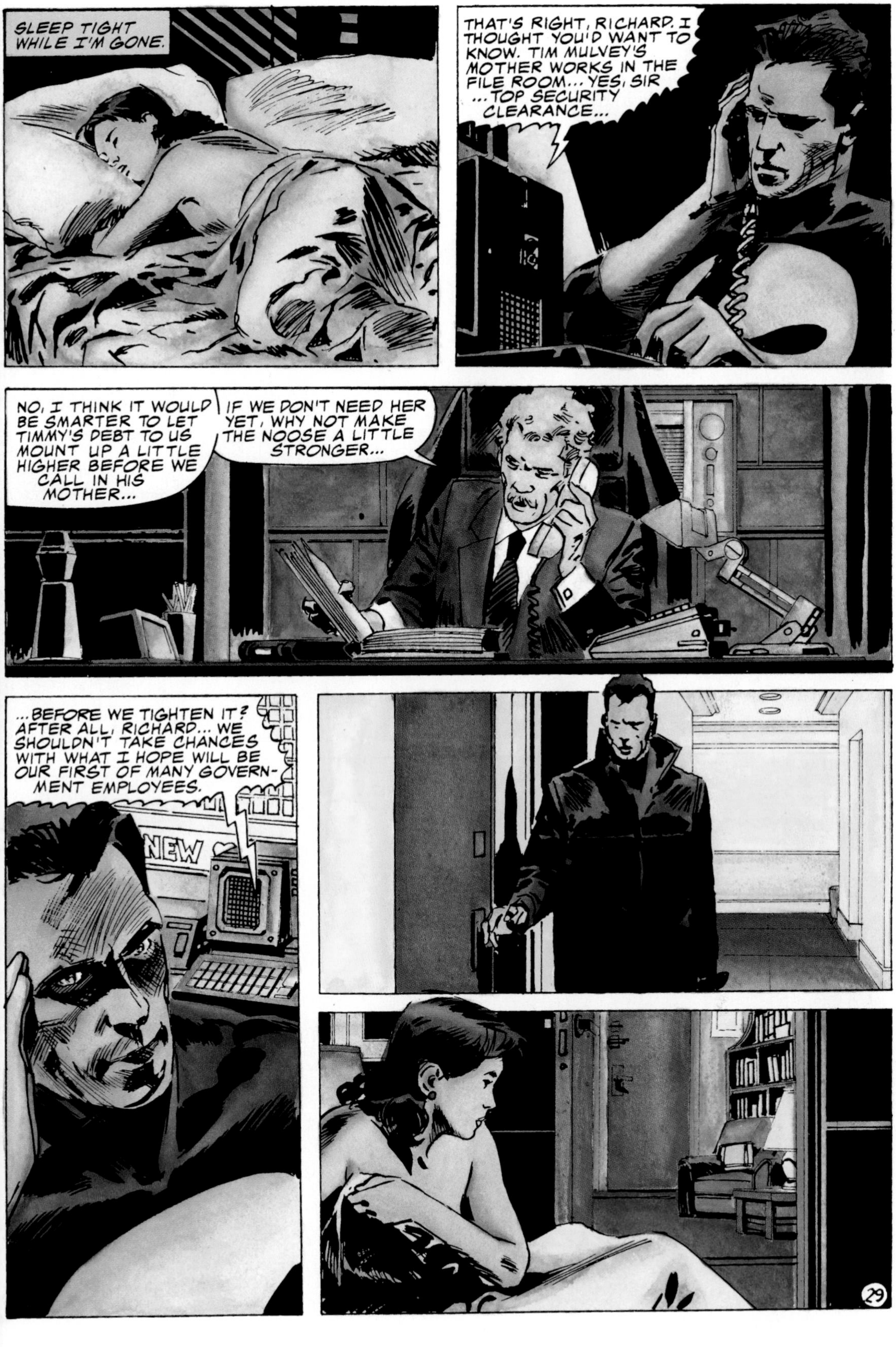
SLEEP TIGHT WHILE I'M GONE.
THAT'S RIGHT, RICHARD. I THOUGHT YOU'D WANT TO KNOW. TIM MULVEY'S MOTHER WORKS IN THE FILE ROOM... YES, SIR ...TOP SECURITY CLEARANCE...
NO, I THINK IT WOULD BE SMARTER TO LET TIMMY'S DEBT TO US MOUNT UP A LITTLE HIGHER BEFORE WE CALL IN HIS MOTHER...
IF WE DON'T NEED HER YET, WHY NOT MAKE THE NOOSE A LITTLE STRONGER...
...BEFORE WE TIGHTEN IT? AFTER ALL, RICHARD... WE SHOULDN'T TAKE CHANCES WITH WHAT I HOPE WILL BE OUR FIRST OF MANY GOVERNMENT EMPLOYEES.
NEW
29

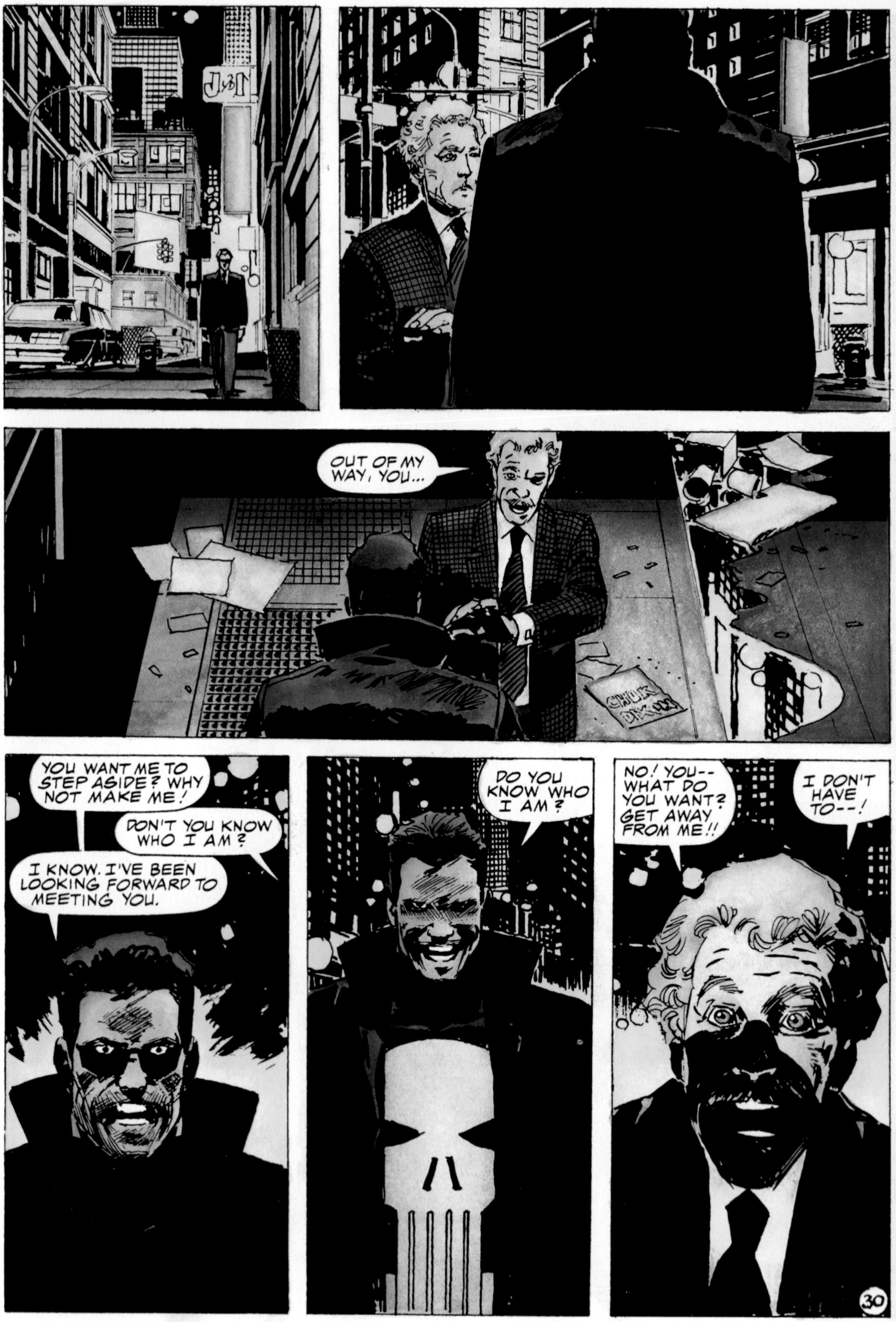
OUT OF MY WAY, YOU...
YOU WANT ME TO STEP ASIDE? WHY NOT MAKE ME!
DON'T YOU KNOW WHO I AM?
I KNOW. I'VE BEEN LOOKING FORWARD TO MEETING YOU.
DO YOU KNOW WHO I AM?
NO! YOU-- WHAT DO YOU WANT? GET AWAY FROM ME!!
I DON'T HAVE TO--!
30

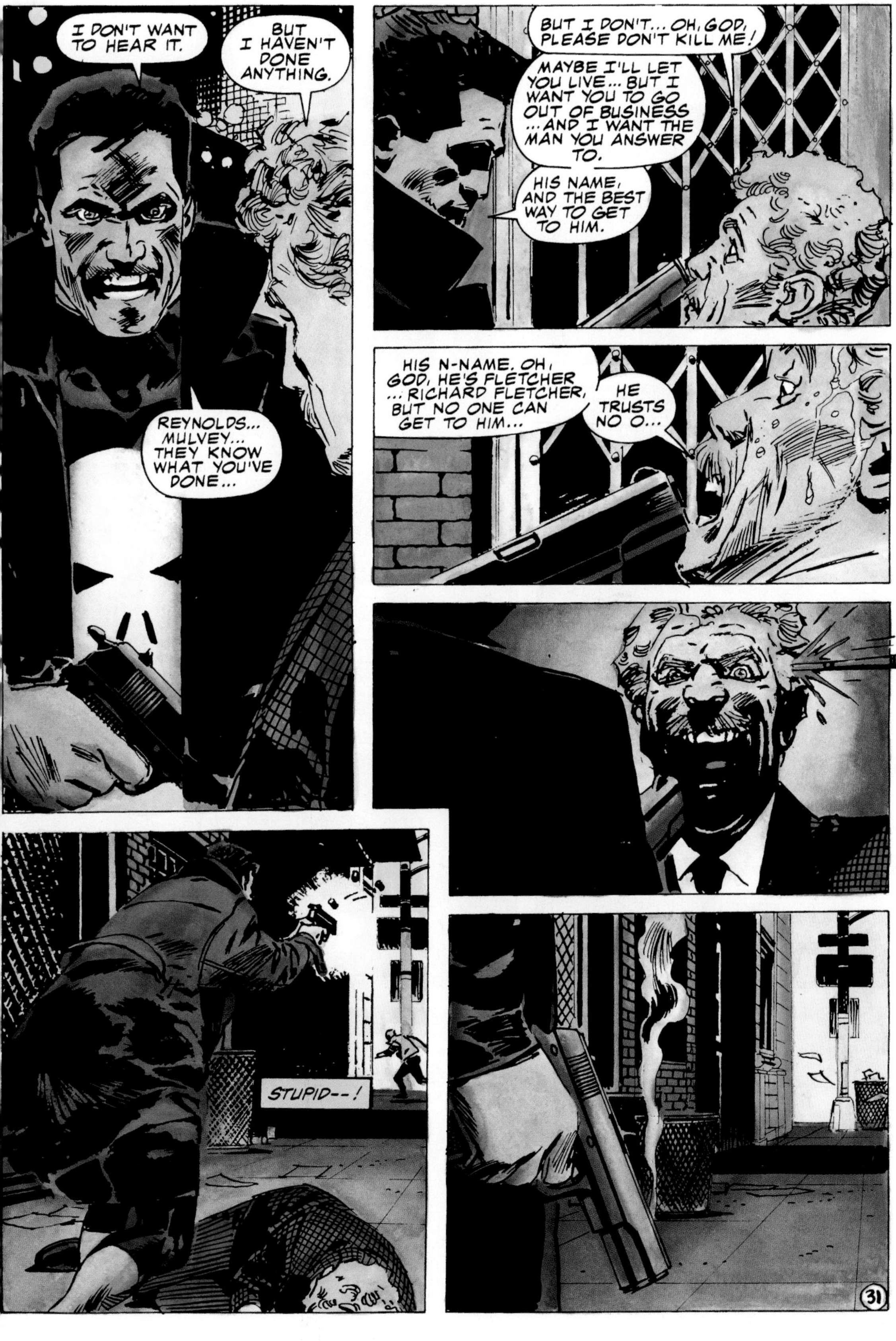
I DON'T WANT TO HEAR IT.
BUT I HAVEN'T DONE ANYTHING.
REYNOLDS... MULVEY... THEY KNOW WHAT YOU'VE DONE...
BUT I DON'T... OH, GOD, PLEASE DON'T KILL ME!
MAYBE I'LL LET YOU LIVE... BUT I WANT YOU TO GO OUT OF BUSINESS ...AND I WANT THE MAN YOU ANSWER TO.
HIS NAME, AND THE BEST WAY TO GET TO HIM.
HIS N-NAME. OH, GOD, HE'S FLETCHER ...RICHARD FLETCHER, BUT NO ONE CAN GET TO HIM...
HE TRUSTS NO O...
STUPID--!
31

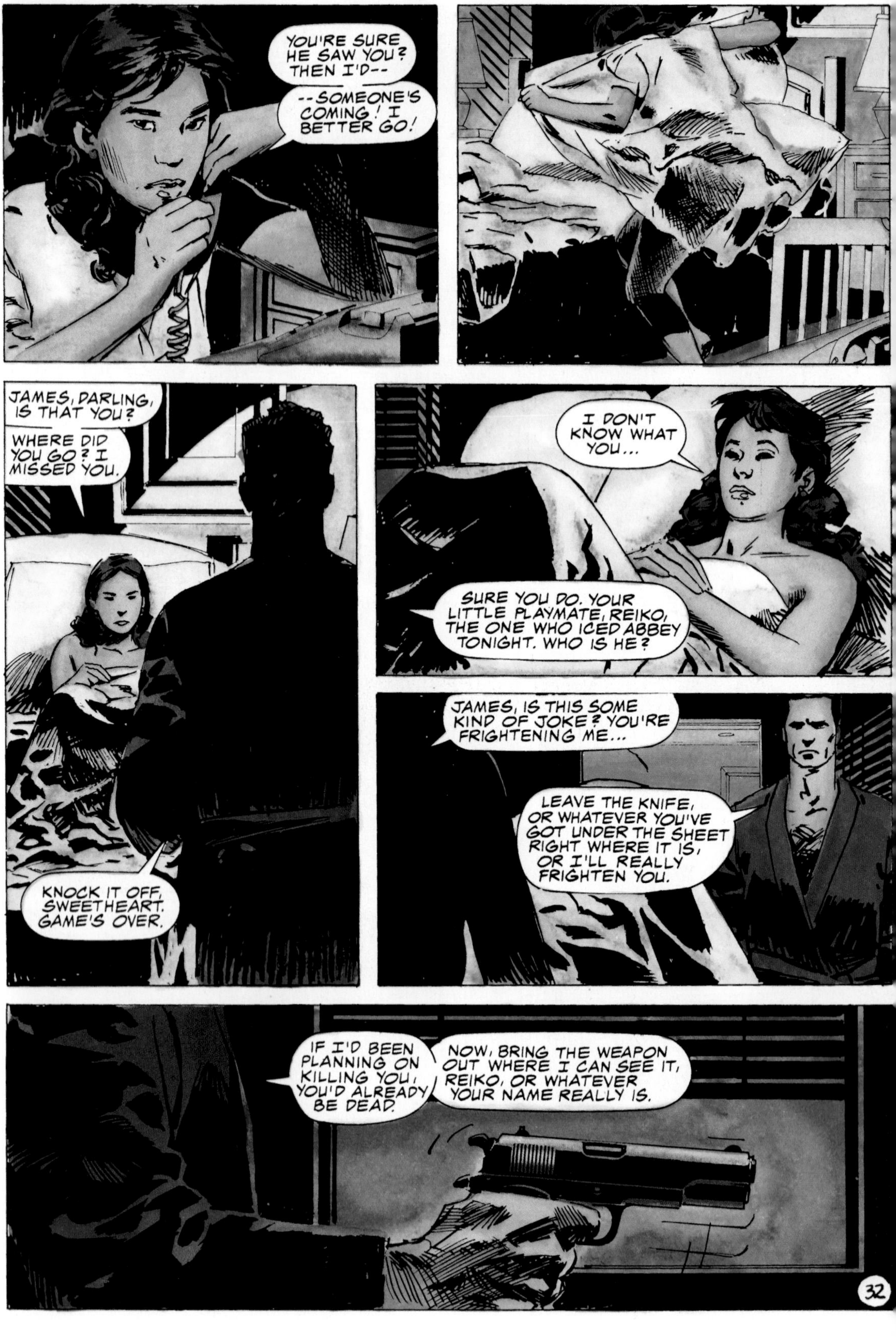
YOU'RE SURE HE SAW YOU? THEN I'D--
--SOMEONE'S COMING! I BETTER GO!
JAMES, DARLING, IS THAT YOU?
WHERE DID YOU GO? I MISSED YOU.
KNOCK IT OFF, SWEETHEART. GAME'S OVER.
I DON'T KNOW WHAT YOU...
SURE YOU DO. YOUR LITTLE PLAYMATE, REIKO, THE ONE WHO ICED ABBEY TONIGHT. WHO IS HE?
JAMES, IS THIS SOME KIND OF JOKE? YOU'RE FRIGHTENING ME...
LEAVE THE KNIFE, OR WHATEVER YOU'VE GOT UNDER THE SHEET RIGHT WHERE IT IS, OR I'LL REALLY FRIGHTEN YOU.
IF I'D BEEN PLANNING ON KILLING YOU, YOU'D ALREADY BE DEAD.
NOW, BRING THE WEAPON OUT WHERE I CAN SEE IT, REIKO, OR WHATEVER YOUR NAME REALLY IS.
32

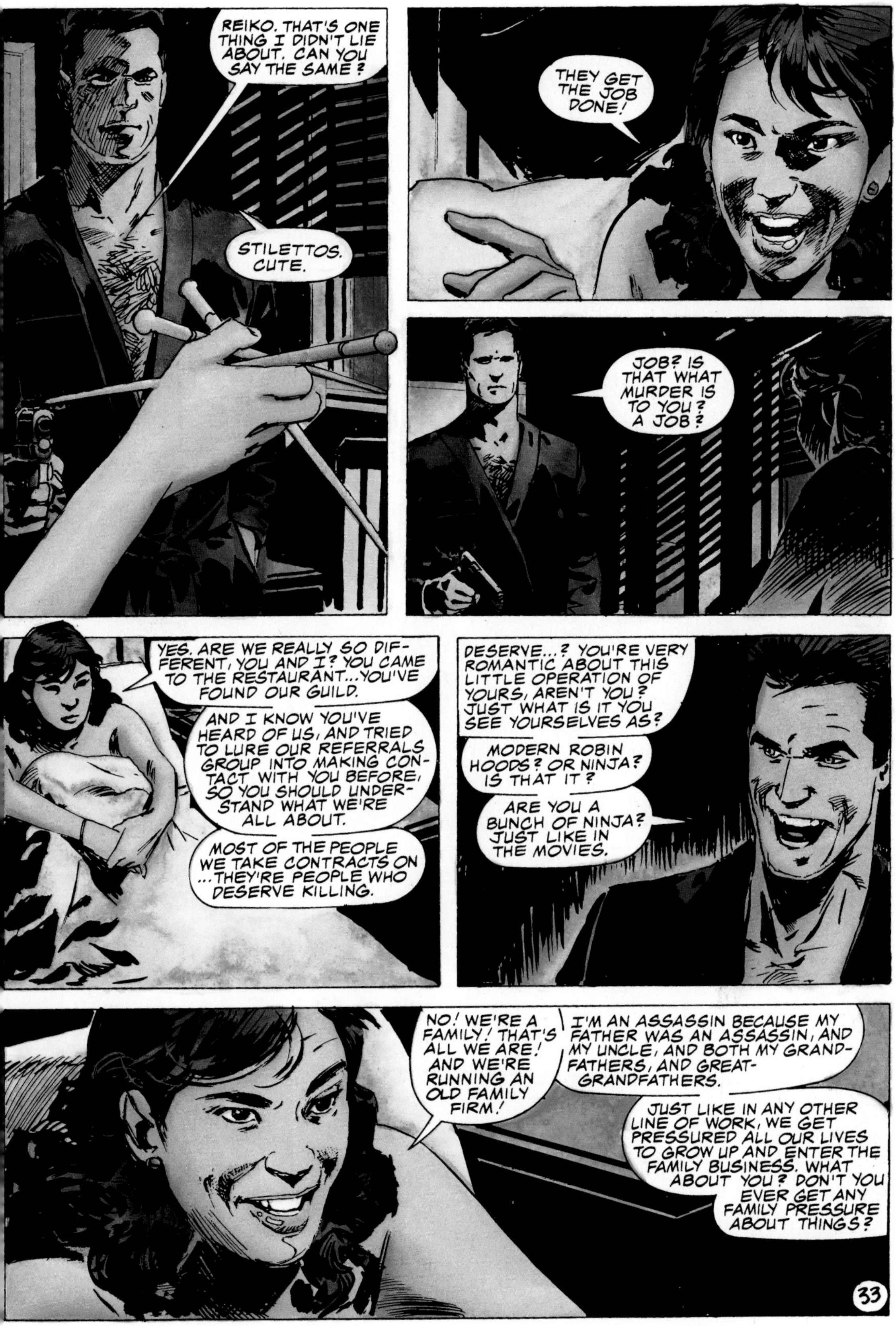
REIKO. THAT'S ONE THING I DIDN'T LIE ABOUT. CAN YOU SAY THE SAME?
STILETTOS. CUTE.
THEY GET THE JOB DONE!
JOB? IS THAT WHAT MURDER IS TO YOU? A JOB?
YES. ARE WE REALLY SO DIFFERENT, YOU AND I? YOU CAME TO THE RESTAURANT...YOU'VE FOUND OUR GUILD.
AND I KNOW YOU'VE HEARD OF US, AND TRIED TO LURE OUR REFERRALS GROUP INTO MAKING CONTACT WITH YOU BEFORE, SO YOU SHOULD UNDERSTAND WHAT WE'RE ALL ABOUT.
MOST OF THE PEOPLE WE TAKE CONTRACTS ON ...THEY'RE PEOPLE WHO DESERVE KILLING.
DESERVE...? YOU'RE VERY ROMANTIC ABOUT THIS LITTLE OPERATION OF YOURS, AREN'T YOU? JUST WHAT IS IT YOU SEE YOURSELVES AS?
MODERN ROBIN HOODS? OR NINJA? IS THAT IT?
ARE YOU A BUNCH OF NINJA? JUST LIKE IN THE MOVIES.
NO! WE'RE A FAMILY! THAT'S ALL WE ARE! AND WE'RE RUNNING AN OLD FAMILY FIRM!
I'M AN ASSASSIN BECAUSE MY FATHER WAS AN ASSASSIN, AND MY UNCLE, AND BOTH MY GRANDFATHERS, AND GREAT-GRANDFATHERS.
JUST LIKE IN ANY OTHER LINE OF WORK, WE GET PRESSURED ALL OUR LIVES TO GROW UP AND ENTER THE FAMILY BUSINESS. WHAT ABOUT YOU? DON'T YOU EVER GET ANY FAMILY PRESSURE ABOUT THINGS?
33

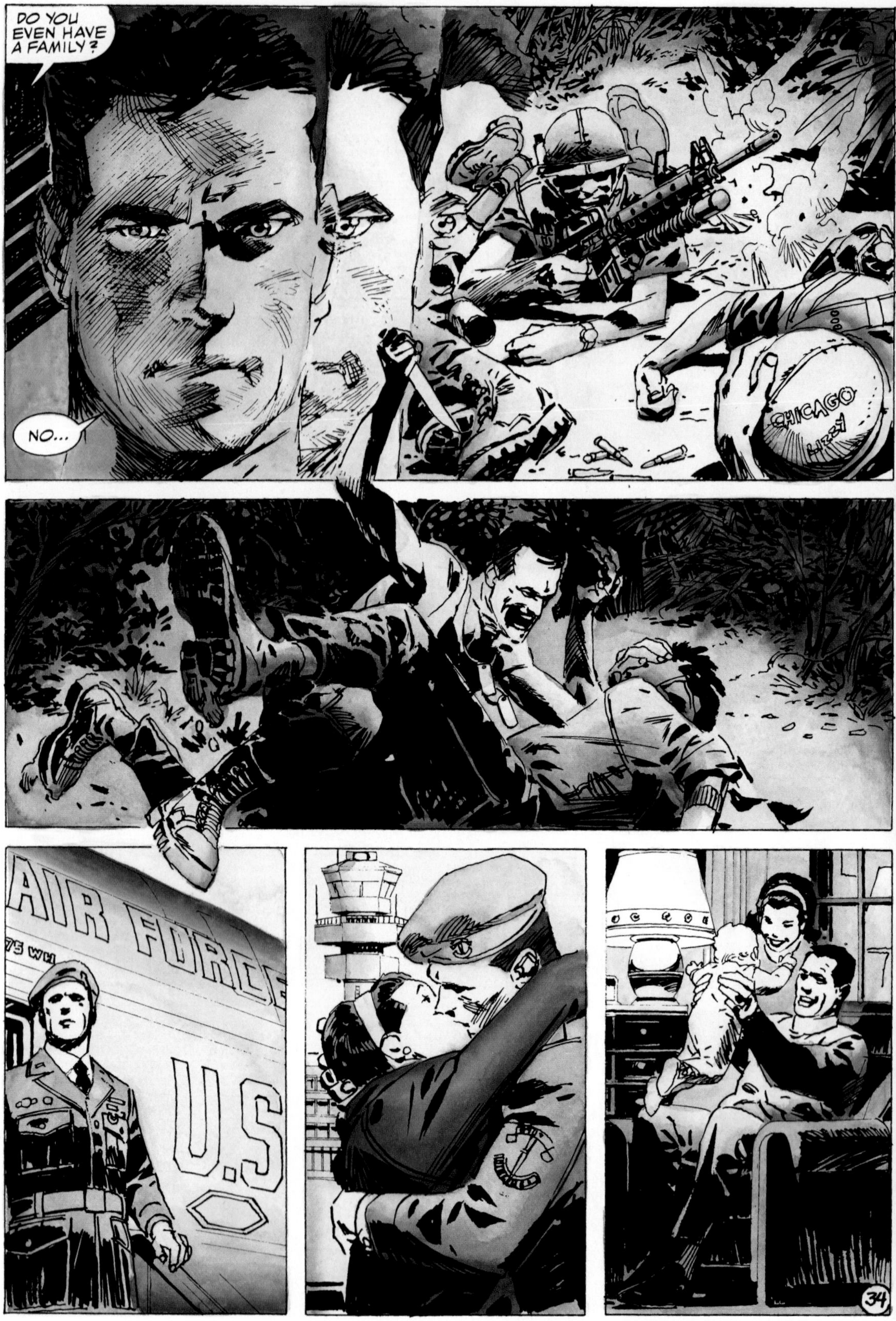
DO YOU EVEN HAVE A FAMILY?
NO...
CHICAGO
AIR FORCE
U.S
34

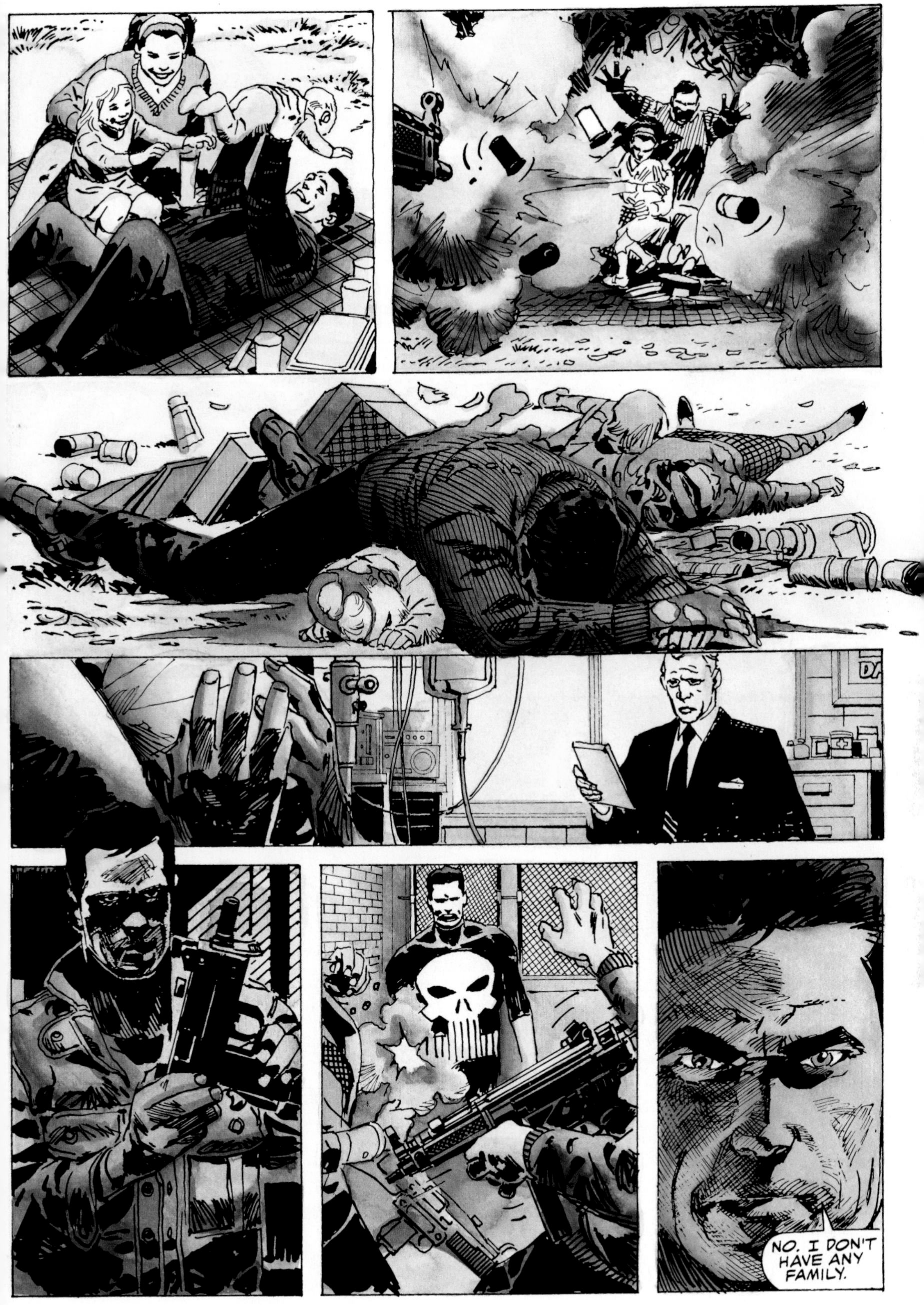
NO. I DON'T HAVE ANY FAMILY.

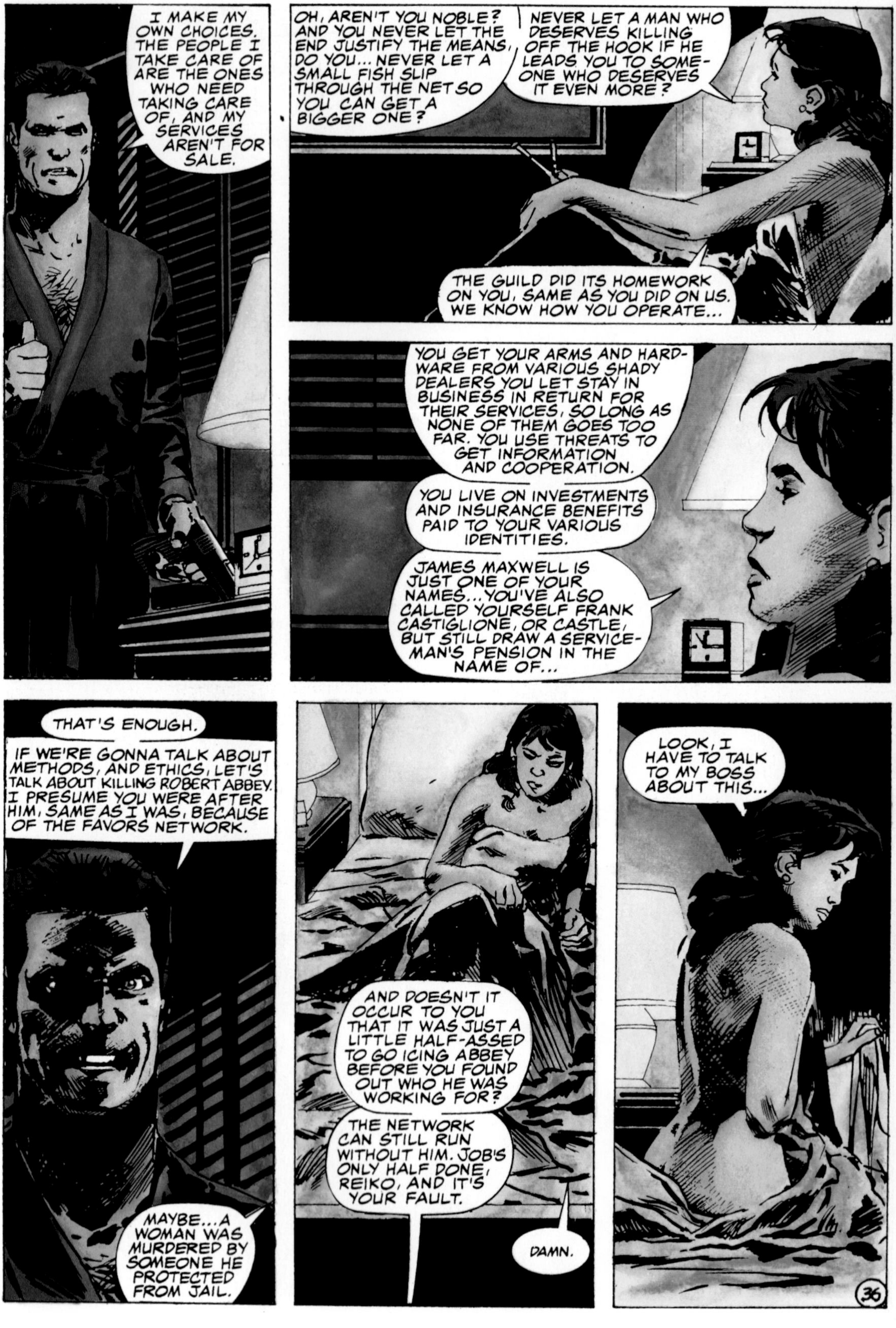
I MAKE MY OWN CHOICES. THE PEOPLE I TAKE CARE OF ARE THE ONES WHO NEED TAKING CARE OF, AND MY SERVICES AREN'T FOR SALE.
OH, AREN'T YOU NOBLE? AND YOU NEVER LET THE END JUSTIFY THE MEANS, DO YOU... NEVER LET A SMALL FISH SLIP THROUGH THE NET SO YOU CAN GET A BIGGER ONE?
NEVER LET A MAN WHO DESERVES KILLING OFF THE HOOK IF HE LEADS YOU TO SOMEONE WHO DESERVES IT EVEN MORE?
THE GUILD DID ITS HOMEWORK ON YOU, SAME AS YOU DID ON US. WE KNOW HOW YOU OPERATE...
YOU GET YOUR ARMS AND HARDWARE FROM VARIOUS SHADY DEALERS YOU LET STAY IN BUSINESS IN RETURN FOR THEIR SERVICES, SO LONG AS NONE OF THEM GOES TOO FAR. YOU USE THREATS TO GET INFORMATION AND COOPERATION.
YOU LIVE ON INVESTMENTS AND INSURANCE BENEFITS PAID TO YOUR VARIOUS IDENTITIES.
JAMES MAXWELL IS JUST ONE OF YOUR NAMES... YOU'VE ALSO CALLED YOURSELF FRANK CASTIGLIONE, OR CASTLE, BUT STILL DRAW A SERVICEMAN'S PENSION IN THE NAME OF...
THAT'S ENOUGH.
IF WE'RE GONNA TALK ABOUT METHODS, AND ETHICS, LET'S TALK ABOUT KILLING ROBERT ABBEY. I PRESUME YOU WERE AFTER HIM, SAME AS I WAS, BECAUSE OF THE FAVORS NETWORK.
MAYBE... A WOMAN WAS MURDERED BY SOMEONE HE PROTECTED FROM JAIL.
AND DOESN'T IT OCCUR TO YOU THAT IT WAS JUST A LITTLE HALF-ASSED TO GO ICING ABBEY BEFORE YOU FOUND OUT WHO HE WAS WORKING FOR?
THE NETWORK CAN STILL RUN WITHOUT HIM. JOB'S ONLY HALF DONE, REIKO, AND IT'S YOUR FAULT.
DAMN.
LOOK, I HAVE TO TALK TO MY BOSS ABOUT THIS...
36

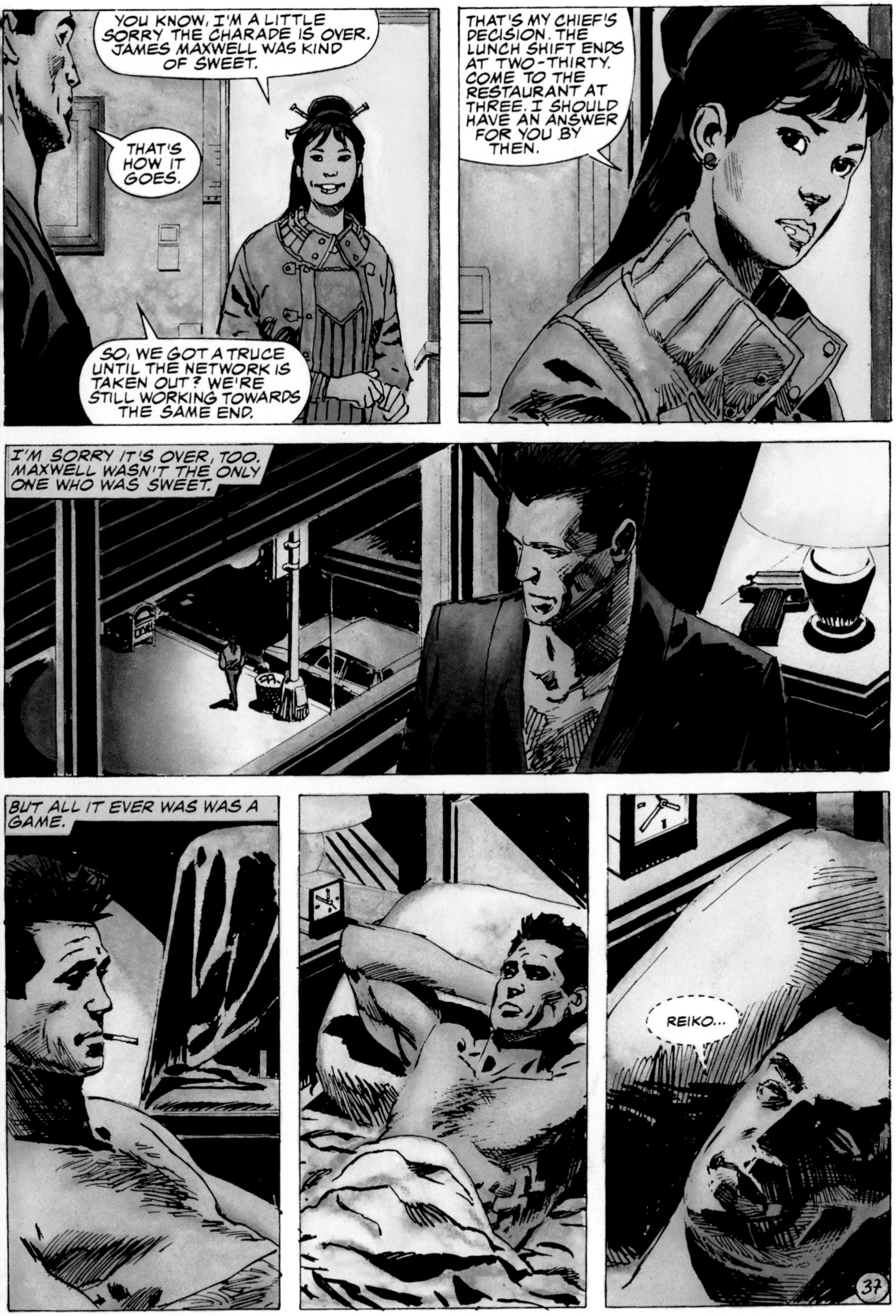
YOU KNOW, I'M A LITTLE SORRY THE CHARADE IS OVER. JAMES MAXWELL WAS KIND OF SWEET.
THAT'S HOW IT GOES.
SO, WE GOT A TRUCE UNTIL THE NETWORK IS TAKEN OUT? WE'RE STILL WORKING TOWARDS THE SAME END.
THAT'S MY CHIEF'S DECISION. THE LUNCH SHIFT ENDS AT TWO-THIRTY. COME TO THE RESTAURANT AT THREE. I SHOULD HAVE AN ANSWER FOR YOU BY THEN.
I'M SORRY IT'S OVER, TOO. MAXWELL WASN'T THE ONLY ONE WHO WAS SWEET.
BUT ALL IT EVER WAS WAS A GAME.
REIKO...
37

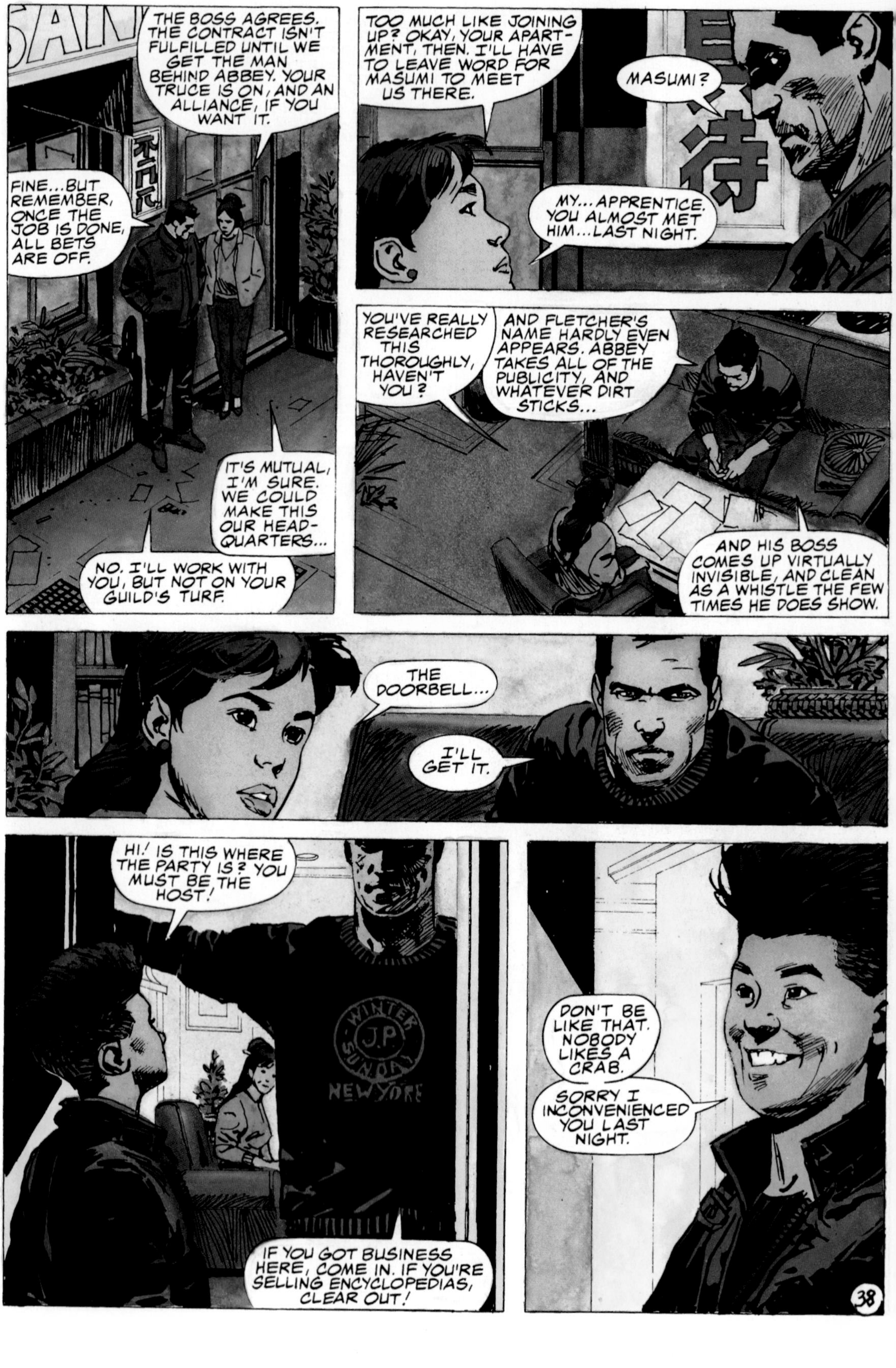
THE BOSS AGREES. THE CONTRACT ISN'T FULFILLED UNTIL WE GET THE MAN BEHIND ABBEY. YOUR TRUCE IS ON, AND AN ALLIANCE, IF YOU WANT IT.
FINE...BUT REMEMBER, ONCE THE JOB IS DONE, ALL BETS ARE OFF.
IT'S MUTUAL, I'M SURE. WE COULD MAKE THIS OUR HEAD-QUARTERS...
NO. I'LL WORK WITH YOU, BUT NOT ON YOUR GUILD'S TURF.
TOO MUCH LIKE JOINING UP? OKAY, YOUR APART-MENT, THEN. I'LL HAVE TO LEAVE WORD FOR MASUMI TO MEET US THERE.
MASUMI?
MY...APPRENTICE. YOU ALMOST MET HIM...LAST NIGHT.
YOU'VE REALLY RESEARCHED THIS THOROUGHLY, HAVEN'T YOU?
AND FLETCHER'S NAME HARDLY EVEN APPEARS. ABBEY TAKES ALL OF THE PUBLICITY, AND WHATEVER DIRT STICKS...
AND HIS BOSS COMES UP VIRTUALLY INVISIBLE, AND CLEAN AS A WHISTLE THE FEW TIMES HE DOES SHOW.
THE DOORBELL...
I'LL GET IT.
HI! IS THIS WHERE THE PARTY IS? YOU MUST BE THE HOST!
WINTER
J.P.
SUNDAY
NEW YORK
IF YOU GOT BUSINESS HERE, COME IN. IF YOU'RE SELLING ENCYCLOPEDIAS, CLEAR OUT!
DON'T BE LIKE THAT. NOBODY LIKES A CRAB.
SORRY I INCONVENIENCED YOU LAST NIGHT.
38

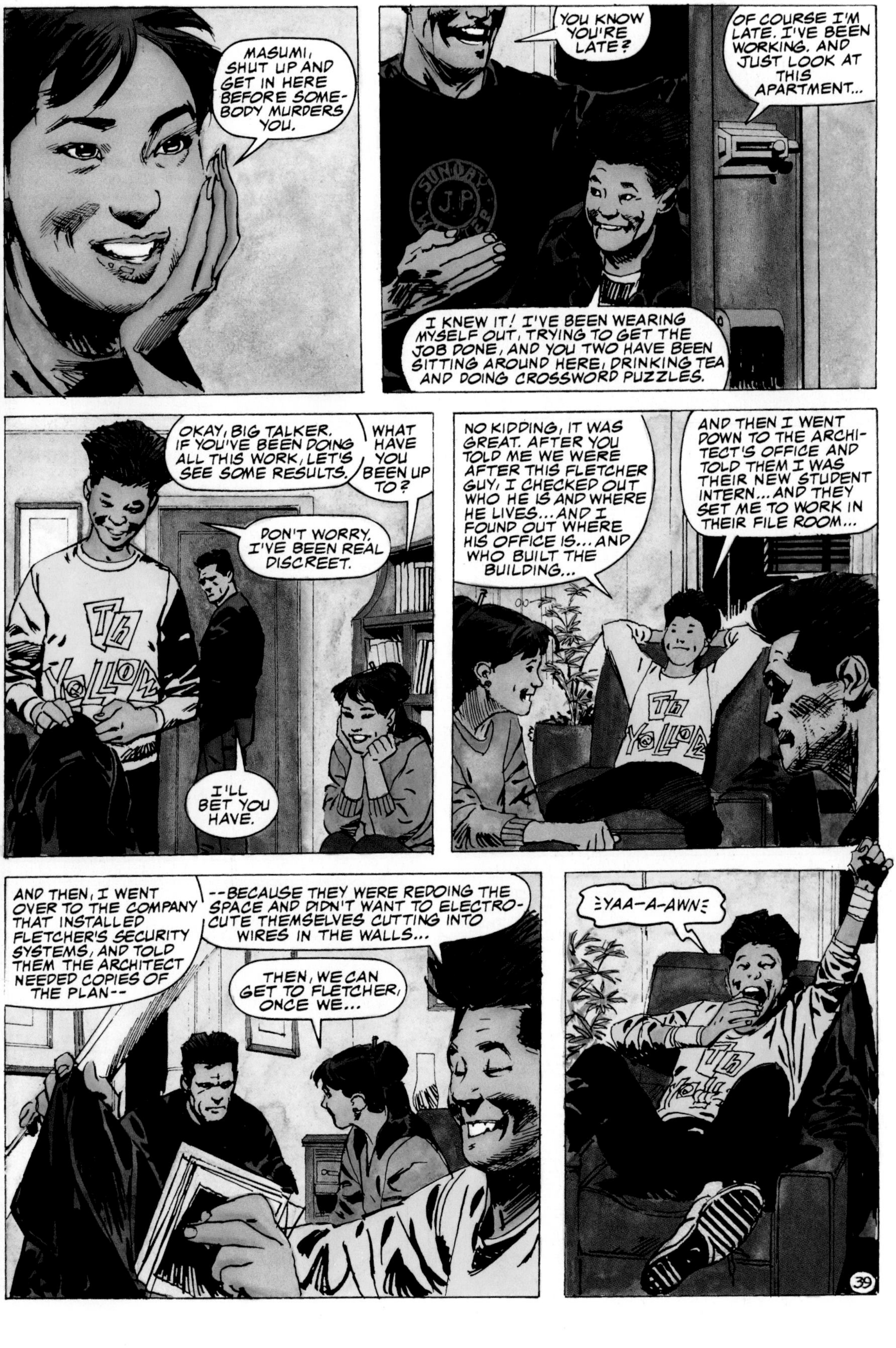

MASUMI, SHUT UP AND GET IN HERE BEFORE SOMEBODY MURDERS YOU.
YOU KNOW YOU'RE LATE?
OF COURSE I'M LATE. I'VE BEEN WORKING. AND JUST LOOK AT THIS APARTMENT...
I KNEW IT! I'VE BEEN WEARING MYSELF OUT, TRYING TO GET THE JOB DONE, AND YOU TWO HAVE BEEN SITTING AROUND HERE, DRINKING TEA AND DOING CROSSWORD PUZZLES.
OKAY, BIG TALKER. IF YOU'VE BEEN DOING ALL THIS WORK, LET'S SEE SOME RESULTS.
WHAT HAVE YOU BEEN UP TO?
DON'T WORRY. I'VE BEEN REAL DISCREET.
I'LL BET YOU HAVE.
NO KIDDING, IT WAS GREAT. AFTER YOU TOLD ME WE WERE AFTER THIS FLETCHER GUY, I CHECKED OUT WHO HE IS AND WHERE HE LIVES... AND I FOUND OUT WHERE HIS OFFICE IS... AND WHO BUILT THE BUILDING...
AND THEN I WENT DOWN TO THE ARCHITECT'S OFFICE AND TOLD THEM I WAS THEIR NEW STUDENT INTERN... AND THEY SET ME TO WORK IN THEIR FILE ROOM...
AND THEN, I WENT OVER TO THE COMPANY THAT INSTALLED FLETCHER'S SECURITY SYSTEMS, AND TOLD THEM THE ARCHITECT NEEDED COPIES OF THE PLAN--
--BECAUSE THEY WERE REDOING THE SPACE AND DIDN'T WANT TO ELECTROCUTE THEMSELVES CUTTING INTO WIRES IN THE WALLS...
THEN, WE CAN GET TO FLETCHER, ONCE WE...
YAA-A-AWN
39

YEAH. THIS LOOKS LIKE JUST WHAT WE NEEDED.

YOU'RE WELCOME.

WHY YOU SO PLEASED WITH YOURSELF? JUST WHAT WILL THAT ARCHITECT THINK WHEN HIS INTERN NEVER SHOWS UP FOR WORK AGAIN?

THAT I'M A FLAKE, LIKE ALL KIDS.

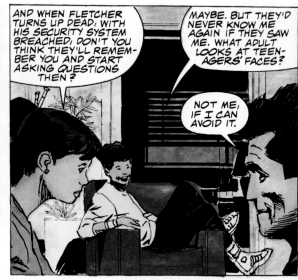

AND WHEN FLETCHER TURNS UP DEAD, WITH HIS SECURITY SYSTEM BREACHED, DON'T YOU THINK THEY'LL REMEMBER YOU AND START ASKING QUESTIONS THEN?

MAYBE. BUT THEY'D NEVER KNOW ME AGAIN IF THEY SAW ME. WHAT ADULT LOOKS AT TEEN-AGERS' FACES?

NOT ME, IF I CAN AVOID IT.

SO... HE HAS THE TOP TEN FLOORS OF THE ENTIRE BUILDING...

METAL DETECTOR, AND A PRIVATE ELEVATOR...

PROBABLY PRIVATE GUARDS, AS WELL...

LOOKS LIKE THERE ARE TV CAMERAS THROUGHOUT THE HALLS...

WHAT ABOUT THE FIRE STAIRS...?

IT LOOKS LIKE IT COULD BE DONE.

ONLY IF WE GO IN AFTER HOURS ...WHEN THE REST OF THE BUILDING IS EMPTY...

BUT... HOW CAN WE GET IN AT NIGHT, WITHOUT THEM KNOWING?

THAT PART'LL BE A CINCH.

40

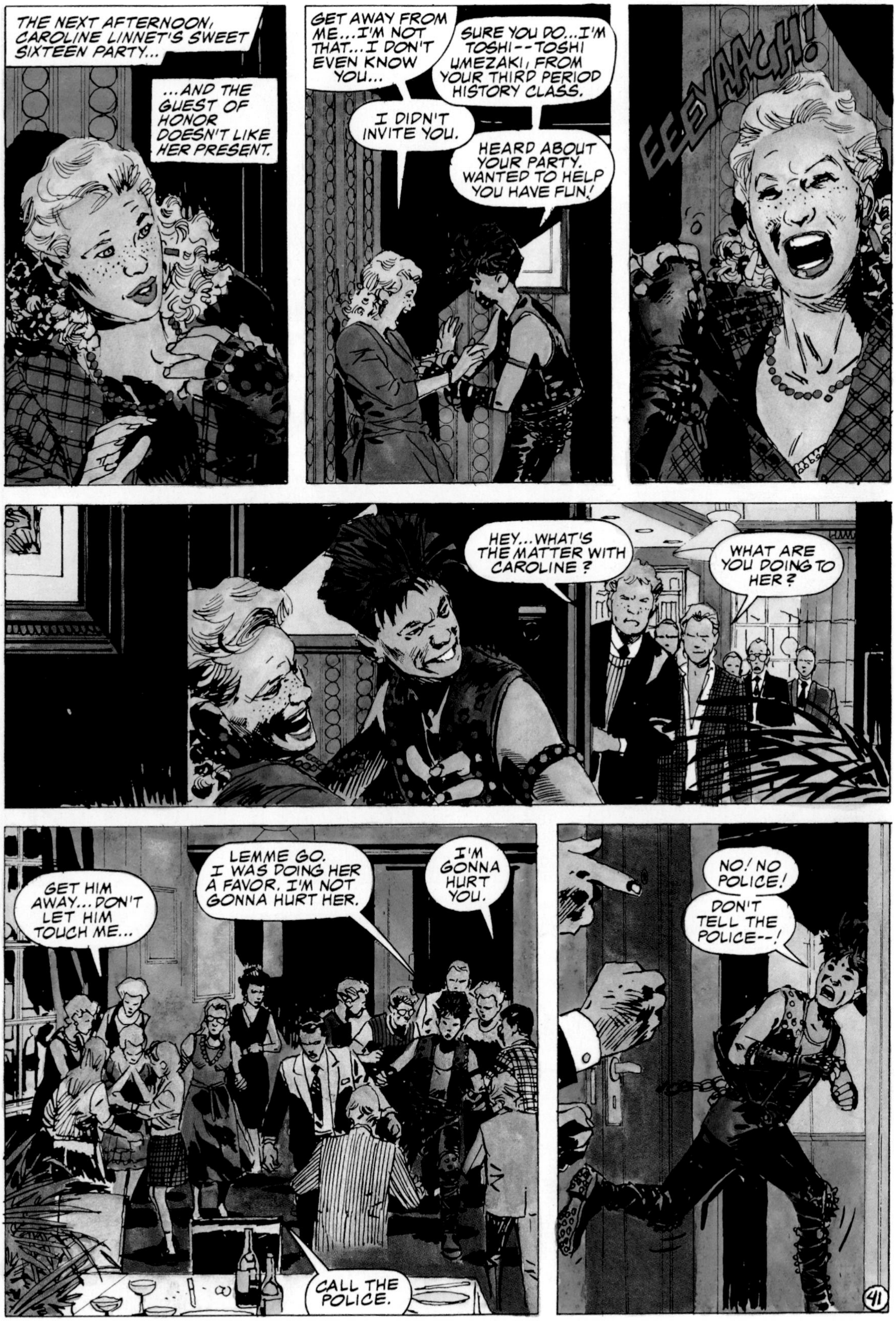
THE NEXT AFTERNOON, CAROLINE LINNET'S SWEET SIXTEEN PARTY...
...AND THE GUEST OF HONOR DOESN'T LIKE HER PRESENT.
GET AWAY FROM ME...I'M NOT THAT...I DON'T EVEN KNOW YOU...
SURE YOU DO...I'M TOSHI--TOSHI UMEZAKI, FROM YOUR THIRD PERIOD HISTORY CLASS.
I DIDN'T INVITE YOU.
HEARD ABOUT YOUR PARTY. WANTED TO HELP YOU HAVE FUN!
EEEYAACH!
HEY...WHAT'S THE MATTER WITH CAROLINE?
WHAT ARE YOU DOING TO HER?
GET HIM AWAY...DON'T LET HIM TOUCH ME...
LEMME GO. I WAS DOING HER A FAVOR. I'M NOT GONNA HURT HER.
I'M GONNA HURT YOU.
CALL THE POLICE.
NO! NO POLICE!
DON'T TELL THE POLICE--!
41

NOW, WHERE EXACTLY DID YOU GET MY NAME?

WE NEED HELP... WE TRIED TO GO TO MR. ABBEY... AND THEY TOLD US HE WAS DEAD...

I'D HEARD...

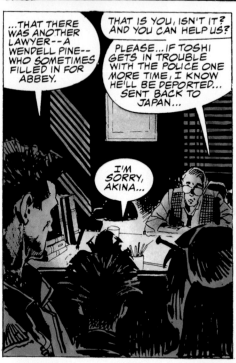

...THAT THERE WAS ANOTHER LAWYER--A WENDELL PINE-- WHO SOMETIMES FILLED IN FOR ABBEY.

THAT IS YOU, ISN'T IT? AND YOU CAN HELP US?

PLEASE...IF TOSHI GETS IN TROUBLE WITH THE POLICE ONE MORE TIME, I KNOW HE'LL BE DEPORTED... SENT BACK TO JAPAN...

I'M SORRY, AKINA...

PLEASE, MRS. MAXWELL. AFTER YOUR HUSBAND CALLED ME, I TOOK THE LIBERTY OF CONFERRING WITH MY IMMEDIATE SUPERIOR...

IT'S UNORTHODOX, BUT... DUE TO THE URGENT NATURE OF THE PROBLEM, MR. FLETCHER HAS AGREED TO SEE YOU TONIGHT, IF YOU'LL GO DIRECTLY TO THE FOLLOWING ADDRESS...

SIXTH AVENUE, IN THE LOW FORTIES. A VERY EXPENSIVE ADDRESS, FOR THIS MAN WHO'S BUILT AN EMPIRE ON HELPING PEOPLE AVOID PAYING THE PRICE FOR THEIR MISTAKES...

AND THEN SHOWING THEM THAT NOT TAKING RESPONSIBILITY FOR WHAT THEY DO CAN COST THEM EVEN MORE IN THE LONG RUN.

HEY, WHEN WE FINISH THE JOB, YOU WANT TO TAKE IN A MOVIE? "NINJA IN THE BAHAMAS" IS PLAYING AT THE RKO.

I HEAR IT'S GREAT...THE NINJA LOOK REALLY CUTE, RUNNING AROUND IN BROAD DAYLIGHT, WEARING FIFTEENTH-CENTURY BLACK PAJAMAS...PLEASE?

TO MAKE YOUR BROTHER-IN-LAW HAPPY?

KNOCK IT OFF, OR I WILL LET THEM DEPORT YOU.

OH, YOU'RE NO FUN ANYMORE! ANYWAY, REIKO AN' I WERE BOTH BORN HERE.

42

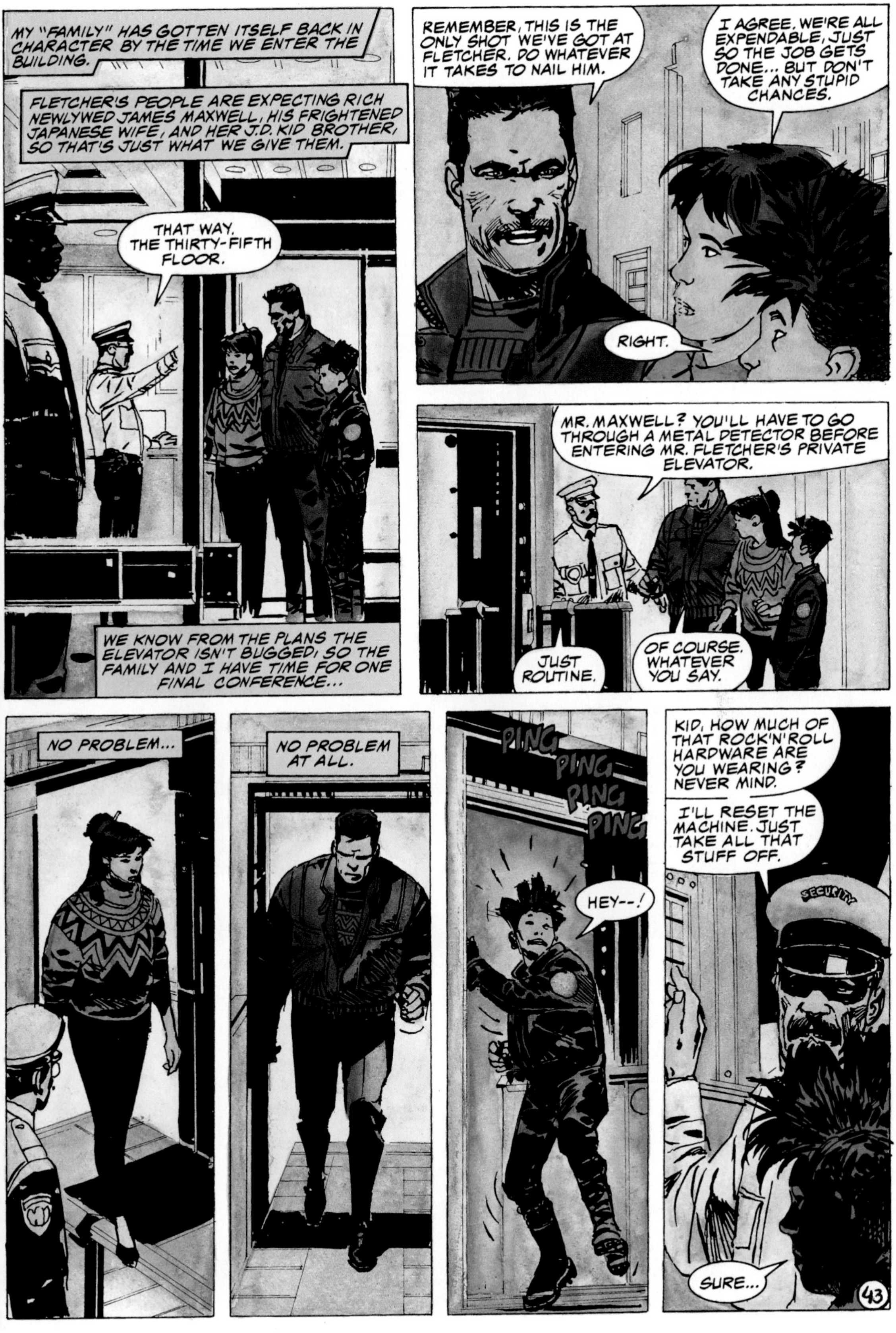
MY "FAMILY" HAS GOTTEN ITSELF BACK IN CHARACTER BY THE TIME WE ENTER THE BUILDING.
FLETCHER'S PEOPLE ARE EXPECTING RICH NEWLYWED JAMES MAXWELL, HIS FRIGHTENED JAPANESE WIFE, AND HER J.D. KID BROTHER, SO THAT'S JUST WHAT WE GIVE THEM.
THAT WAY. THE THIRTY-FIFTH FLOOR.
WE KNOW FROM THE PLANS THE ELEVATOR ISN'T BUGGED, SO THE FAMILY AND I HAVE TIME FOR ONE FINAL CONFERENCE...
REMEMBER, THIS IS THE ONLY SHOT WE'VE GOT AT FLETCHER. DO WHATEVER IT TAKES TO NAIL HIM.
I AGREE. WE'RE ALL EXPENDABLE, JUST SO THE JOB GETS DONE... BUT DON'T TAKE ANY STUPID CHANCES.
RIGHT.
MR. MAXWELL? YOU'LL HAVE TO GO THROUGH A METAL DETECTOR BEFORE ENTERING MR. FLETCHER'S PRIVATE ELEVATOR.
JUST ROUTINE.
OF COURSE. WHATEVER YOU SAY.
NO PROBLEM...
NO PROBLEM AT ALL.
PING PING PING PING
HEY--!
KID, HOW MUCH OF THAT ROCK'N'ROLL HARDWARE ARE YOU WEARING? NEVER MIND.
I'LL RESET THE MACHINE. JUST TAKE ALL THAT STUFF OFF.
SECURITY
SURE...
43

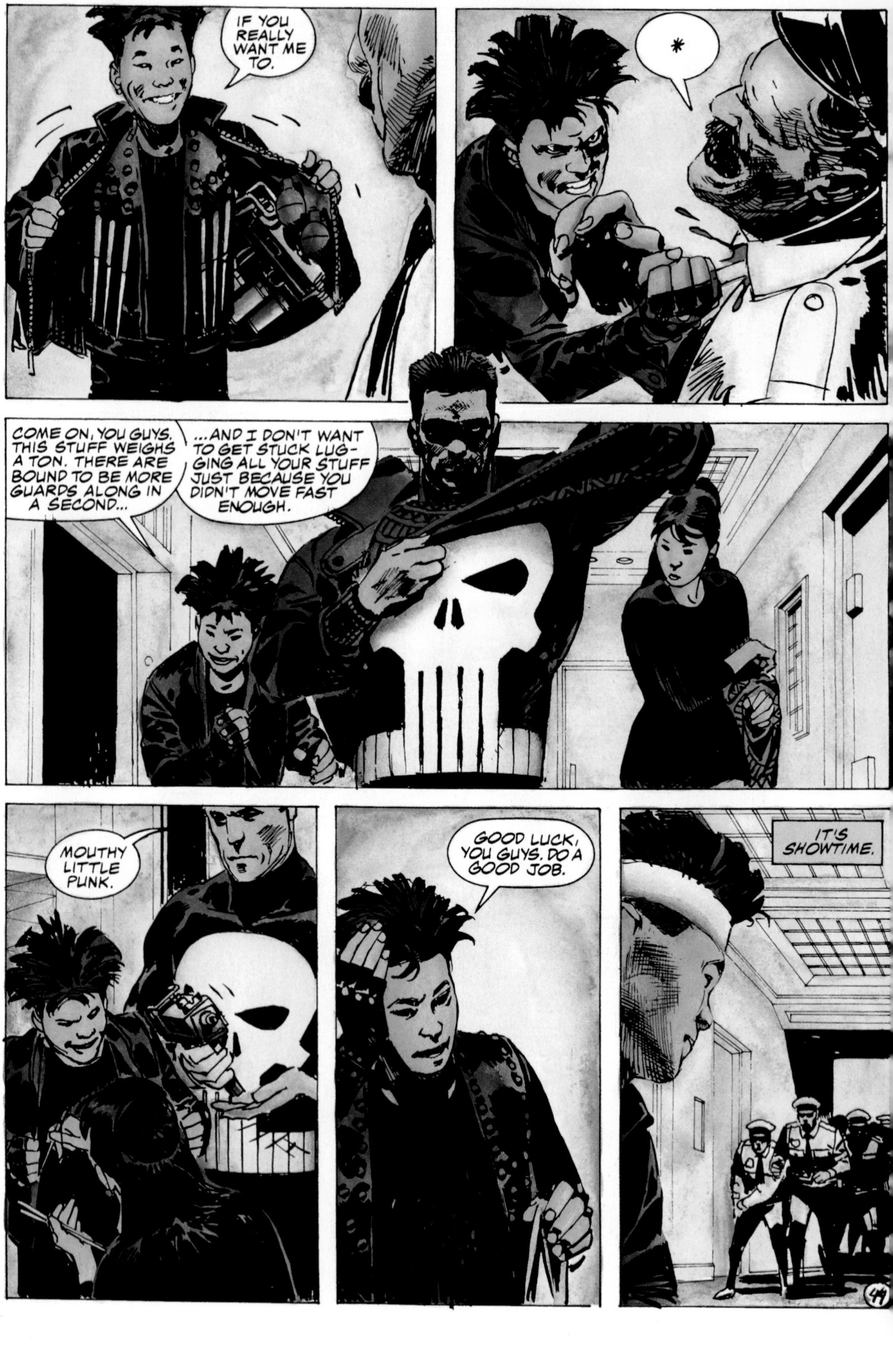
IF YOU REALLY WANT ME TO.
*
COME ON, YOU GUYS. THIS STUFF WEIGHS A TON. THERE ARE BOUND TO BE MORE GUARDS ALONG IN A SECOND...
...AND I DON'T WANT TO GET STUCK LUGGING ALL YOUR STUFF JUST BECAUSE YOU DIDN'T MOVE FAST ENOUGH.
MOUTHY LITTLE PUNK.
GOOD LUCK, YOU GUYS. DO A GOOD JOB.
IT'S SHOWTIME.
49

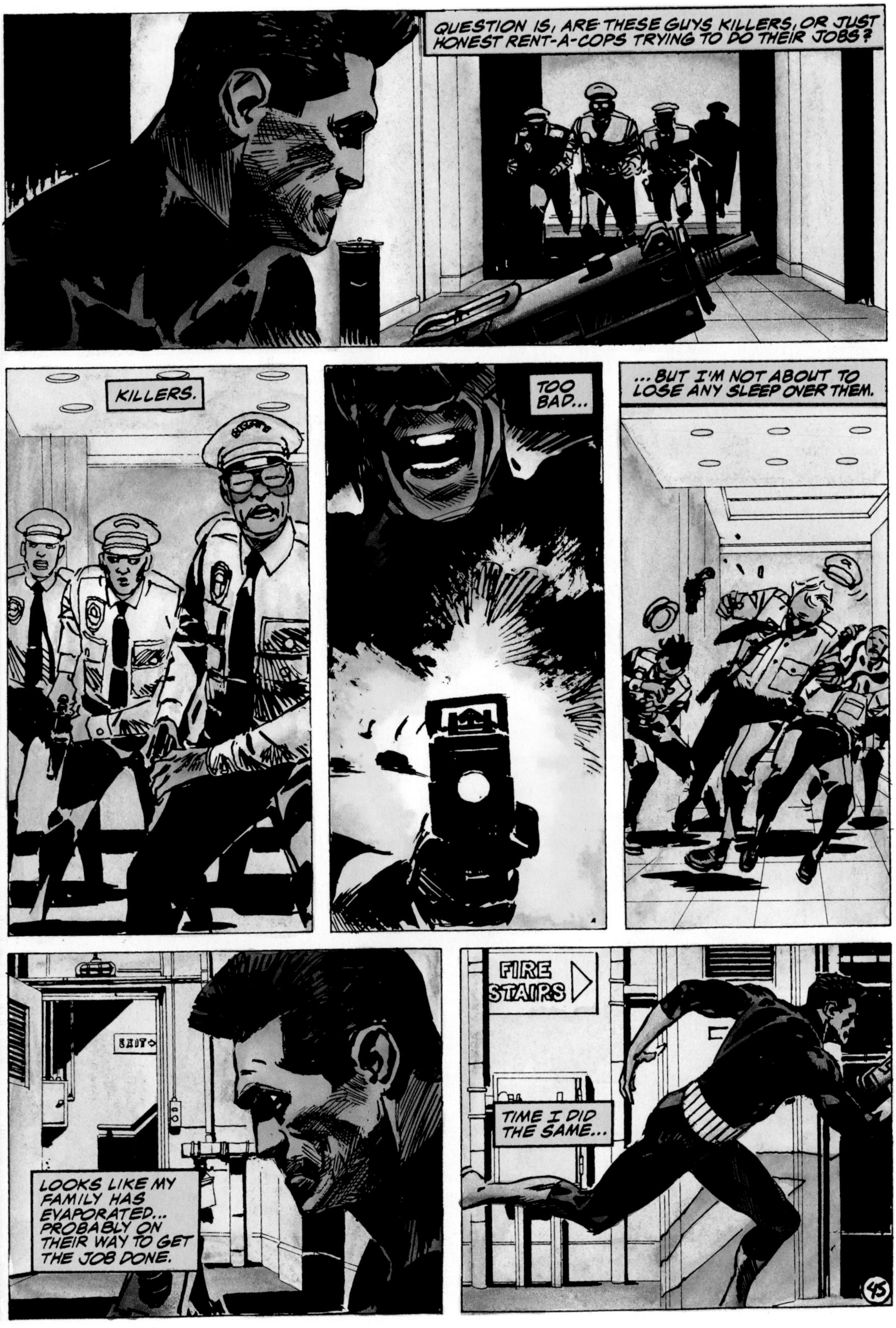
QUESTION IS, ARE THESE GUYS KILLERS, OR JUST HONEST RENT-A-COPS TRYING TO DO THEIR JOBS?
KILLERS.
TOO BAD...
...BUT I'M NOT ABOUT TO LOSE ANY SLEEP OVER THEM.
LOOKS LIKE MY FAMILY HAS EVAPORATED... PROBABLY ON THEIR WAY TO GET THE JOB DONE.
FIRE STAIRS
TIME I DID THE SAME...
45

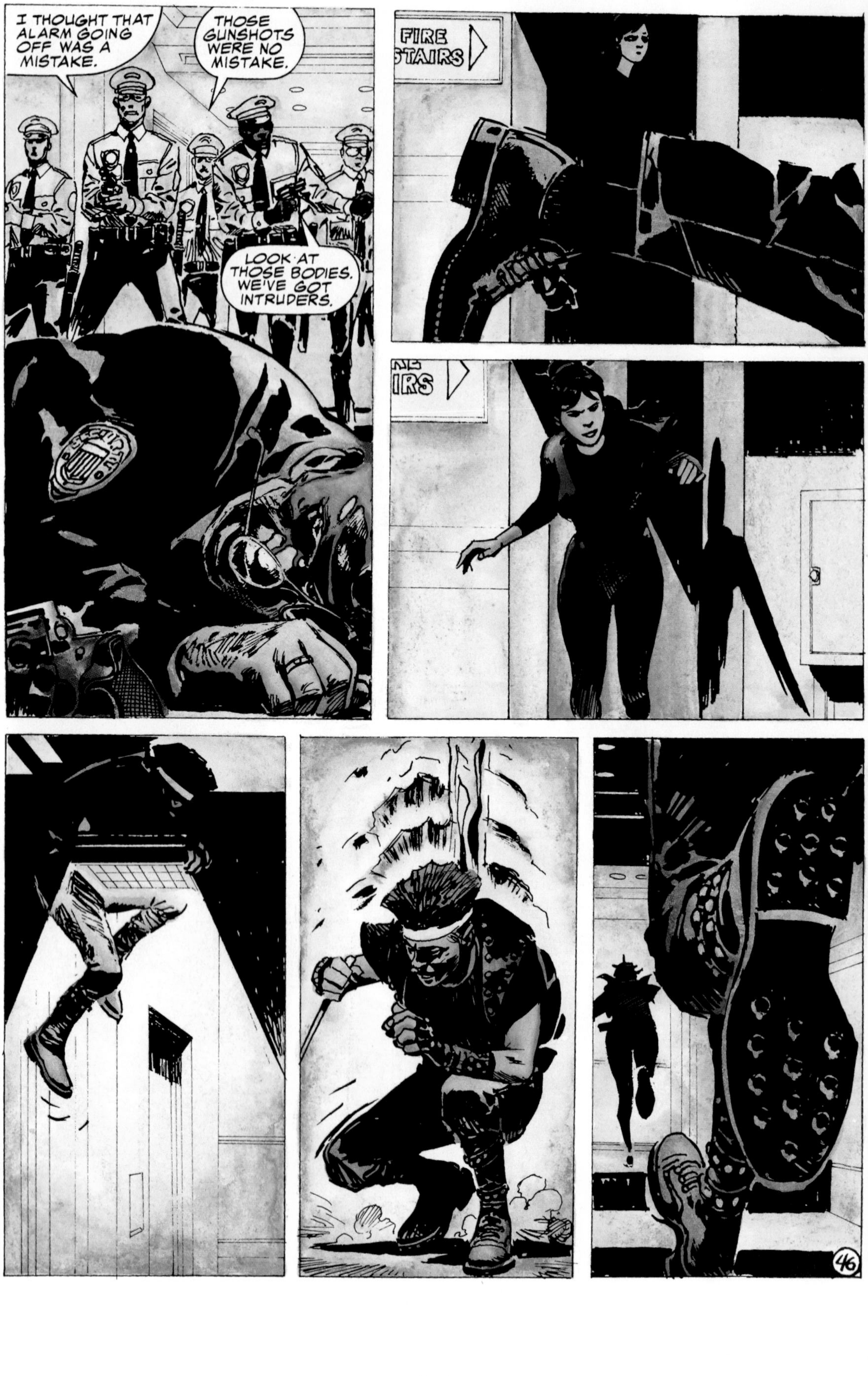
I THOUGHT THAT ALARM GOING OFF WAS A MISTAKE.
THOSE GUNSHOTS WERE NO MISTAKE.
LOOK AT THOSE BODIES. WE'VE GOT INTRUDERS.
FIRE STAIRS
IRS
46

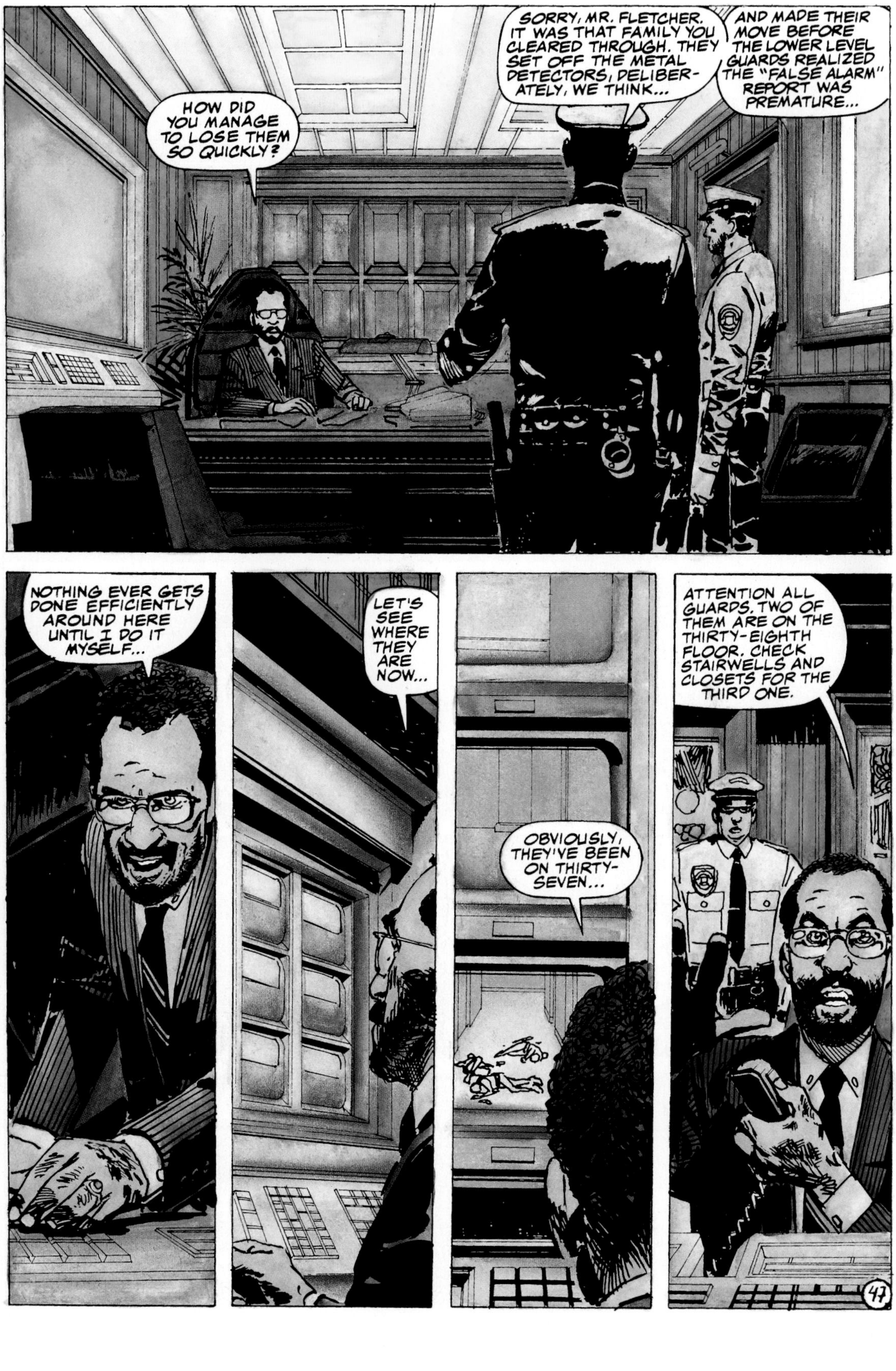
HOW DID YOU MANAGE TO LOSE THEM SO QUICKLY?
SORRY, MR. FLETCHER. IT WAS THAT FAMILY YOU CLEARED THROUGH. THEY SET OFF THE METAL DETECTORS, DELIBERATELY, WE THINK...
AND MADE THEIR MOVE BEFORE THE LOWER LEVEL GUARDS REALIZED THE "FALSE ALARM" REPORT WAS PREMATURE...
NOTHING EVER GETS DONE EFFICIENTLY AROUND HERE UNTIL I DO IT MYSELF...
LET'S SEE WHERE THEY ARE NOW...
OBVIOUSLY, THEY'VE BEEN ON THIRTY-SEVEN...
ATTENTION ALL GUARDS. TWO OF THEM ARE ON THE THIRTY-EIGHTH FLOOR. CHECK STAIRWELLS AND CLOSETS FOR THE THIRD ONE.
47

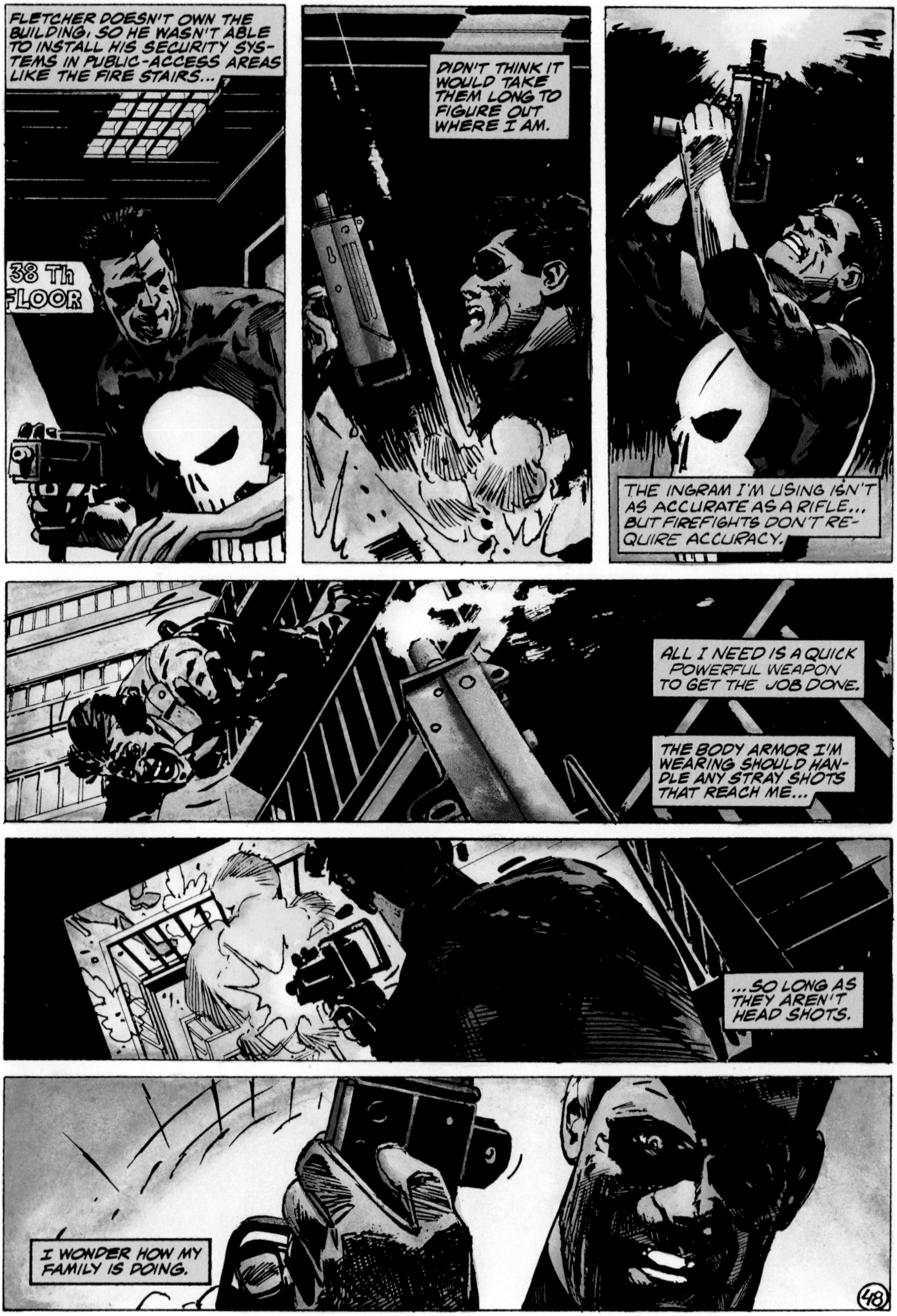
FLETCHER DOESN'T OWN THE BUILDING, SO HE WASN'T ABLE TO INSTALL HIS SECURITY SYSTEMS IN PUBLIC-ACCESS AREAS LIKE THE FIRE STAIRS...
38 Th FLOOR
DIDN'T THINK IT WOULD TAKE THEM LONG TO FIGURE OUT WHERE I AM.
THE INGRAM I'M USING ISN'T AS ACCURATE AS A RIFLE... BUT FIREFIGHTS DON'T REQUIRE ACCURACY.
ALL I NEED IS A QUICK POWERFUL WEAPON TO GET THE JOB DONE.
THE BODY ARMOR I'M WEARING SHOULD HANDLE ANY STRAY SHOTS THAT REACH ME...
...SO LONG AS THEY AREN'T HEAD SHOTS.
I WONDER HOW MY FAMILY IS DOING.
48

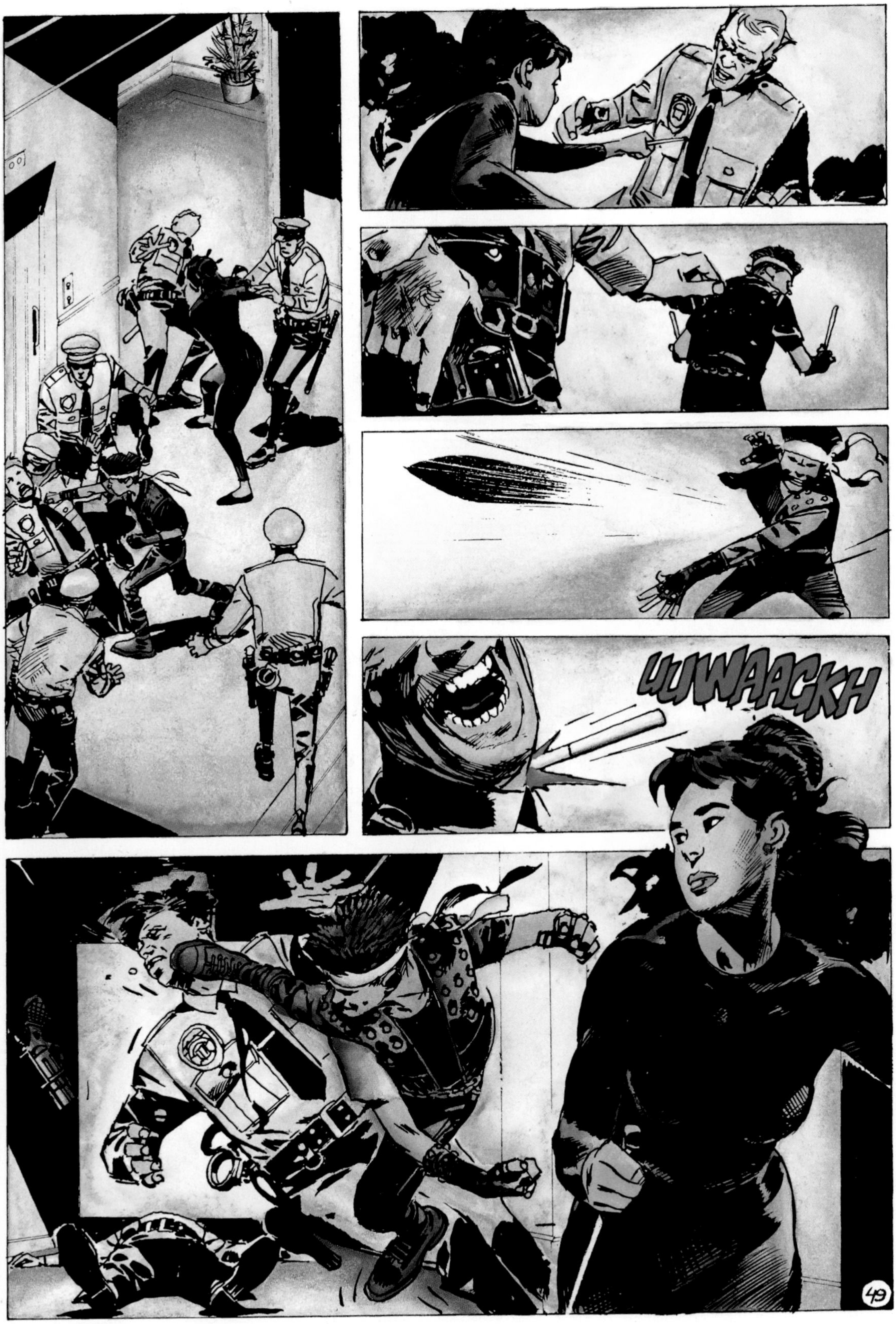
UUWAAGKH
49

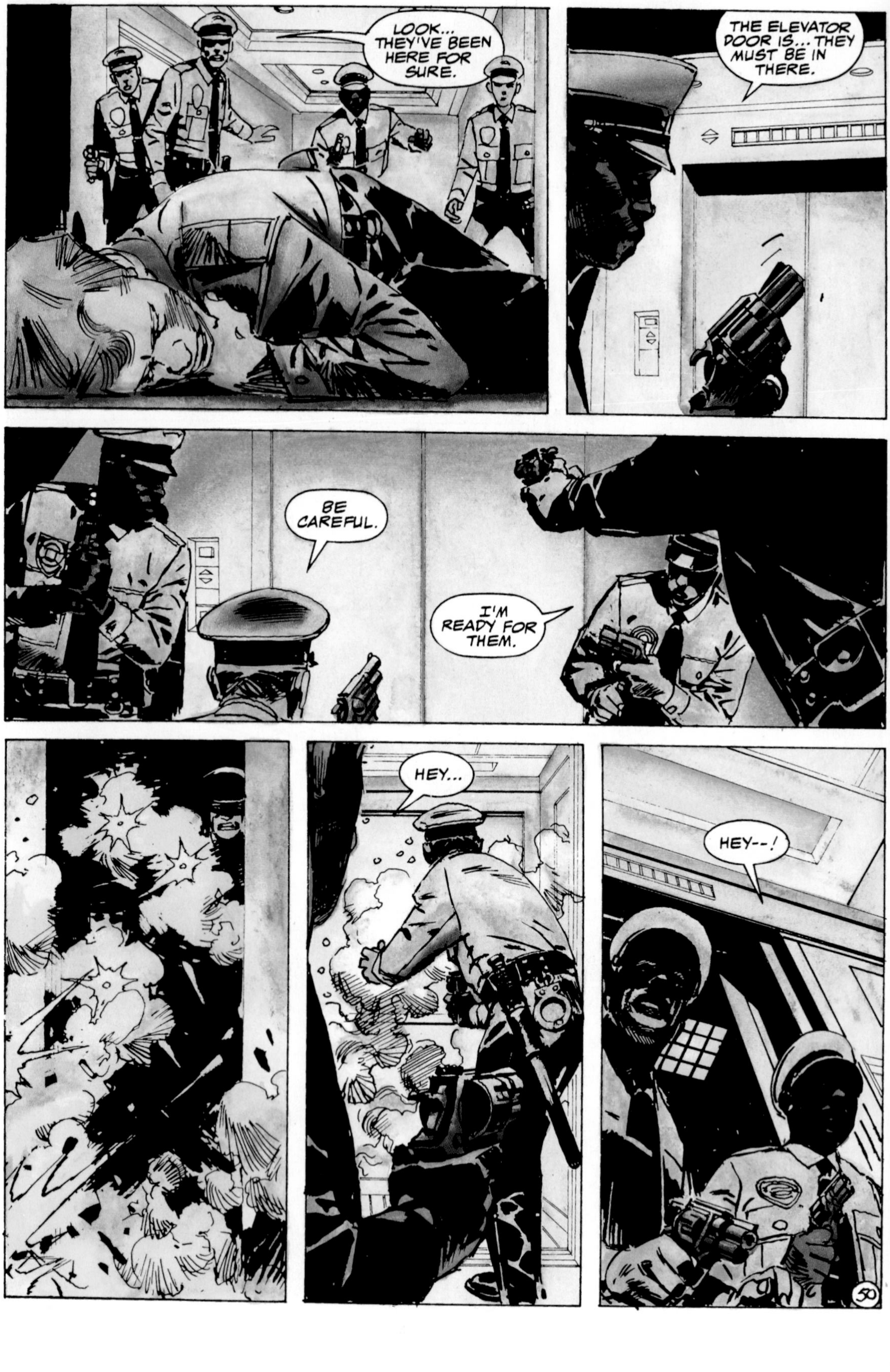
LOOK... THEY'VE BEEN HERE FOR SURE.
THE ELEVATOR DOOR IS... THEY MUST BE IN THERE.
BE CAREFUL.
I'M READY FOR THEM.
HEY...
HEY--!
50

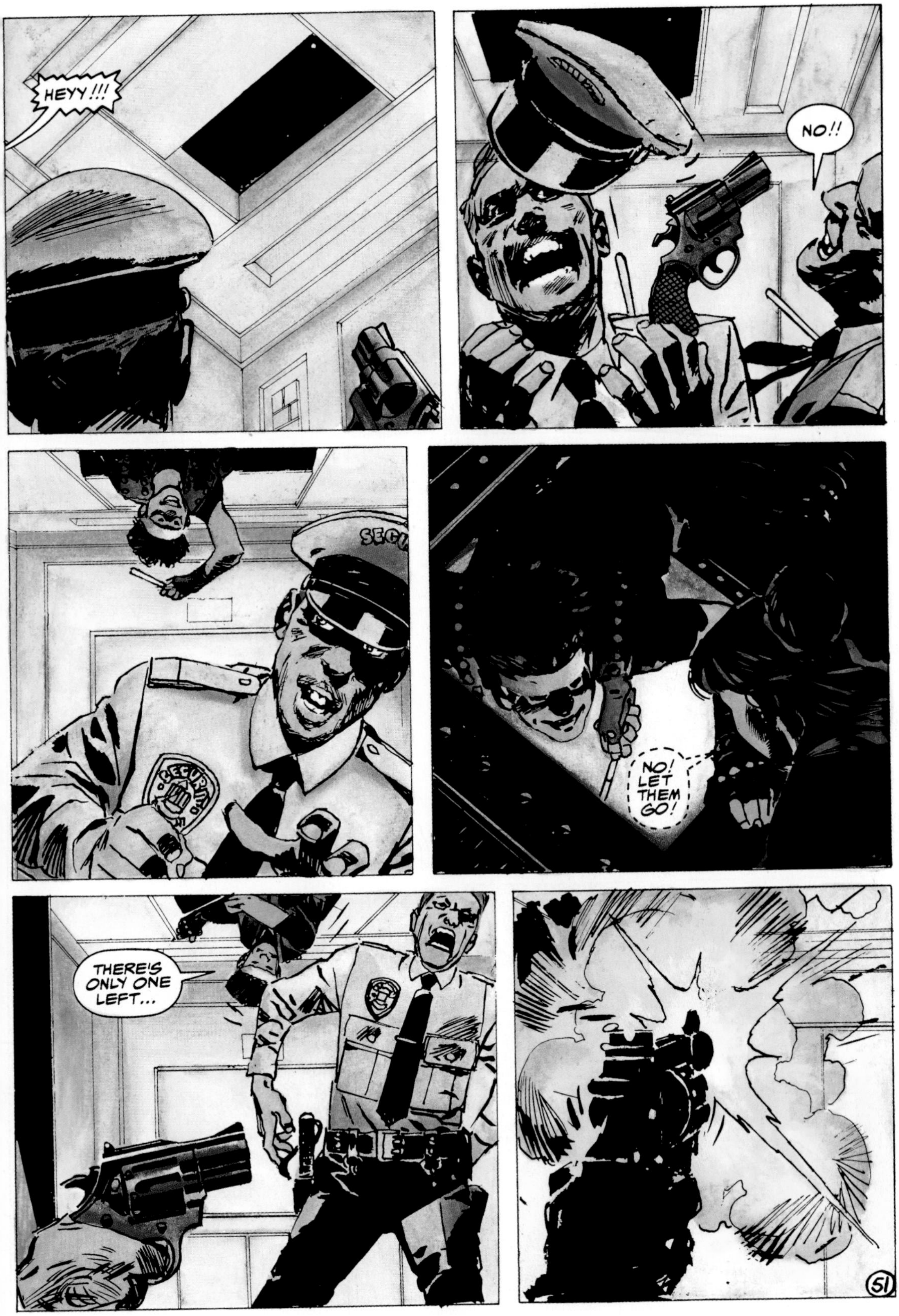
HEYY!!!
NO!!
SEGU
NO! LET THEM GO!
THERE'S ONLY ONE LEFT...
51

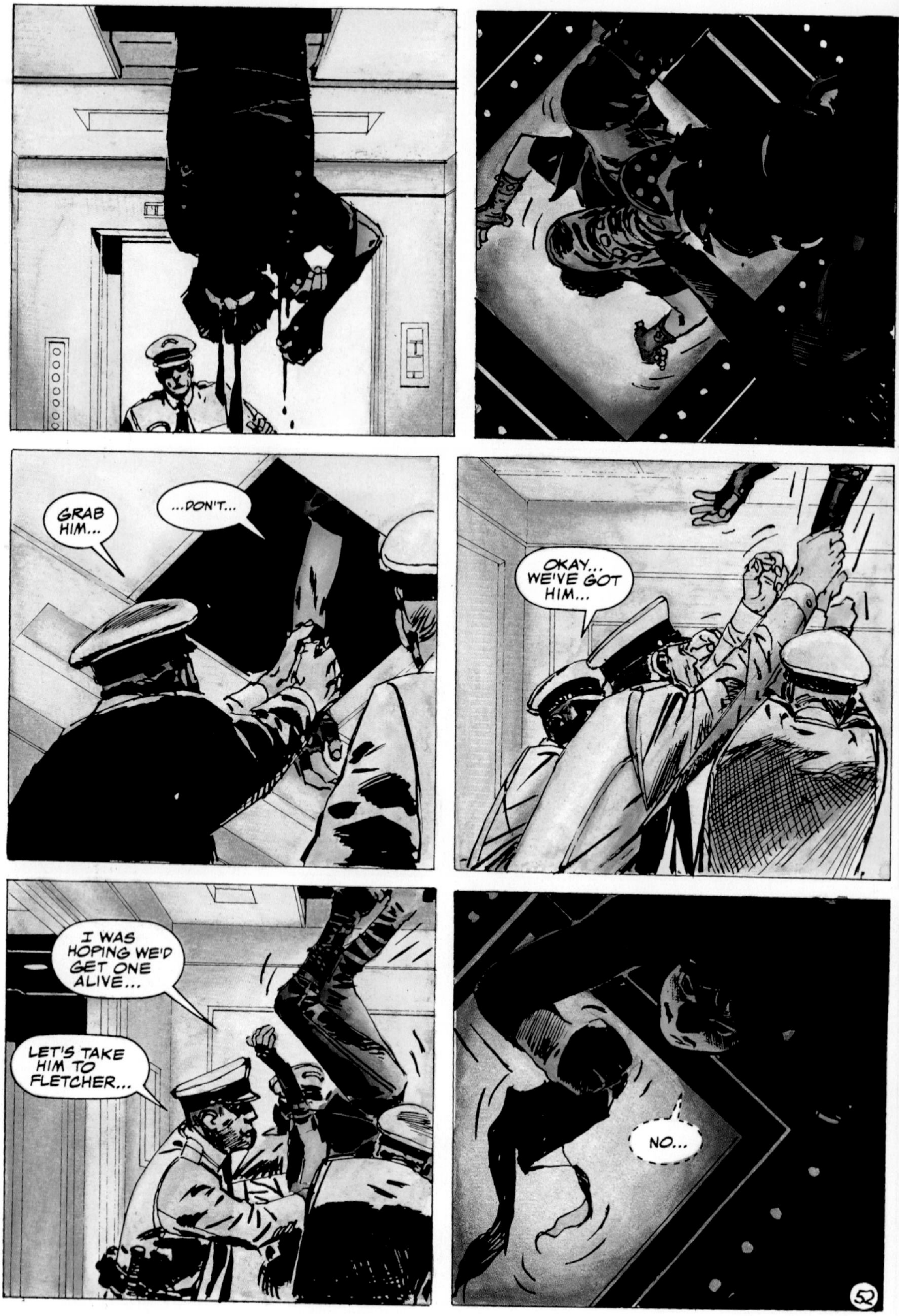
GRAB HIM...
...DON'T...
OKAY... WE'VE GOT HIM...
I WAS HOPING WE'D GET ONE ALIVE...
LET'S TAKE HIM TO FLETCHER...
NO...
52

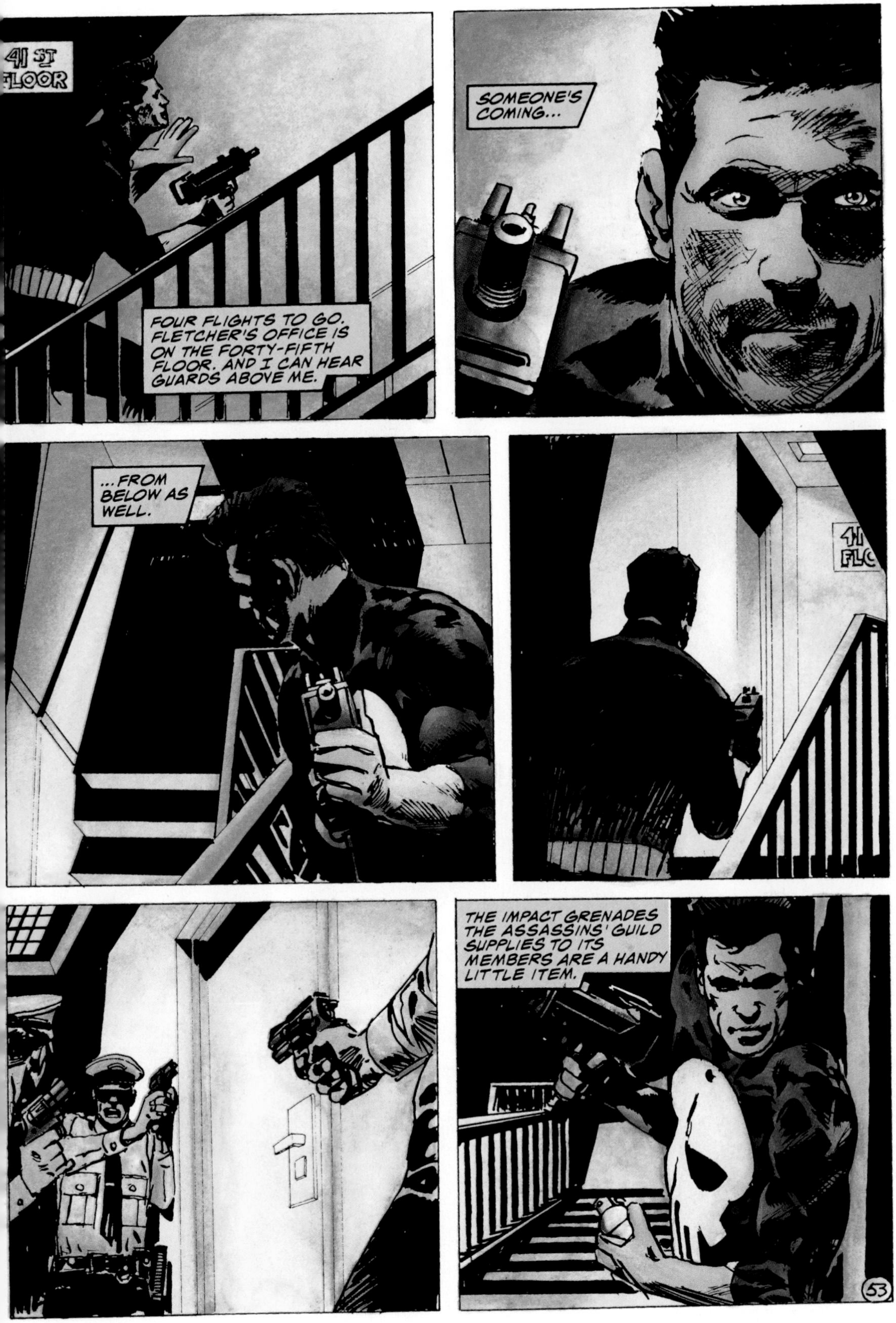
41 ST FLOOR
FOUR FLIGHTS TO GO. FLETCHER'S OFFICE IS ON THE FORTY-FIFTH FLOOR. AND I CAN HEAR GUARDS ABOVE ME.
SOMEONE'S COMING...
...FROM BELOW AS WELL.
THE IMPACT GRENADES THE ASSASSINS' GUILD SUPPLIES TO ITS MEMBERS ARE A HANDY LITTLE ITEM.
53

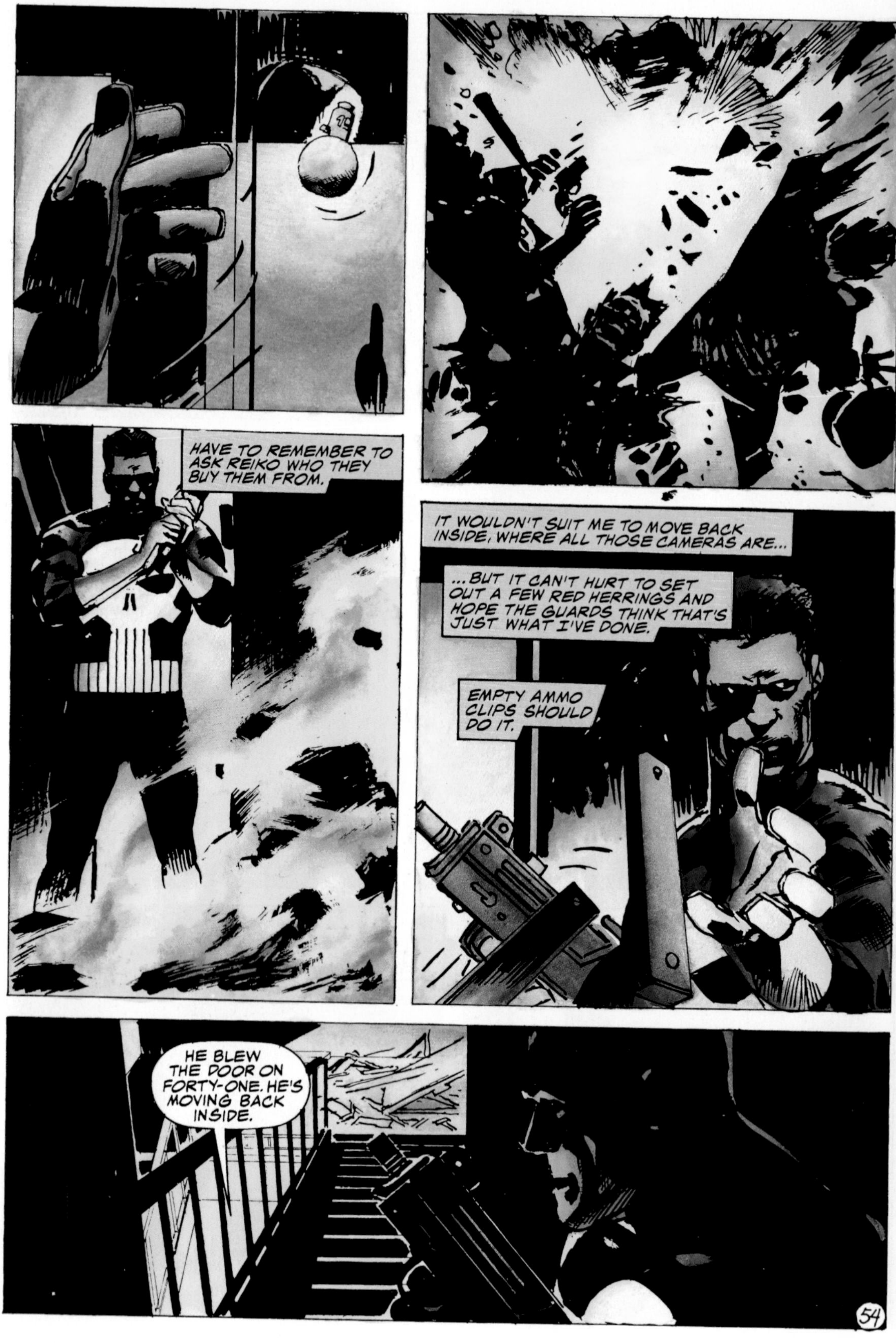
HAVE TO REMEMBER TO ASK REIKO WHO THEY BUY THEM FROM.
IT WOULDN'T SUIT ME TO MOVE BACK INSIDE, WHERE ALL THOSE CAMERAS ARE...
...BUT IT CAN'T HURT TO SET OUT A FEW RED HERRINGS AND HOPE THE GUARDS THINK THAT'S JUST WHAT I'VE DONE.
EMPTY AMMO CLIPS SHOULD DO IT.
HE BLEW THE DOOR ON FORTY-ONE. HE'S MOVING BACK INSIDE.
54

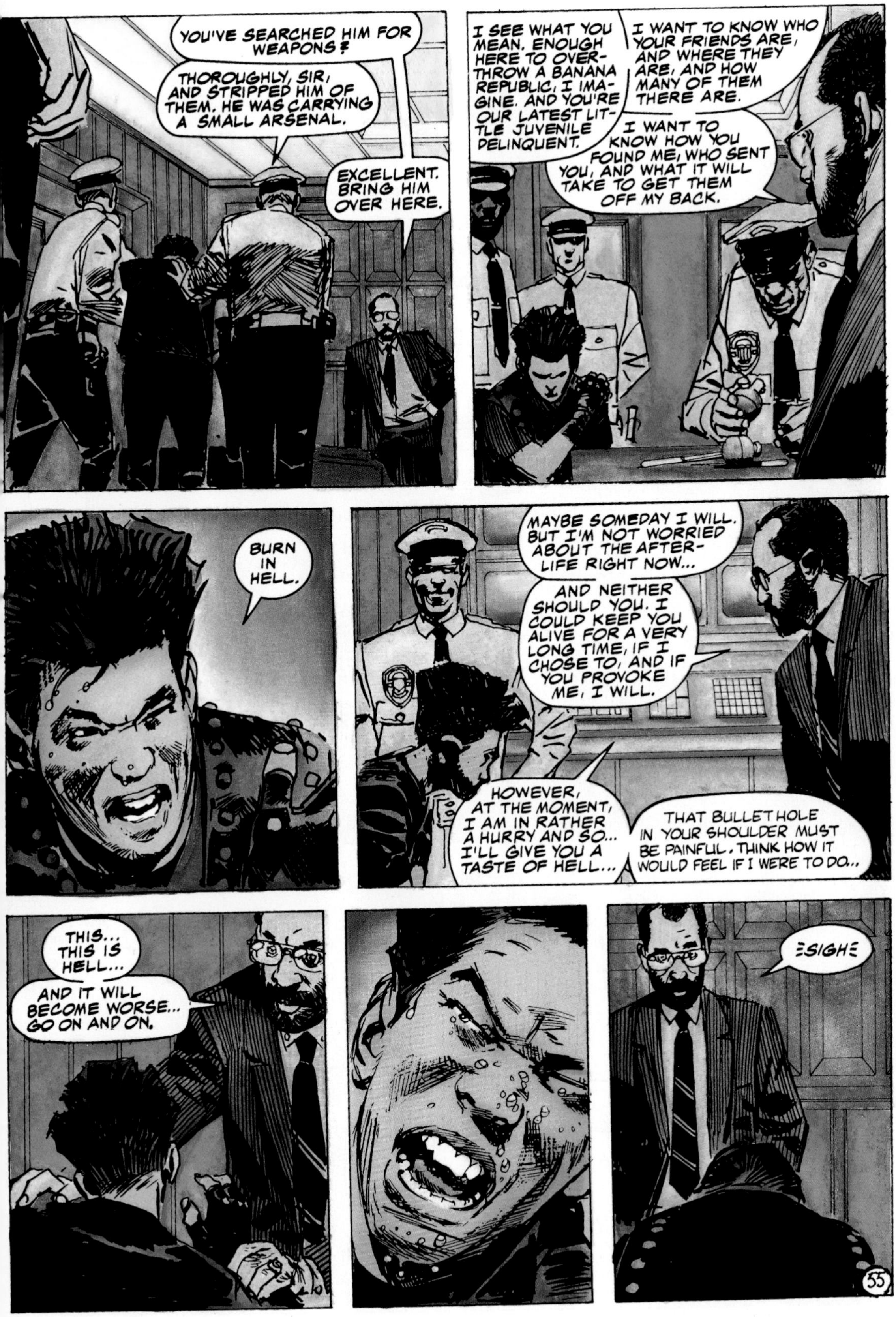
YOU'VE SEARCHED HIM FOR WEAPONS?
THOROUGHLY, SIR, AND STRIPPED HIM OF THEM. HE WAS CARRYING A SMALL ARSENAL.
EXCELLENT. BRING HIM OVER HERE.
I SEE WHAT YOU MEAN. ENOUGH HERE TO OVERTHROW A BANANA REPUBLIC, I IMAGINE. AND YOU'RE OUR LATEST LITTLE JUVENILE DELINQUENT.
I WANT TO KNOW WHO YOUR FRIENDS ARE, AND WHERE THEY ARE, AND HOW MANY OF THEM THERE ARE.
I WANT TO KNOW HOW YOU FOUND ME, WHO SENT YOU, AND WHAT IT WILL TAKE TO GET THEM OFF MY BACK.
BURN IN HELL.
MAYBE SOMEDAY I WILL. BUT I'M NOT WORRIED ABOUT THE AFTER-LIFE RIGHT NOW...
AND NEITHER SHOULD YOU. I COULD KEEP YOU ALIVE FOR A VERY LONG TIME, IF I CHOSE TO, AND IF YOU PROVOKE ME, I WILL.
HOWEVER, AT THE MOMENT, I AM IN RATHER A HURRY AND SO... I'LL GIVE YOU A TASTE OF HELL...
THAT BULLET HOLE IN YOUR SHOULDER MUST BE PAINFUL. THINK HOW IT WOULD FEEL IF I WERE TO DO...
THIS... THIS IS HELL...
AND IT WILL BECOME WORSE... GO ON AND ON.
SIGH
55

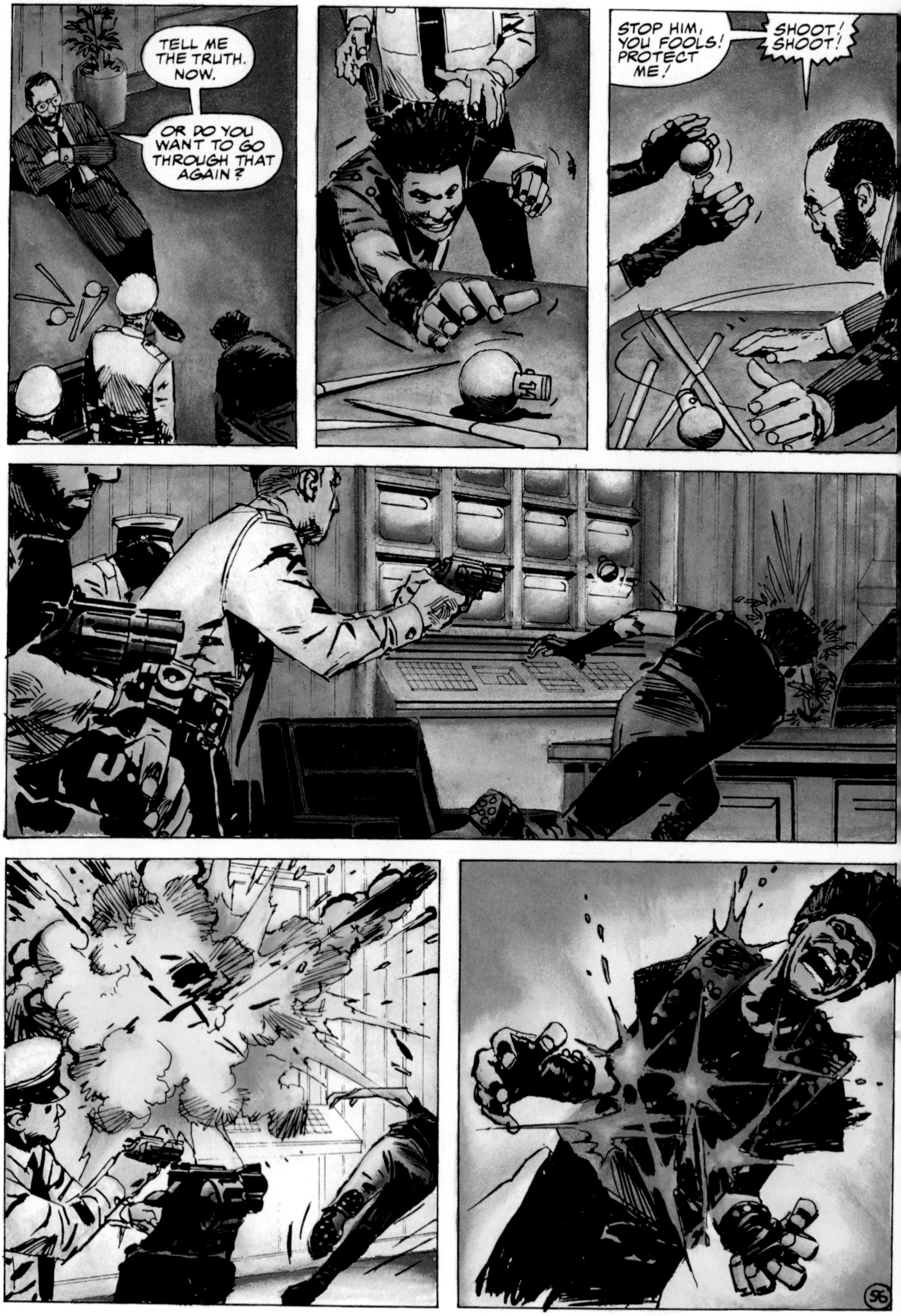
TELL ME THE TRUTH. NOW.
OR DO YOU WANT TO GO THROUGH THAT AGAIN?
STOP HIM, YOU FOOLS! PROTECT ME!
SHOOT! SHOOT!
56

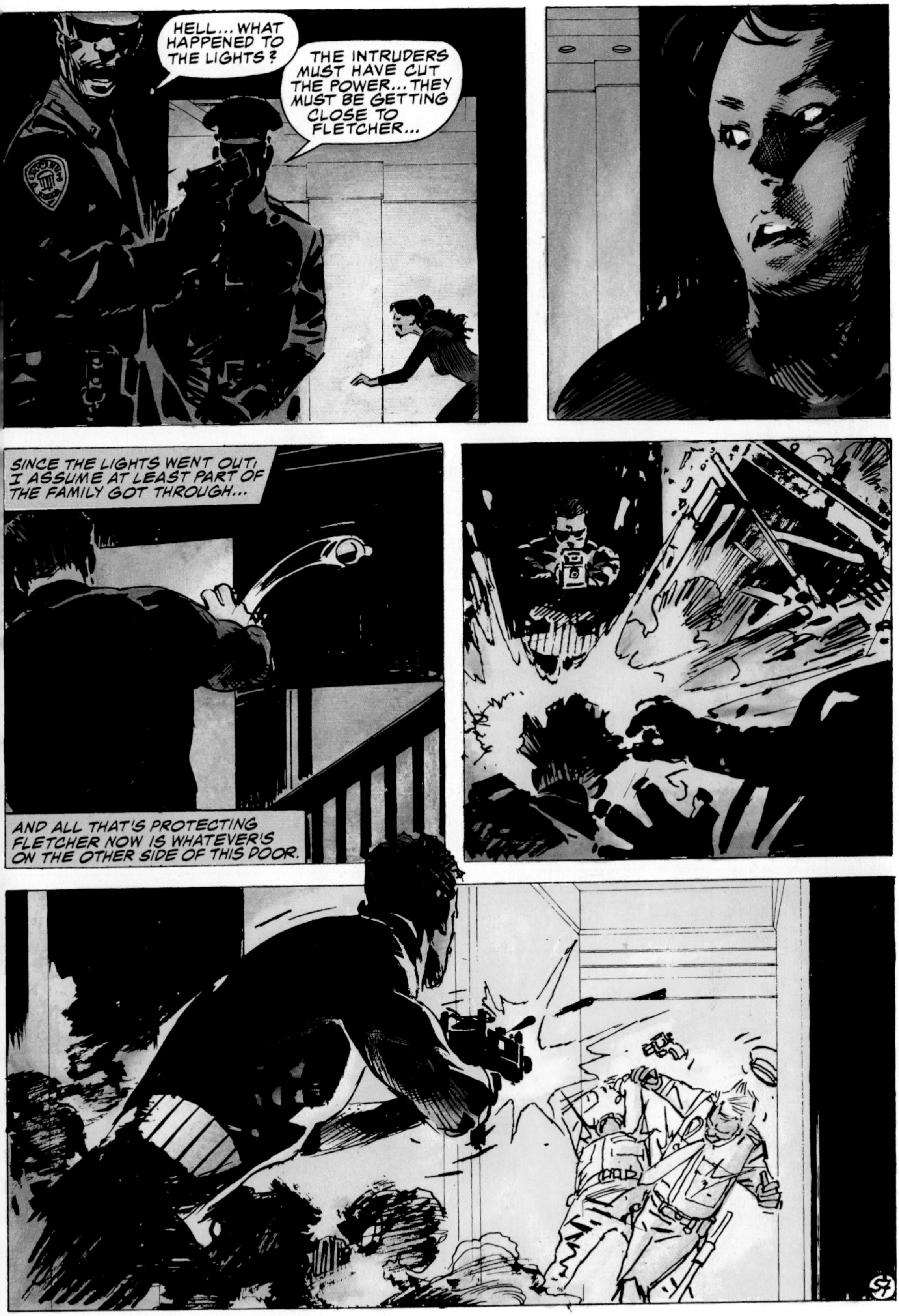
HELL... WHAT HAPPENED TO THE LIGHTS?
THE INTRUDERS MUST HAVE CUT THE POWER... THEY MUST BE GETTING CLOSE TO FLETCHER...
SINCE THE LIGHTS WENT OUT, I ASSUME AT LEAST PART OF THE FAMILY GOT THROUGH...
AND ALL THAT'S PROTECTING FLETCHER NOW IS WHATEVER'S ON THE OTHER SIDE OF THIS DOOR.

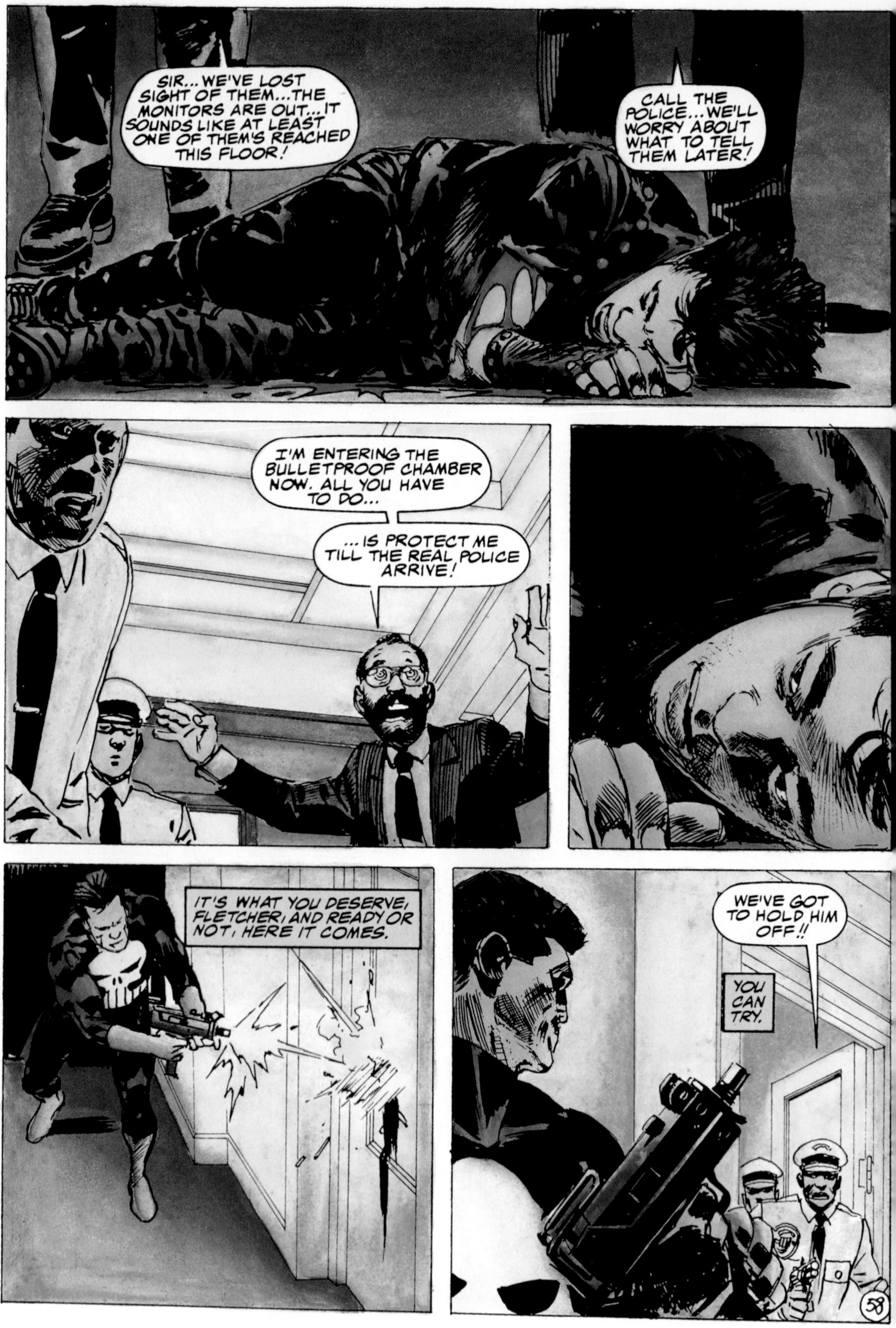
SIR... WE'VE LOST SIGHT OF THEM... THE MONITORS ARE OUT... IT SOUNDS LIKE AT LEAST ONE OF THEM'S REACHED THIS FLOOR!
CALL THE POLICE... WE'LL WORRY ABOUT WHAT TO TELL THEM LATER!
I'M ENTERING THE BULLETPROOF CHAMBER NOW. ALL YOU HAVE TO DO...
...IS PROTECT ME TILL THE REAL POLICE ARRIVE!
IT'S WHAT YOU DESERVE, FLETCHER, AND READY OR NOT, HERE IT COMES.
WE'VE GOT TO HOLD HIM OFF!!
YOU CAN TRY.
58

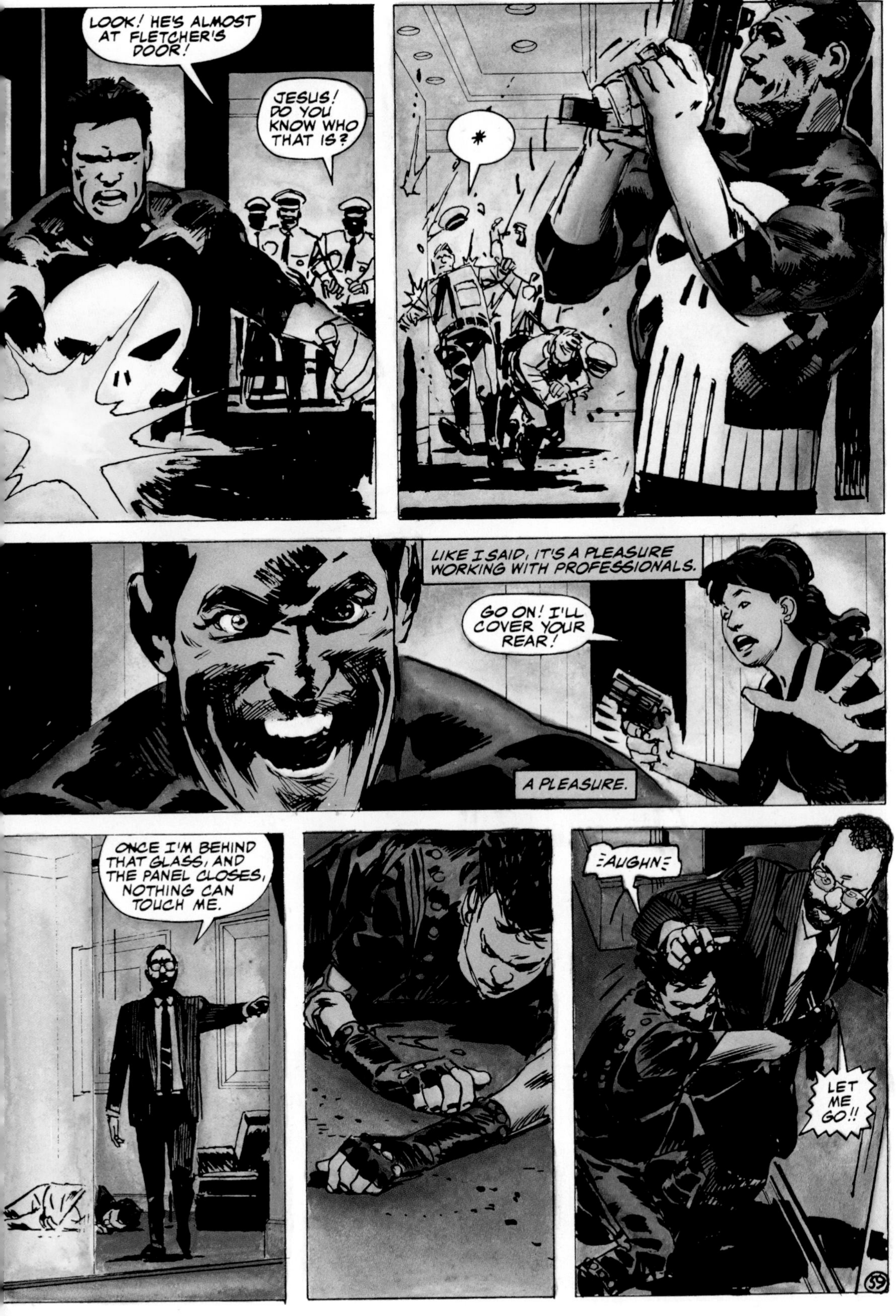

LOOK! HE'S ALMOST AT FLETCHER'S DOOR!
JESUS! DO YOU KNOW WHO THAT IS?
*
LIKE I SAID, IT'S A PLEASURE WORKING WITH PROFESSIONALS.
GO ON! I'LL COVER YOUR REAR!
A PLEASURE.
ONCE I'M BEHIND THAT GLASS, AND THE PANEL CLOSES, NOTHING CAN TOUCH ME.
AUGHN
LET ME GO!!
59

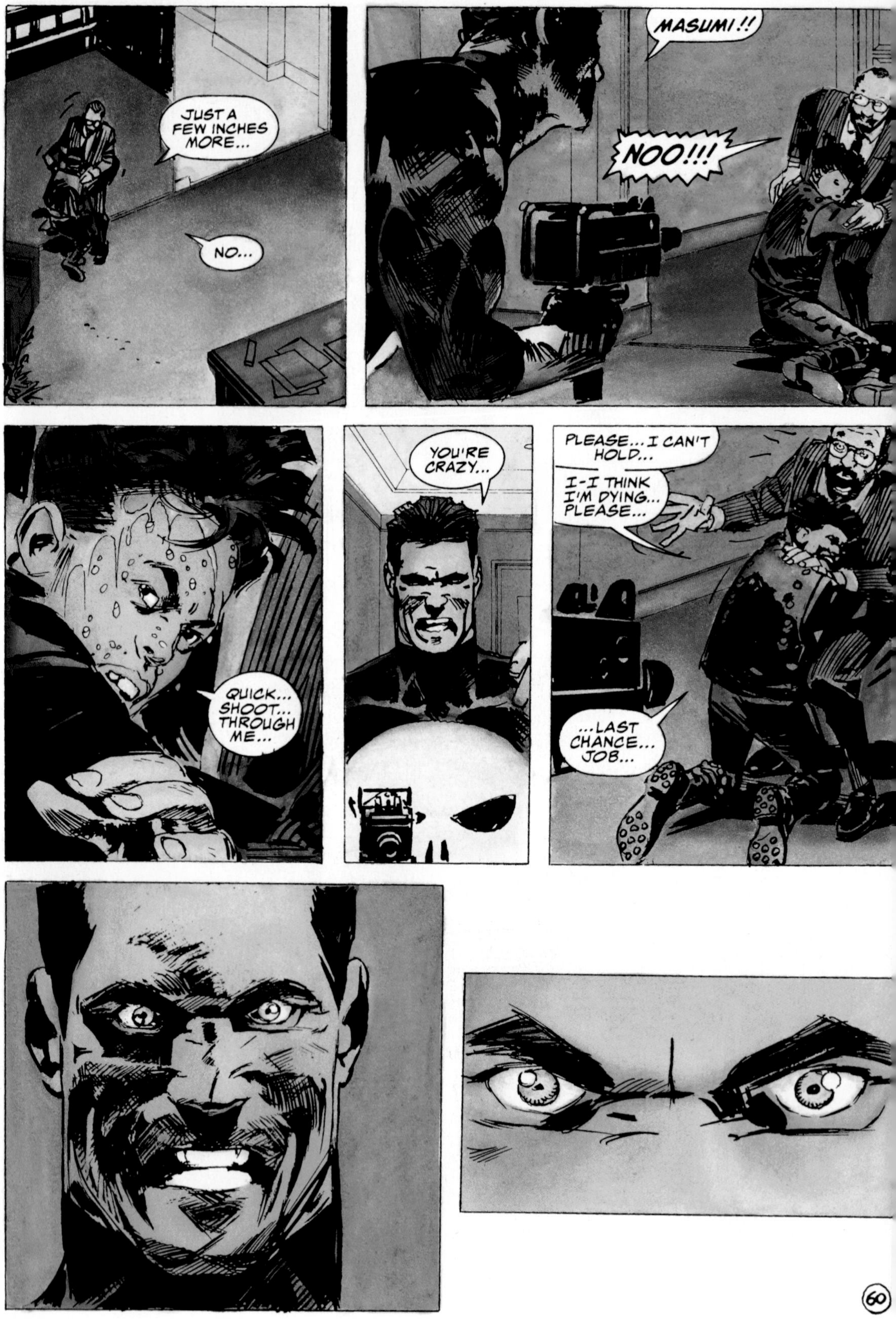
JUST A FEW INCHES MORE...
NO...
MASUMI!!
NOO!!!
QUICK... SHOOT... THROUGH ME...
YOU'RE CRAZY...
PLEASE... I CAN'T HOLD...
I-I THINK I'M DYING... PLEASE...
...LAST CHANCE... JOB...
60

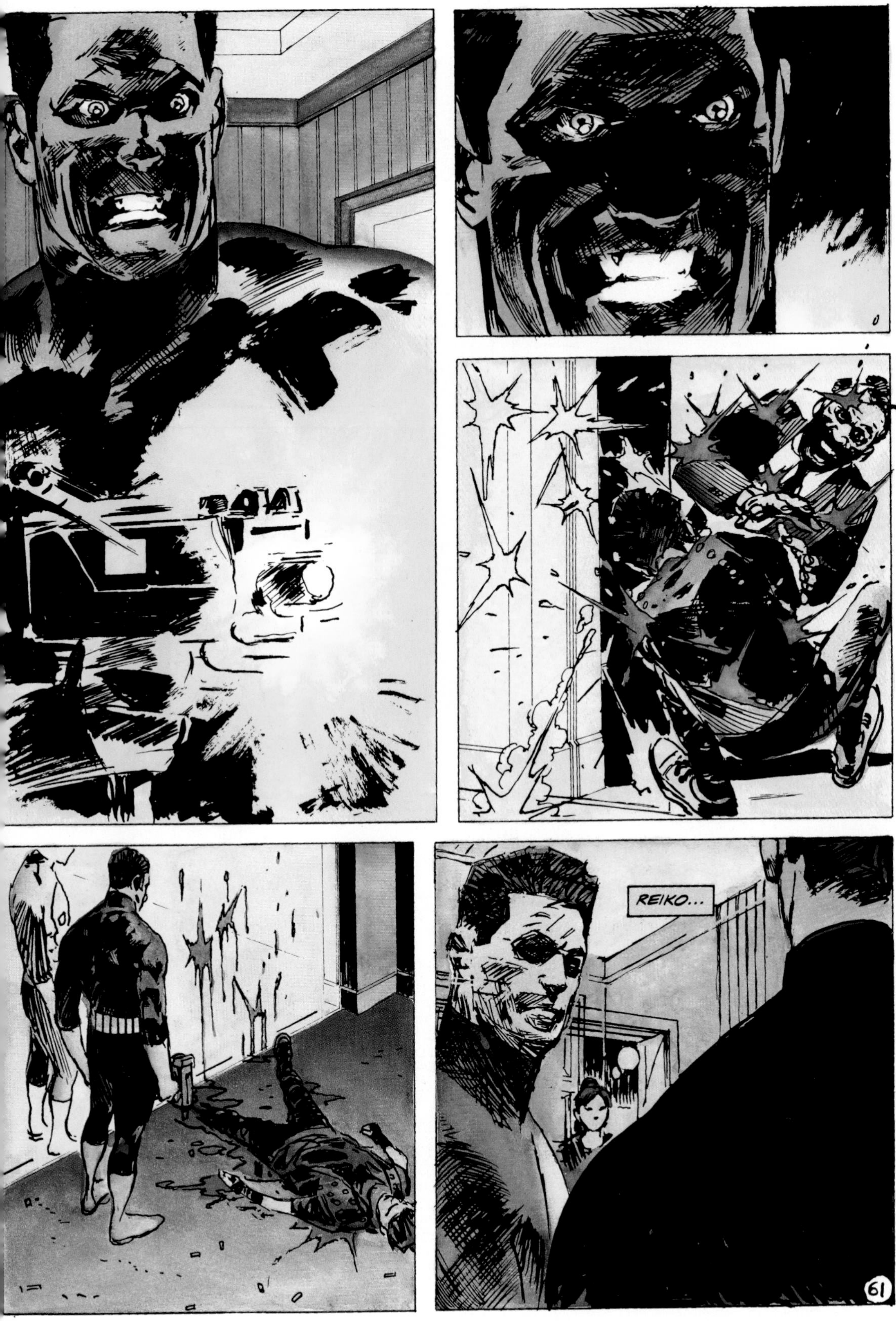
REIKO...
61

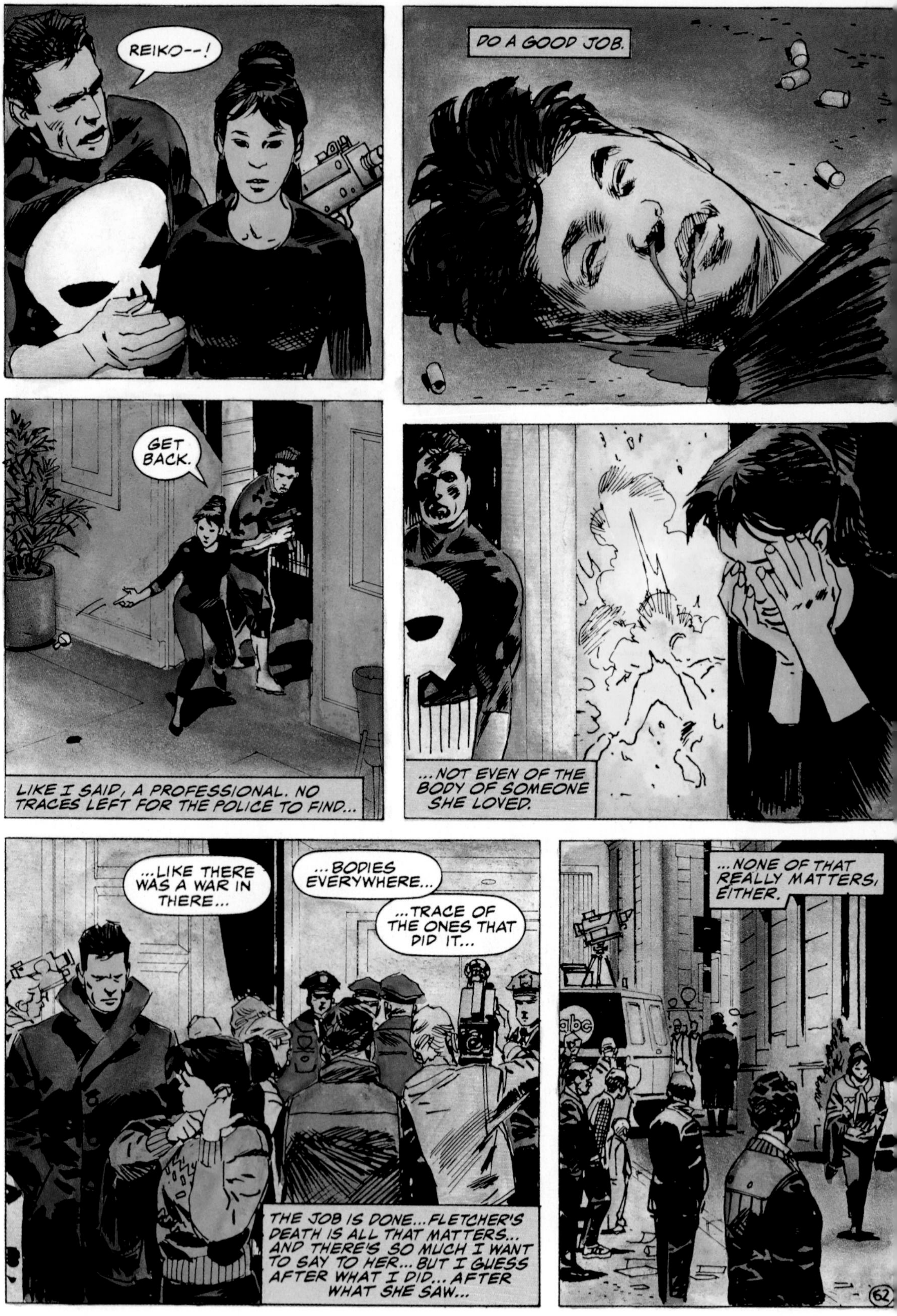
REIKO--!
DO A GOOD JOB.
GET BACK.
LIKE I SAID, A PROFESSIONAL. NO TRACES LEFT FOR THE POLICE TO FIND...
...NOT EVEN OF THE BODY OF SOMEONE SHE LOVED.
...LIKE THERE WAS A WAR IN THERE...
...BODIES EVERYWHERE...
...TRACE OF THE ONES THAT DID IT...
THE JOB IS DONE...FLETCHER'S DEATH IS ALL THAT MATTERS... AND THERE'S SO MUCH I WANT TO SAY TO HER... BUT I GUESS AFTER WHAT I DID... AFTER WHAT SHE SAW...
...NONE OF THAT REALLY MATTERS, EITHER.
abc
62

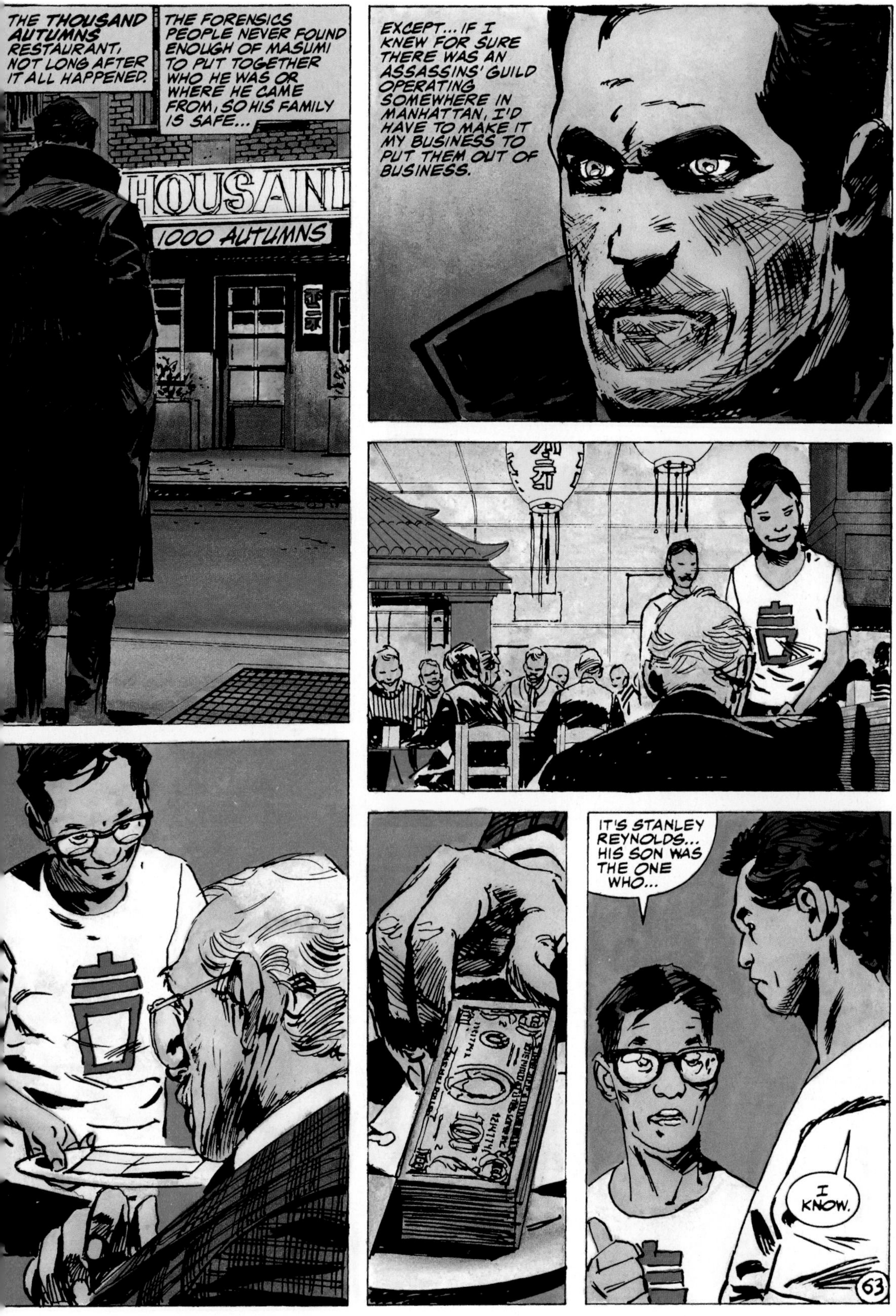
THE THOUSAND AUTUMNS RESTAURANT, NOT LONG AFTER IT ALL HAPPENED.
THE FORENSICS PEOPLE NEVER FOUND ENOUGH OF MASUMI TO PUT TOGETHER WHO HE WAS OR WHERE HE CAME FROM, SO HIS FAMILY IS SAFE...
1000 AUTUMNS
EXCEPT... IF I KNEW FOR SURE THERE WAS AN ASSASSINS' GUILD OPERATING SOMEWHERE IN MANHATTAN, I'D HAVE TO MAKE IT MY BUSINESS TO PUT THEM OUT OF BUSINESS.
IT'S STANLEY REYNOLDS... HIS SON WAS THE ONE WHO...
I KNOW.
63

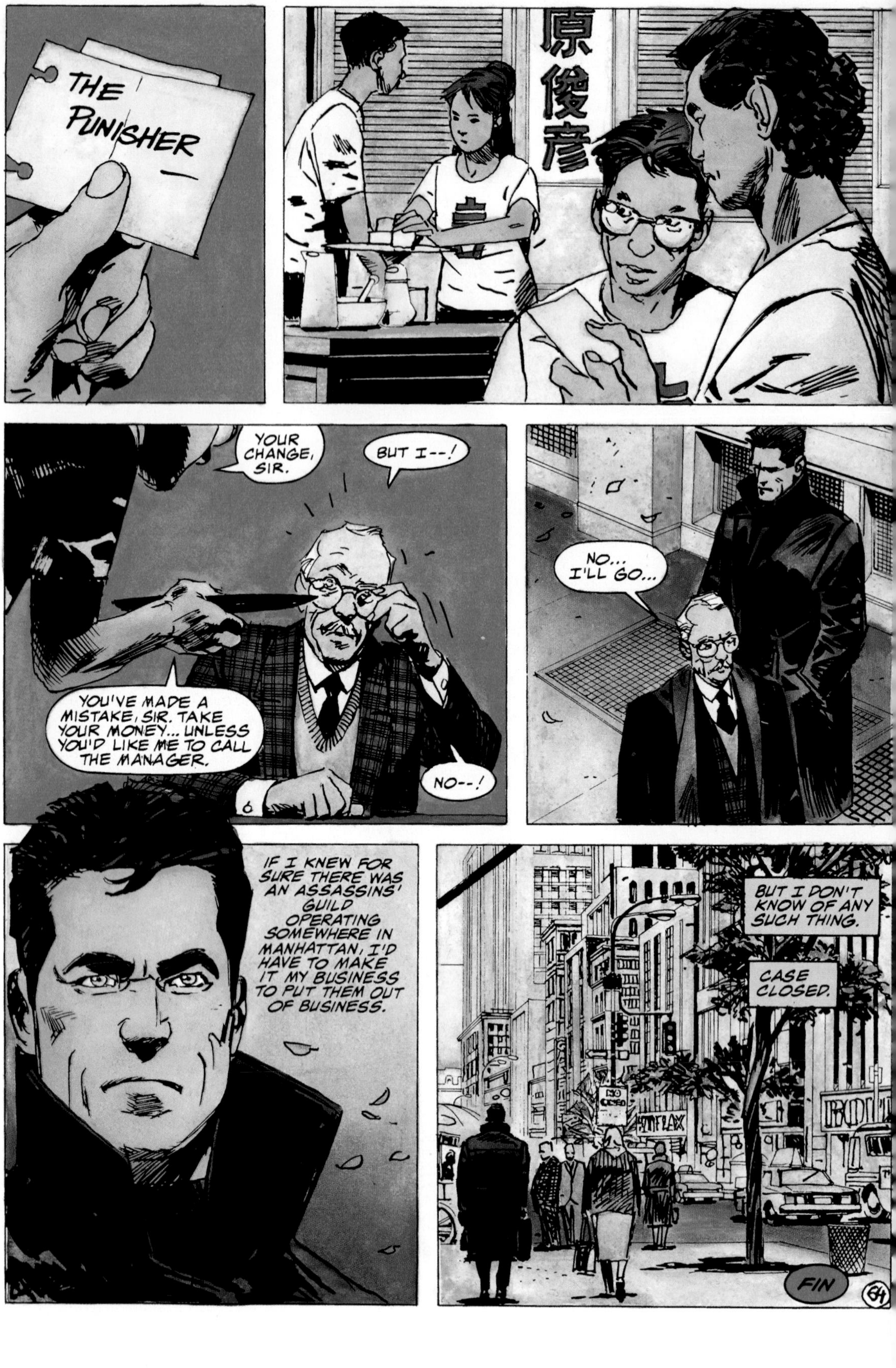
THE PUNISHER
原俊彦
YOUR CHANGE, SIR.
BUT I--!
YOU'VE MADE A MISTAKE, SIR. TAKE YOUR MONEY... UNLESS YOU'D LIKE ME TO CALL THE MANAGER.
NO--!
NO... I'LL GO...
IF I KNEW FOR SURE THERE WAS AN ASSASSINS' GUILD OPERATING SOMEWHERE IN MANHATTAN, I'D HAVE TO MAKE IT MY BUSINESS TO PUT THEM OUT OF BUSINESS.
BUT I DON'T KNOW OF ANY SUCH THING.
CASE CLOSED.
FIN
64

Jo Duffy—was born in Queens, New York in 1954. From 1977 until late in 1986, she worked on the editorial staff of Marvel Comics, becoming an editor on Marvel's Epic Comics line at the end of 1980.

Duffy's comics writing credits include <u>Power Man and Iron Fist</u>, <u>Star Wars</u>, and the <u>Fallen Angels</u> mini-series, as well as an upcoming <u>Fallen Angels</u> sequel, and she is currently at work on the second volume of a trilogy of fantasy novels.

Jorge Zaffino—was born in Buenos Aires, Argentina in 1959 and has been a professional artist since the age of sixteen. In addition to illustrating comics, Zaffino also works in advertising, and he is currently studying painting and working on pieces for gallery shows.

His North America comics debut was on <u>Winterworld</u>—a three-issue limited series written by Chuck Dixon.

Zaffino is happily married and the father of two.

Julie Michel—was born in Greeley, Colorado in 1959 and studied at the Corcoran School of Art. She made her comics coloring debut in 1986 on <u>Fashion in Action</u>, written and illustrated by her close friend John Snyder. Other comics credits include the three-issue <u>Winterworld</u> mini-series, which was illustrated by Jorge Zaffino.

Michel also works as a sculptor and hopes, in the future, to work in children's book illustration.

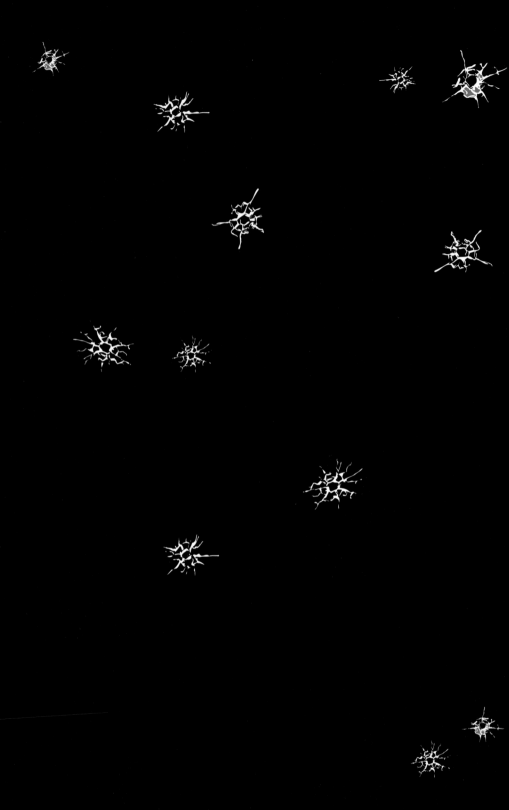

MARVEL®
GRAPHIC NOVEL
$14.95 US
$19.95 CAN
THE PUNISHER™
W.REINHOLD·89
INTRUDER™
by
Mike Baron
Bill Reinhold
Linda Lessmann

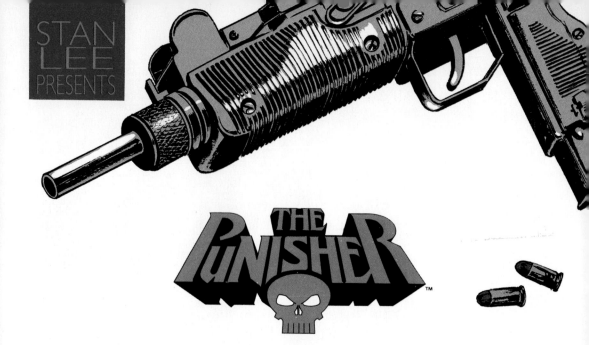

THE PUNISHER

in

INTRUDER

MIKE BARON — story

BILL REINHOLD — art

WILLIE SCHUBERT — letters

LINDA LESSMAN — colors

carl potts — EDITOR/TITLES DESIGN
marc mclaurin — ASSISTANT EDITOR
tom defalco — EDITOR IN CHIEF

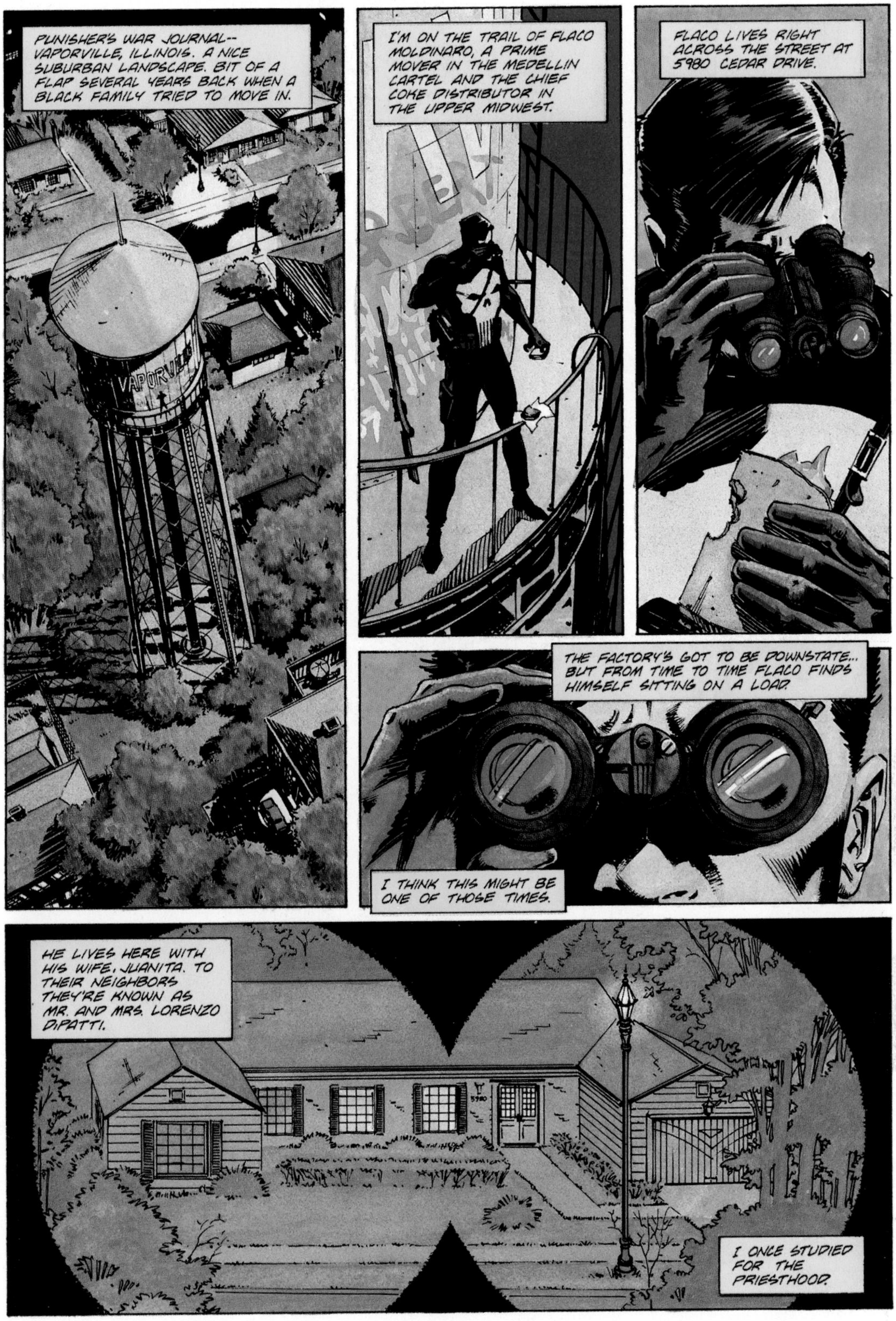
PUNISHER'S WAR JOURNAL--
VAPORVILLE, ILLINOIS. A NICE SUBURBAN LANDSCAPE. BIT OF A FLAP SEVERAL YEARS BACK WHEN A BLACK FAMILY TRIED TO MOVE IN.
VAPORVILLE
I'M ON THE TRAIL OF FLACO MOLDINARO, A PRIME MOVER IN THE MEDELLIN CARTEL AND THE CHIEF COKE DISTRIBUTOR IN THE UPPER MIDWEST.
FLACO LIVES RIGHT ACROSS THE STREET AT 5980 CEDAR DRIVE.
THE FACTORY'S GOT TO BE DOWNSTATE... BUT FROM TIME TO TIME FLACO FINDS HIMSELF SITTING ON A LOAD.
I THINK THIS MIGHT BE ONE OF THOSE TIMES.
HE LIVES HERE WITH HIS WIFE, JUANITA. TO THEIR NEIGHBORS THEY'RE KNOWN AS MR. AND MRS. LORENZO DIPATTI.
5980
I ONCE STUDIED FOR THE PRIESTHOOD.

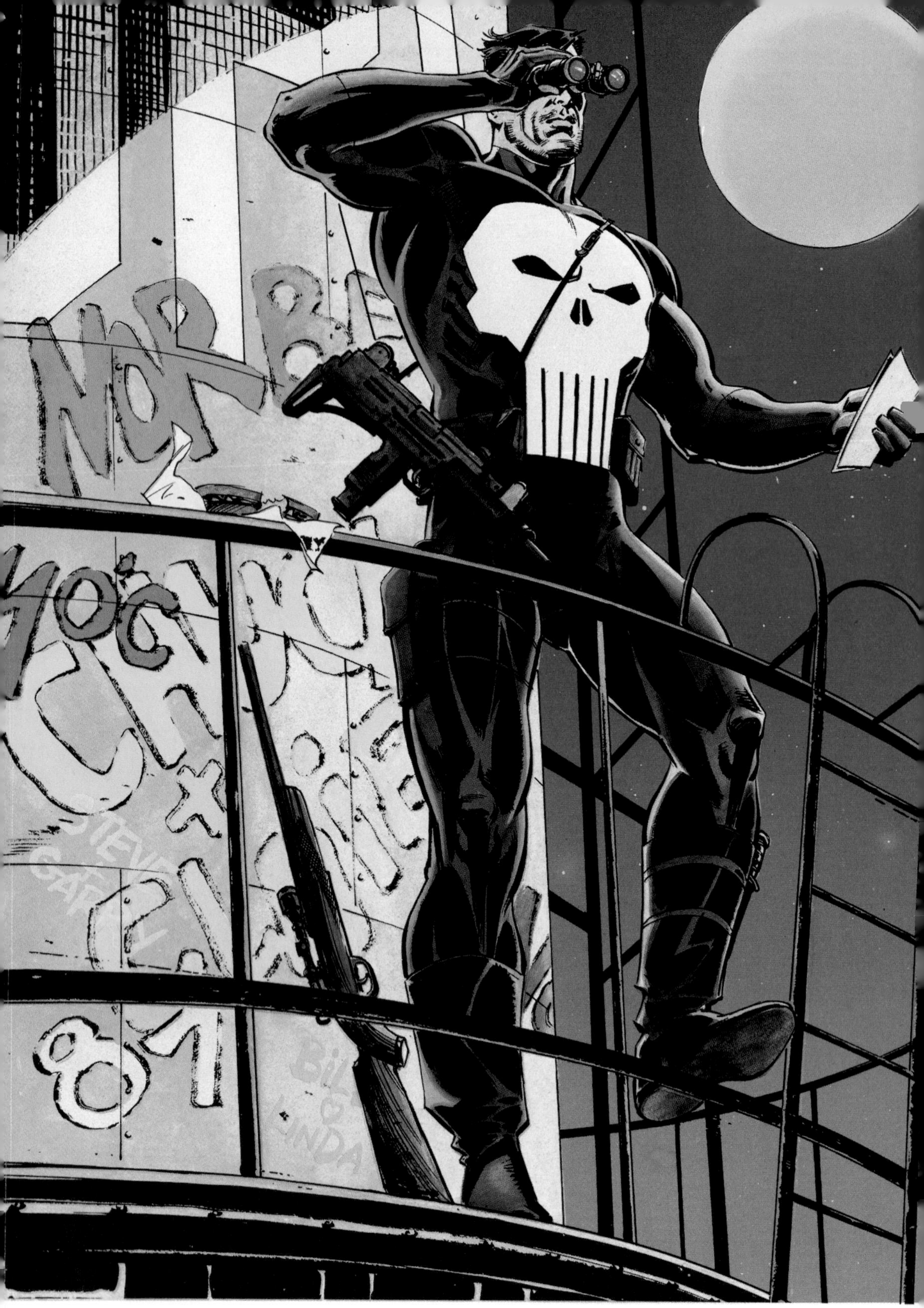

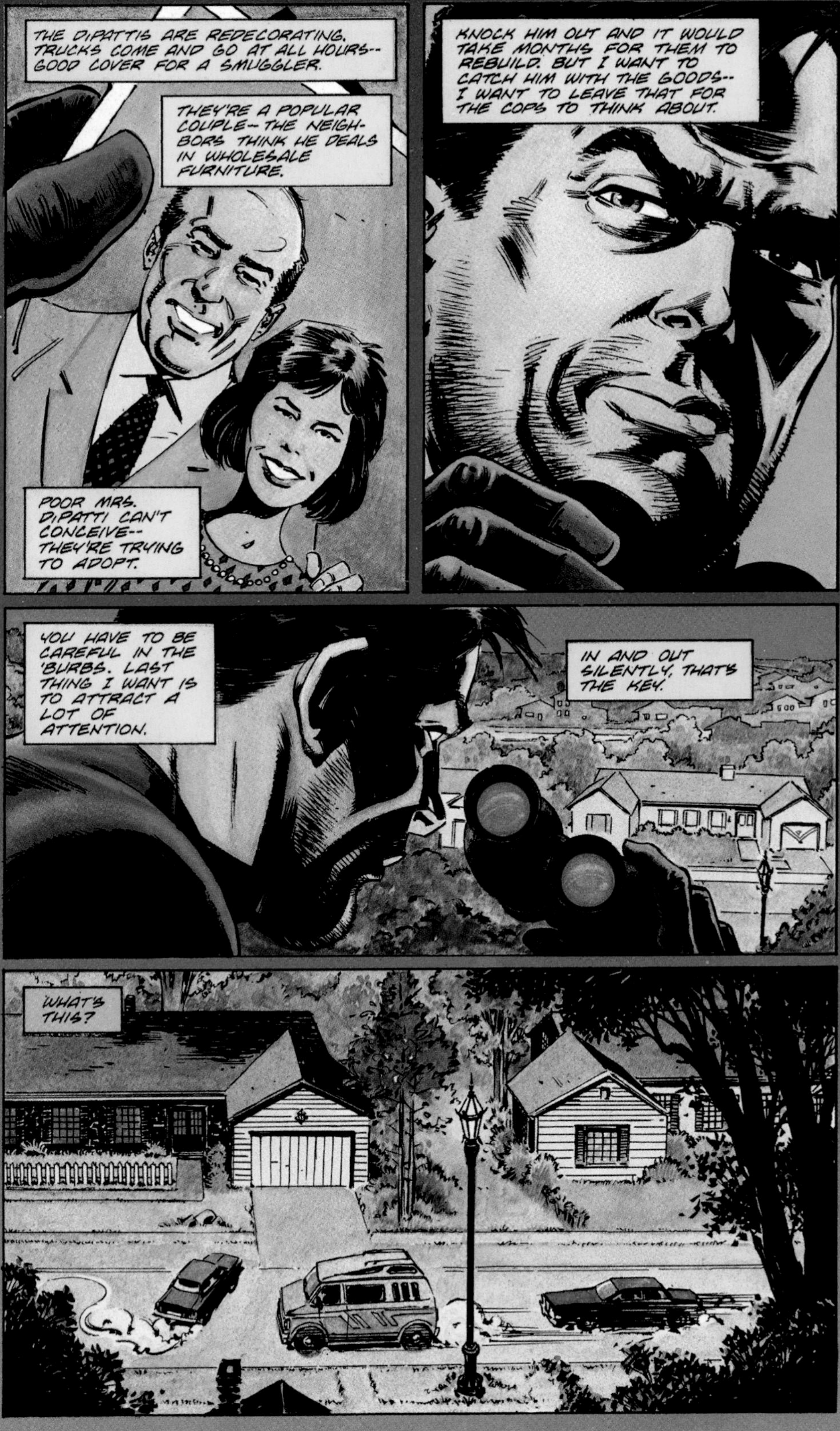
THE DIPATTIS ARE REDECORATING. TRUCKS COME AND GO AT ALL HOURS-- GOOD COVER FOR A SMUGGLER.
THEY'RE A POPULAR COUPLE-- THE NEIGH-BORS THINK HE DEALS IN WHOLESALE FURNITURE.
POOR MRS. DIPATTI CAN'T CONCEIVE-- THEY'RE TRYING TO ADOPT.
KNOCK HIM OUT AND IT WOULD TAKE MONTHS FOR THEM TO REBUILD. BUT I WANT TO CATCH HIM WITH THE GOODS-- I WANT TO LEAVE THAT FOR THE COPS TO THINK ABOUT.
YOU HAVE TO BE CAREFUL IN THE 'BURBS. LAST THING I WANT IS TO ATTRACT A LOT OF ATTENTION.
IN AND OUT SILENTLY, THAT'S THE KEY.
WHAT'S THIS?

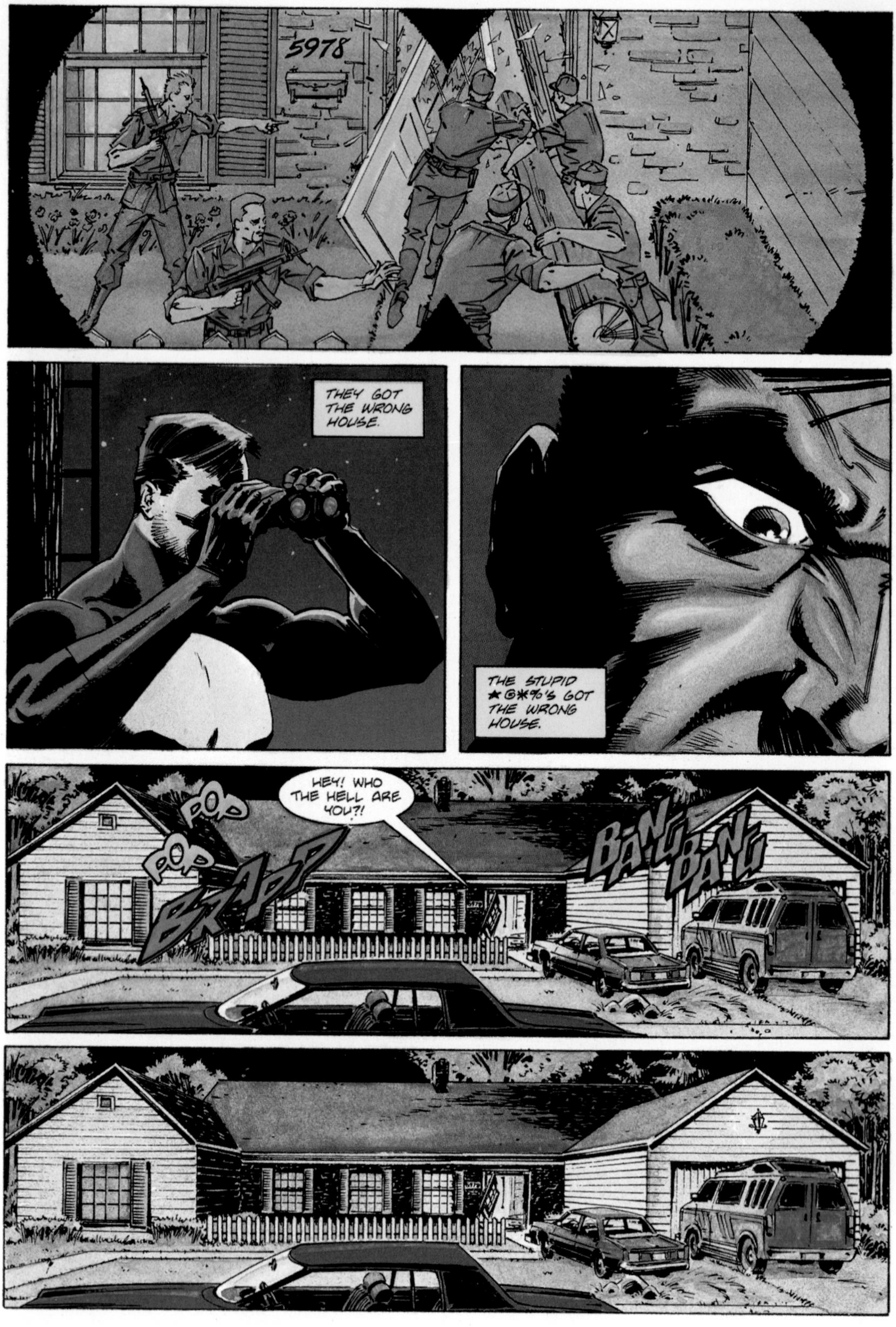

5978
THEY GOT THE WRONG HOUSE.
THE STUPID ★@✱%'s GOT THE WRONG HOUSE.
POP
POP
BRAPP
HEY! WHO THE HELL ARE YOU?!
BANG BANG

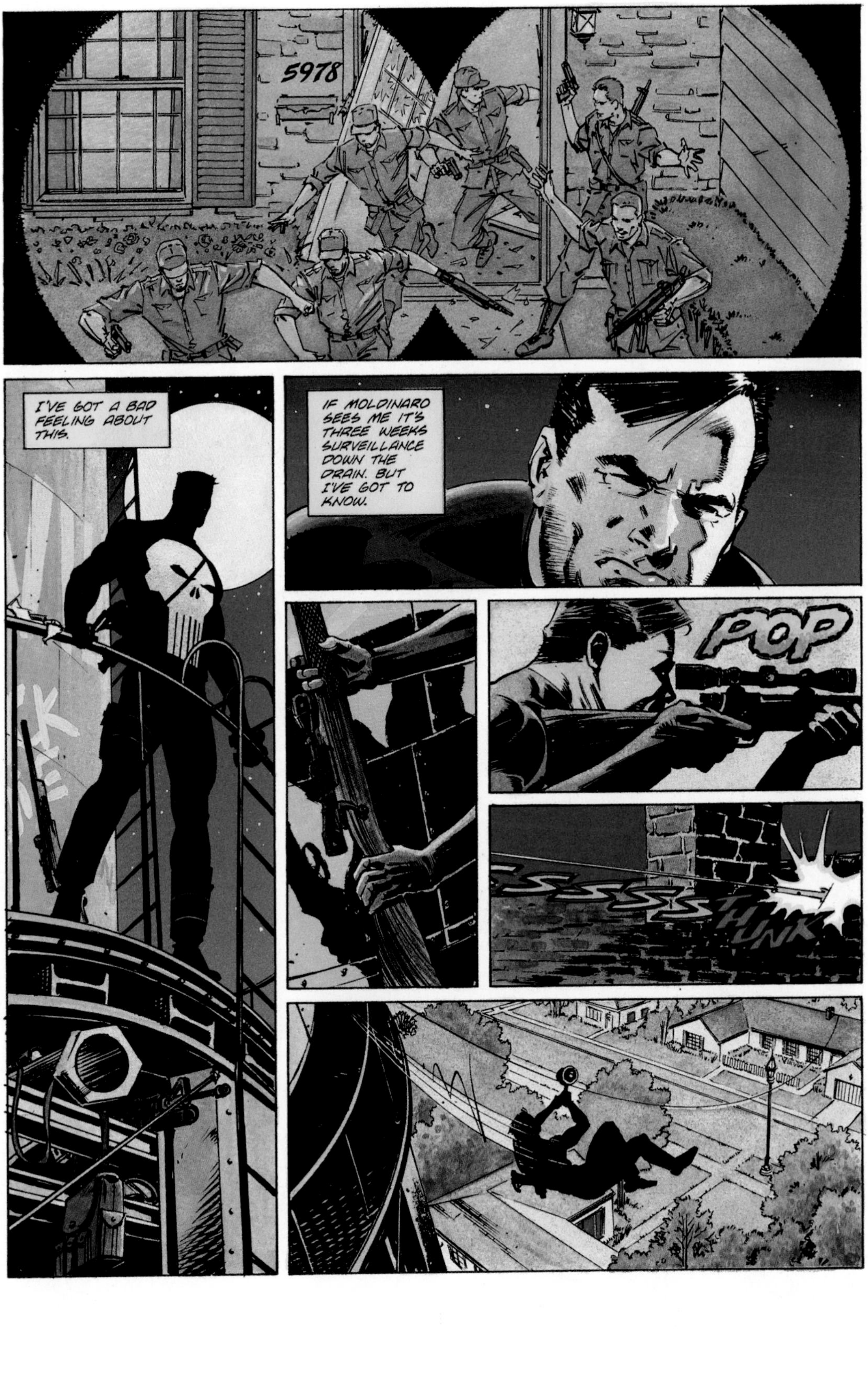
5978
I'VE GOT A BAD FEELING ABOUT THIS.
IF MOLDINARO SEES ME IT'S THREE WEEKS SURVEILLANCE DOWN THE DRAIN. BUT I'VE GOT TO KNOW.
POP
SSSSSS
THUNK

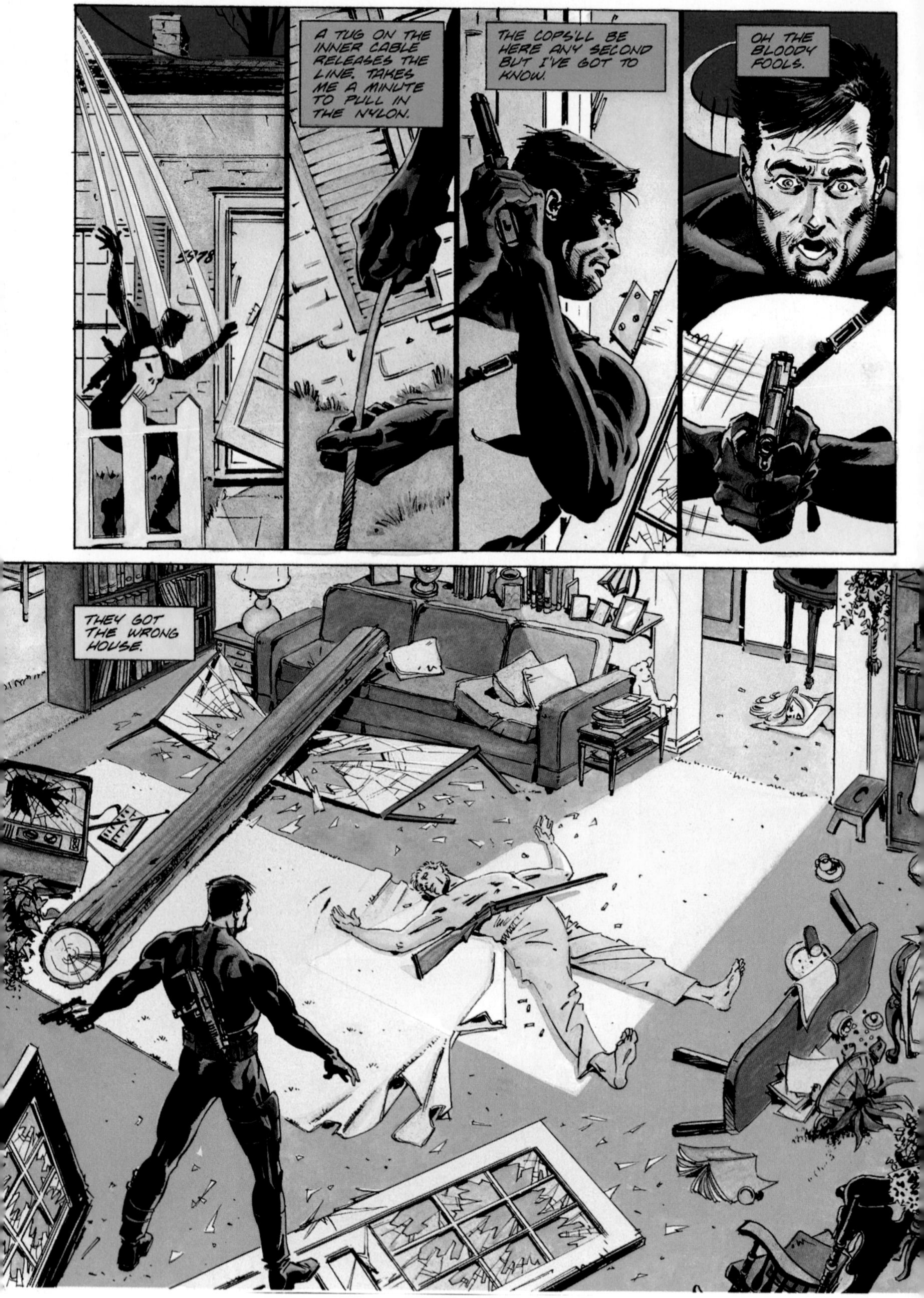
A TUG ON THE INNER CABLE RELEASES THE LINE. TAKES ME A MINUTE TO PULL IN THE NYLON.
THE COPS'LL BE HERE ANY SECOND BUT I'VE GOT TO KNOW.
OH THE BLOODY FOOLS.
THEY GOT THE WRONG HOUSE.

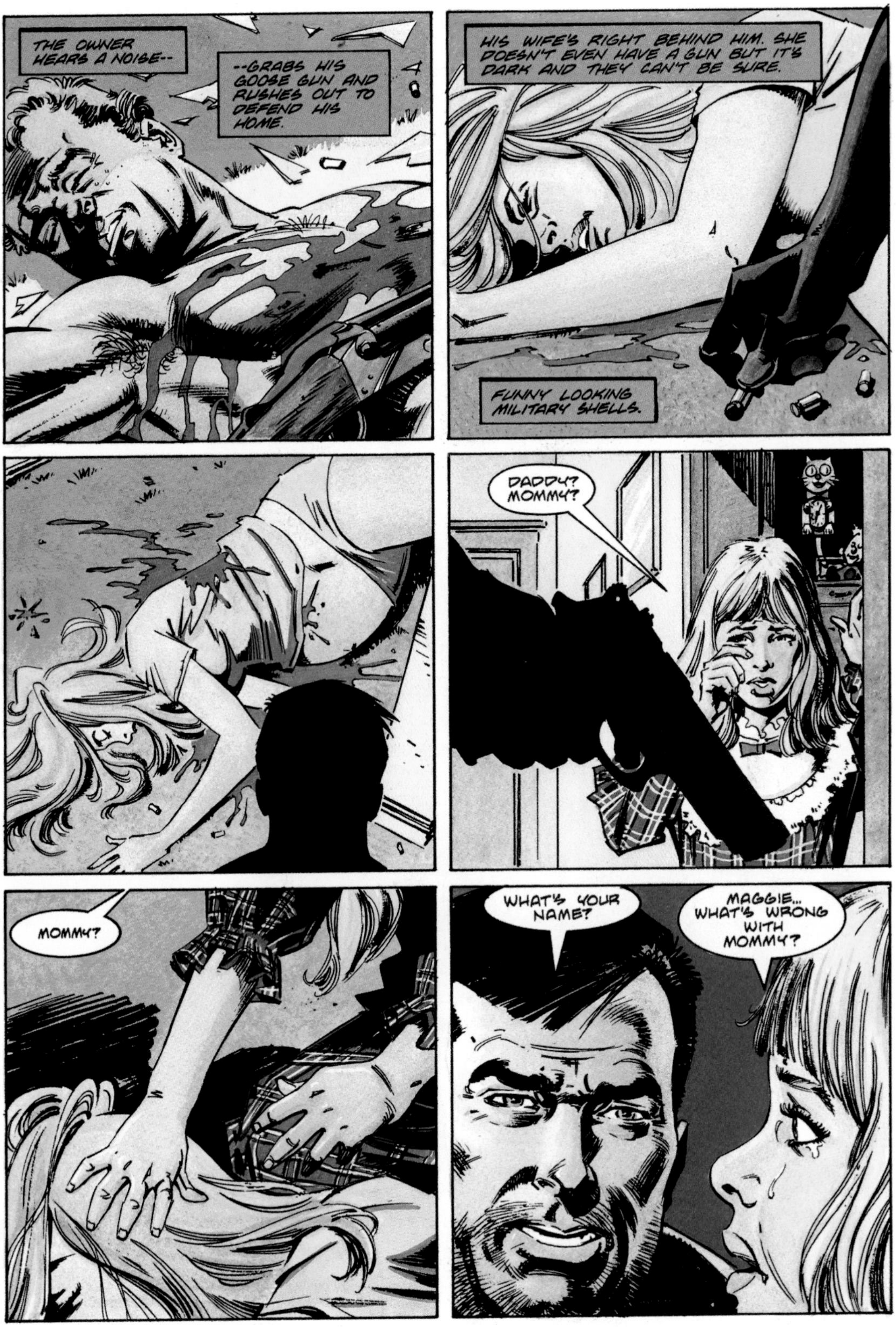
THE OWNER HEARS A NOISE--
--GRABS HIS GOOSE GUN AND RUSHES OUT TO DEFEND HIS HOME.
HIS WIFE'S RIGHT BEHIND HIM. SHE DOESN'T EVEN HAVE A GUN BUT IT'S DARK AND THEY CAN'T BE SURE.
FUNNY LOOKING MILITARY SHELLS.
DADDY? MOMMY?
MOMMY?
WHAT'S YOUR NAME?
MAGGIE... WHAT'S WRONG WITH MOMMY?

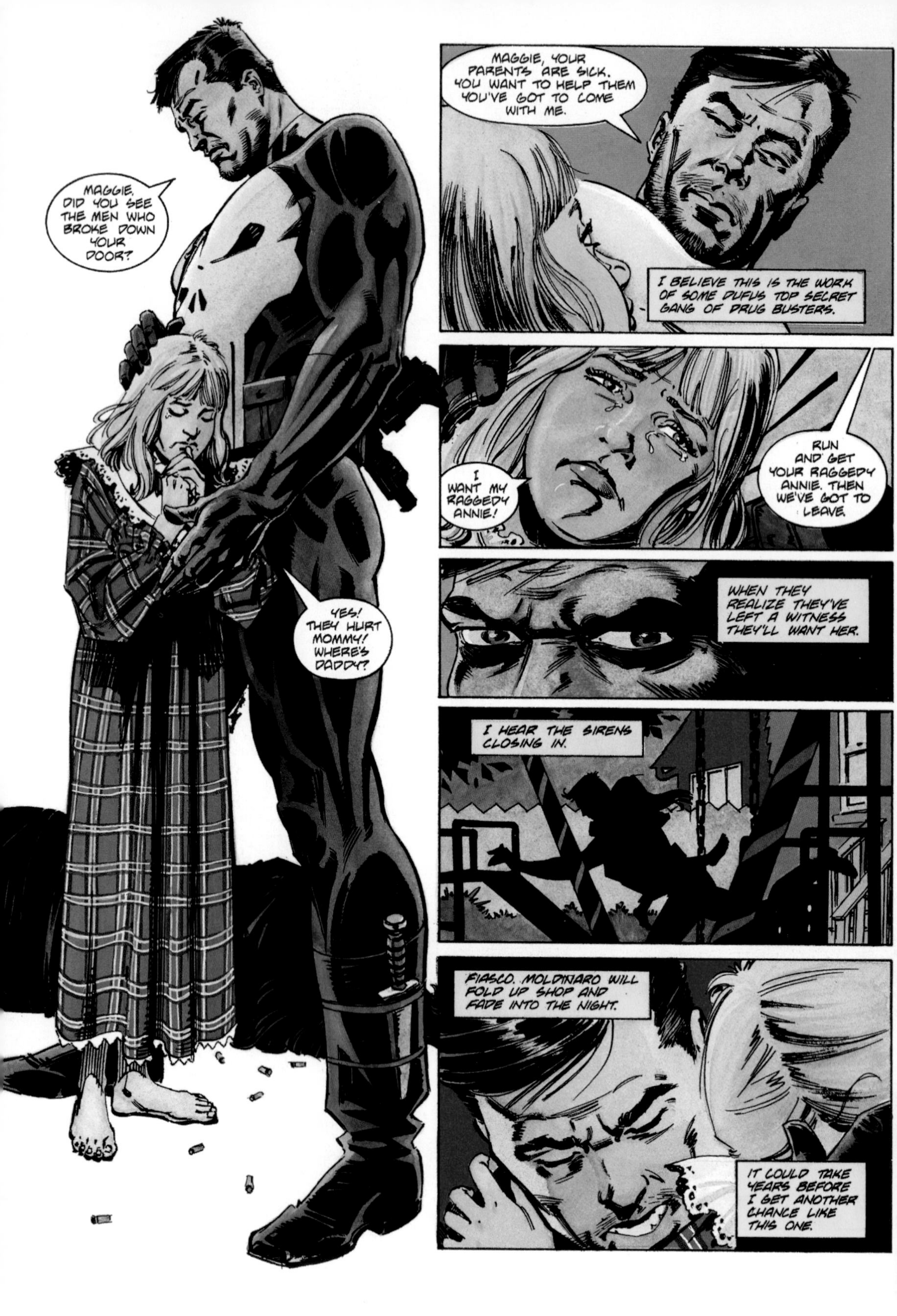
MAGGIE. DID YOU SEE THE MEN WHO BROKE DOWN YOUR DOOR?
YES! THEY HURT MOMMY! WHERE'S DADDY?
MAGGIE, YOUR PARENTS ARE SICK. YOU WANT TO HELP THEM YOU'VE GOT TO COME WITH ME.
I BELIEVE THIS IS THE WORK OF SOME DUFUS TOP SECRET GANG OF DRUG BUSTERS.
I WANT MY RAGGEDY ANNIE!
RUN AND GET YOUR RAGGEDY ANNIE. THEN WE'VE GOT TO LEAVE.
WHEN THEY REALIZE THEY'VE LEFT A WITNESS THEY'LL WANT HER.
I HEAR THE SIRENS CLOSING IN.
FIASCO. MOLDINARO WILL FOLD UP SHOP AND FADE INTO THE NIGHT.
IT COULD TAKE YEARS BEFORE I GET ANOTHER CHANCE LIKE THIS ONE.

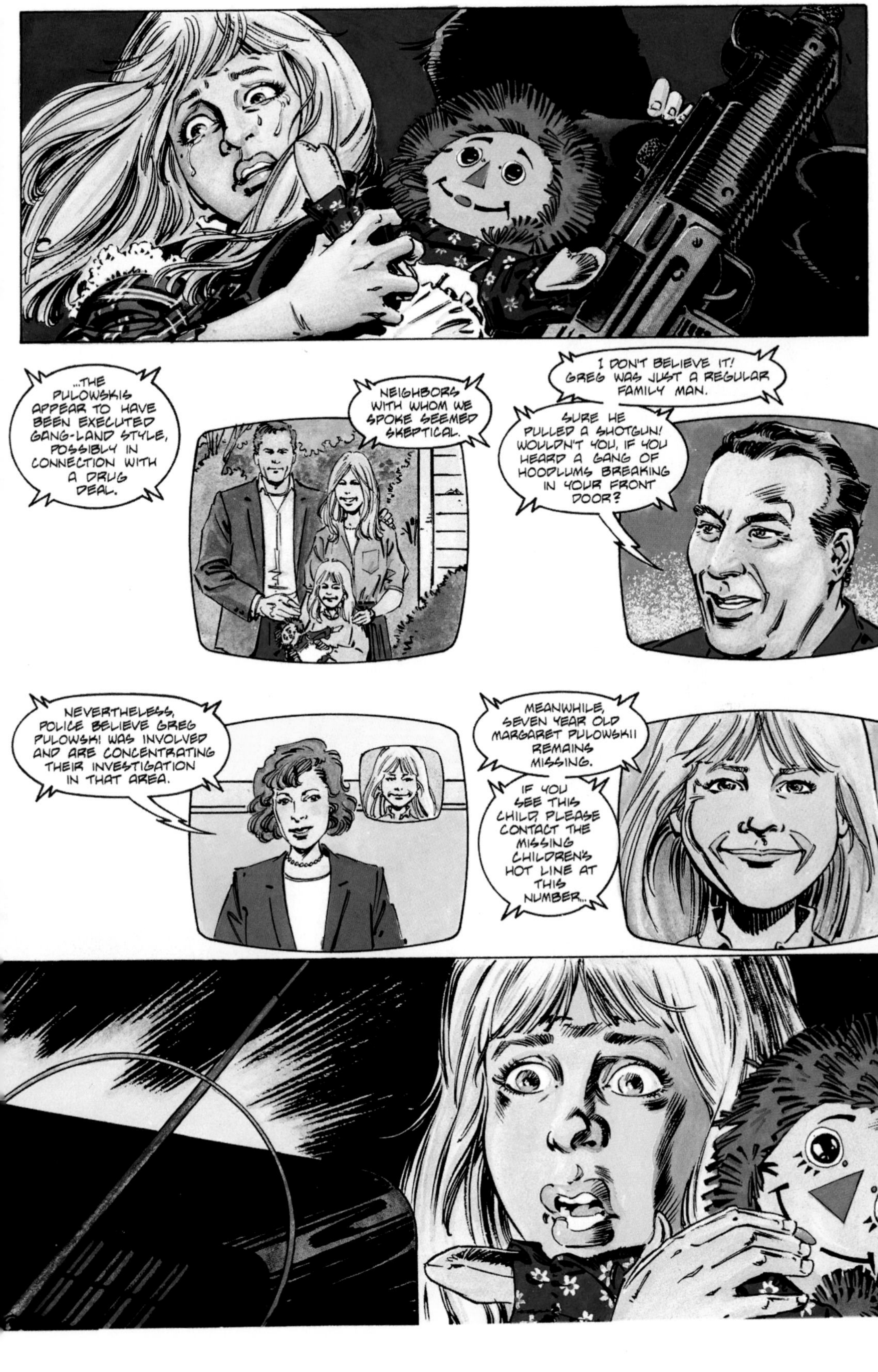
...THE PULOWSKIS APPEAR TO HAVE BEEN EXECUTED GANG-LAND STYLE, POSSIBLY IN CONNECTION WITH A DRUG DEAL.
NEIGHBORS WITH WHOM WE SPOKE SEEMED SKEPTICAL.
I DON'T BELIEVE IT! GREG WAS JUST A REGULAR FAMILY MAN.
SURE HE PULLED A SHOTGUN! WOULDN'T YOU, IF YOU HEARD A GANG OF HOODLUMS BREAKING IN YOUR FRONT DOOR?
NEVERTHELESS, POLICE BELIEVE GREG PULOWSKI WAS INVOLVED AND ARE CONCENTRATING THEIR INVESTIGATION IN THAT AREA.
MEANWHILE, SEVEN YEAR OLD MARGARET PULOWSKII REMAINS MISSING.
IF YOU SEE THIS CHILD, PLEASE CONTACT THE MISSING CHILDREN'S HOT LINE AT THIS NUMBER...

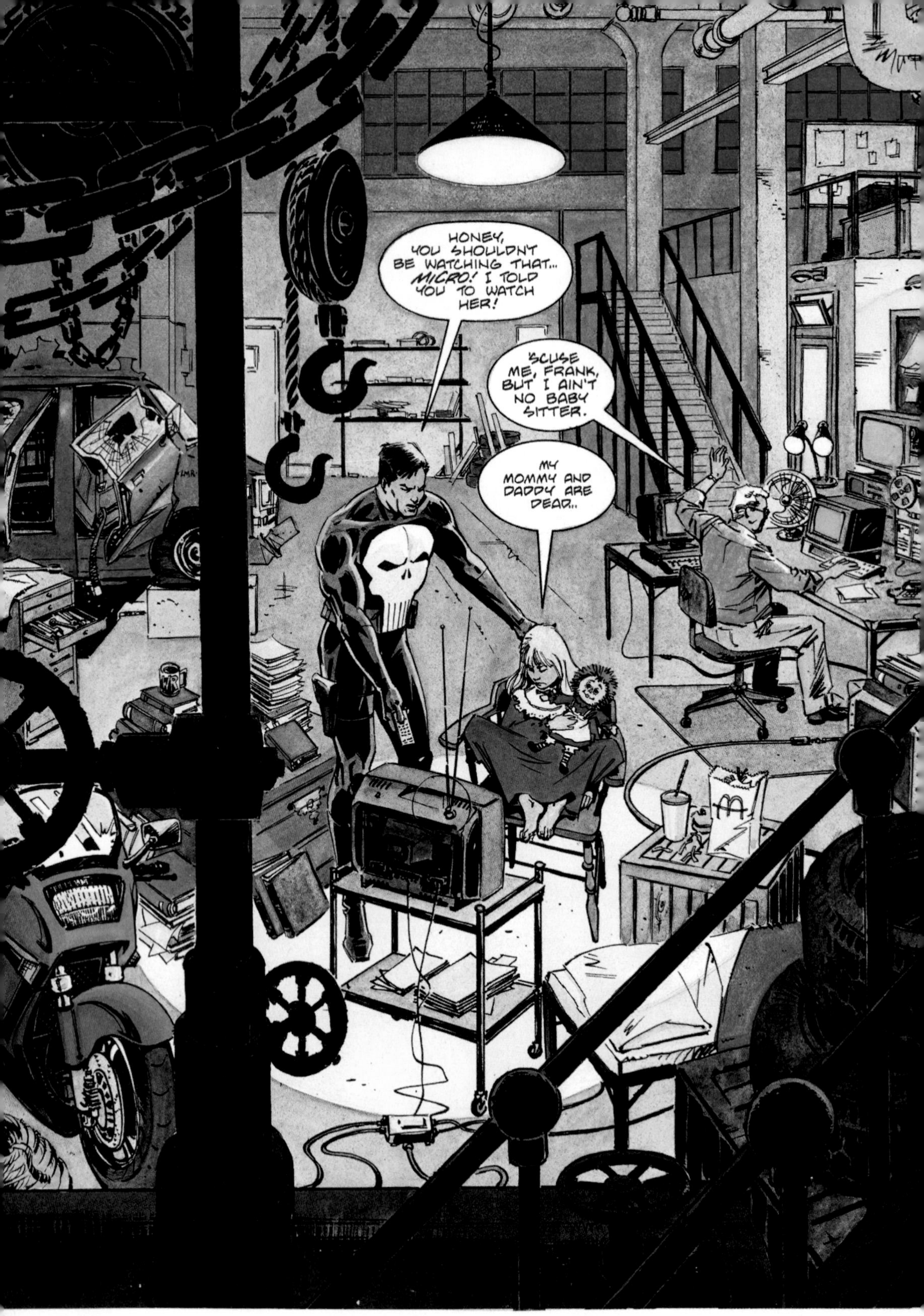
HONEY, YOU SHOULDN'T BE WATCHING THAT... MICRO! I TOLD YOU TO WATCH HER!
'SCUSE ME, FRANK, BUT I AIN'T NO BABY SITTER.
MY MOMMY AND DADDY ARE DEAD...

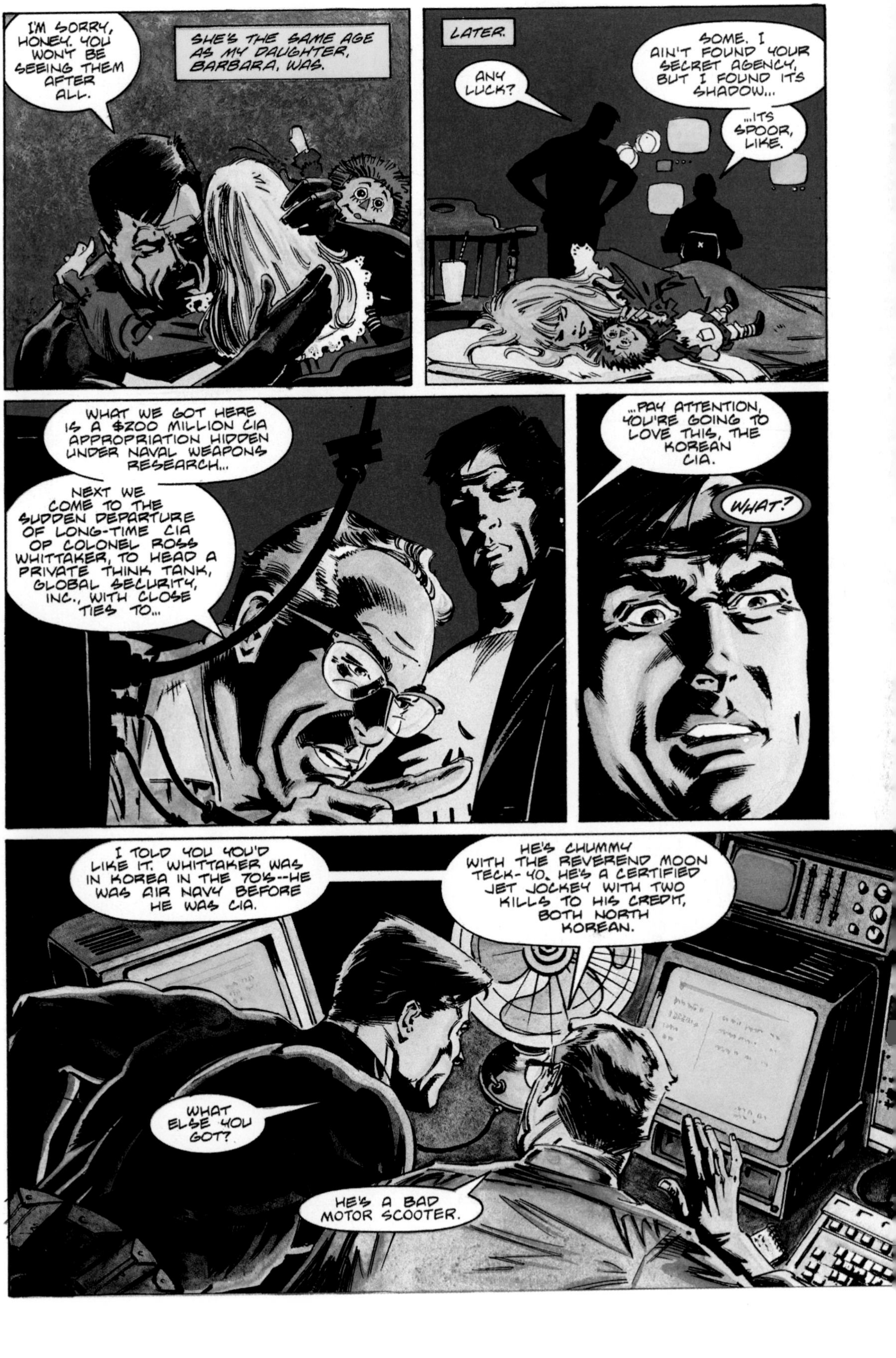
I'M SORRY, HONEY. YOU WON'T BE SEEING THEM AFTER ALL.
SHE'S THE SAME AGE AS MY DAUGHTER, BARBARA, WAS.
LATER.
ANY LUCK?
SOME. I AIN'T FOUND YOUR SECRET AGENCY, BUT I FOUND ITS SHADOW...
...ITS SPOOR, LIKE.
WHAT WE GOT HERE IS A $200 MILLION CIA APPROPRIATION HIDDEN UNDER NAVAL WEAPONS RESEARCH...
NEXT WE COME TO THE SUDDEN DEPARTURE OF LONG-TIME CIA OP COLONEL ROSS WHITTAKER, TO HEAD A PRIVATE THINK TANK, GLOBAL SECURITY, INC., WITH CLOSE TIES TO...
...PAY ATTENTION, YOU'RE GOING TO LOVE THIS, THE KOREAN CIA.
WHAT?
I TOLD YOU YOU'D LIKE IT. WHITTAKER WAS IN KOREA IN THE 70'S--HE WAS AIR NAVY BEFORE HE WAS CIA.
HE'S CHUMMY WITH THE REVEREND MOON TECK-YO. HE'S A CERTIFIED JET JOCKEY WITH TWO KILLS TO HIS CREDIT, BOTH NORTH KOREAN.
WHAT ELSE YOU GOT?
HE'S A BAD MOTOR SCOOTER.

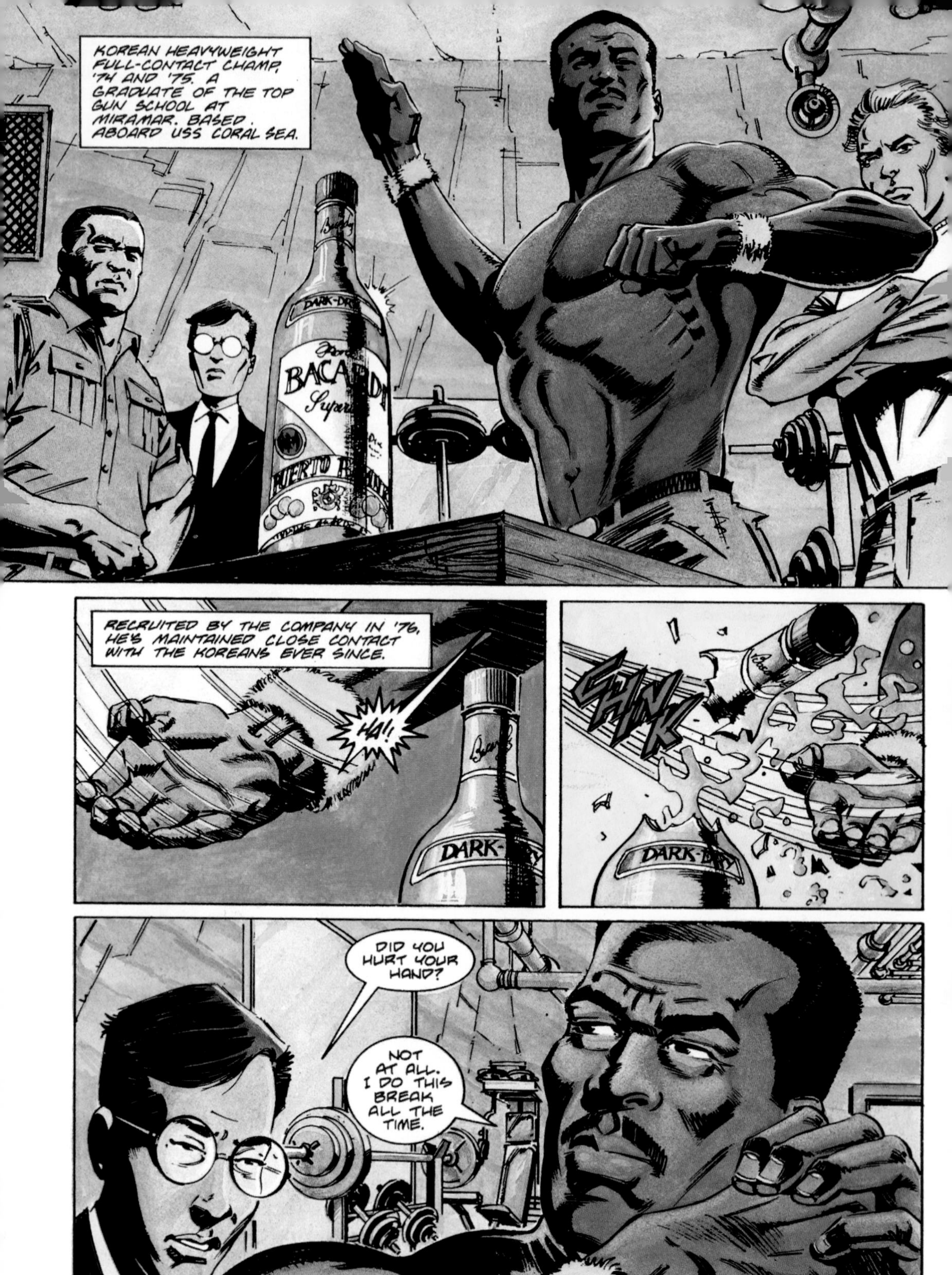
KOREAN HEAVYWEIGHT FULL-CONTACT CHAMP, '74 AND '75. A GRADUATE OF THE TOP GUN SCHOOL AT MIRAMAR. BASED ABOARD USS CORAL SEA.
RECRUITED BY THE COMPANY IN '76, HE'S MAINTAINED CLOSE CONTACT WITH THE KOREANS EVER SINCE.
HA!!
CHNK
DID YOU HURT YOUR HAND?
NOT AT ALL. I DO THIS BREAK ALL THE TIME.

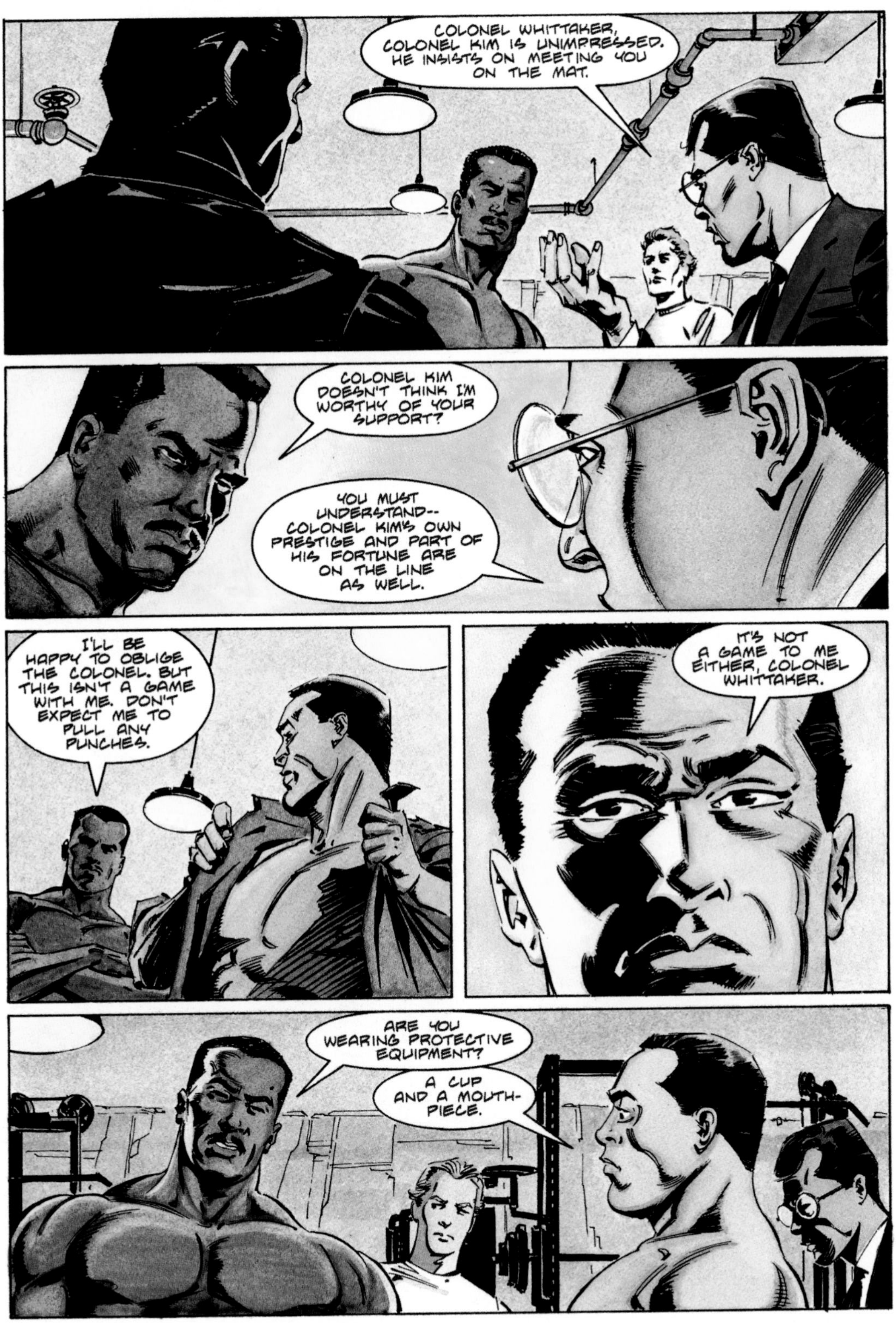
COLONEL WHITTAKER, COLONEL KIM IS UNIMPRESSED. HE INSISTS ON MEETING YOU ON THE MAT.
COLONEL KIM DOESN'T THINK I'M WORTHY OF YOUR SUPPORT?
YOU MUST UNDERSTAND-- COLONEL KIM'S OWN PRESTIGE AND PART OF HIS FORTUNE ARE ON THE LINE AS WELL.
I'LL BE HAPPY TO OBLIGE THE COLONEL. BUT THIS ISN'T A GAME WITH ME. DON'T EXPECT ME TO PULL ANY PUNCHES.
IT'S NOT A GAME TO ME EITHER, COLONEL WHITTAKER.
ARE YOU WEARING PROTECTIVE EQUIPMENT?
A CUP AND A MOUTH-PIECE.

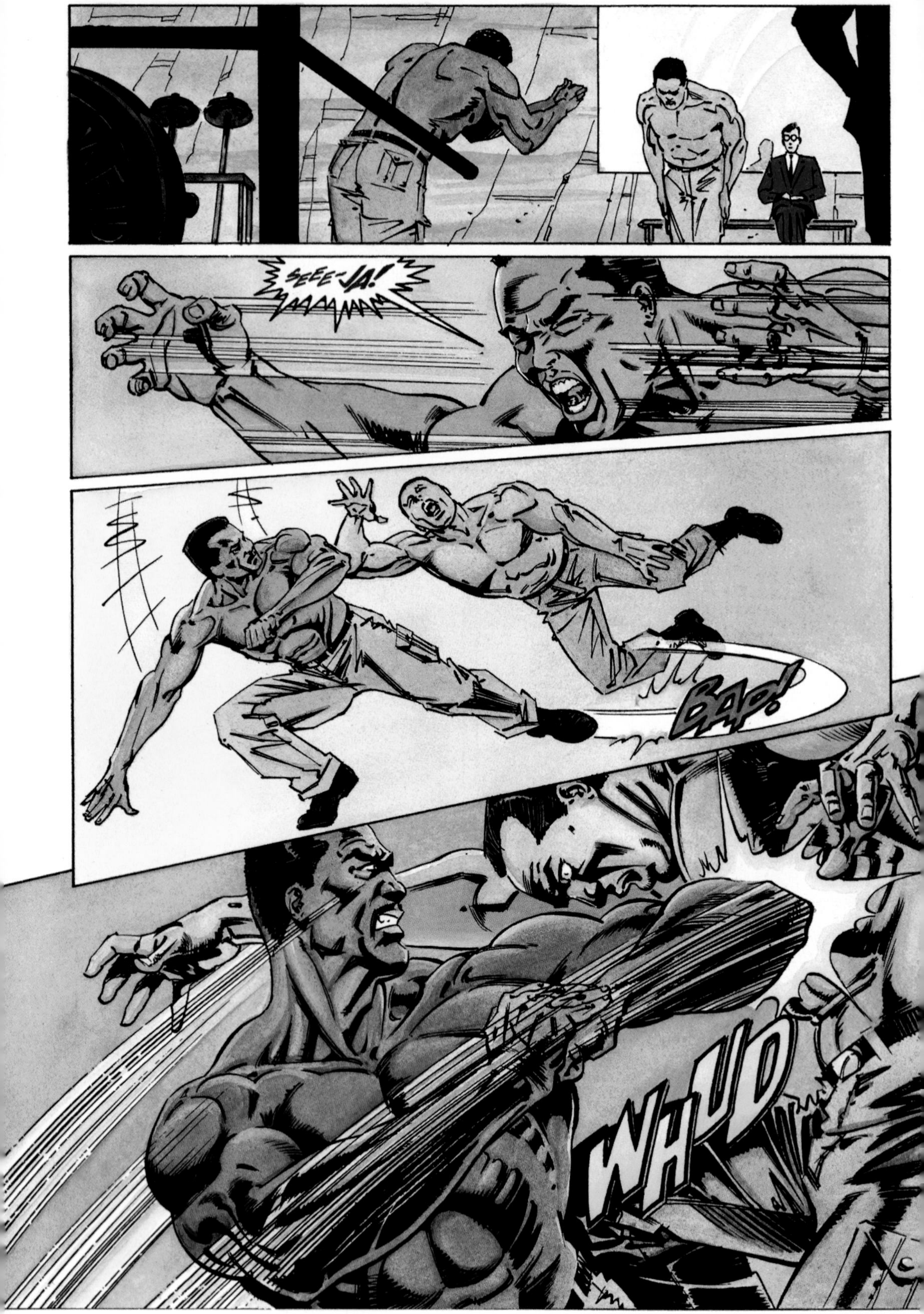
SEEE-JA!
BAP!
WHUD

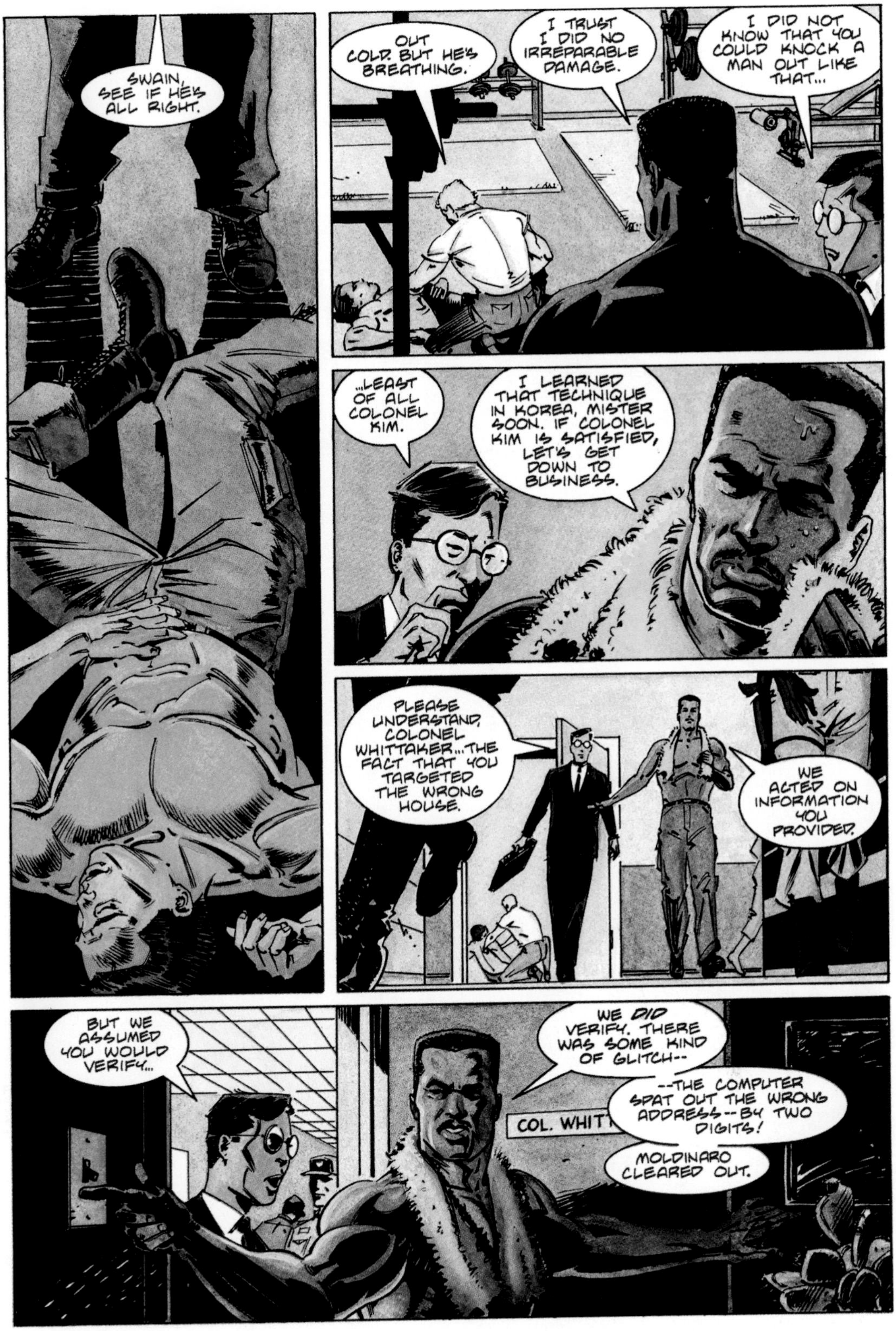
SWAIN, SEE IF HE'S ALL RIGHT.
OUT COLD. BUT HE'S BREATHING.
I TRUST I DID NO IRREPARABLE DAMAGE.
I DID NOT KNOW THAT YOU COULD KNOCK A MAN OUT LIKE THAT...
...LEAST OF ALL COLONEL KIM.
I LEARNED THAT TECHNIQUE IN KOREA, MISTER SOON. IF COLONEL KIM IS SATISFIED, LET'S GET DOWN TO BUSINESS.
PLEASE UNDERSTAND, COLONEL WHITTAKER...THE FACT THAT YOU TARGETED THE WRONG HOUSE.
WE ACTED ON INFORMATION YOU PROVIDED.
BUT WE ASSUMED YOU WOULD VERIFY...
WE *DID* VERIFY. THERE WAS SOME KIND OF GLITCH--
--THE COMPUTER SPAT OUT THE WRONG ADDRESS--BY TWO DIGITS!
MOLDINARO CLEARED OUT.
COL. WHITT

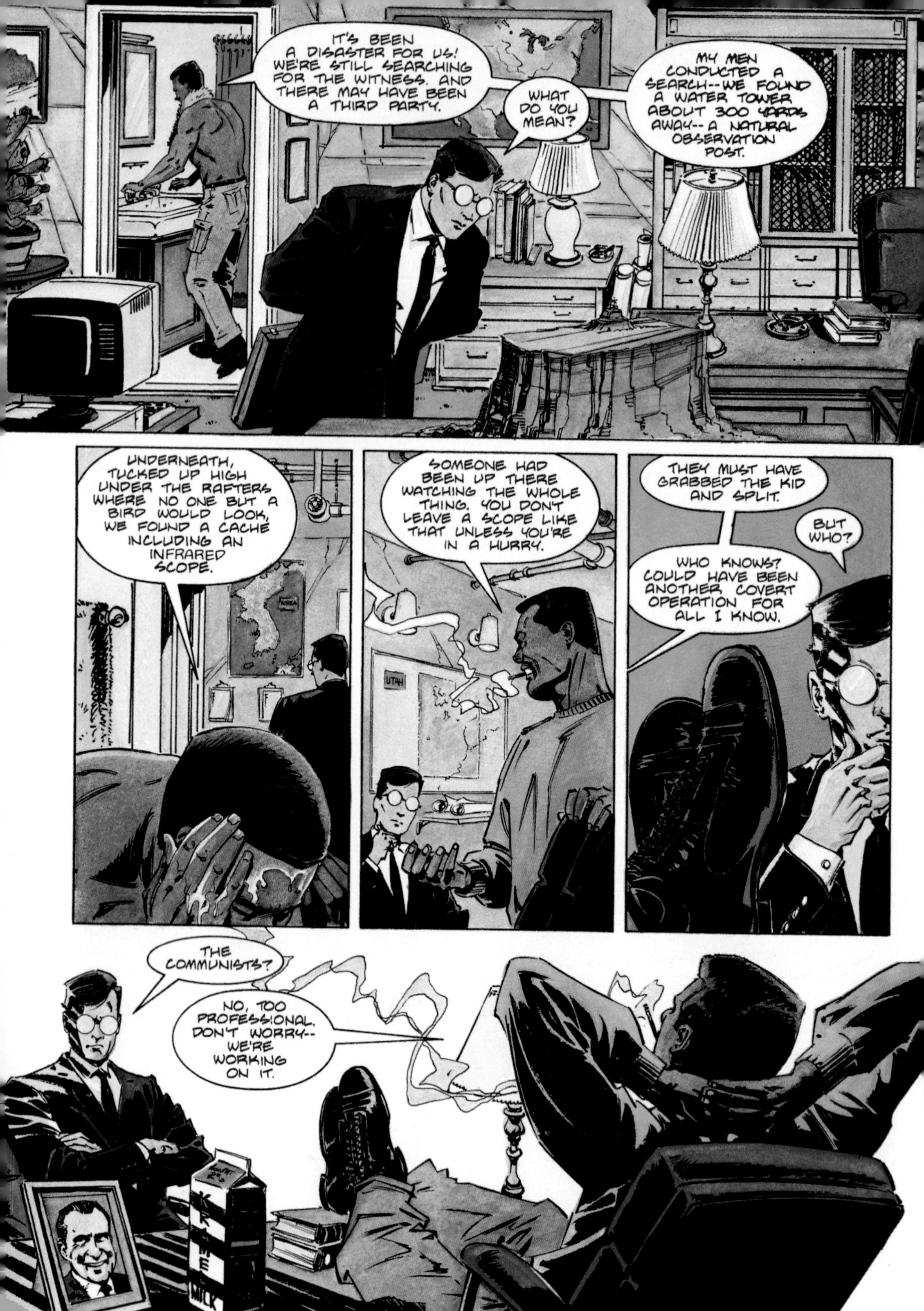
IT'S BEEN A DISASTER FOR US! WE'RE STILL SEARCHING FOR THE WITNESS. AND THERE MAY HAVE BEEN A THIRD PARTY.
WHAT DO YOU MEAN?
MY MEN CONDUCTED A SEARCH--WE FOUND A WATER TOWER ABOUT 300 YARDS AWAY--A NATURAL OBSERVATION POST.
UNDERNEATH, TUCKED UP HIGH UNDER THE RAFTERS WHERE NO ONE BUT A BIRD WOULD LOOK, WE FOUND A CACHE INCLUDING AN INFRARED SCOPE.
SOMEONE HAD BEEN UP THERE WATCHING THE WHOLE THING. YOU DON'T LEAVE A SCOPE LIKE THAT UNLESS YOU'RE IN A HURRY.
UTAH
THEY MUST HAVE GRABBED THE KID AND SPLIT.
BUT WHO?
WHO KNOWS? COULD HAVE BEEN ANOTHER COVERT OPERATION FOR ALL I KNOW.
THE COMMUNISTS?
NO, TOO PROFESSIONAL. DON'T WORRY--WE'RE WORKING ON IT.
MILK

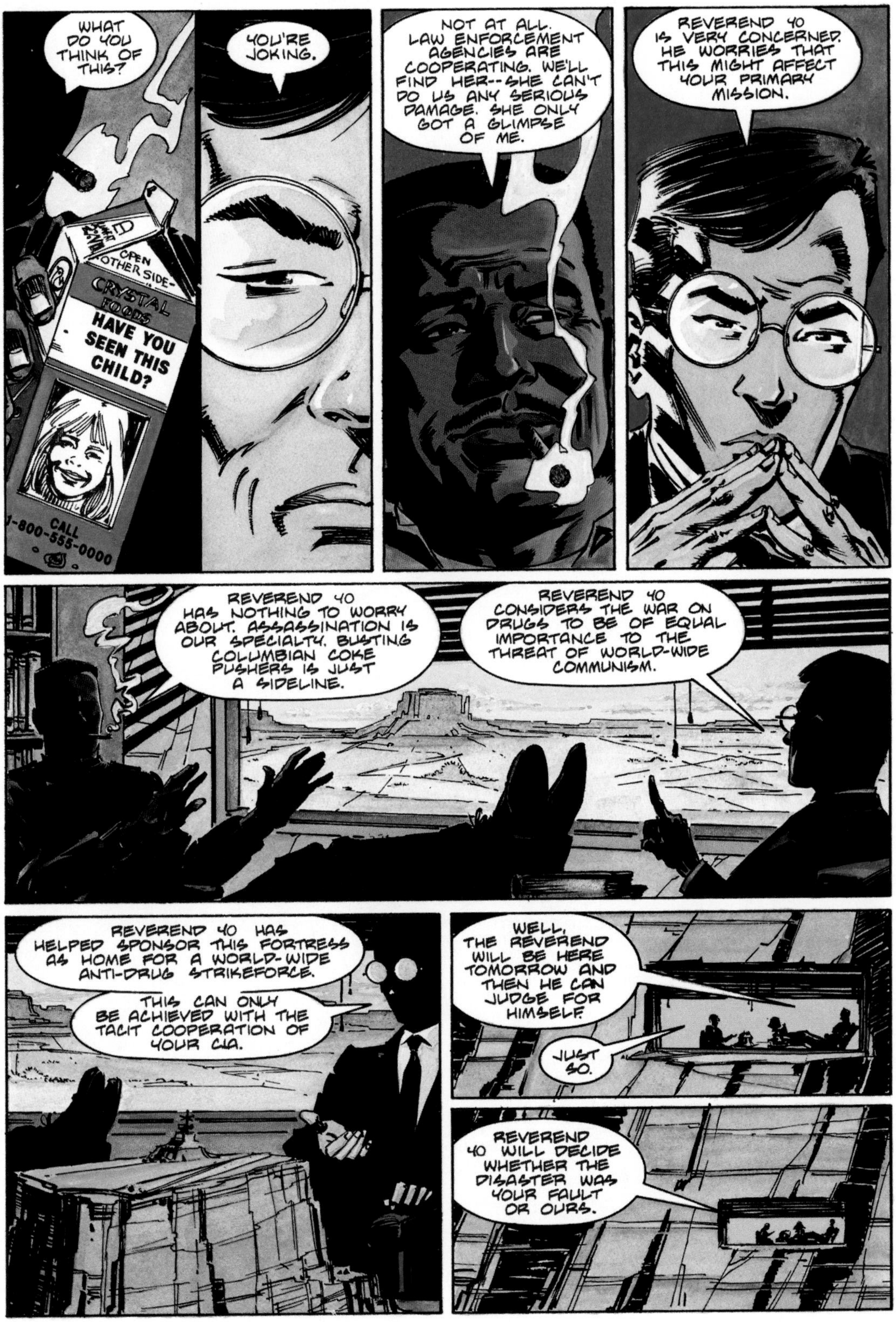
WHAT DO YOU THINK OF THIS?
OPEN OTHER SIDE
CRYSTAL FOODS
HAVE YOU SEEN THIS CHILD?
CALL 1-800-555-0000
YOU'RE JOKING.
NOT AT ALL. LAW ENFORCEMENT AGENCIES ARE COOPERATING. WE'LL FIND HER--SHE CAN'T DO US ANY SERIOUS DAMAGE. SHE ONLY GOT A GLIMPSE OF ME.
REVEREND YO IS VERY CONCERNED. HE WORRIES THAT THIS MIGHT AFFECT YOUR PRIMARY MISSION.
REVEREND YO HAS NOTHING TO WORRY ABOUT. ASSASSINATION IS OUR SPECIALTY. BUSTING COLUMBIAN COKE PUSHERS IS JUST A SIDELINE.
REVEREND YO CONSIDERS THE WAR ON DRUGS TO BE OF EQUAL IMPORTANCE TO THE THREAT OF WORLD-WIDE COMMUNISM.
REVEREND YO HAS HELPED SPONSOR THIS FORTRESS AS HOME FOR A WORLD-WIDE ANTI-DRUG STRIKEFORCE.
THIS CAN ONLY BE ACHIEVED WITH THE TACIT COOPERATION OF YOUR CIA.
WELL, THE REVEREND WILL BE HERE TOMORROW AND THEN HE CAN JUDGE FOR HIMSELF.
JUST SO.
REVEREND YO WILL DECIDE WHETHER THE DISASTER WAS YOUR FAULT OR OURS.

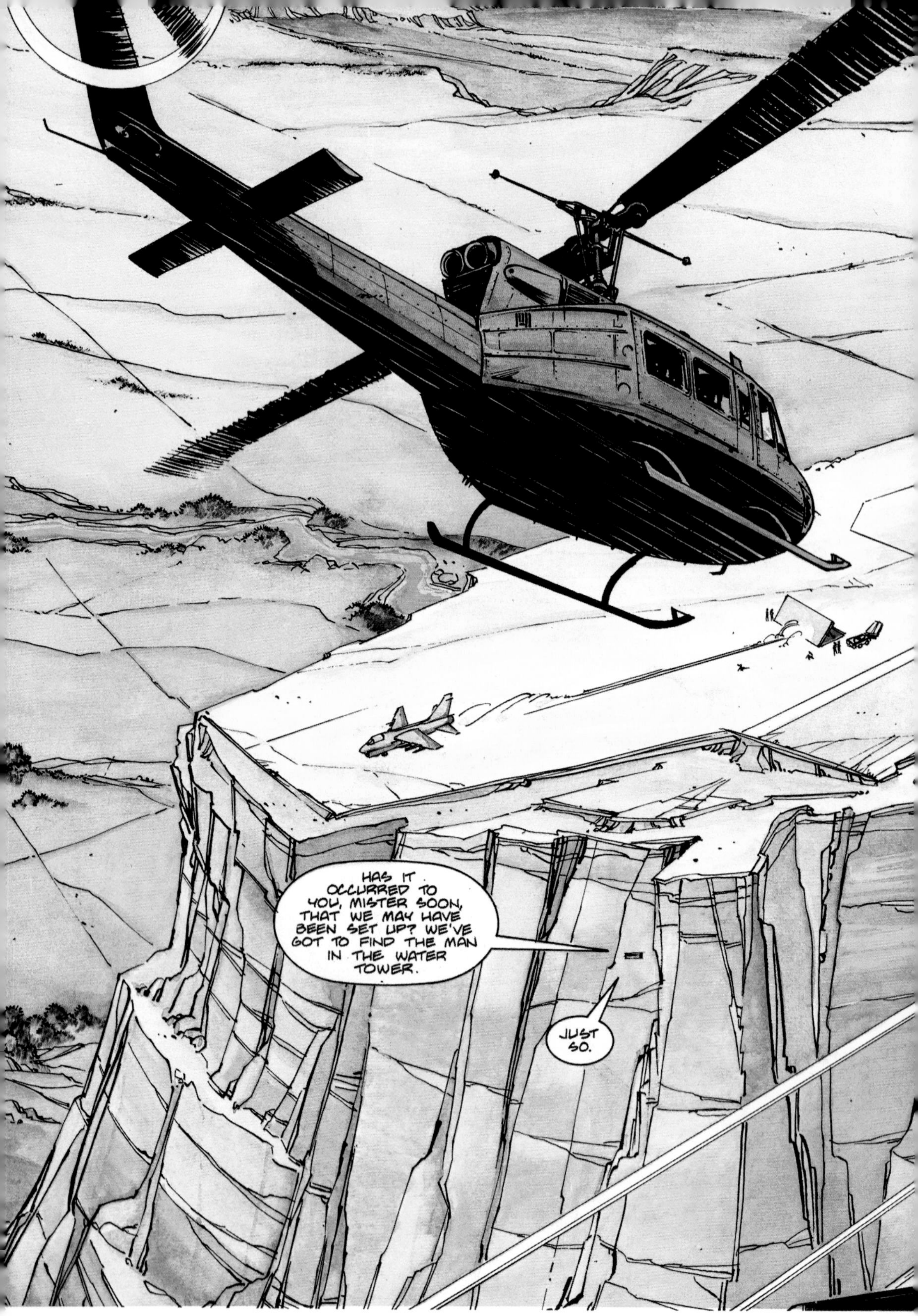
HAS IT OCCURRED TO YOU, MISTER SOON, THAT WE MAY HAVE BEEN SET UP? WE'VE GOT TO FIND THE MAN IN THE WATER TOWER.
JUST SO.

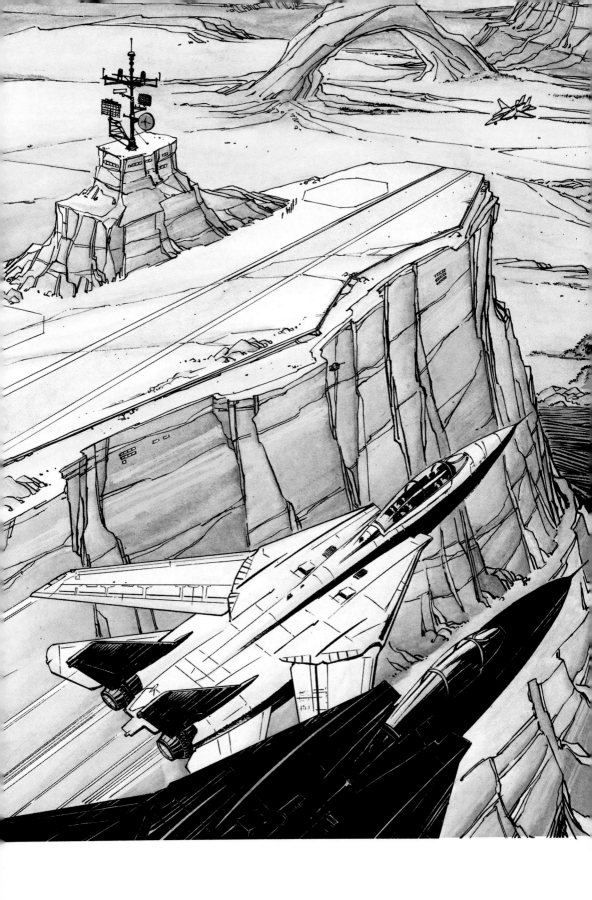

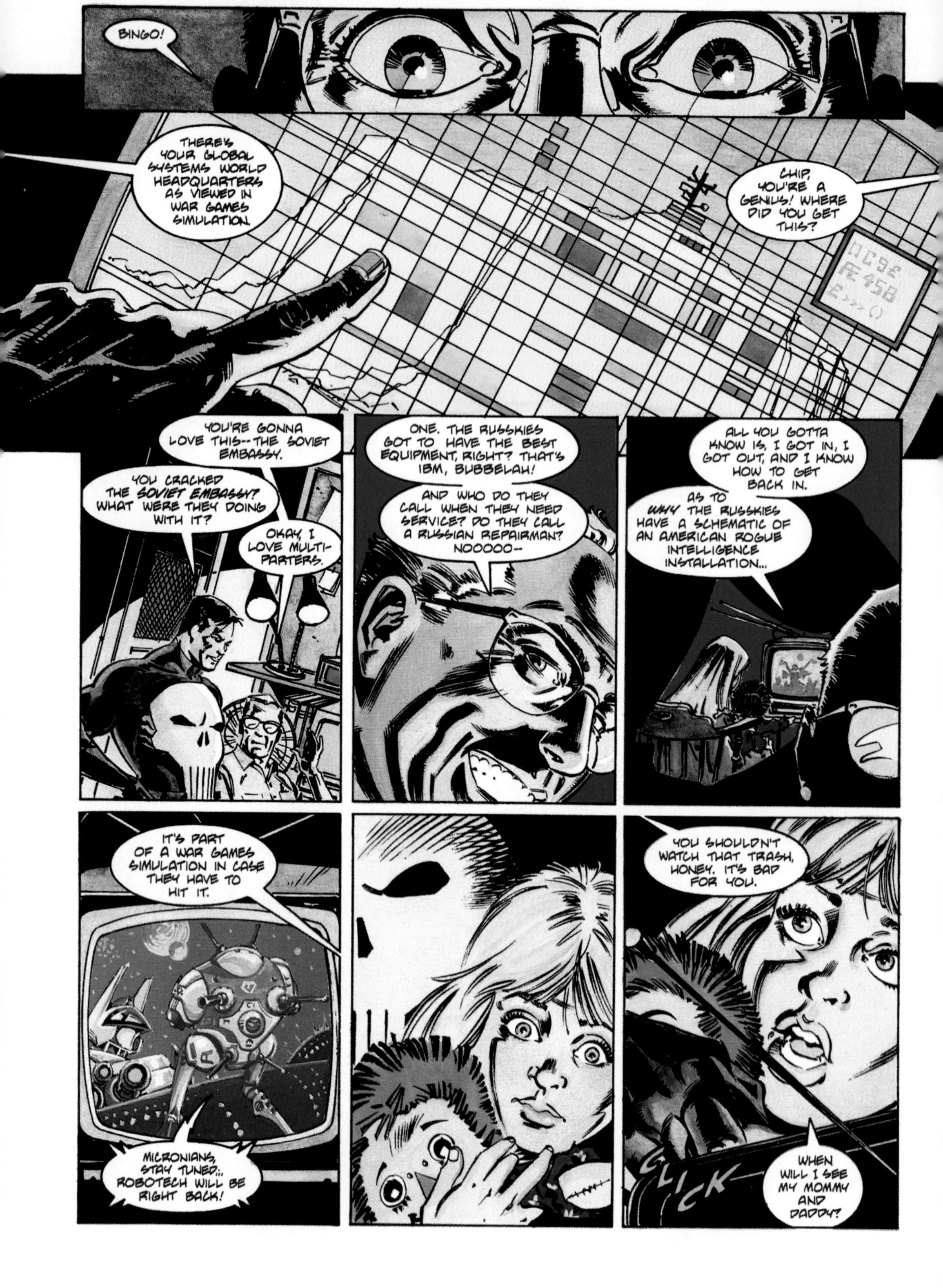
BINGO!
THERE'S YOUR GLOBAL SYSTEMS WORLD HEADQUARTERS AS VIEWED IN WAR GAMES SIMULATION.
CHIP, YOU'RE A GENIUS! WHERE DID YOU GET THIS?
YOU'RE GONNA LOVE THIS--THE SOVIET EMBASSY.
YOU CRACKED THE SOVIET EMBASSY? WHAT WERE THEY DOING WITH IT?
OKAY, I LOVE MULTI-PARTERS.
ONE. THE RUSSKIES GOT TO HAVE THE BEST EQUIPMENT, RIGHT? THAT'S IBM, BUBBELAH!
AND WHO DO THEY CALL WHEN THEY NEED SERVICE? DO THEY CALL A RUSSIAN REPAIRMAN? NOOOOO--
ALL YOU GOTTA KNOW IS, I GOT IN, I GOT OUT, AND I KNOW HOW TO GET BACK IN.
AS TO WHY THE RUSSKIES HAVE A SCHEMATIC OF AN AMERICAN ROGUE INTELLIGENCE INSTALLATION...
IT'S PART OF A WAR GAMES SIMULATION IN CASE THEY HAVE TO HIT IT.
MICRONIANS, STAY TUNED... ROBOTECH WILL BE RIGHT BACK!
YOU SHOULDN'T WATCH THAT TRASH, HONEY. IT'S BAD FOR YOU.
CLICK
WHEN WILL I SEE MY MOMMY AND DADDY?

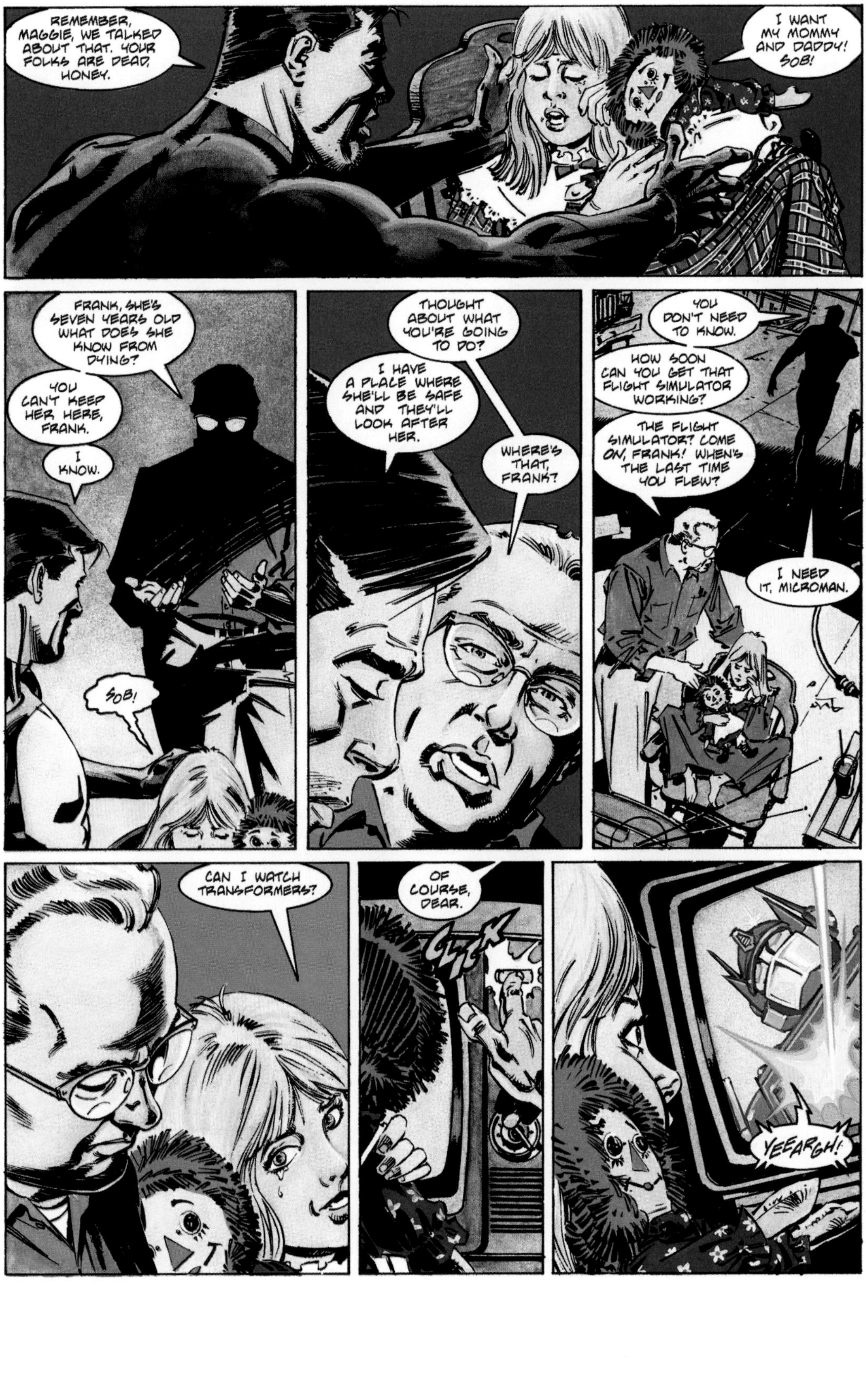

REMEMBER, MAGGIE, WE TALKED ABOUT THAT. YOUR FOLKS ARE DEAD, HONEY.
I WANT MY MOMMY AND DADDY! SOB!
FRANK, SHE'S SEVEN YEARS OLD WHAT DOES SHE KNOW FROM DYING?
YOU CAN'T KEEP HER HERE, FRANK.
I KNOW.
SOB!
THOUGHT ABOUT WHAT YOU'RE GOING TO DO?
I HAVE A PLACE WHERE SHE'LL BE SAFE AND THEY'LL LOOK AFTER HER.
WHERE'S THAT, FRANK?
YOU DON'T NEED TO KNOW.
HOW SOON CAN YOU GET THAT FLIGHT SIMULATOR WORKING?
THE FLIGHT SIMULATOR? COME ON, FRANK! WHEN'S THE LAST TIME YOU FLEW?
I NEED IT, MICROMAN.
CAN I WATCH TRANSFORMERS?
OF COURSE, DEAR.
CLICK
YEEARGH!

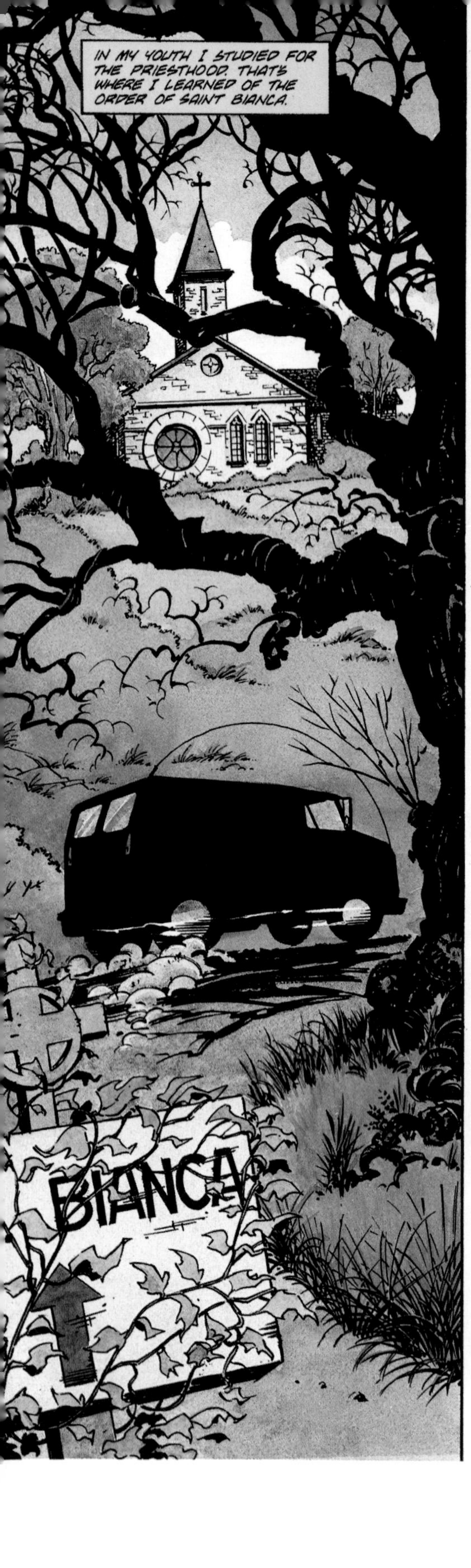
IN MY YOUTH I STUDIED FOR THE PRIESTHOOD. THAT'S WHERE I LEARNED OF THE ORDER OF SAINT BIANCA.
BIANCA

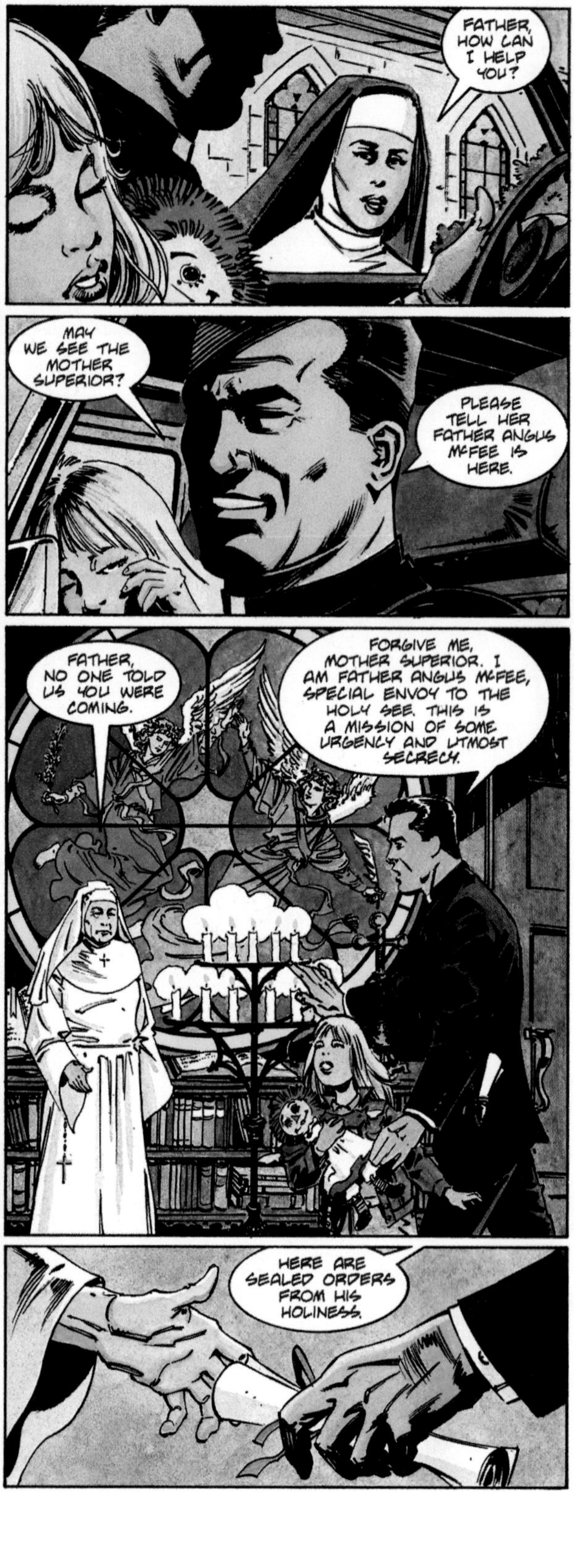
FATHER, HOW CAN I HELP YOU?
MAY WE SEE THE MOTHER SUPERIOR?
PLEASE TELL HER FATHER ANGUS McFEE IS HERE.
FATHER, NO ONE TOLD US YOU WERE COMING.
FORGIVE ME, MOTHER SUPERIOR. I AM FATHER ANGUS McFEE, SPECIAL ENVOY TO THE HOLY SEE. THIS IS A MISSION OF SOME URGENCY AND UTMOST SECRECY.
HERE ARE SEALED ORDERS FROM HIS HOLINESS.

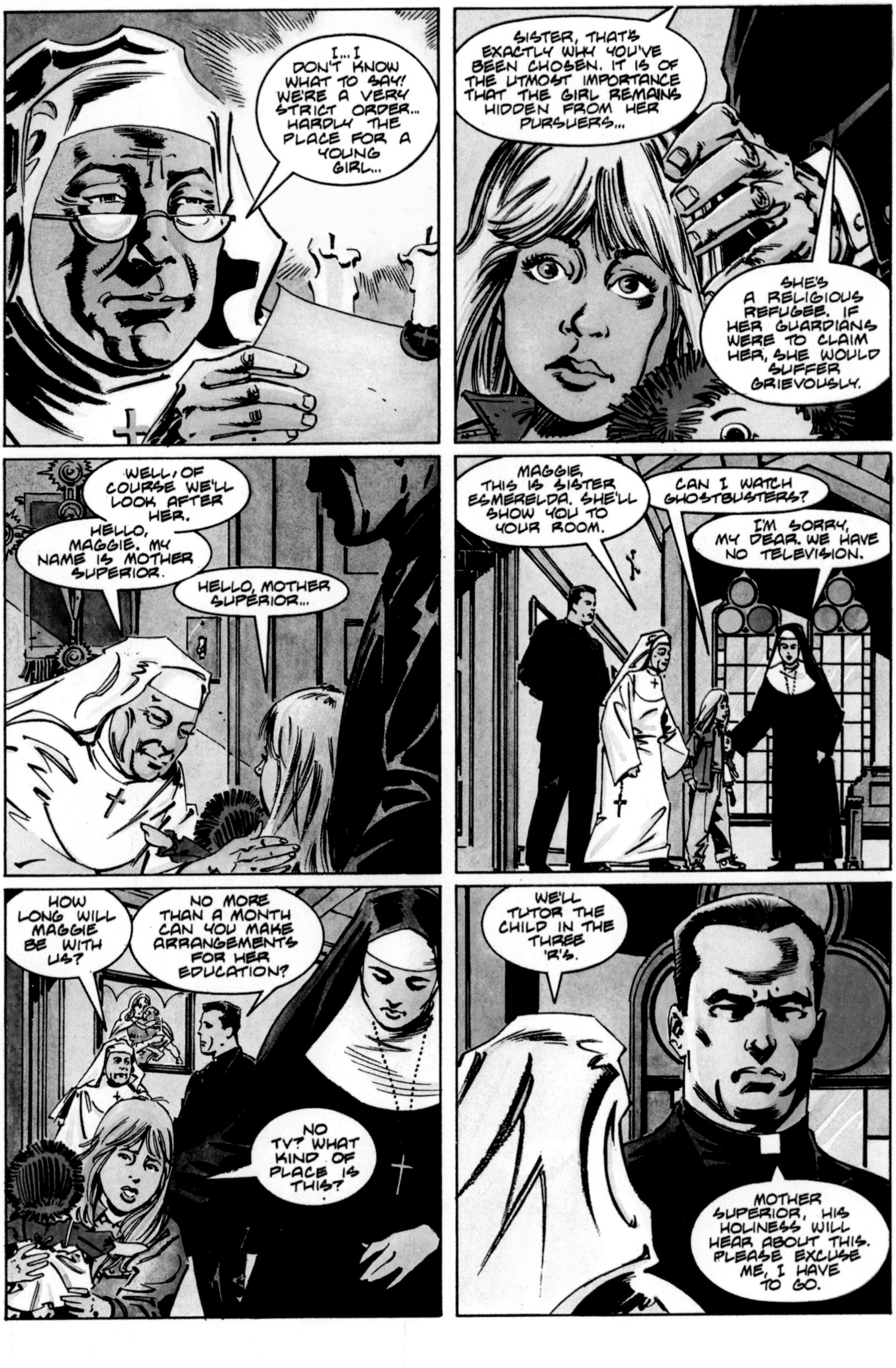
I... I DON'T KNOW WHAT TO SAY! WE'RE A VERY STRICT ORDER... HARDLY THE PLACE FOR A YOUNG GIRL...
SISTER, THAT'S EXACTLY WHY YOU'VE BEEN CHOSEN. IT IS OF THE UTMOST IMPORTANCE THAT THE GIRL REMAINS HIDDEN FROM HER PURSUERS...
SHE'S A RELIGIOUS REFUGEE. IF HER GUARDIANS WERE TO CLAIM HER, SHE WOULD SUFFER GRIEVOUSLY.
WELL, OF COURSE WE'LL LOOK AFTER HER.
HELLO, MAGGIE. MY NAME IS MOTHER SUPERIOR.
HELLO, MOTHER SUPERIOR...
MAGGIE, THIS IS SISTER ESMERELDA. SHE'LL SHOW YOU TO YOUR ROOM.
CAN I WATCH GHOSTBUSTERS?
I'M SORRY, MY DEAR. WE HAVE NO TELEVISION.
HOW LONG WILL MAGGIE BE WITH US?
NO MORE THAN A MONTH CAN YOU MAKE ARRANGEMENTS FOR HER EDUCATION?
NO TV? WHAT KIND OF PLACE IS THIS?
WE'LL TUTOR THE CHILD IN THE THREE 'R'S.
MOTHER SUPERIOR, HIS HOLINESS WILL HEAR ABOUT THIS. PLEASE EXCUSE ME, I HAVE TO GO.

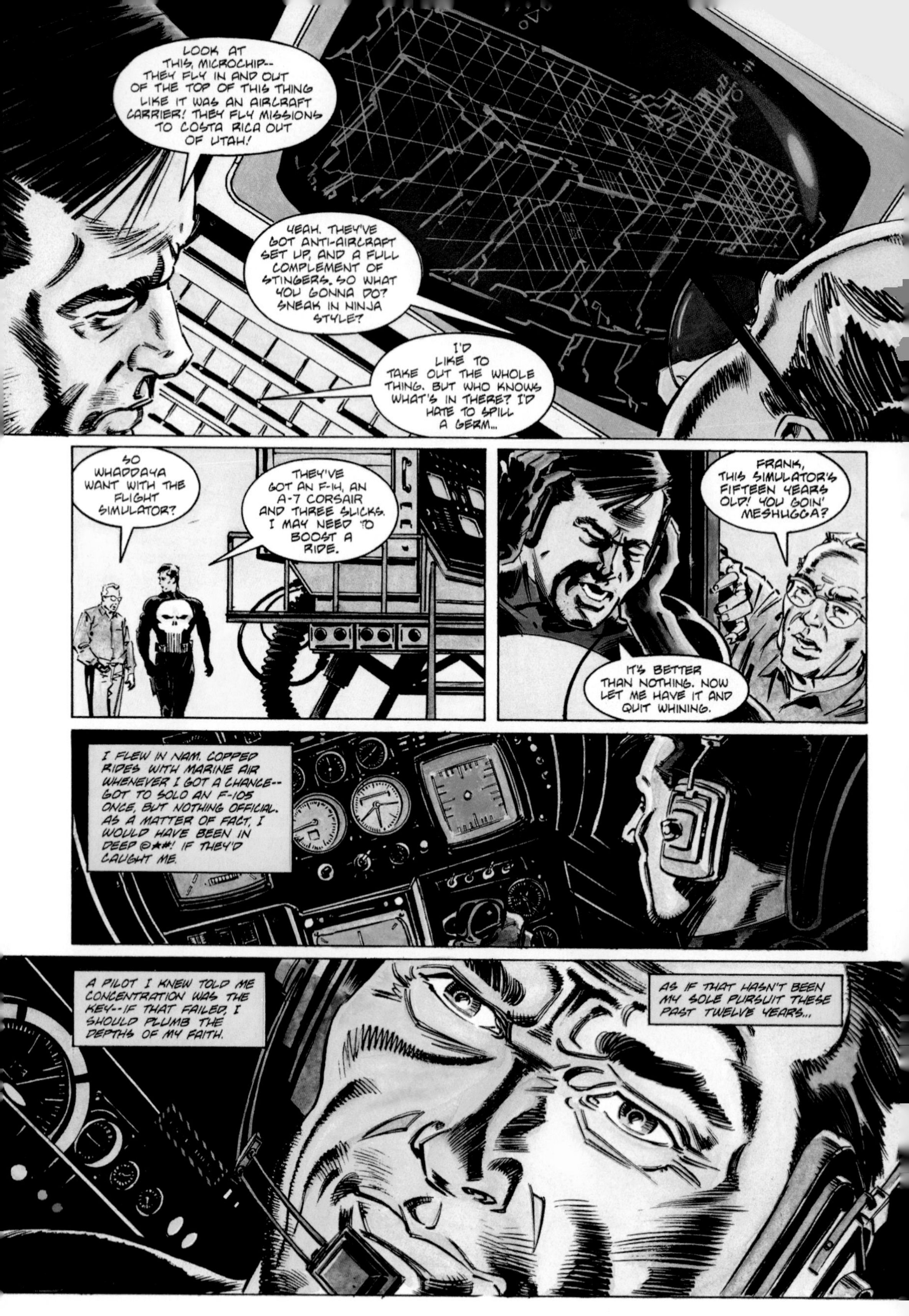
LOOK AT THIS, MICROCHIP-- THEY FLY IN AND OUT OF THE TOP OF THIS THING LIKE IT WAS AN AIRCRAFT CARRIER! THEY FLY MISSIONS TO COSTA RICA OUT OF UTAH!
YEAH. THEY'VE GOT ANTI-AIRCRAFT SET UP, AND A FULL COMPLEMENT OF STINGERS. SO WHAT YOU GONNA DO? SNEAK IN NINJA STYLE?
I'D LIKE TO TAKE OUT THE WHOLE THING. BUT WHO KNOWS WHAT'S IN THERE? I'D HATE TO SPILL A GERM...
SO WHADDAYA WANT WITH THE FLIGHT SIMULATOR?
THEY'VE GOT AN F-14, AN A-7 CORSAIR AND THREE SLICKS. I MAY NEED TO BOOST A RIDE.
FRANK, THIS SIMULATOR'S FIFTEEN YEARS OLD! YOU GOIN' MESHUGGA?
IT'S BETTER THAN NOTHING. NOW LET ME HAVE IT AND QUIT WHINING.
I FLEW IN NAM. COPPED RIDES WITH MARINE AIR WHENEVER I GOT A CHANCE-- GOT TO SOLO AN F-105 ONCE, BUT NOTHING OFFICIAL. AS A MATTER OF FACT, I WOULD HAVE BEEN IN DEEP ©★#! IF THEY'D CAUGHT ME.
A PILOT I KNEW TOLD ME CONCENTRATION WAS THE KEY--IF THAT FAILED, I SHOULD PLUMB THE DEPTHS OF MY FAITH.
AS IF THAT HASN'T BEEN MY SOLE PURSUIT THESE PAST TWELVE YEARS...

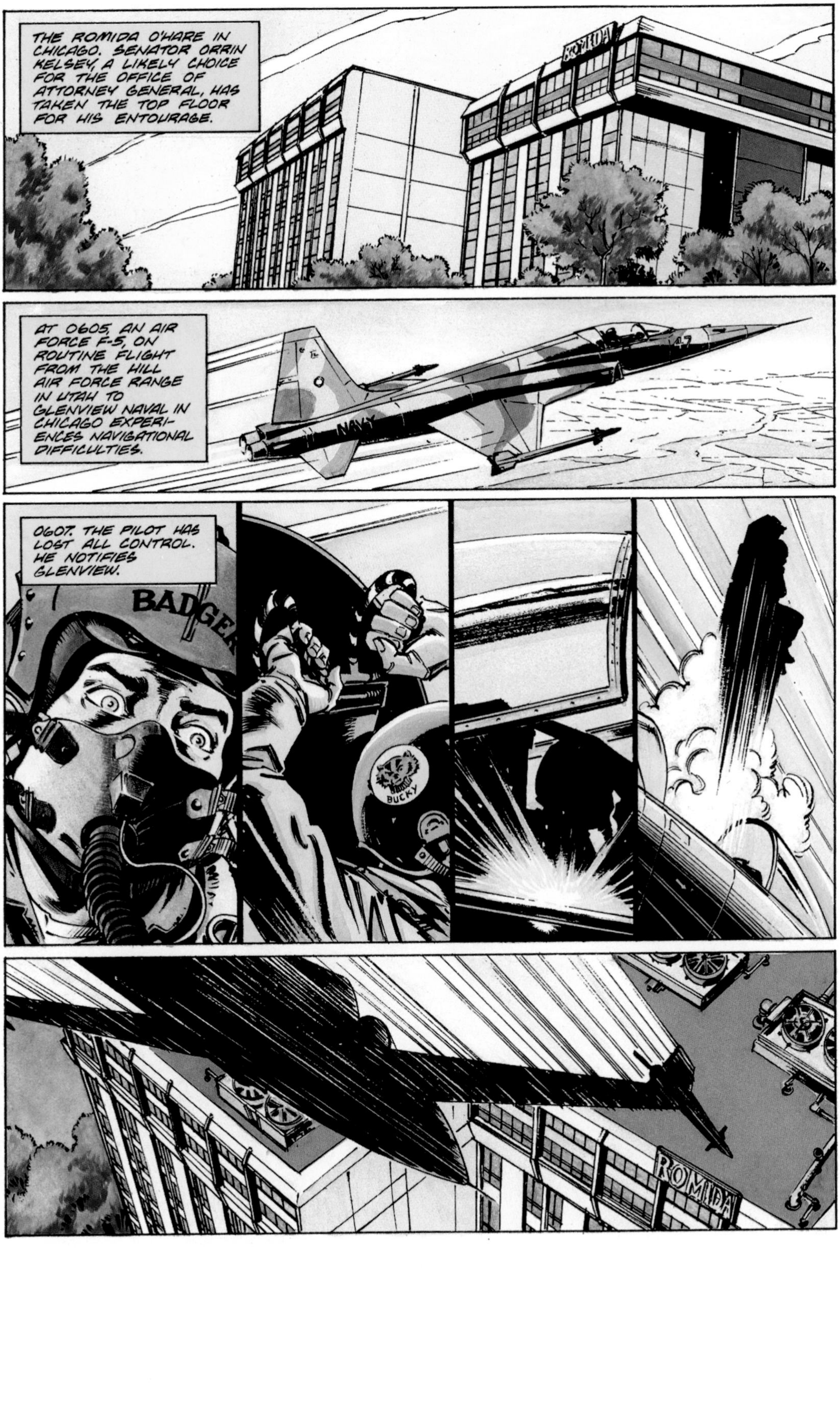
THE ROMIDA O'HARE IN CHICAGO. SENATOR ORRIN KELSEY, A LIKELY CHOICE FOR THE OFFICE OF ATTORNEY GENERAL, HAS TAKEN THE TOP FLOOR FOR HIS ENTOURAGE.
AT 0605, AN AIR FORCE F-5, ON ROUTINE FLIGHT FROM THE HILL AIR FORCE RANGE IN UTAH TO GLENVIEW NAVAL IN CHICAGO EXPERIENCES NAVIGATIONAL DIFFICULTIES.
NAVY
47
0607. THE PILOT HAS LOST ALL CONTROL. HE NOTIFIES GLENVIEW.
BADGER
BUCKY
ROMIDA

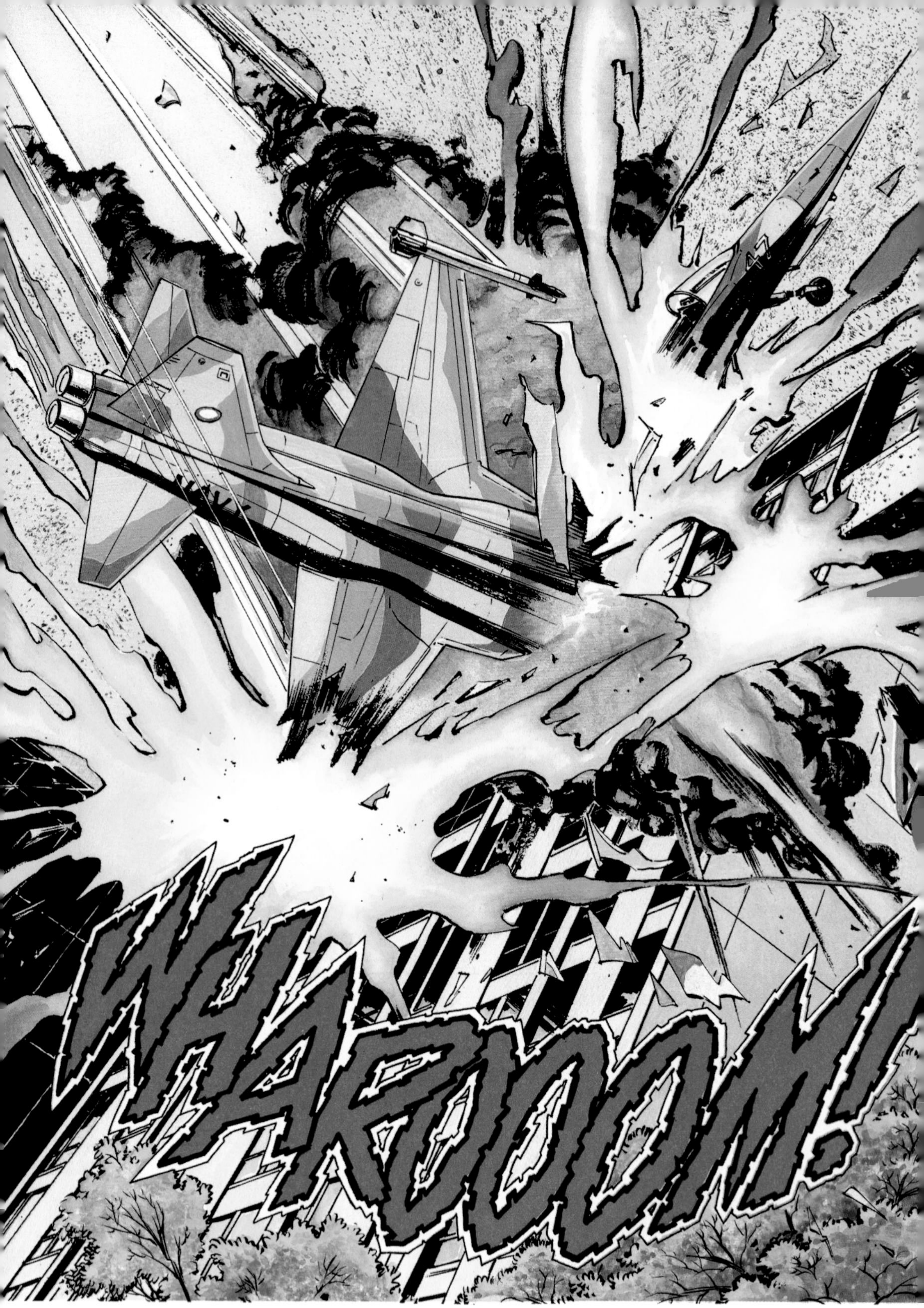
WHABOOM!

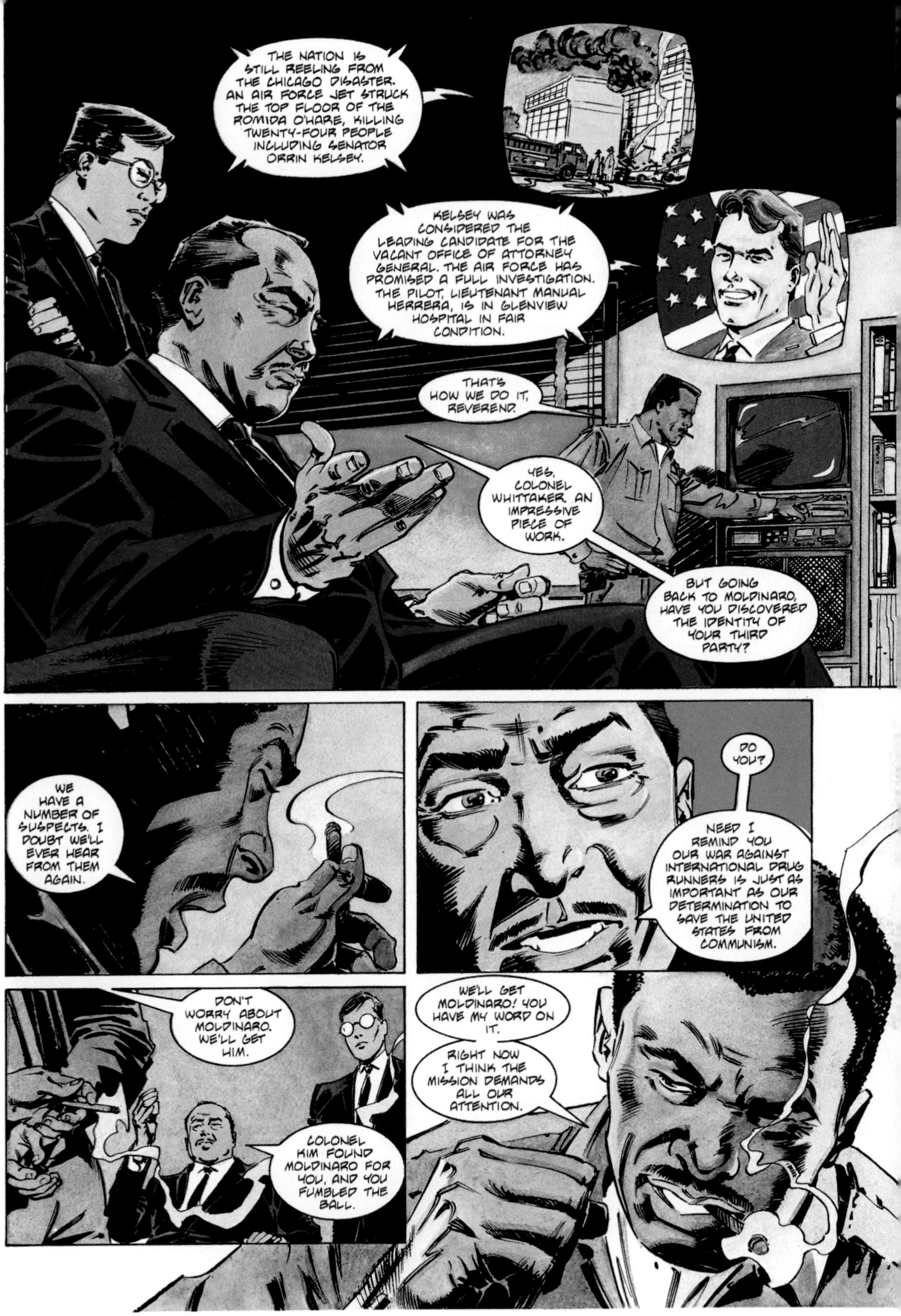

THE NATION IS STILL REELING FROM THE CHICAGO DISASTER. AN AIR FORCE JET STRUCK THE TOP FLOOR OF THE ROMIDA O'HARE, KILLING TWENTY-FOUR PEOPLE INCLUDING SENATOR ORRIN KELSEY.
KELSEY WAS CONSIDERED THE LEADING CANDIDATE FOR THE VACANT OFFICE OF ATTORNEY GENERAL. THE AIR FORCE HAS PROMISED A FULL INVESTIGATION. THE PILOT, LIEUTENANT MANUAL HERRERA, IS IN GLENVIEW HOSPITAL IN FAIR CONDITION.
THAT'S HOW WE DO IT, REVEREND.
YES, COLONEL WHITTAKER. AN IMPRESSIVE PIECE OF WORK.
BUT GOING BACK TO MOLDINARO, HAVE YOU DISCOVERED THE IDENTITY OF YOUR THIRD PARTY?
WE HAVE A NUMBER OF SUSPECTS. I DOUBT WE'LL EVER HEAR FROM THEM AGAIN.
DO YOU?
NEED I REMIND YOU OUR WAR AGAINST INTERNATIONAL DRUG RUNNERS IS JUST AS IMPORTANT AS OUR DETERMINATION TO SAVE THE UNITED STATES FROM COMMUNISM.
DON'T WORRY ABOUT MOLDINARO. WE'LL GET HIM.
COLONEL KIM FOUND MOLDINARO FOR YOU, AND YOU FUMBLED THE BALL.
WE'LL GET MOLDINARO! YOU HAVE MY WORD ON IT.
RIGHT NOW I THINK THE MISSION DEMANDS ALL OUR ATTENTION.

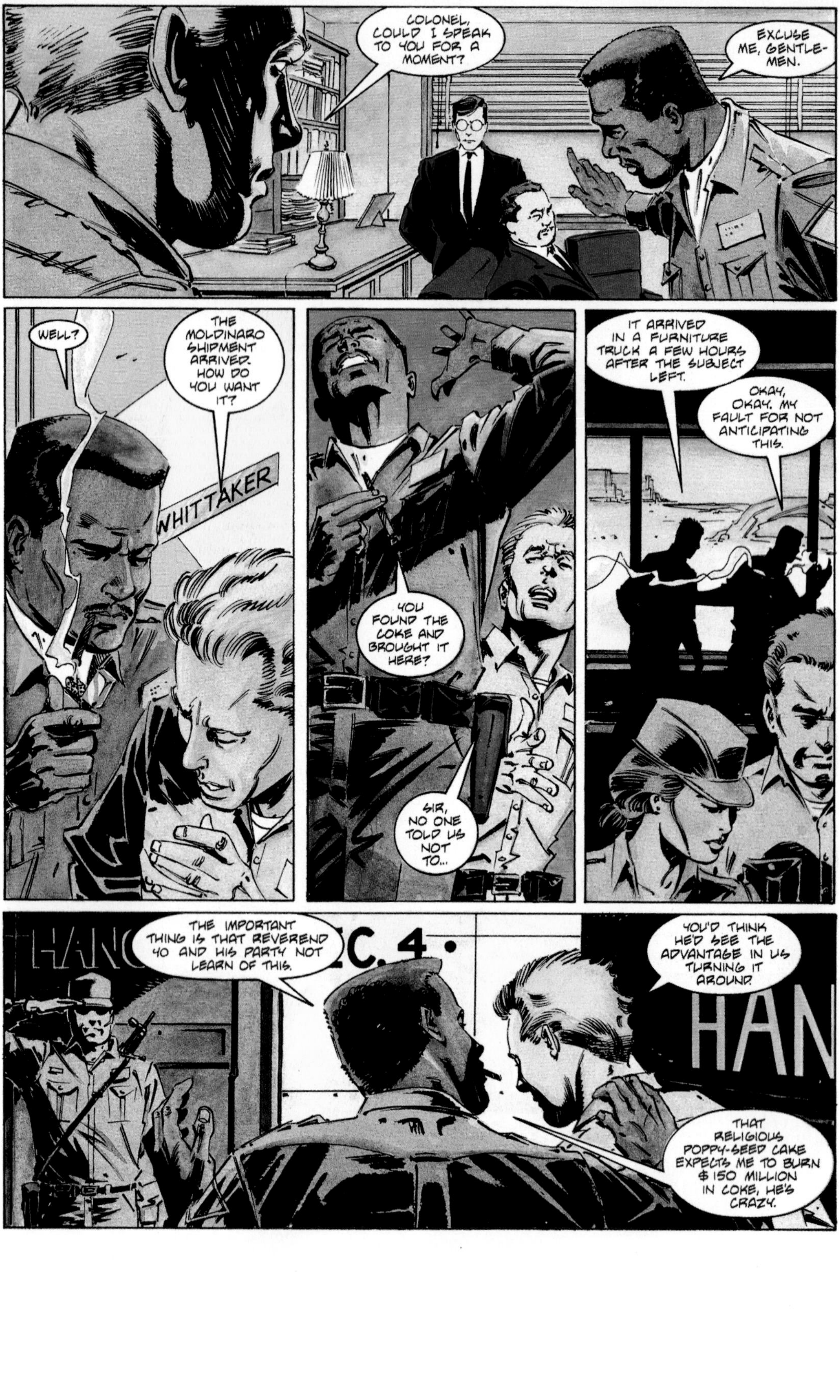
COLONEL, COULD I SPEAK TO YOU FOR A MOMENT?
EXCUSE ME, GENTLE-MEN.
WELL?
THE MOLDINARO SHIPMENT ARRIVED. HOW DO YOU WANT IT?
WHITTAKER
YOU FOUND THE COKE AND BROUGHT IT HERE?
SIR, NO ONE TOLD US NOT TO...
IT ARRIVED IN A FURNITURE TRUCK A FEW HOURS AFTER THE SUBJECT LEFT.
OKAY, OKAY. MY FAULT FOR NOT ANTICIPATING THIS.
THE IMPORTANT THING IS THAT REVEREND YO AND HIS PARTY NOT LEARN OF THIS.
YOU'D THINK HE'D SEE THE ADVANTAGE IN US TURNING IT AROUND.
THAT RELIGIOUS POPPY-SEED CAKE EXPECTS ME TO BURN $ 150 MILLION IN COKE, HE'S CRAZY.
HAN

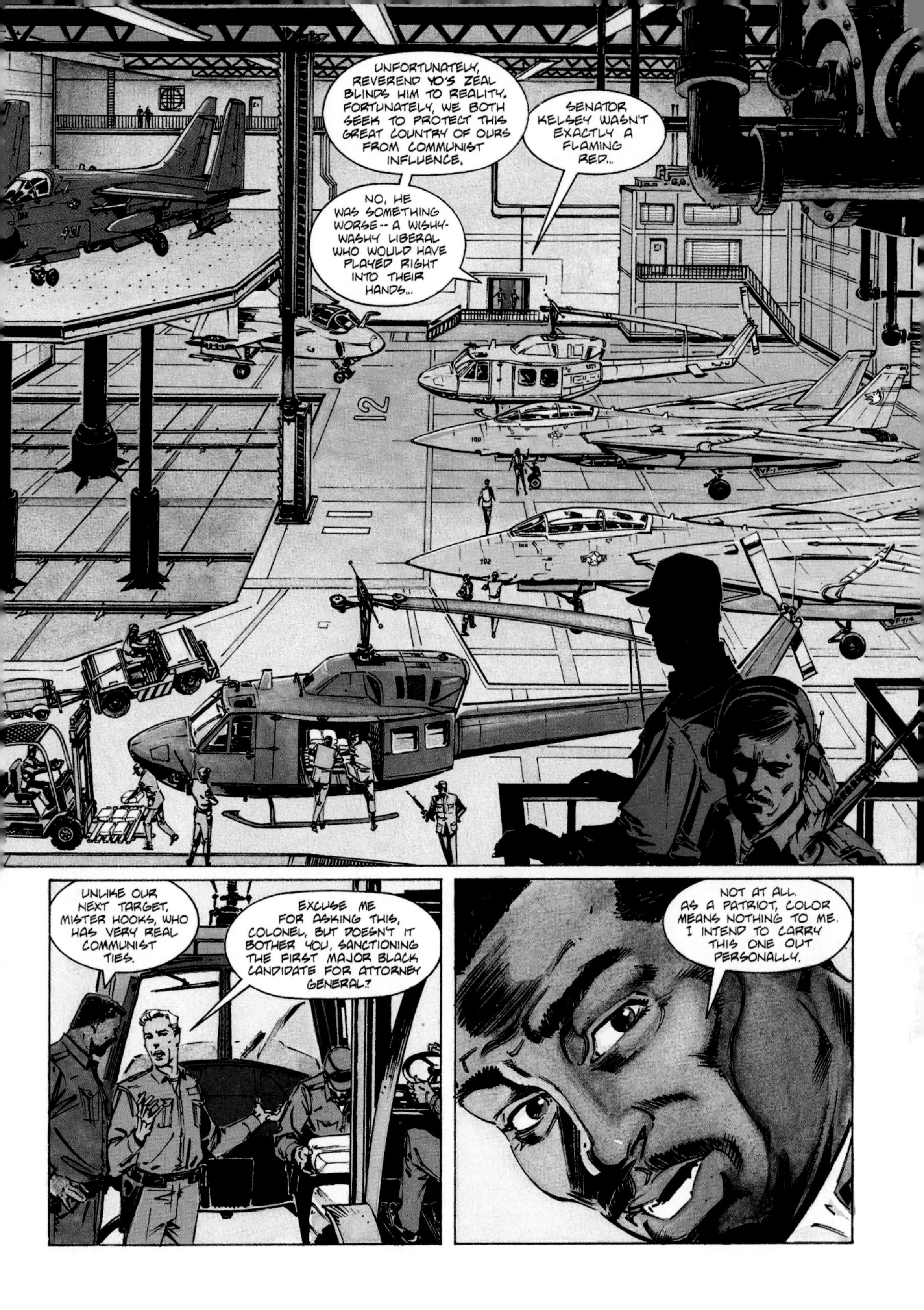
UNFORTUNATELY, REVEREND YO'S ZEAL BLINDS HIM TO REALITY. FORTUNATELY, WE BOTH SEEK TO PROTECT THIS GREAT COUNTRY OF OURS FROM COMMUNIST INFLUENCE.
SENATOR KELSEY WASN'T EXACTLY A FLAMING RED...
NO, HE WAS SOMETHING WORSE-- A WISHY-WASHY LIBERAL WHO WOULD HAVE PLAYED RIGHT INTO THEIR HANDS...
UNLIKE OUR NEXT TARGET, MISTER HOOKS, WHO HAS VERY REAL COMMUNIST TIES.
EXCUSE ME FOR ASKING THIS, COLONEL, BUT DOESN'T IT BOTHER YOU, SANCTIONING THE FIRST MAJOR BLACK CANDIDATE FOR ATTORNEY GENERAL?
NOT AT ALL. AS A PATRIOT, COLOR MEANS NOTHING TO ME. I INTEND TO CARRY THIS ONE OUT PERSONALLY.

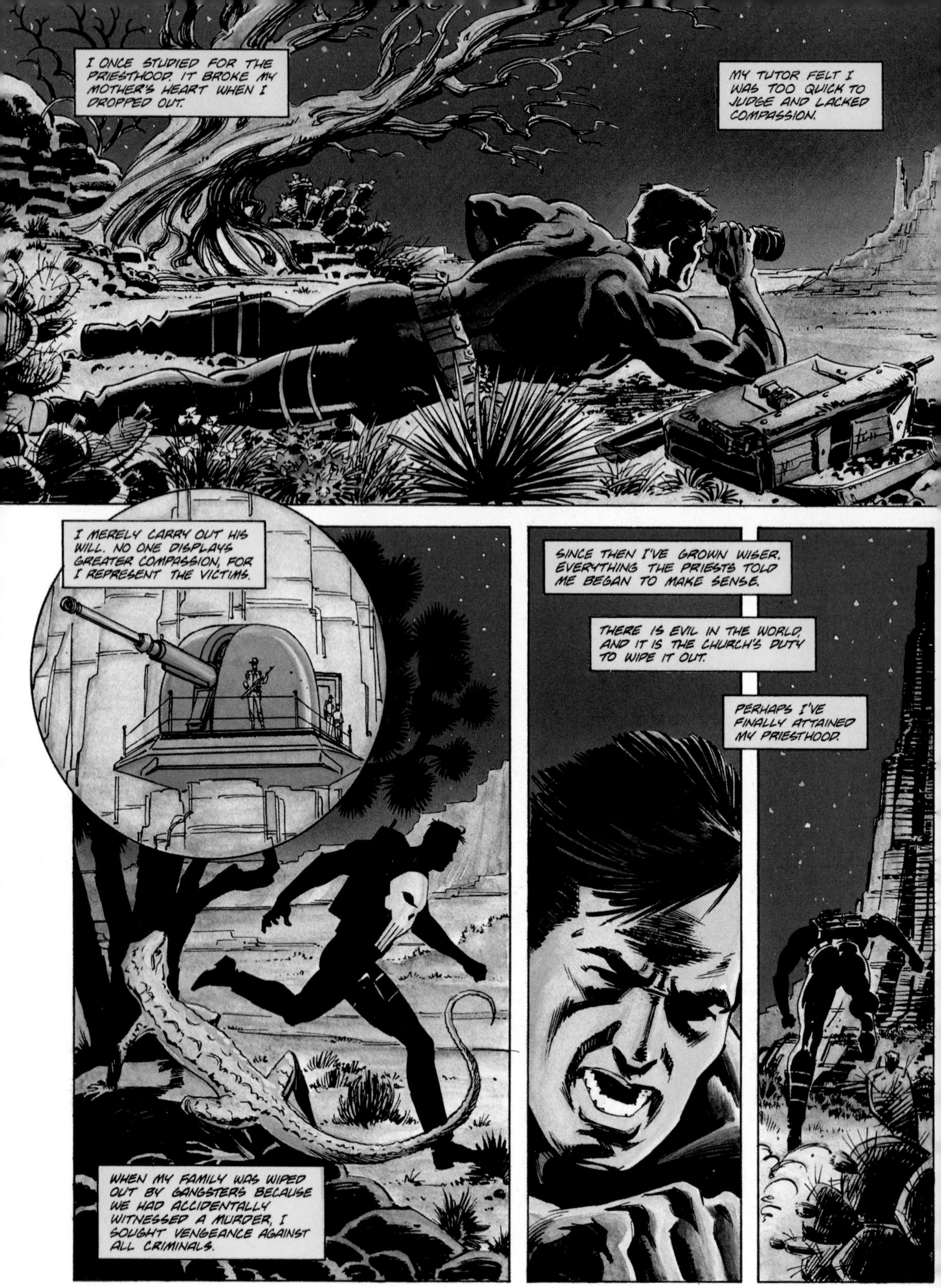
I ONCE STUDIED FOR THE PRIESTHOOD. IT BROKE MY MOTHER'S HEART WHEN I DROPPED OUT.
MY TUTOR FELT I WAS TOO QUICK TO JUDGE AND LACKED COMPASSION.
I MERELY CARRY OUT HIS WILL. NO ONE DISPLAYS GREATER COMPASSION, FOR I REPRESENT THE VICTIMS.
WHEN MY FAMILY WAS WIPED OUT BY GANGSTERS BECAUSE WE HAD ACCIDENTALLY WITNESSED A MURDER, I SOUGHT VENGEANCE AGAINST ALL CRIMINALS.
SINCE THEN I'VE GROWN WISER. EVERYTHING THE PRIESTS TOLD ME BEGAN TO MAKE SENSE.
THERE IS EVIL IN THE WORLD, AND IT IS THE CHURCH'S DUTY TO WIPE IT OUT.
PERHAPS I'VE FINALLY ATTAINED MY PRIESTHOOD.

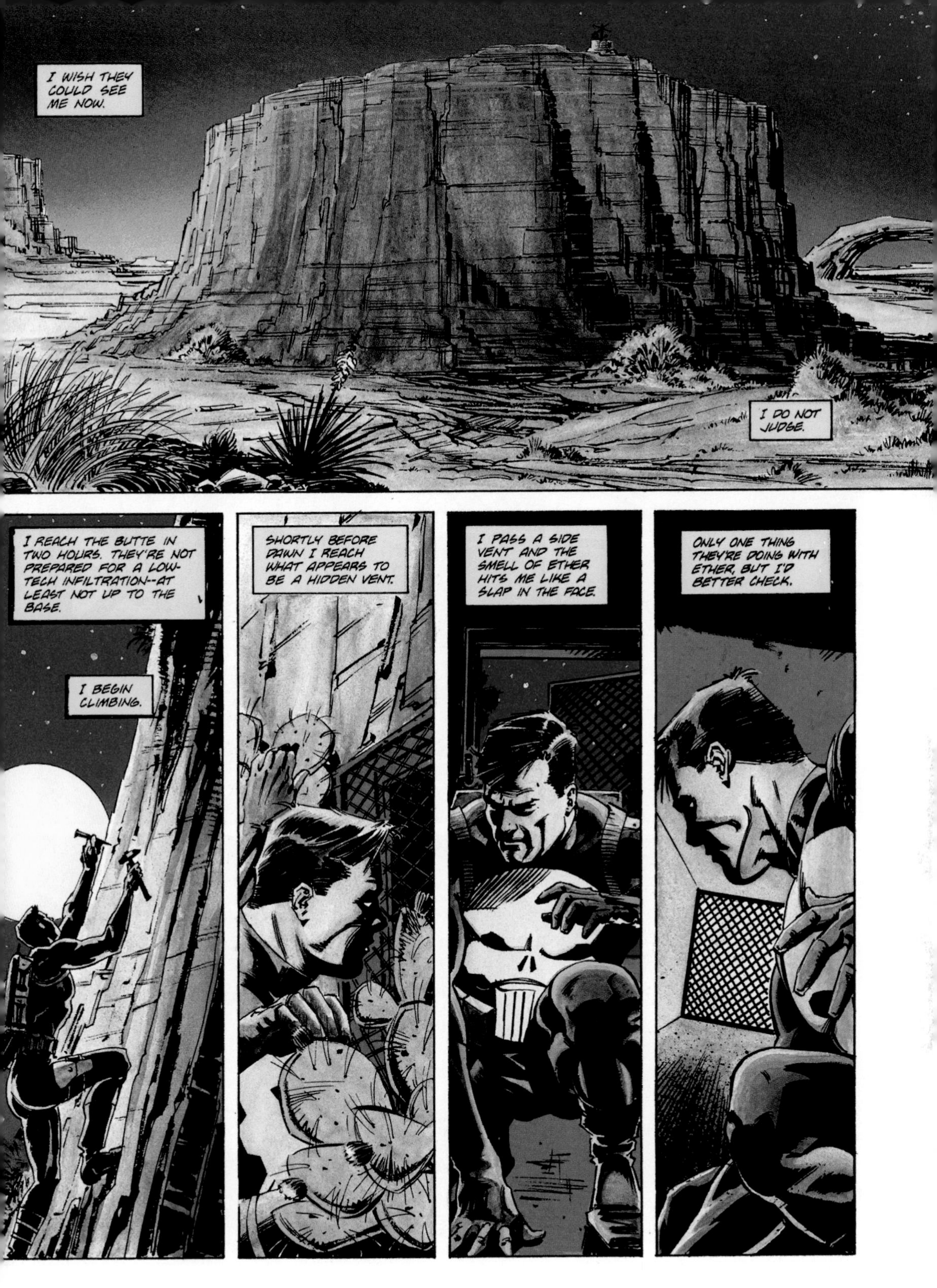

I WISH THEY COULD SEE ME NOW.
I DO NOT JUDGE.
I REACH THE BUTTE IN TWO HOURS. THEY'RE NOT PREPARED FOR A LOW-TECH INFILTRATION--AT LEAST NOT UP TO THE BASE.
I BEGIN CLIMBING.
SHORTLY BEFORE DAWN I REACH WHAT APPEARS TO BE A HIDDEN VENT.
I PASS A SIDE VENT AND THE SMELL OF ETHER HITS ME LIKE A SLAP IN THE FACE.
ONLY ONE THING THEY'RE DOING WITH ETHER, BUT I'D BETTER CHECK.

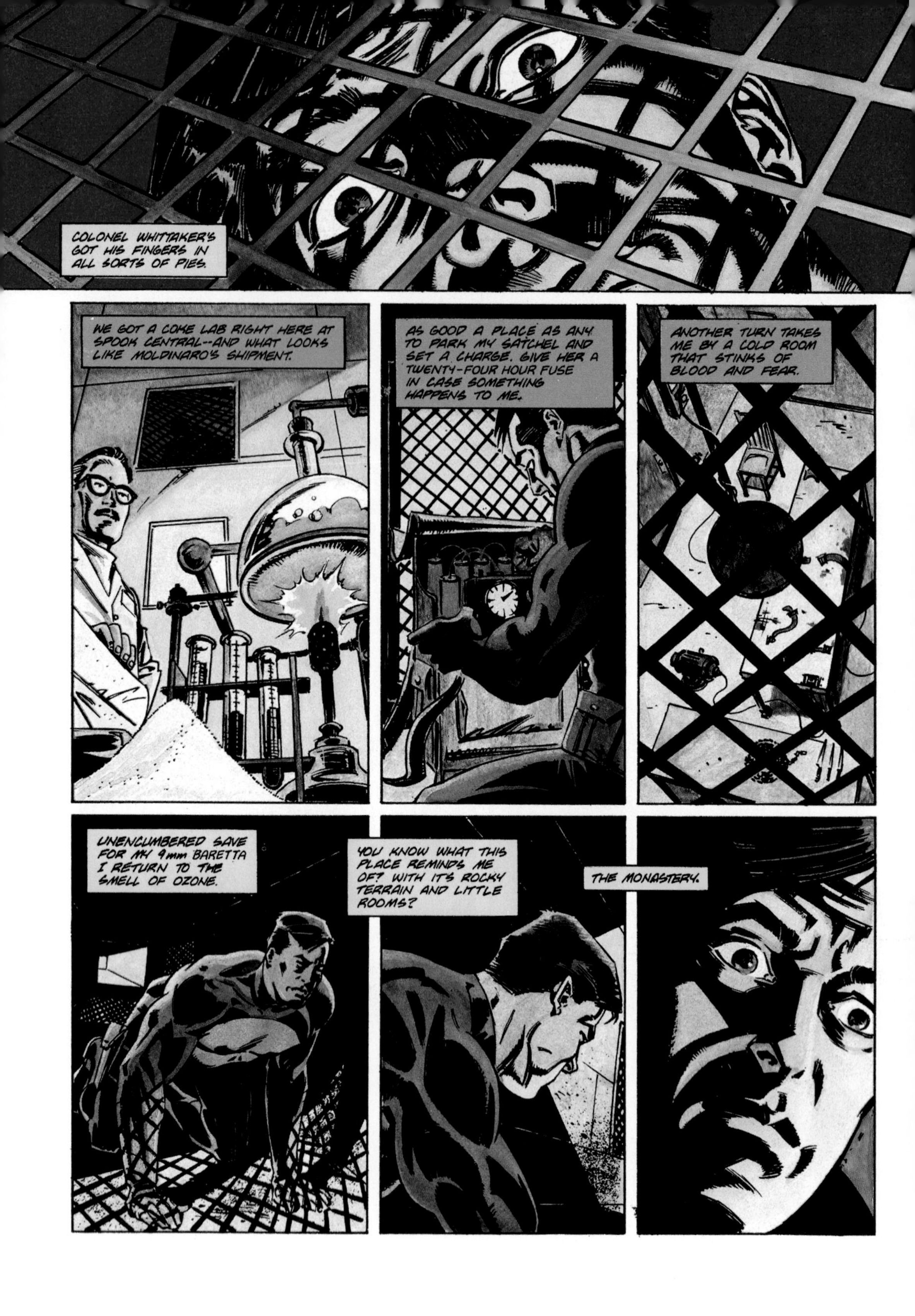
COLONEL WHITTAKER'S GOT HIS FINGERS IN ALL SORTS OF PIES.
WE GOT A COKE LAB RIGHT HERE AT SPOOK CENTRAL--AND WHAT LOOKS LIKE MOLDINARO'S SHIPMENT.
AS GOOD A PLACE AS ANY TO PARK MY SATCHEL AND SET A CHARGE. GIVE HER A TWENTY-FOUR HOUR FUSE IN CASE SOMETHING HAPPENS TO ME.
ANOTHER TURN TAKES ME BY A COLD ROOM THAT STINKS OF BLOOD AND FEAR.
UNENCUMBERED SAVE FOR MY 9mm BARETTA I RETURN TO THE SMELL OF OZONE.
YOU KNOW WHAT THIS PLACE REMINDS ME OF? WITH IT'S ROCKY TERRAIN AND LITTLE ROOMS?
THE MONASTERY.

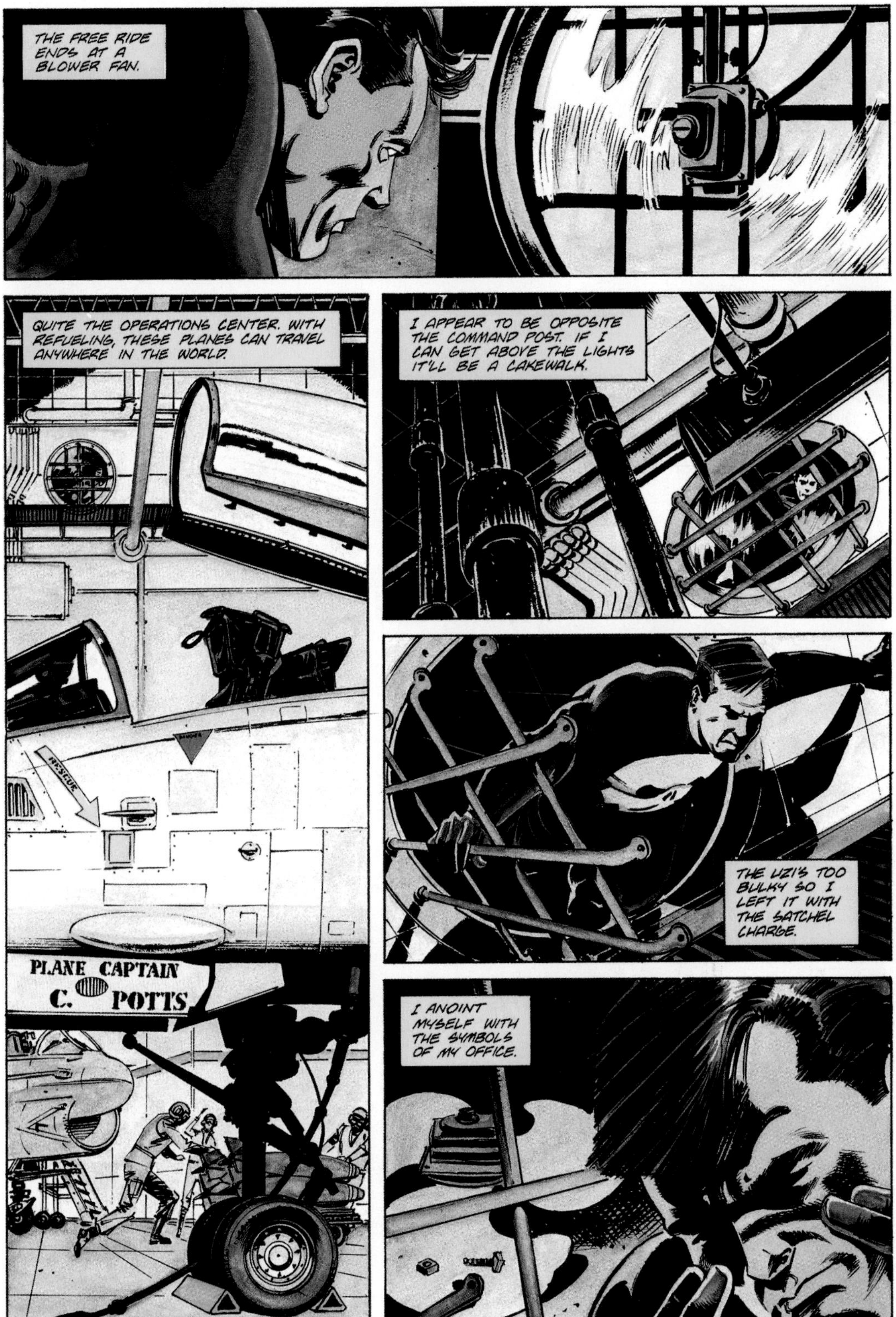
THE FREE RIDE ENDS AT A BLOWER FAN.
QUITE THE OPERATIONS CENTER. WITH REFUELING, THESE PLANES CAN TRAVEL ANYWHERE IN THE WORLD.
PLANE CAPTAIN
C. POTTS
I APPEAR TO BE OPPOSITE THE COMMAND POST. IF I CAN GET ABOVE THE LIGHTS IT'LL BE A CAKEWALK.
THE UZI'S TOO BULKY SO I LEFT IT WITH THE SATCHEL CHARGE.
I ANOINT MYSELF WITH THE SYMBOLS OF MY OFFICE.

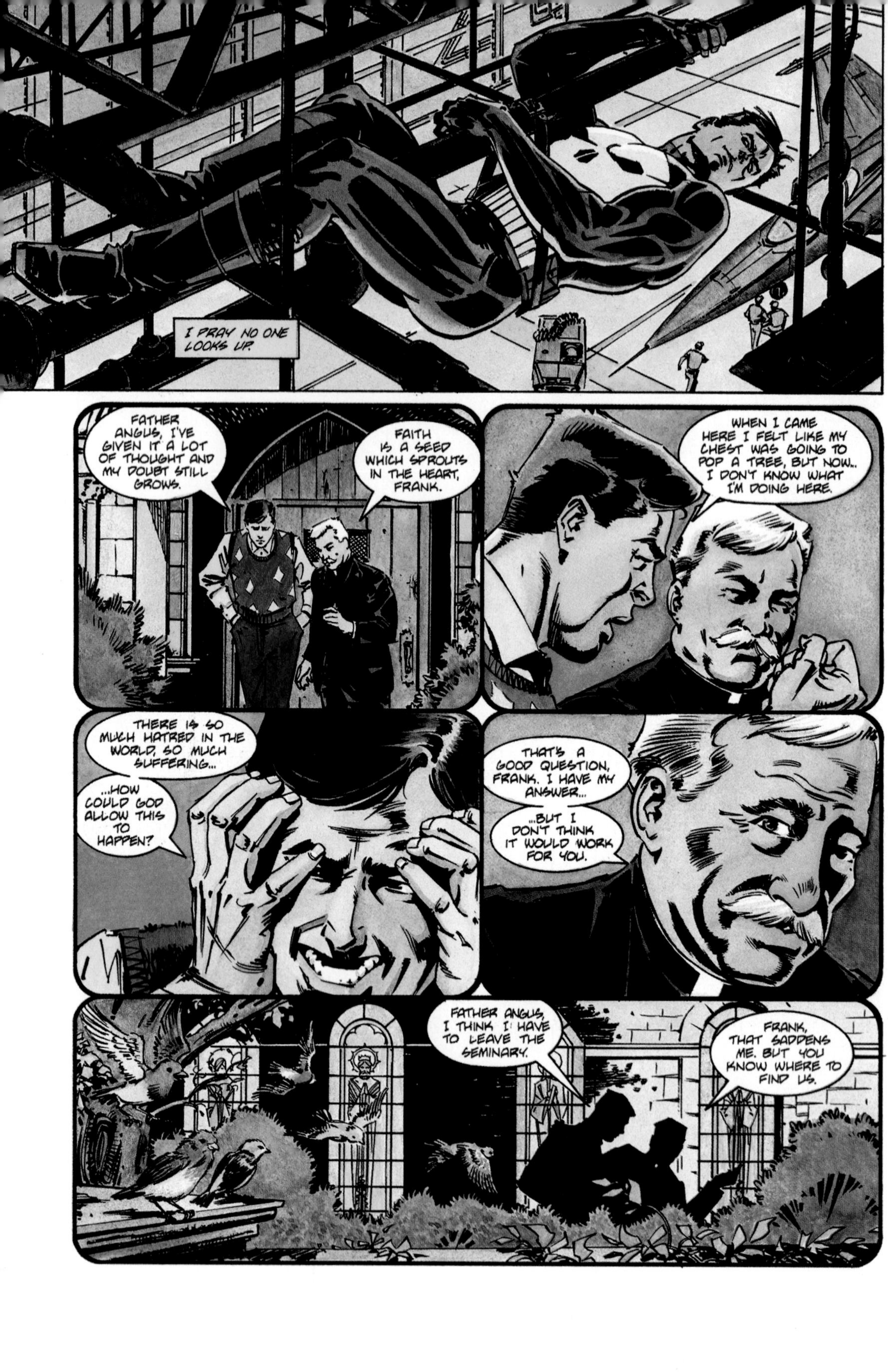
I PRAY NO ONE LOOKS UP.
FATHER ANGUS, I'VE GIVEN IT A LOT OF THOUGHT AND MY DOUBT STILL GROWS.
FAITH IS A SEED WHICH SPROUTS IN THE HEART, FRANK.
WHEN I CAME HERE I FELT LIKE MY CHEST WAS GOING TO POP A TREE, BUT NOW.. I DON'T KNOW WHAT I'M DOING HERE.
THERE IS SO MUCH HATRED IN THE WORLD, SO MUCH SUFFERING...
...HOW COULD GOD ALLOW THIS TO HAPPEN?
THAT'S A GOOD QUESTION, FRANK. I HAVE MY ANSWER...
...BUT I DON'T THINK IT WOULD WORK FOR YOU.
FATHER ANGUS, I THINK I HAVE TO LEAVE THE SEMINARY.
FRANK, THAT SADDENS ME. BUT YOU KNOW WHERE TO FIND US.

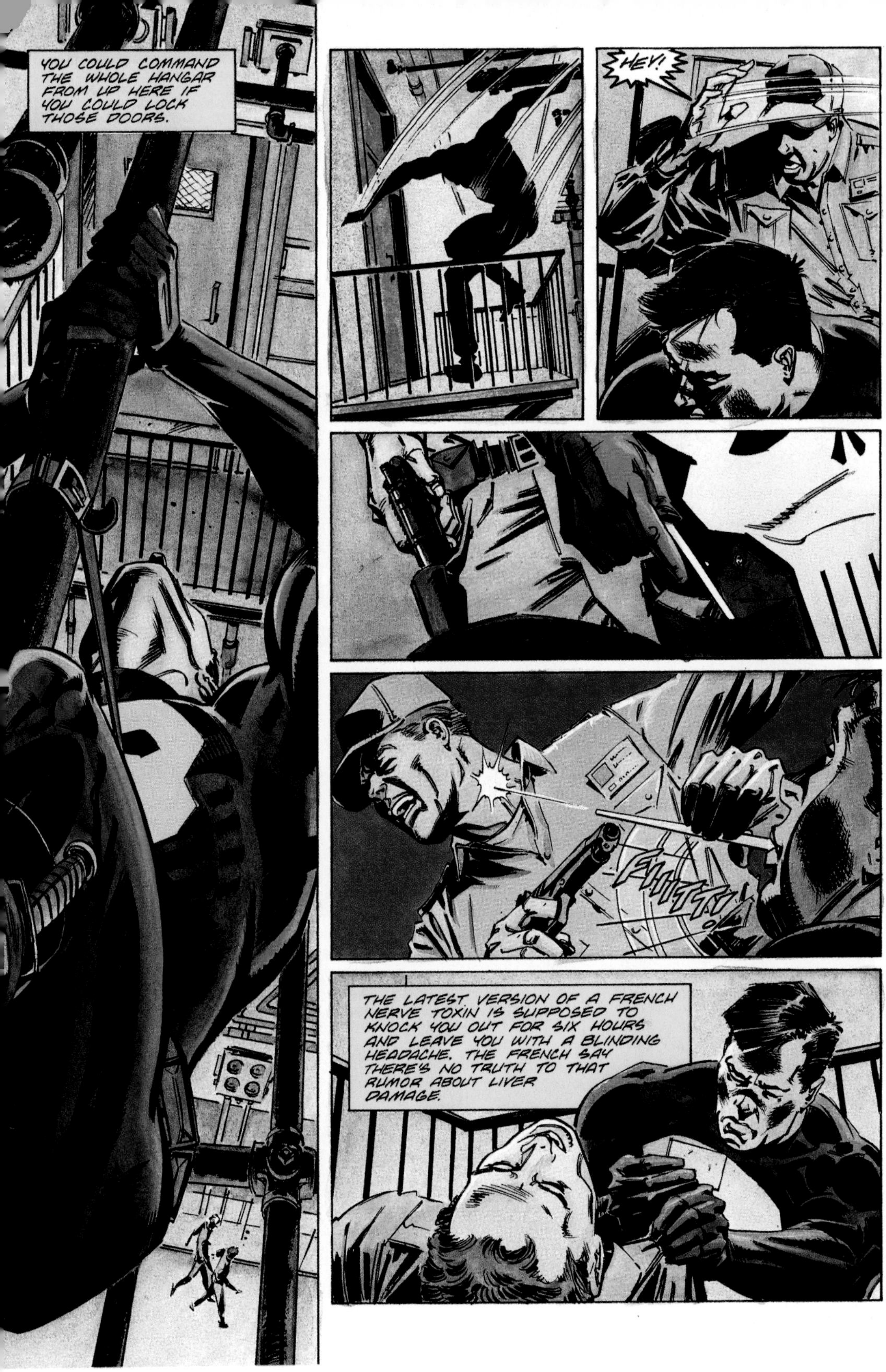
YOU COULD COMMAND THE WHOLE HANGAR FROM UP HERE IF YOU COULD LOCK THOSE DOORS.
HEY!
THE LATEST VERSION OF A FRENCH NERVE TOXIN IS SUPPOSED TO KNOCK YOU OUT FOR SIX HOURS AND LEAVE YOU WITH A BLINDING HEADACHE. THE FRENCH SAY THERE'S NO TRUTH TO THAT RUMOR ABOUT LIVER DAMAGE.

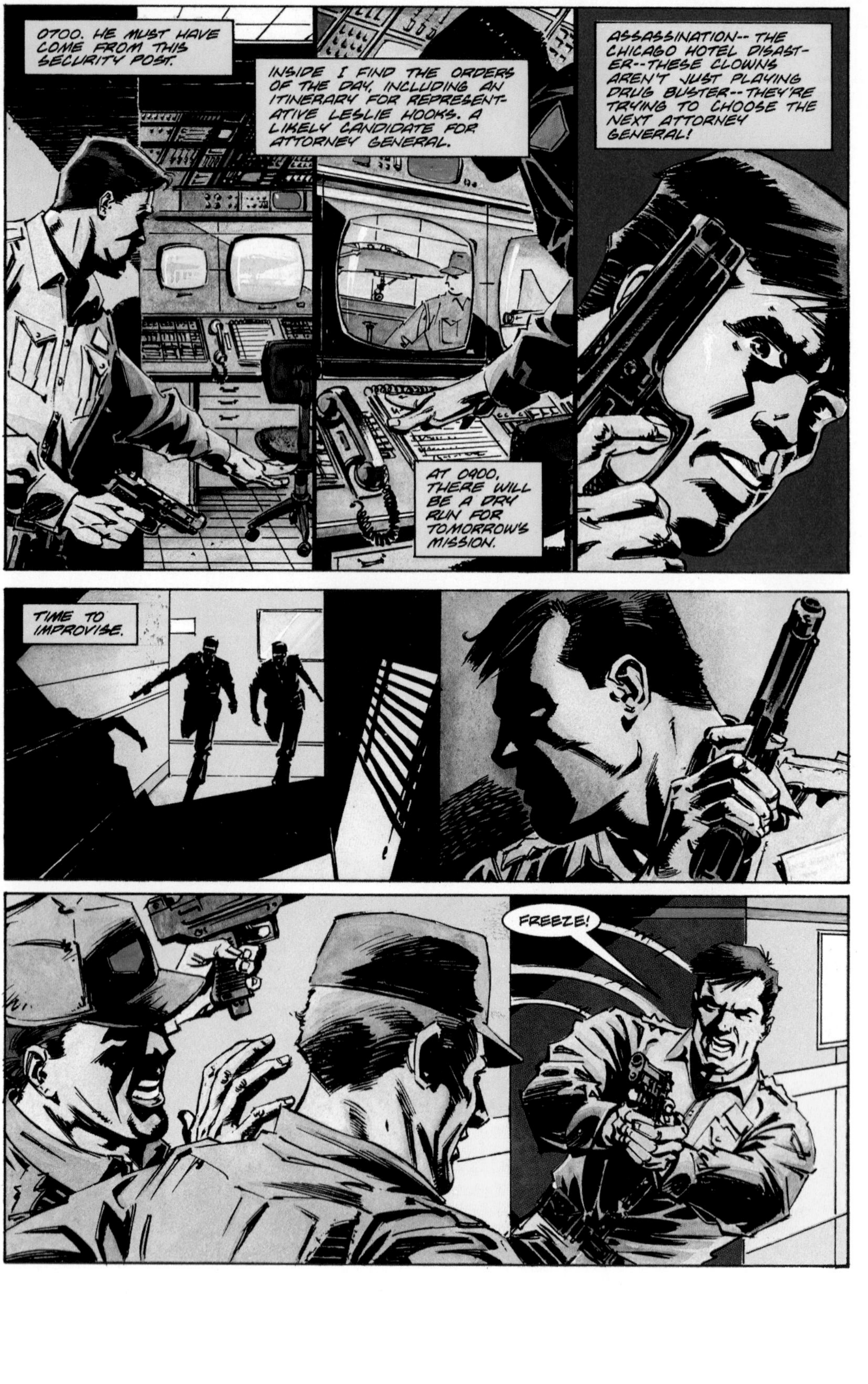

0700. HE MUST HAVE COME FROM THIS SECURITY POST.
INSIDE I FIND THE ORDERS OF THE DAY, INCLUDING AN ITINERARY FOR REPRESENTATIVE LESLIE HOOKS. A LIKELY CANDIDATE FOR ATTORNEY GENERAL.
AT 0900, THERE WILL BE A DRY RUN FOR TOMORROW'S MISSION.
ASSASSINATION-- THE CHICAGO HOTEL DISASTER--THESE CLOWNS AREN'T JUST PLAYING DRUG BUSTER--THEY'RE TRYING TO CHOOSE THE NEXT ATTORNEY GENERAL!
TIME TO IMPROVISE.
FREEZE!

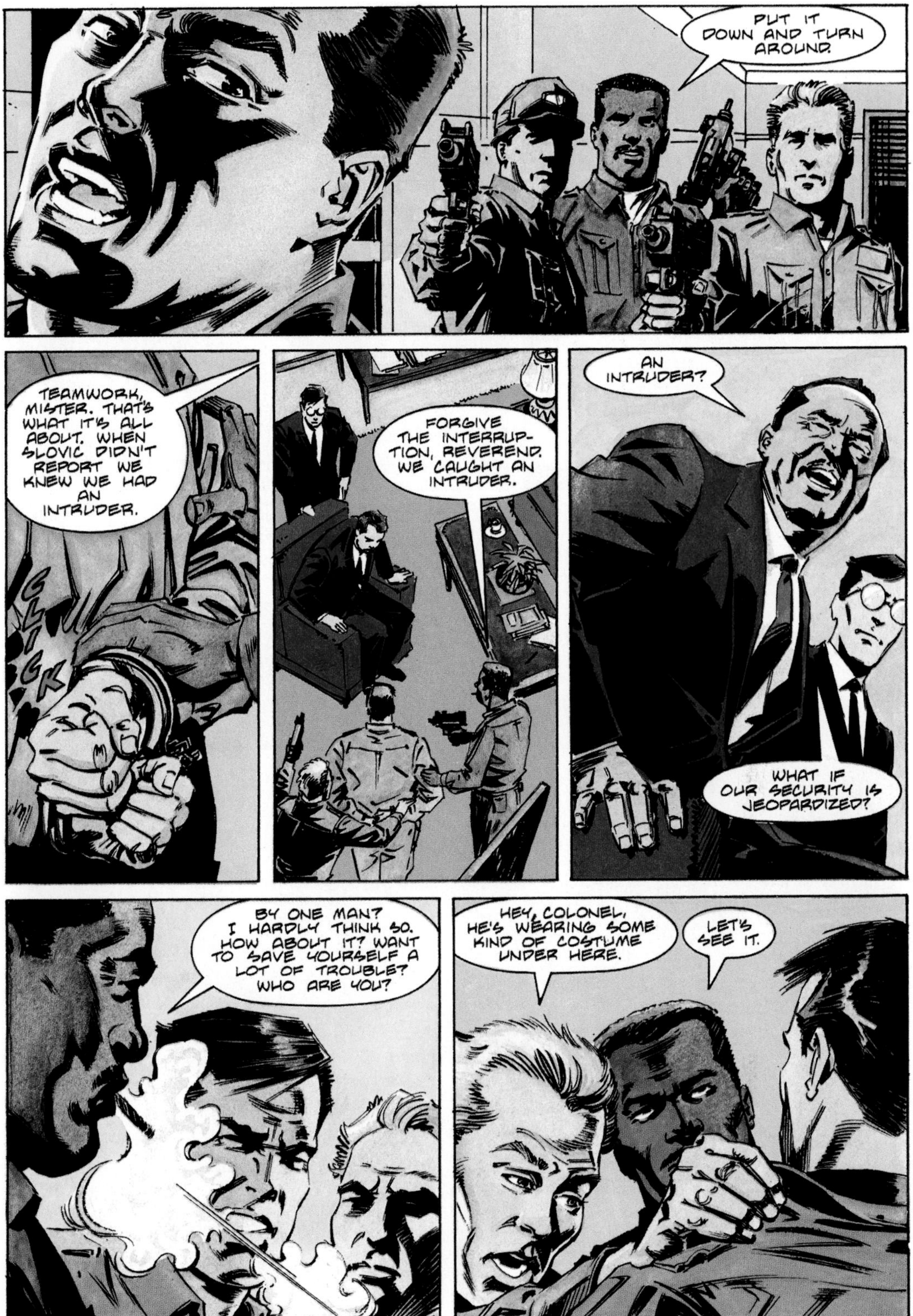
PUT IT DOWN AND TURN AROUND.
TEAMWORK, MISTER. THAT'S WHAT IT'S ALL ABOUT. WHEN SLOVIC DIDN'T REPORT WE KNEW WE HAD AN INTRUDER.
CLICK
FORGIVE THE INTERRUPTION, REVEREND. WE CAUGHT AN INTRUDER.
AN INTRUDER?
WHAT IF OUR SECURITY IS JEOPARDIZED?
BY ONE MAN? I HARDLY THINK SO. HOW ABOUT IT? WANT TO SAVE YOURSELF A LOT OF TROUBLE? WHO ARE YOU?
HEY, COLONEL, HE'S WEARING SOME KIND OF COSTUME UNDER HERE.
LET'S SEE IT.

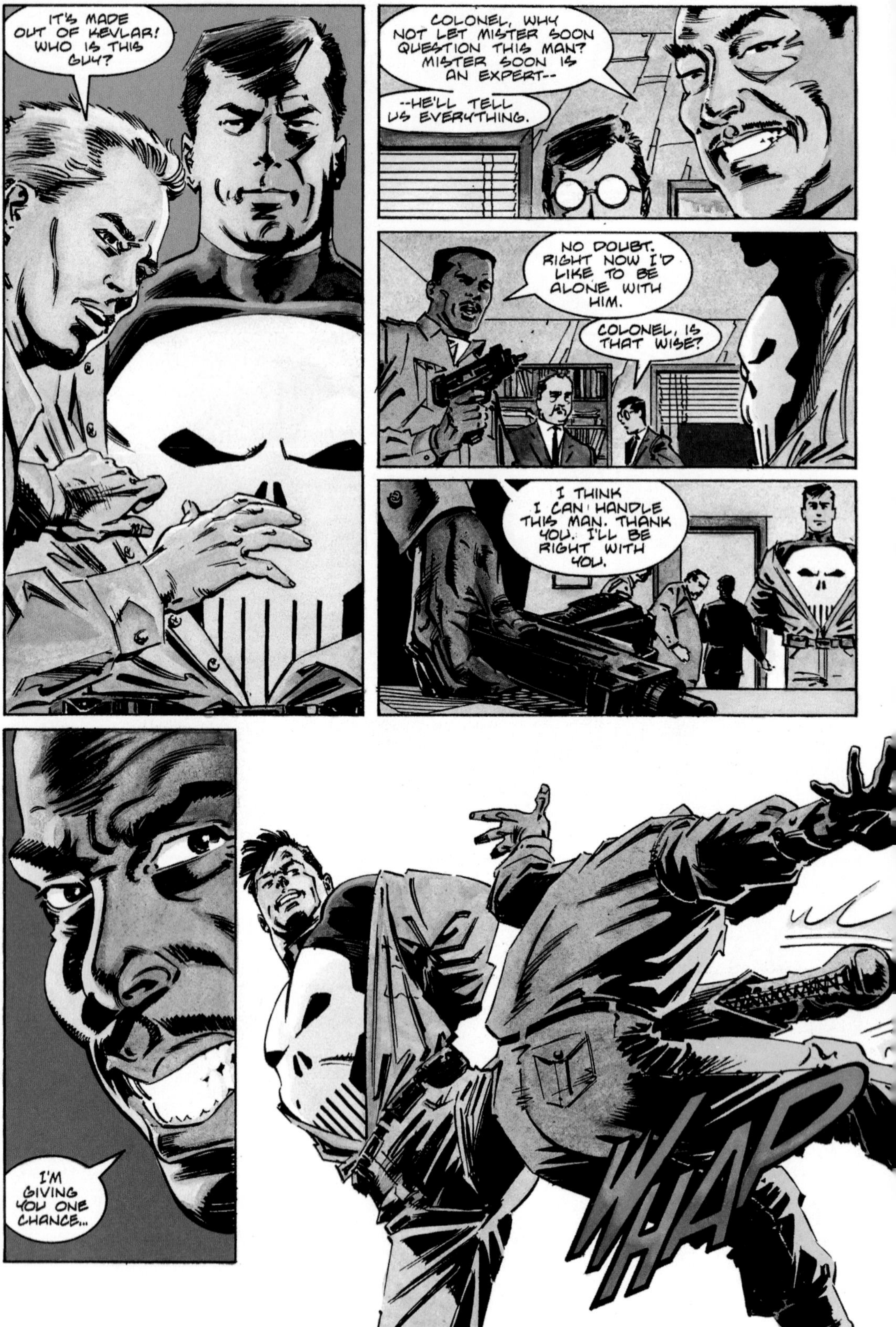
IT'S MADE OUT OF KEVLAR! WHO IS THIS GUY?
COLONEL, WHY NOT LET MISTER SOON QUESTION THIS MAN? MISTER SOON IS AN EXPERT--
--HE'LL TELL US EVERYTHING.
NO DOUBT. RIGHT NOW I'D LIKE TO BE ALONE WITH HIM.
COLONEL, IS THAT WISE?
I THINK I CAN HANDLE THIS MAN. THANK YOU. I'LL BE RIGHT WITH YOU.
I'M GIVING YOU ONE CHANCE...
WHAP

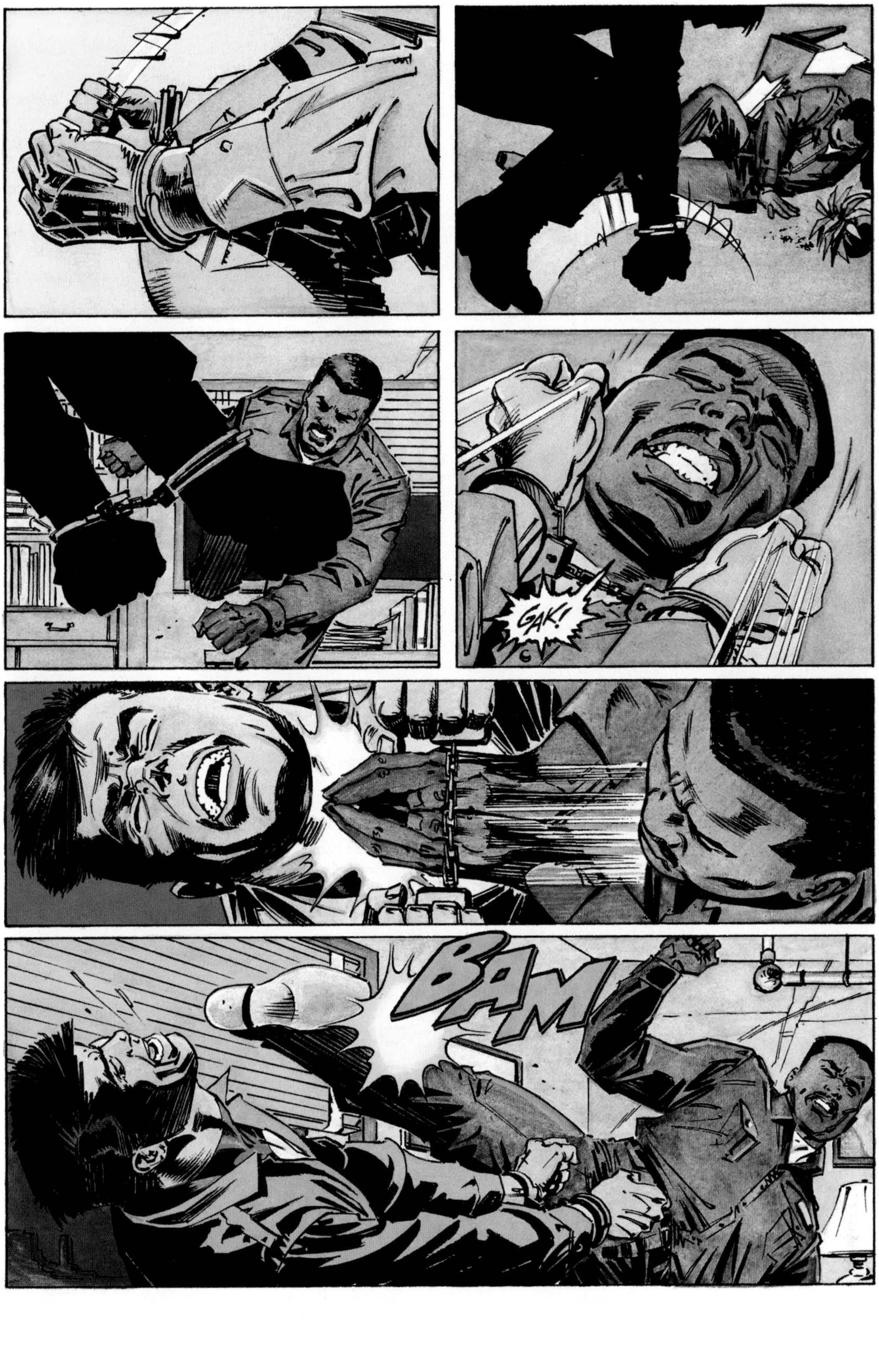
GAK!
BAM

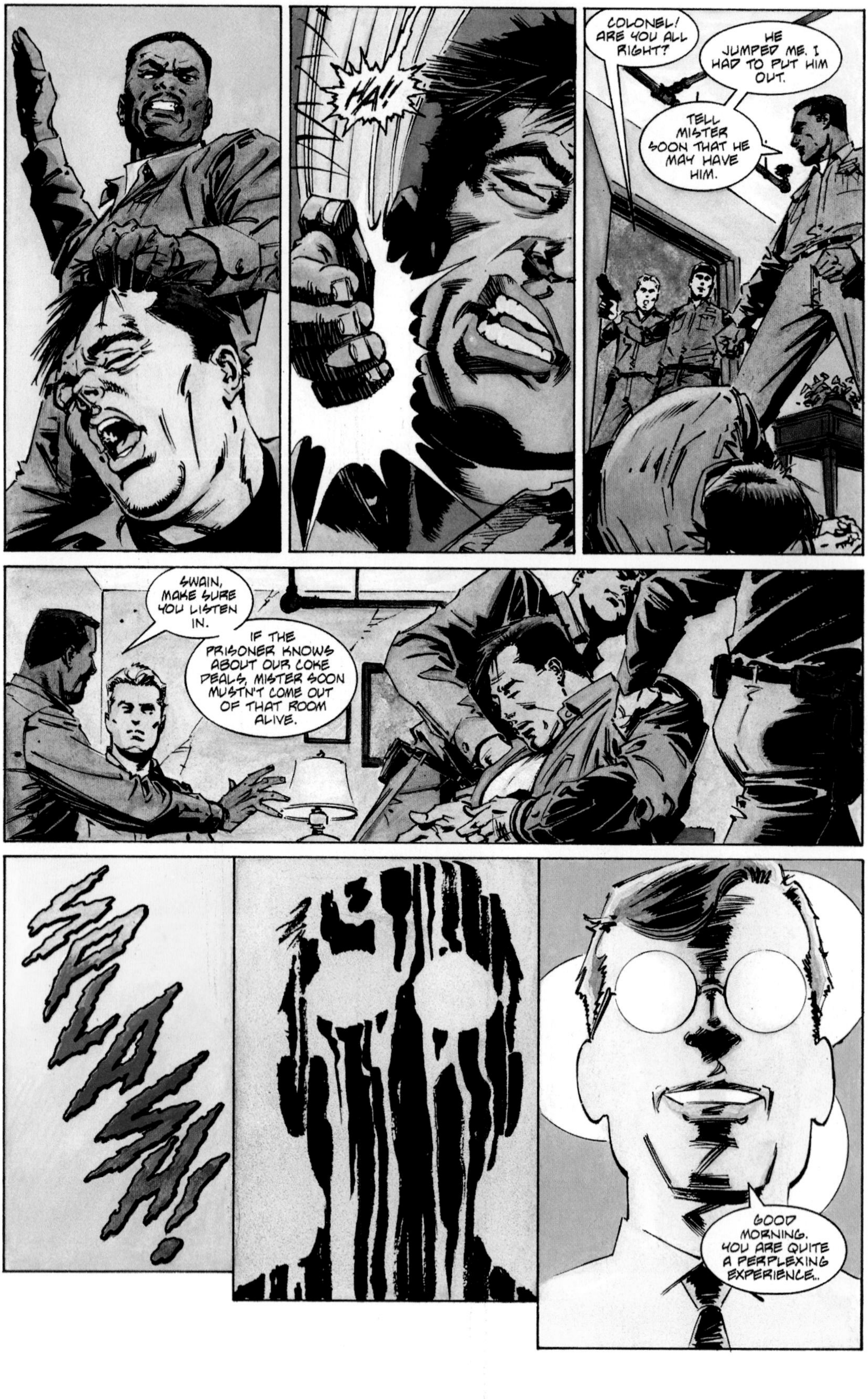

HA!!
COLONEL! ARE YOU ALL RIGHT?
HE JUMPED ME. I HAD TO PUT HIM OUT.
TELL MISTER SOON THAT HE MAY HAVE HIM.
SWAIN, MAKE SURE YOU LISTEN IN.
IF THE PRISONER KNOWS ABOUT OUR COKE DEALS, MISTER SOON MUSTN'T COME OUT OF THAT ROOM ALIVE.
SPLASH!
GOOD MORNING. YOU ARE QUITE A PERPLEXING EXPERIENCE..

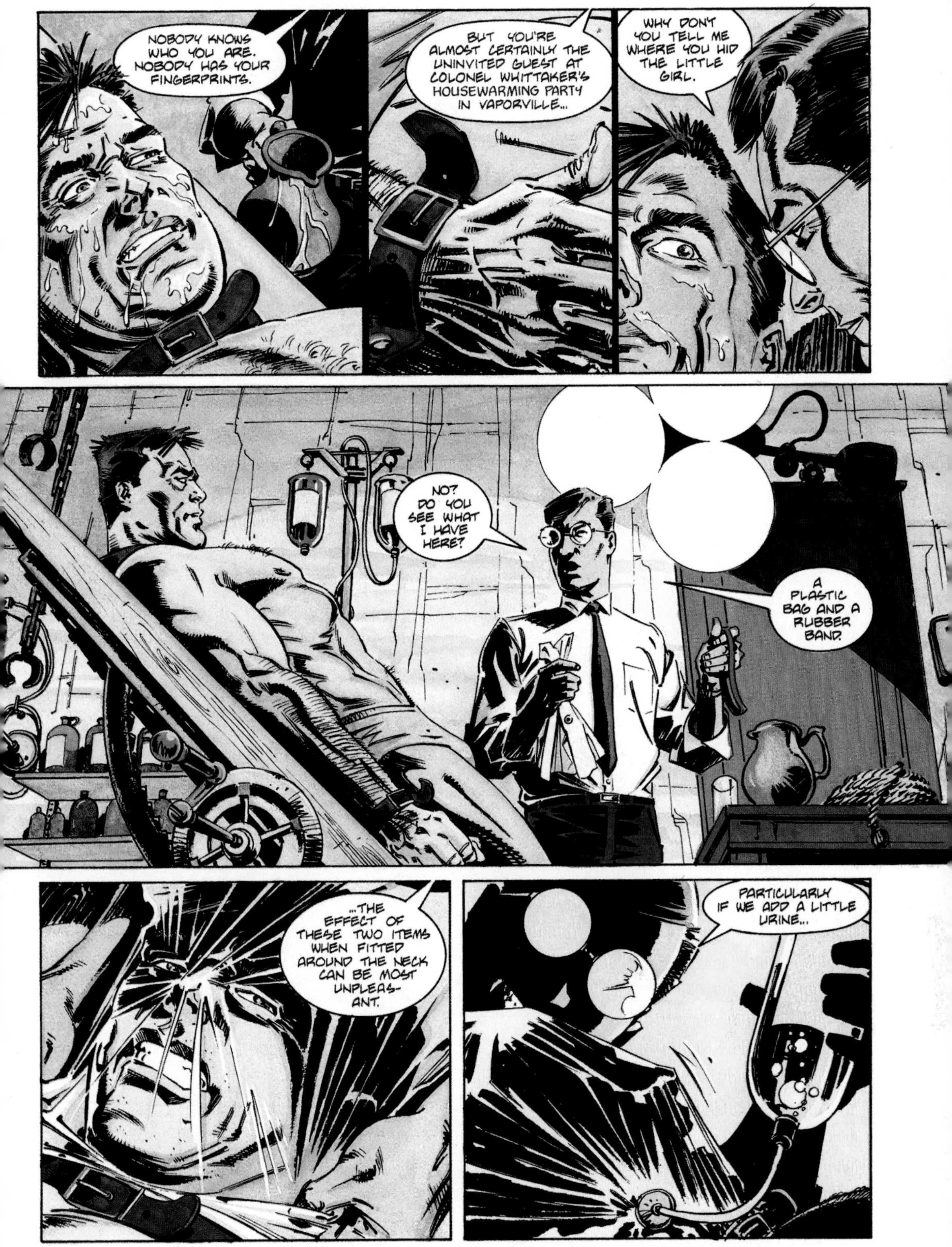
NOBODY KNOWS WHO YOU ARE. NOBODY HAS YOUR FINGERPRINTS.
BUT YOU'RE ALMOST CERTAINLY THE UNINVITED GUEST AT COLONEL WHITTAKER'S HOUSEWARMING PARTY IN VAPORVILLE...
WHY DON'T YOU TELL ME WHERE YOU HID THE LITTLE GIRL.
NO? DO YOU SEE WHAT I HAVE HERE?
A PLASTIC BAG AND A RUBBER BAND.
...THE EFFECT OF THESE TWO ITEMS WHEN FITTED AROUND THE NECK CAN BE MOST UNPLEAS-ANT.
PARTICULARLY IF WE ADD A LITTLE URINE...

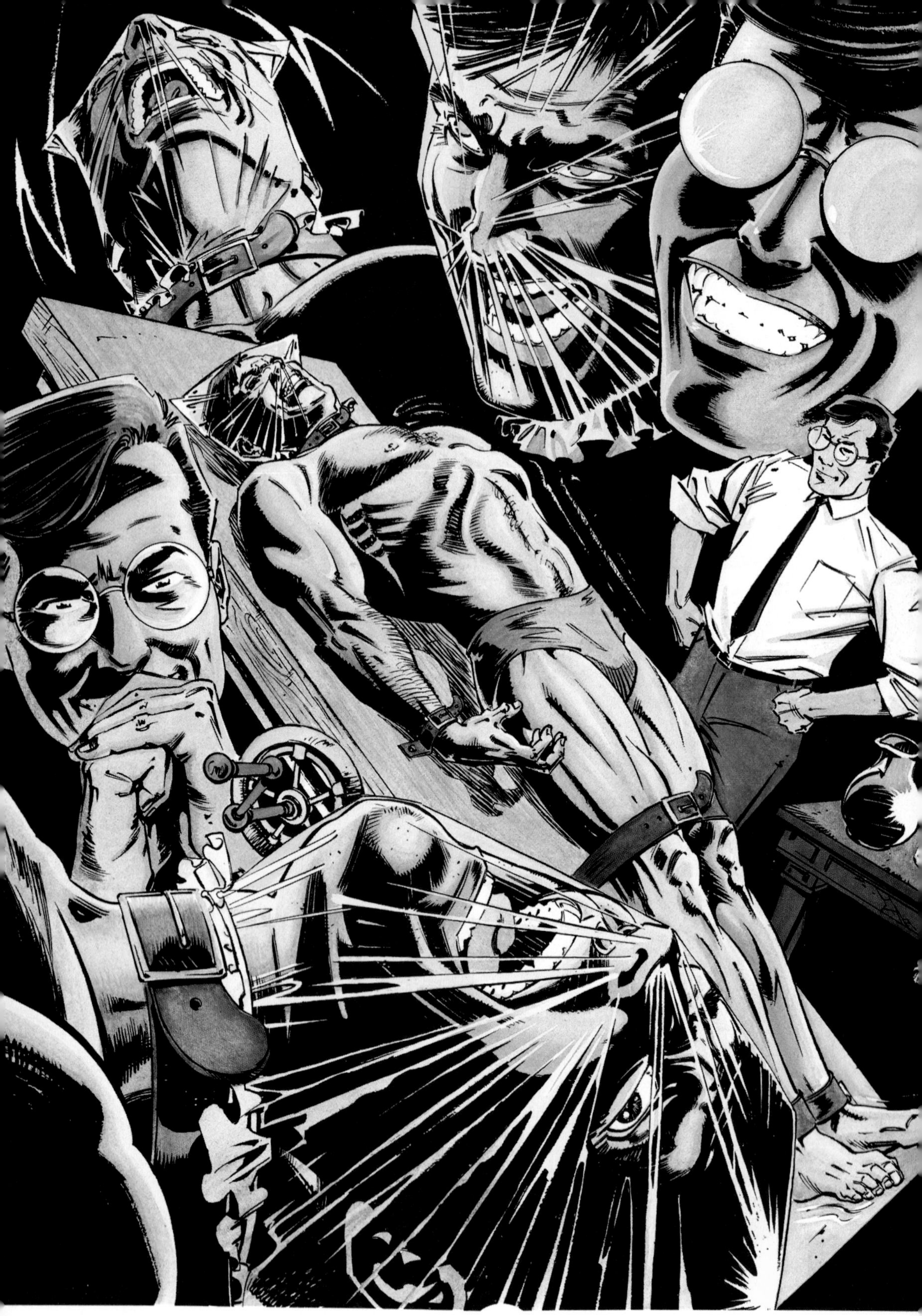

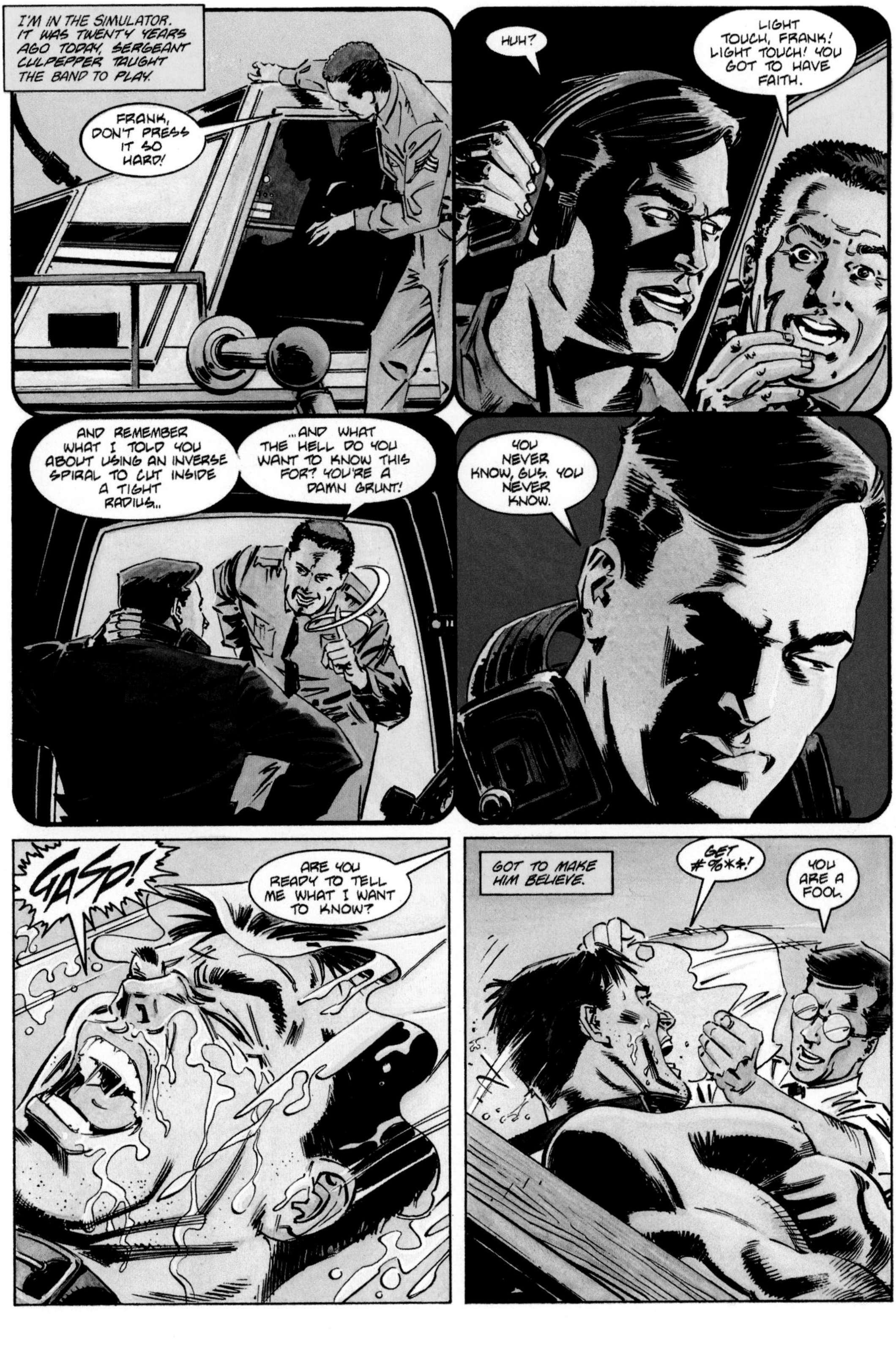
I'M IN THE SIMULATOR. IT WAS TWENTY YEARS AGO TODAY, SERGEANT CULPEPPER TAUGHT THE BAND TO PLAY.
FRANK, DON'T PRESS IT SO HARD!
HUH?
LIGHT TOUCH, FRANK! LIGHT TOUCH! YOU GOT TO HAVE FAITH.
AND REMEMBER WHAT I TOLD YOU ABOUT USING AN INVERSE SPIRAL TO CUT INSIDE A TIGHT RADIUS...
...AND WHAT THE HELL DO YOU WANT TO KNOW THIS FOR? YOU'RE A DAMN GRUNT!
YOU NEVER KNOW, GUS. YOU NEVER KNOW.
GASP!
ARE YOU READY TO TELL ME WHAT I WANT TO KNOW?
GOT TO MAKE HIM BELIEVE.
GET #%*$!
YOU ARE A FOOL.

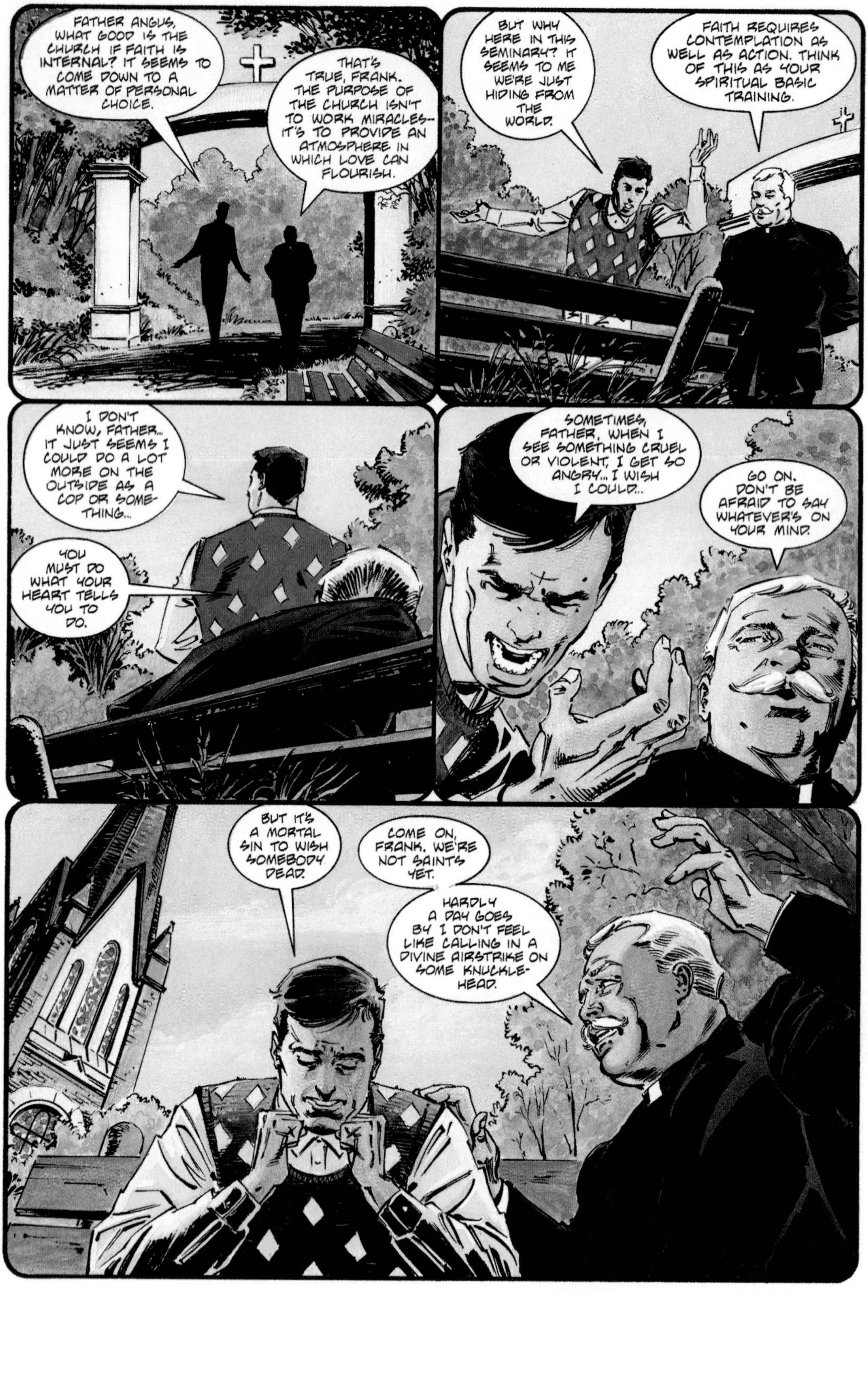
FATHER ANGUS, WHAT GOOD IS THE CHURCH IF FAITH IS INTERNAL? IT SEEMS TO COME DOWN TO A MATTER OF PERSONAL CHOICE.
THAT'S TRUE, FRANK. THE PURPOSE OF THE CHURCH ISN'T TO WORK MIRACLES-- IT'S TO PROVIDE AN ATMOSPHERE IN WHICH LOVE CAN FLOURISH.
BUT WHY HERE IN THIS SEMINARY? IT SEEMS TO ME WE'RE JUST HIDING FROM THE WORLD.
FAITH REQUIRES CONTEMPLATION AS WELL AS ACTION. THINK OF THIS AS YOUR SPIRITUAL BASIC TRAINING.
I DON'T KNOW, FATHER... IT JUST SEEMS I COULD DO A LOT MORE ON THE OUTSIDE AS A COP OR SOMETHING...
YOU MUST DO WHAT YOUR HEART TELLS YOU TO DO.
SOMETIMES, FATHER, WHEN I SEE SOMETHING CRUEL OR VIOLENT, I GET SO ANGRY... I WISH I COULD...
GO ON. DON'T BE AFRAID TO SAY WHATEVER'S ON YOUR MIND.
BUT IT'S A MORTAL SIN TO WISH SOMEBODY DEAD.
COME ON, FRANK. WE'RE NOT SAINTS YET.
HARDLY A DAY GOES BY I DON'T FEEL LIKE CALLING IN A DIVINE AIRSTRIKE ON SOME KNUCKLE-HEAD.

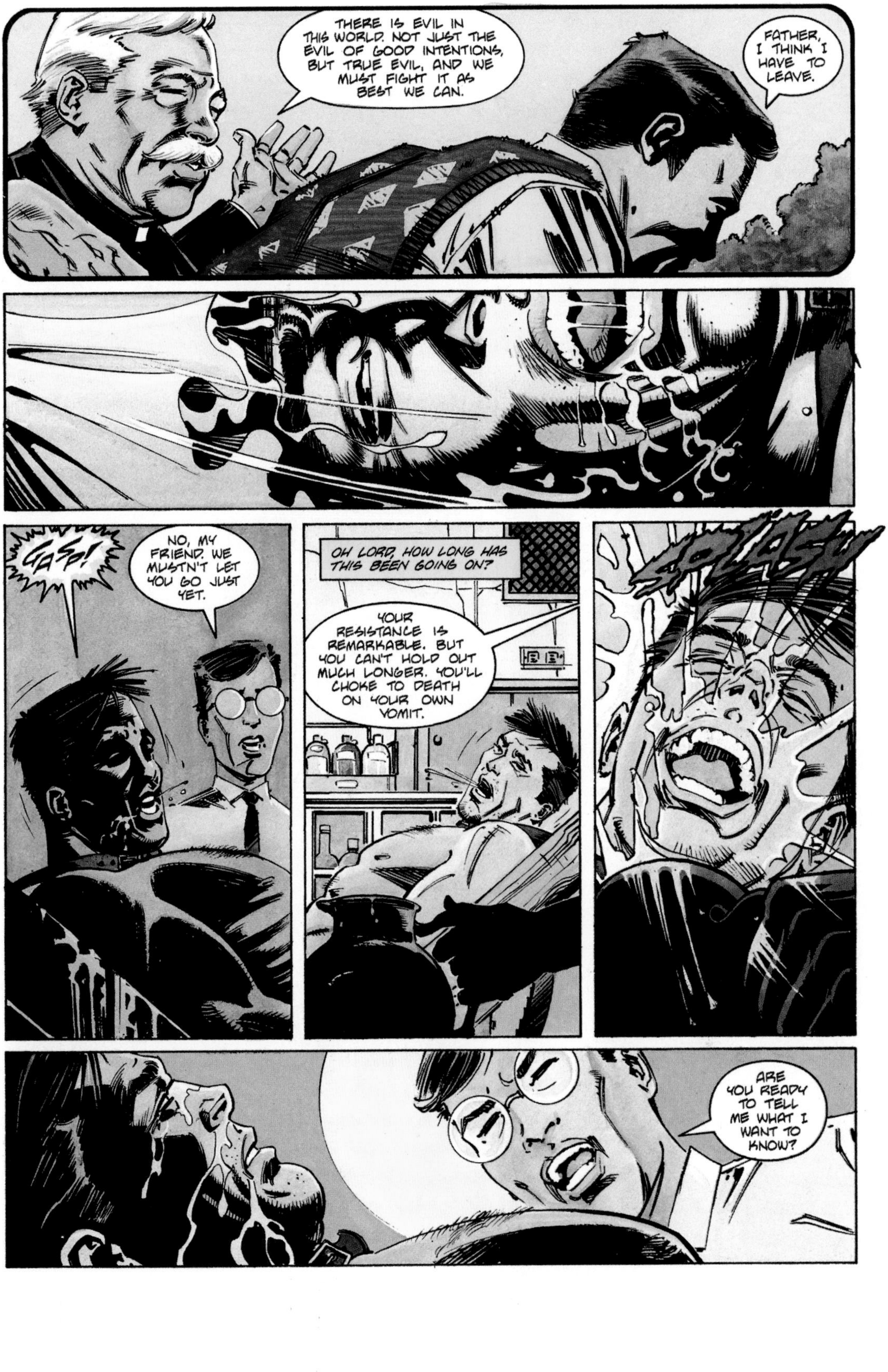

THERE IS EVIL IN THIS WORLD. NOT JUST THE EVIL OF GOOD INTENTIONS, BUT TRUE EVIL, AND WE MUST FIGHT IT AS BEST WE CAN.
FATHER, I THINK I HAVE TO LEAVE.
GASP!
NO, MY FRIEND. WE MUSTN'T LET YOU GO JUST YET.
OH LORD, HOW LONG HAS THIS BEEN GOING ON?
YOUR RESISTANCE IS REMARKABLE. BUT YOU CAN'T HOLD OUT MUCH LONGER. YOU'LL CHOKE TO DEATH ON YOUR OWN VOMIT.
SPLASH
ARE YOU READY TO TELL ME WHAT I WANT TO KNOW?

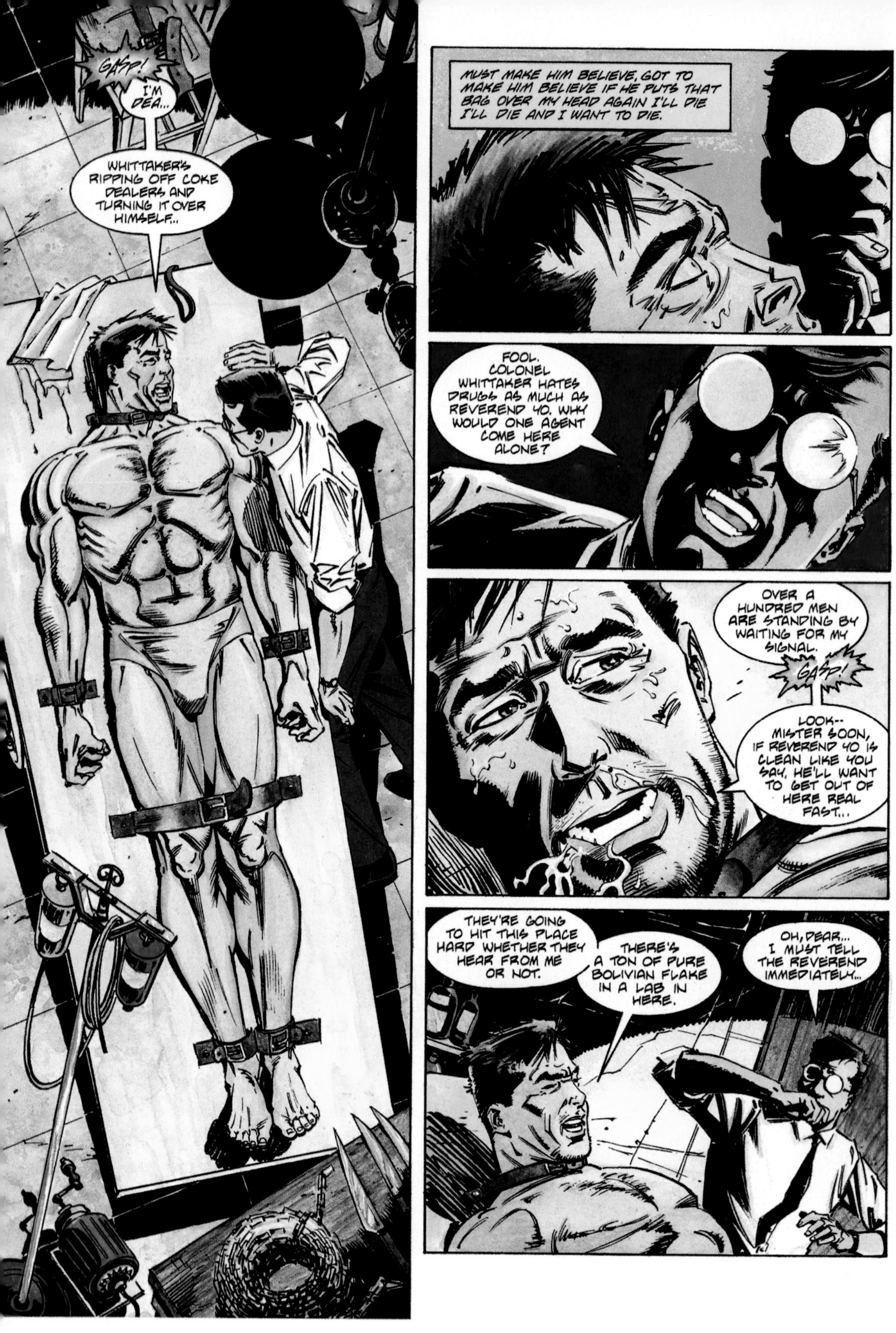
GASP!
I'M DEA...
WHITTAKER'S RIPPING OFF COKE DEALERS AND TURNING IT OVER HIMSELF...
MUST MAKE HIM BELIEVE, GOT TO MAKE HIM BELIEVE IF HE PUTS THAT BAG OVER MY HEAD AGAIN I'LL DIE I'LL DIE AND I WANT TO DIE.
FOOL. COLONEL WHITTAKER HATES DRUGS AS MUCH AS REVEREND YO. WHY WOULD ONE AGENT COME HERE ALONE?
OVER A HUNDRED MEN ARE STANDING BY WAITING FOR MY SIGNAL.
GASP!
LOOK-- MISTER SOON, IF REVEREND YO IS CLEAN LIKE YOU SAY, HE'LL WANT TO GET OUT OF HERE REAL FAST...
THEY'RE GOING TO HIT THIS PLACE HARD WHETHER THEY HEAR FROM ME OR NOT.
THERE'S A TON OF PURE BOLIVIAN FLAKE IN A LAB IN HERE.
OH, DEAR... I MUST TELL THE REVEREND IMMEDIATELY...

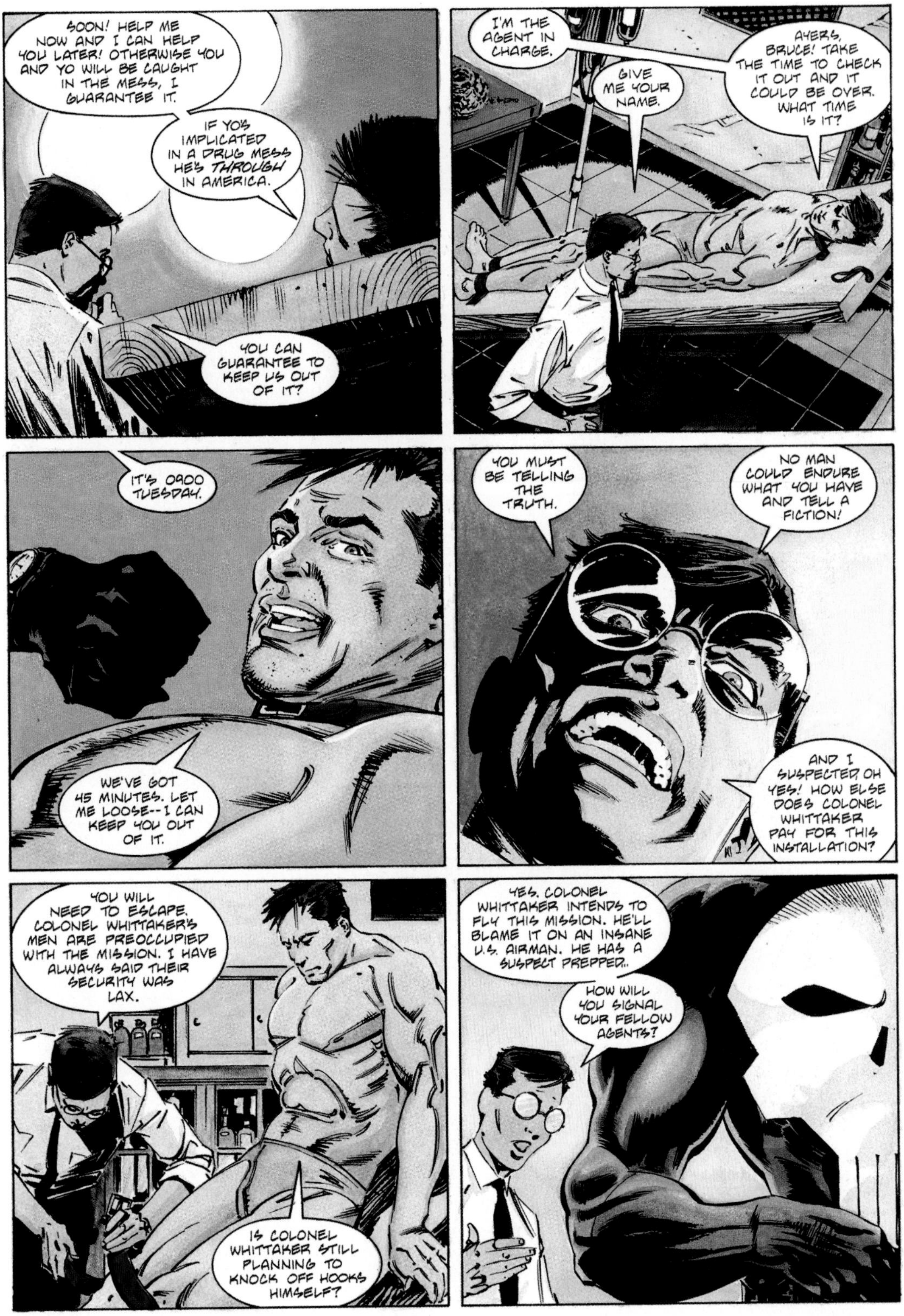
SOON! HELP ME NOW AND I CAN HELP YOU LATER! OTHERWISE YOU AND YO WILL BE CAUGHT IN THE MESS, I GUARANTEE IT.
IF YO'S IMPLICATED IN A DRUG MESS HE'S THROUGH IN AMERICA.
YOU CAN GUARANTEE TO KEEP US OUT OF IT?
I'M THE AGENT IN CHARGE.
GIVE ME YOUR NAME.
AYERS, BRUCE! TAKE THE TIME TO CHECK IT OUT AND IT COULD BE OVER. WHAT TIME IS IT?
IT'S 0900 TUESDAY.
WE'VE GOT 45 MINUTES. LET ME LOOSE--I CAN KEEP YOU OUT OF IT.
YOU MUST BE TELLING THE TRUTH.
NO MAN COULD ENDURE WHAT YOU HAVE AND TELL A FICTION!
AND I SUSPECTED, OH YES! HOW ELSE DOES COLONEL WHITTAKER PAY FOR THIS INSTALLATION?
YOU WILL NEED TO ESCAPE. COLONEL WHITTAKER'S MEN ARE PREOCCUPIED WITH THE MISSION. I HAVE ALWAYS SAID THEIR SECURITY WAS LAX.
IS COLONEL WHITTAKER STILL PLANNING TO KNOCK OFF HOOKS HIMSELF?
YES. COLONEL WHITTAKER INTENDS TO FLY THIS MISSION. HE'LL BLAME IT ON AN INSANE U.S. AIRMAN. HE HAS A SUSPECT PREPPED..
HOW WILL YOU SIGNAL YOUR FELLOW AGENTS?

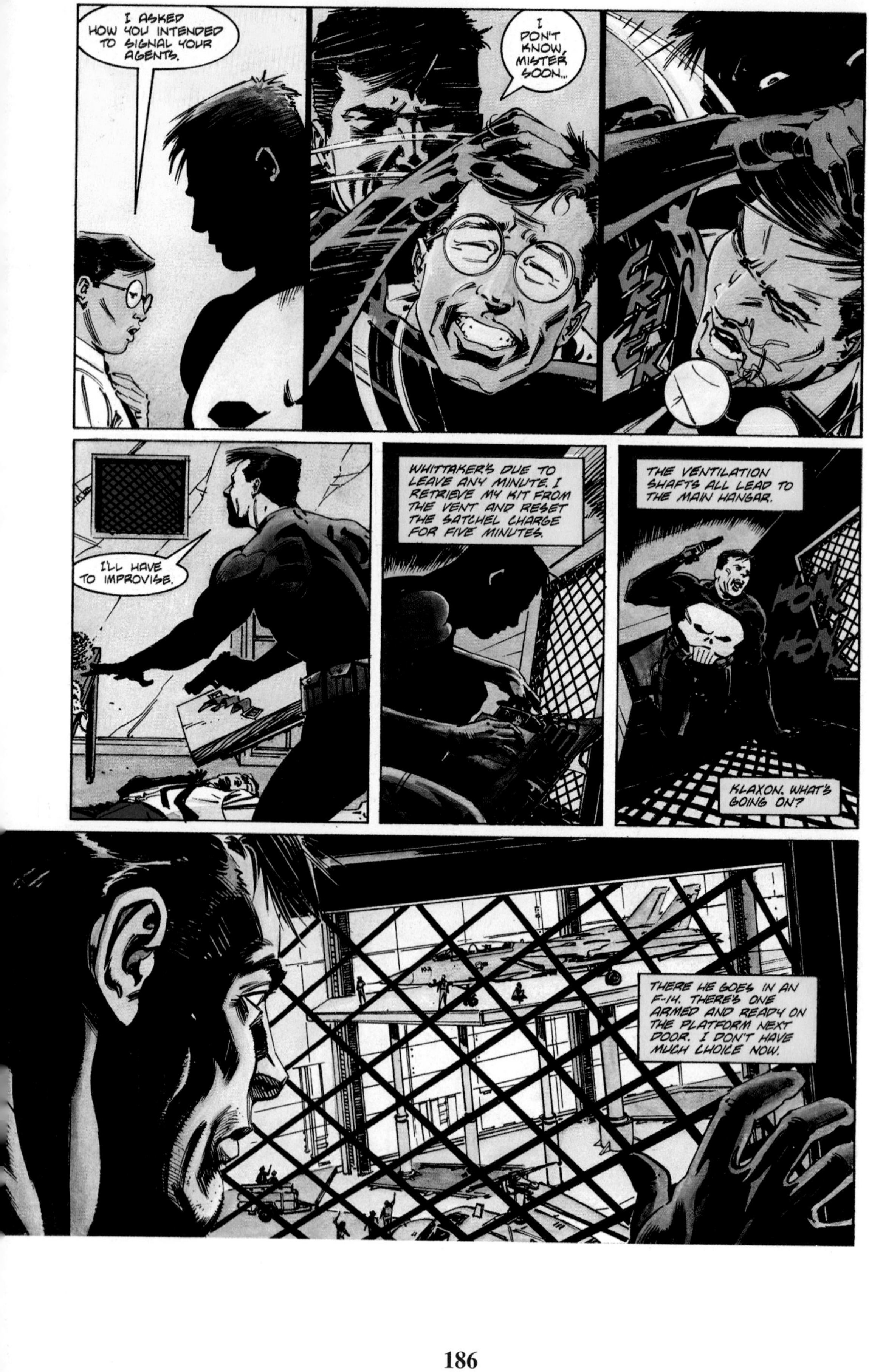
I ASKED HOW YOU INTENDED TO SIGNAL YOUR AGENTS.
I DON'T KNOW, MISTER SOON...
I'LL HAVE TO IMPROVISE.
WHITTAKER'S DUE TO LEAVE ANY MINUTE. I RETRIEVE MY KIT FROM THE VENT AND RESET THE SATCHEL CHARGE FOR FIVE MINUTES.
THE VENTILATION SHAFTS ALL LEAD TO THE MAIN HANGAR.
KLAXON. WHAT'S GOING ON?
THERE HE GOES IN AN F-14. THERE'S ONE ARMED AND READY ON THE PLATFORM NEXT DOOR. I DON'T HAVE MUCH CHOICE NOW.

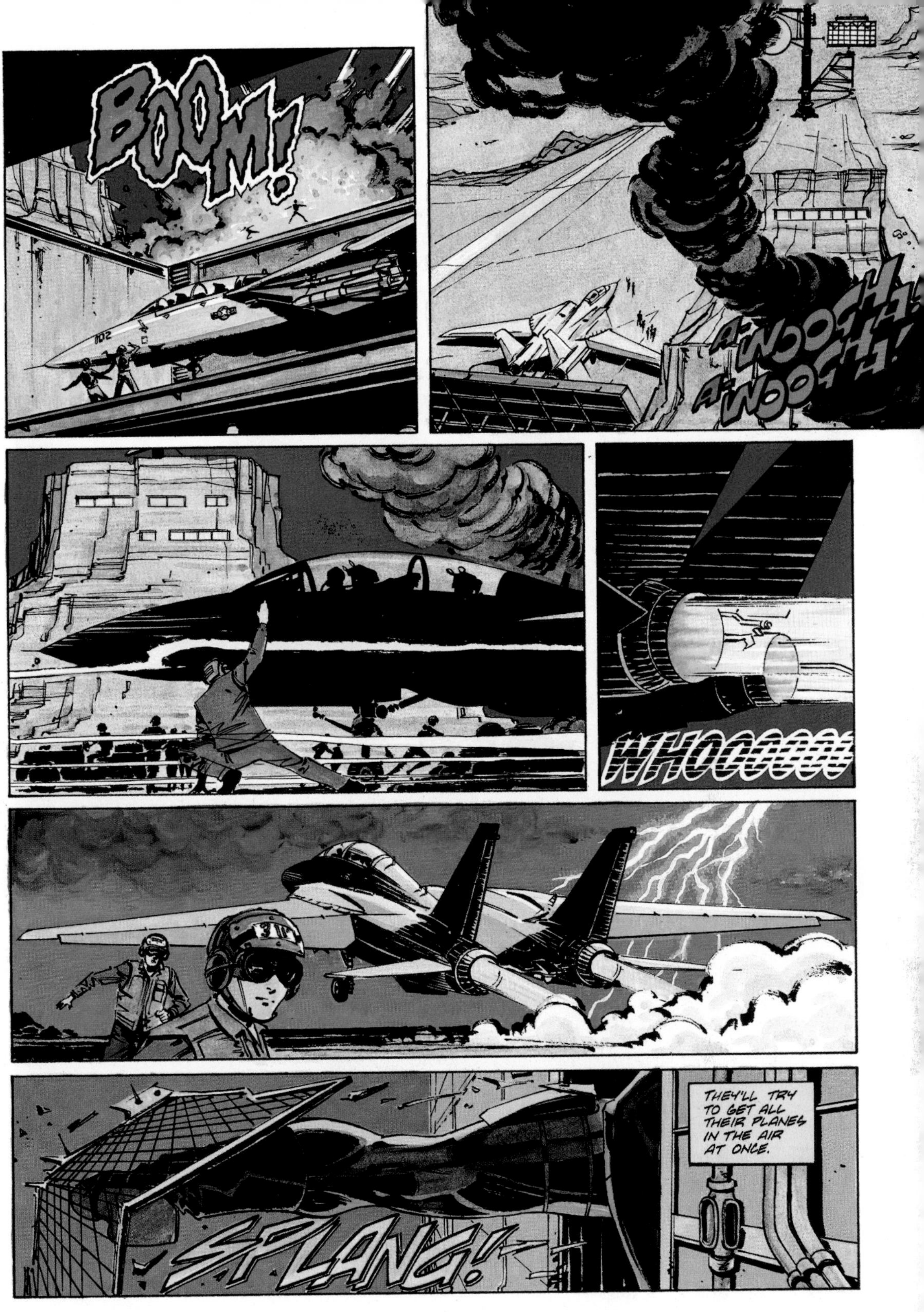
BOOM!
A-WOOSH! A-WOOSH!
WHOOOOOO
THEY'LL TRY TO GET ALL THEIR PLANES IN THE AIR AT ONCE.
SPLANG!

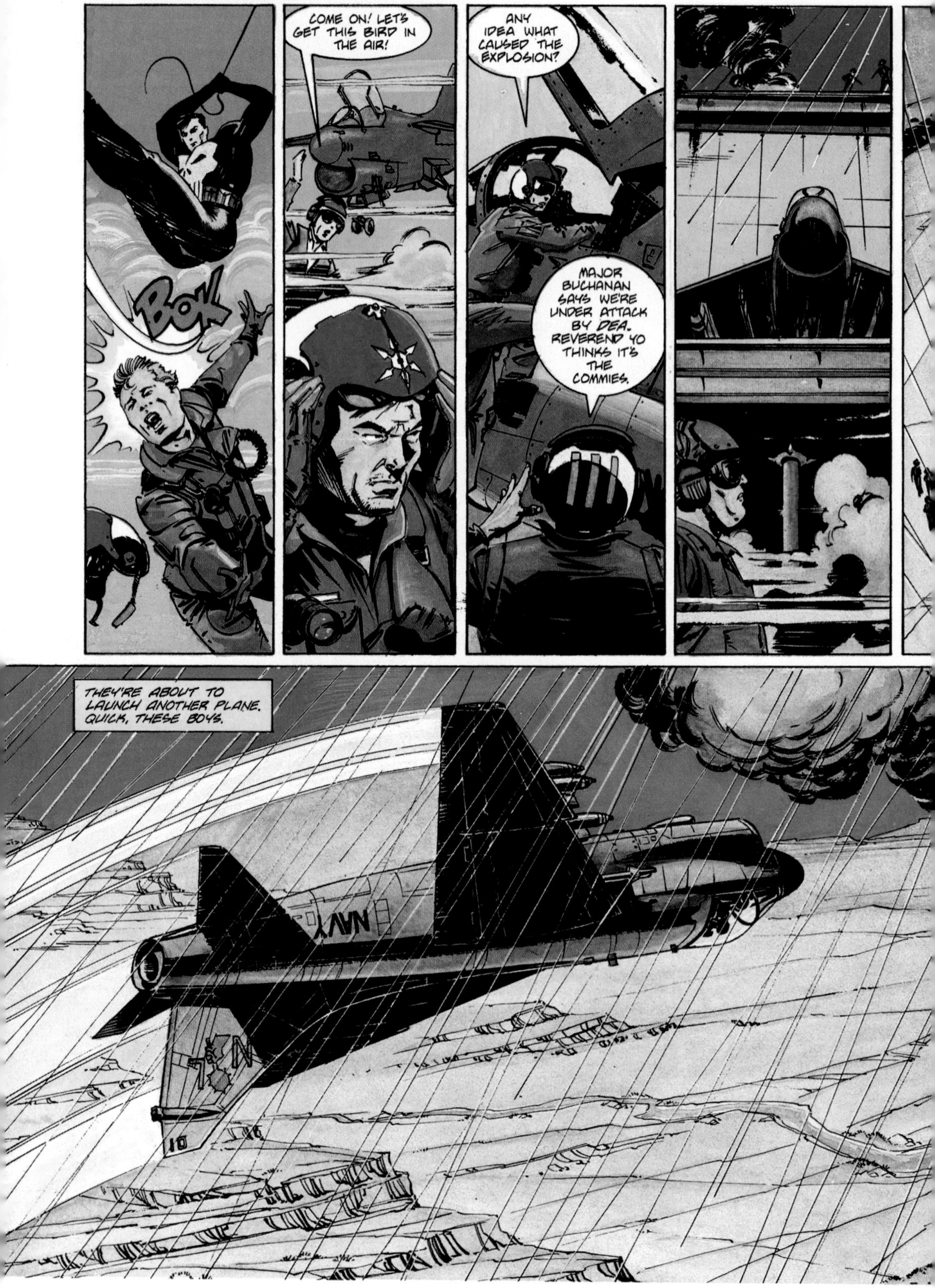
BOK
COME ON! LET'S GET THIS BIRD IN THE AIR!
ANY IDEA WHAT CAUSED THE EXPLOSION?
MAJOR BUCHANAN SAYS WE'RE UNDER ATTACK BY DEA. REVEREND YO THINKS IT'S THE COMMIES.
THEY'RE ABOUT TO LAUNCH ANOTHER PLANE. QUICK, THESE BOYS.
NAVY

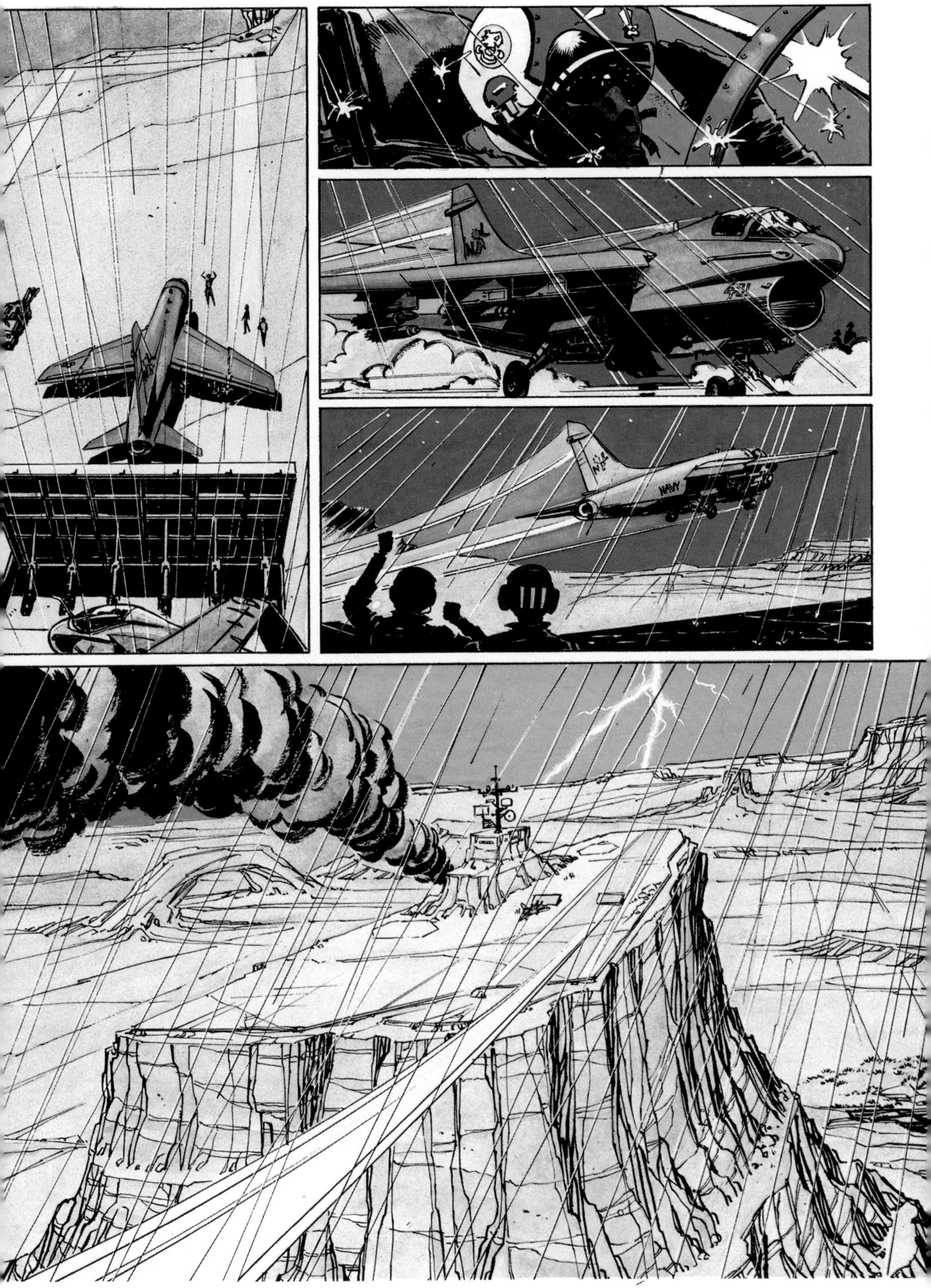
NAVY

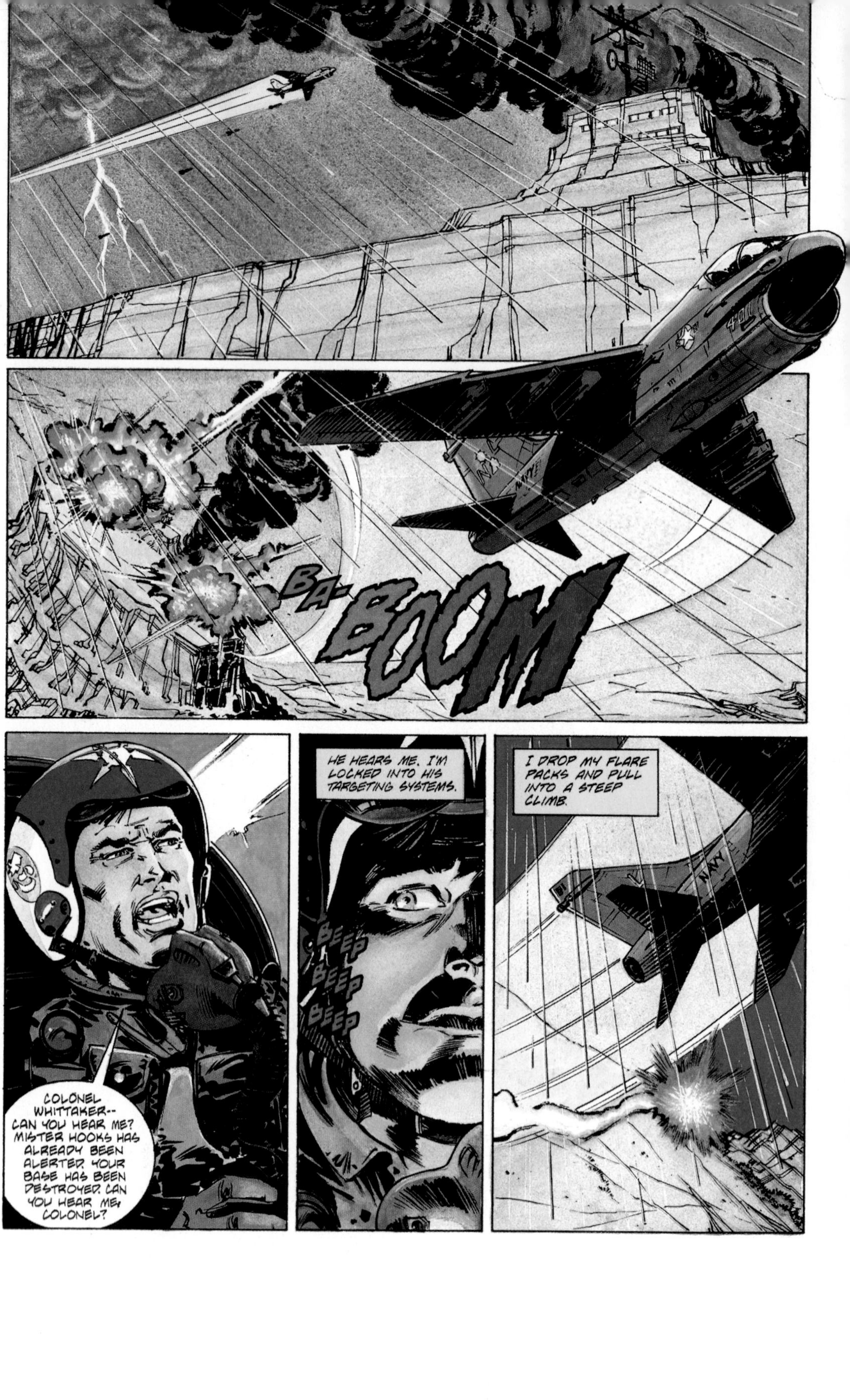
BA-BOOM
COLONEL WHITTAKER-- CAN YOU HEAR ME? MISTER HOOKS HAS ALREADY BEEN ALERTED. YOUR BASE HAS BEEN DESTROYED. CAN YOU HEAR ME, COLONEL?
HE HEARS ME. I'M LOCKED INTO HIS TARGETING SYSTEMS.
BEEP BEEP BEEP
I DROP MY FLARE PACKS AND PULL INTO A STEEP CLIMB.

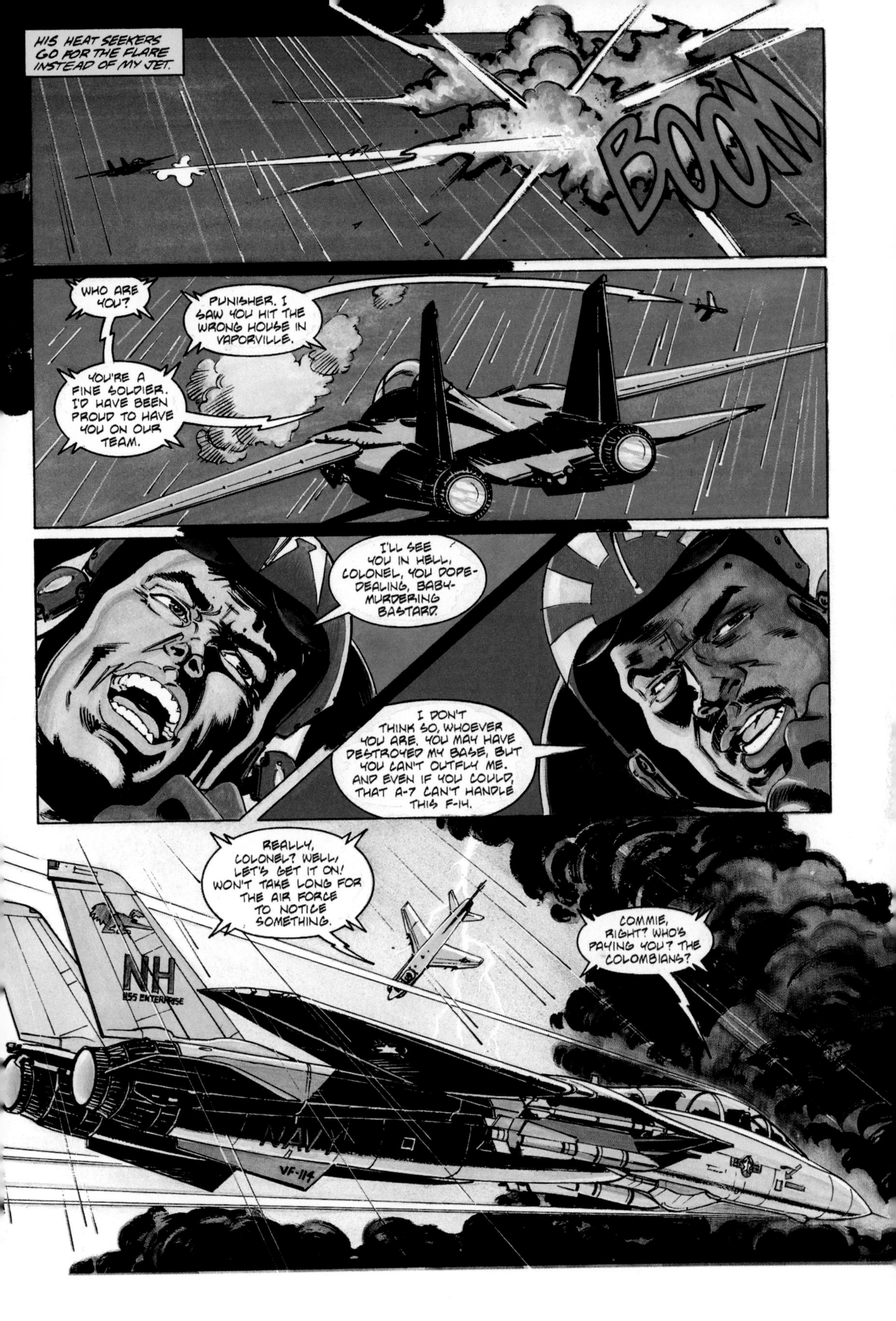
HIS HEAT SEEKERS GO FOR THE FLARE INSTEAD OF MY JET.
BOOM
WHO ARE YOU?
PUNISHER. I SAW YOU HIT THE WRONG HOUSE IN VAPORVILLE.
YOU'RE A FINE SOLDIER. I'D HAVE BEEN PROUD TO HAVE YOU ON OUR TEAM.
I'LL SEE YOU IN HELL, COLONEL, YOU DOPE-DEALING, BABY-MURDERING BASTARD.
I DON'T THINK SO, WHOEVER YOU ARE. YOU MAY HAVE DESTROYED MY BASE, BUT YOU CAN'T OUTFLY ME. AND EVEN IF YOU COULD, THAT A-7 CAN'T HANDLE THIS F-14.
REALLY, COLONEL? WELL, LET'S GET IT ON! WON'T TAKE LONG FOR THE AIR FORCE TO NOTICE SOMETHING.
COMMIE, RIGHT? WHO'S PAYING YOU? THE COLOMBIANS?
NH
USS ENTERPRISE
NAVY
VF-114

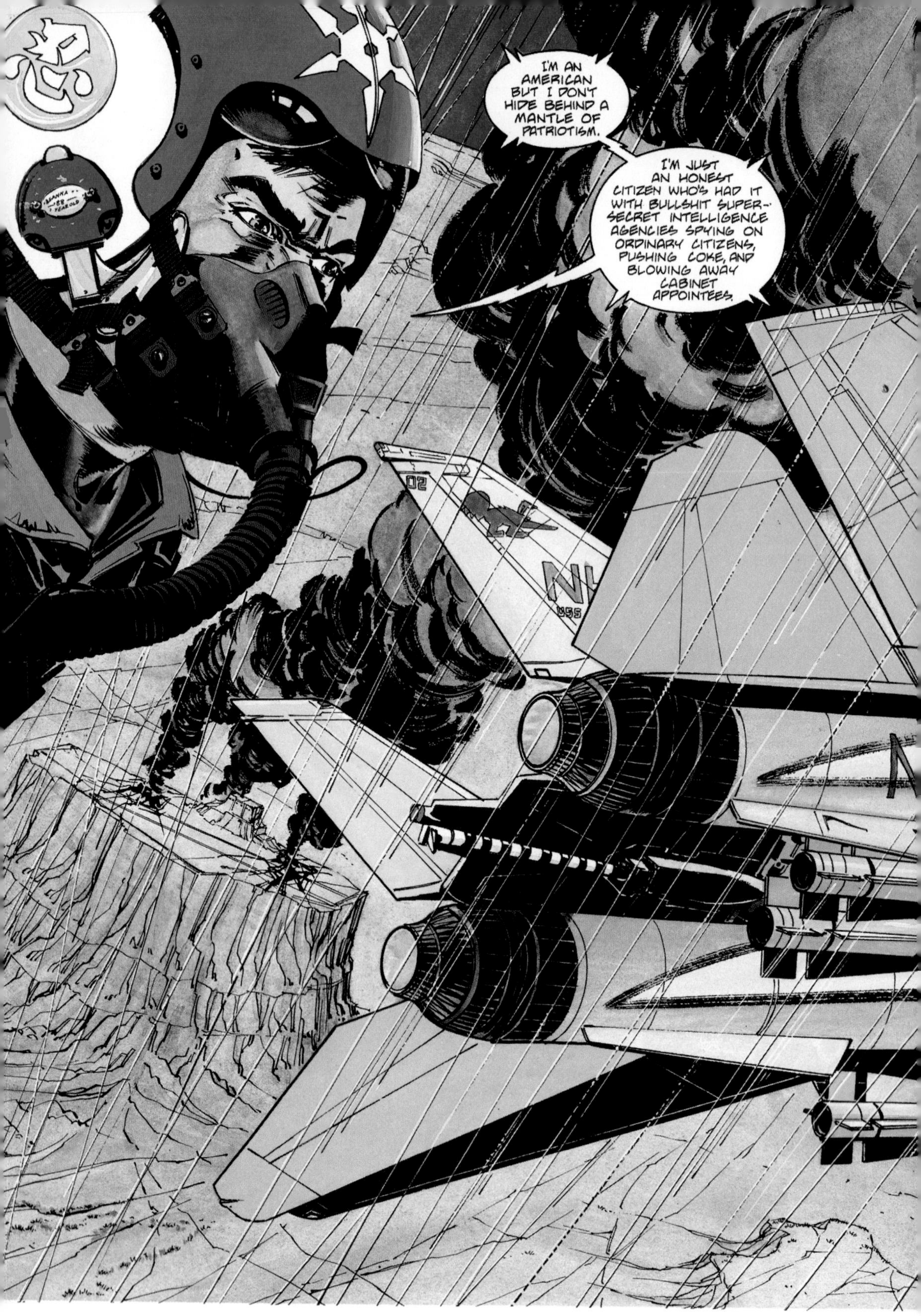
I'M AN AMERICAN BUT I DON'T HIDE BEHIND A MANTLE OF PATRIOTISM.
I'M JUST AN HONEST CITIZEN WHO'S HAD IT WITH BULLSHIT SUPER-SECRET INTELLIGENCE AGENCIES SPYING ON ORDINARY CITIZENS, PUSHING COKE, AND BLOWING AWAY CABINET APPOINTEES.

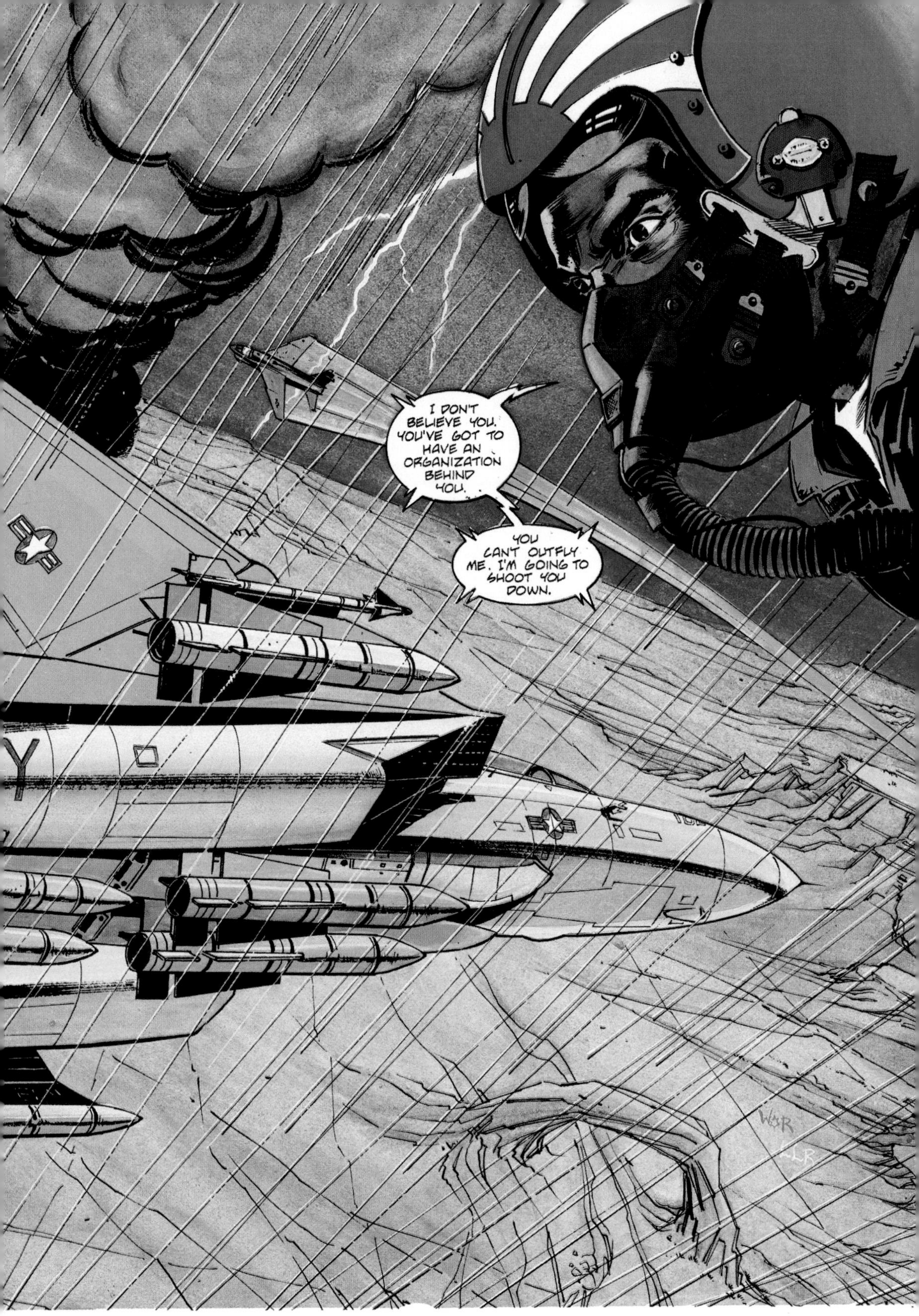
I DON'T BELIEVE YOU. YOU'VE GOT TO HAVE AN ORGANIZATION BEHIND YOU.
YOU CAN'T OUTFLY ME. I'M GOING TO SHOOT YOU DOWN.

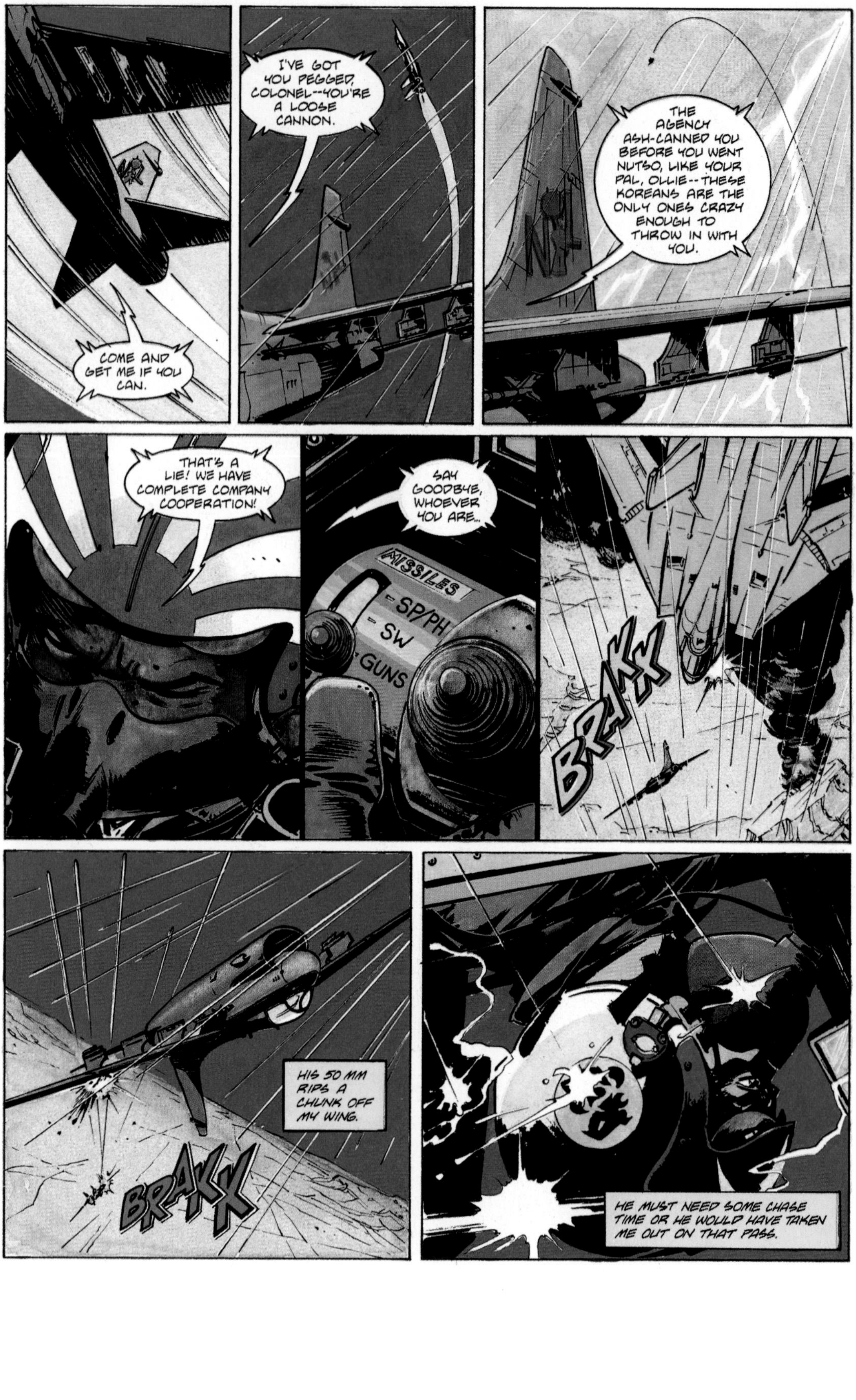
COME AND GET ME IF YOU CAN.
I'VE GOT YOU PEGGED, COLONEL--YOU'RE A LOOSE CANNON.
THE AGENCY ASH-CANNED YOU BEFORE YOU WENT NUTSO, LIKE YOUR PAL, OLLIE--THESE KOREANS ARE THE ONLY ONES CRAZY ENOUGH TO THROW IN WITH YOU.
THAT'S A LIE! WE HAVE COMPLETE COMPANY COOPERATION!
...
SAY GOODBYE, WHOEVER YOU ARE...
MISSILES
SP/PH
SW
GUNS
BRAKK
HIS 50 MM RIPS A CHUNK OFF MY WING.
BRAKK
HE MUST NEED SOME CHASE TIME OR HE WOULD HAVE TAKEN ME OUT ON THAT PASS.

HE LOCKS ME INTO HIS RADAR--THERE'S AN INELUCTABLE STRUCTURE TO HIS TACTICS.

I'VE GOT ONE SIDEWINDER LEFT.

THIS IS IT, MISTER. FIVE SECONDS AND YOU'RE A POWDER BURN.

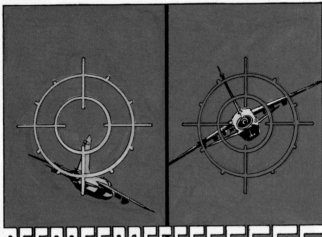

BEEPBEEPBEEEEEEEEEEE

THE COLONEL'S TOO EAGER. I STAND ON THE BRAKES.

WHOOSH

THERE HE GOES.

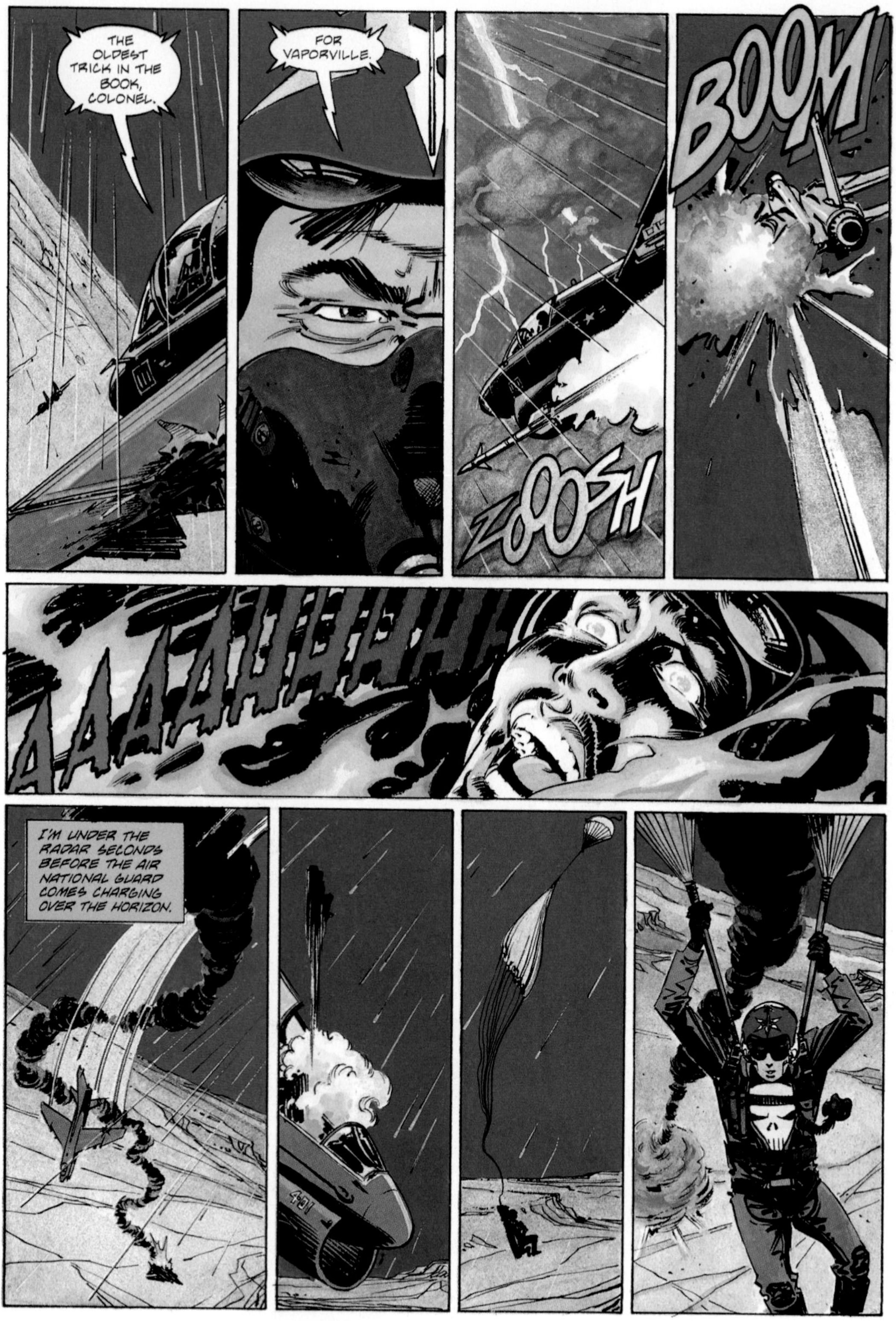
THE OLDEST TRICK IN THE BOOK, COLONEL.
FOR VAPORVILLE.
ZOOOSH
BOOM
AAAAAHHHHH
I'M UNDER THE RADAR SECONDS BEFORE THE AIR NATIONAL GUARD COMES CHARGING OVER THE HORIZON.

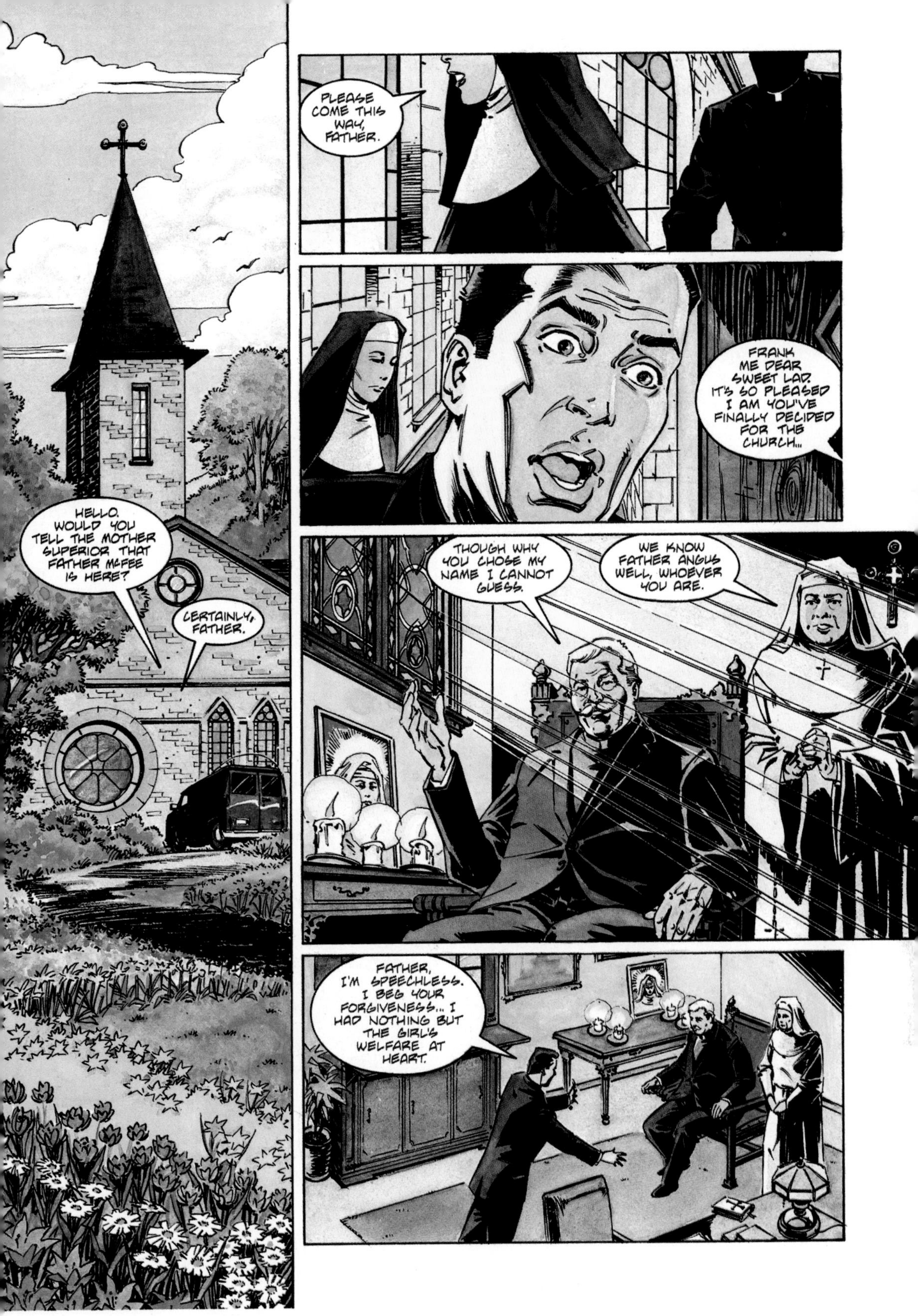
HELLO. WOULD YOU TELL THE MOTHER SUPERIOR THAT FATHER McFEE IS HERE?
CERTAINLY, FATHER.
PLEASE COME THIS WAY, FATHER.
FRANK ME DEAR SWEET LAD. IT'S SO PLEASED I AM YOU'VE FINALLY DECIDED FOR THE CHURCH...
THOUGH WHY YOU CHOSE MY NAME I CANNOT GUESS.
WE KNOW FATHER ANGUS WELL, WHOEVER YOU ARE.
FATHER, I'M SPEECHLESS. I BEG YOUR FORGIVENESS... I HAD NOTHING BUT THE GIRL'S WELFARE AT HEART.

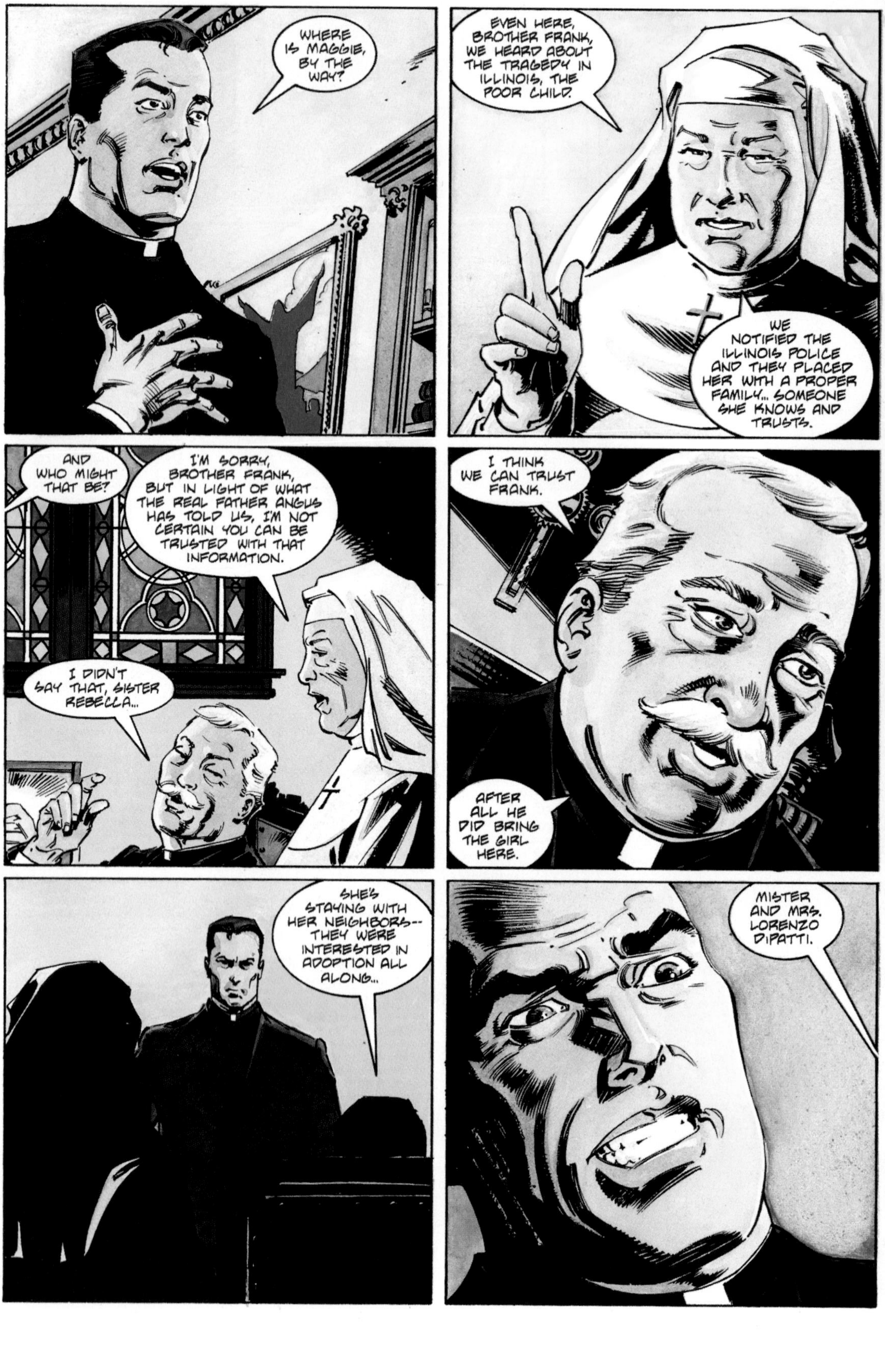
WHERE IS MAGGIE, BY THE WAY?
EVEN HERE, BROTHER FRANK, WE HEARD ABOUT THE TRAGEDY IN ILLINOIS, THE POOR CHILD.
WE NOTIFIED THE ILLINOIS POLICE AND THEY PLACED HER WITH A PROPER FAMILY... SOMEONE SHE KNOWS AND TRUSTS.
AND WHO MIGHT THAT BE?
I'M SORRY, BROTHER FRANK, BUT IN LIGHT OF WHAT THE REAL FATHER ANGUS HAS TOLD US, I'M NOT CERTAIN YOU CAN BE TRUSTED WITH THAT INFORMATION.
I DIDN'T SAY THAT, SISTER REBECCA...
I THINK WE CAN TRUST FRANK.
AFTER ALL HE DID BRING THE GIRL HERE.
SHE'S STAYING WITH HER NEIGHBORS-- THEY WERE INTERESTED IN ADOPTION ALL ALONG...
MISTER AND MRS. LORENZO DIPATTI.

end

mike baron

Mike Baron graduated from the University of Wisconsin with a degree in political science and moved at once to Boston to pursue a career in writing. While working on various Boston weekly newspapers, Baron made regular pilgrimages to comic conventions in New York where he remembers badgering Linda Lessman at a Gorblimey Press exhibit. Baron plowed the flinty fields of journalism from 1971 until 1977, while his interest in comics grew. In 1975, he wrote his first comic, "Tie-Tac," for Warm Neck Funnies.

Returning to hometown Madison, Wisconsin, Baron temporarily gave up on his writing career for another career, with an insurance company. Eventually, he was fired, but by then it was too late—he'd met artist Steve Rude with whom he created Nexus for Capital Comics. Baron also convinced Capital to publish the Badger, a comic about a multiple personality/crime fighter. Jeff Butler helped create the Badger, but when Jeff quit to take a full time job, Bill Reinhold stepped in as the new Badger artist.

In 1987, Marvel editor Carl Potts asked Baron to script the new ongoing Punisher series. Reinhold, a gentle soul with little experience in the real world, was recently persuaded to undertake the task of drawing Baron's punishing tales in exchange for a complete set of the "Freddy the Pig" books. ∎

bill reinhold

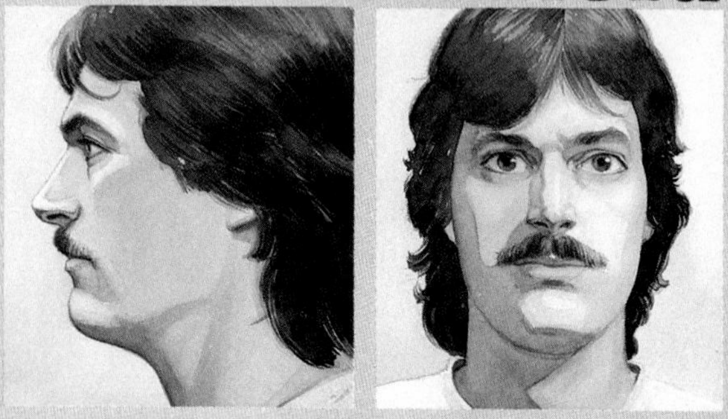

Bill Reinhold was born in Chicago in 1955 and grew up planning to be a rock and roll drummer. Throughout his adolescence he gigged in a succession of garage bands including Hairball, The Grape Stompers, Psychic Debris, Naughty Baby, The Tudpuckers, and Cheese Curd. A tryout with Ultimate Spinach Revival ultimately dashed his hopes and he turned to his second love, drawing.

An inveterate doodler, Bill filled the margins of his high school history texts with endless armies of futuristic warriors clutching rail beams and smart rocks. He attended the American Academy of Art in Chicago, host to many comics professionals.

Bill's first published work appeared in Texas Comics Justice Machine in 1981. Prior to that, Bill had done some work for Charlton. His next job after Justice Machine was penciling Capital's The Badger, which became a First publication before his first published issue. A meticulous craftsman, Bill is fascinated by such minutiae as the number of buttons on the Kingpin's sleeve. Although his mastery of drawing anatomy and lay-out skills frees him from a dependence on reference, he won't draw anything mechanical without a photograph. ∎

linda lessmann

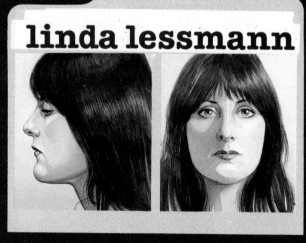

Colorist extraordinaire Linda Lessman broke into comics by accident. She graduated with a bachelor's degree in fine art from Stevens College in Columbia, MO. with advertising on her mind. An early marriage landed Linda in New York where she went to work for Estee Lauder selling make-up. In 1972, with an idea of changing jobs, Linda visited the Marvel offices where she was introduced to various bullpenners. A few weeks later, she received calls from Sol Brodsky, Frank Giacoia, and Morrie Kuramoto all in the same day, asking for her services at Marvel.

"I began free-lancing in production, then working full time. Gradually I phased into coloring under Marie Severin's tutelage. I was on staff for fourteen months." In 1974 she quit Marvel to form Gorblimey Press with Barry Windsor-Smith where she worked for ten years. In 1984, fed up with comics, Linda packed her portfolio looking for a job in advertising. But, in November, she went in for an interview with First Comics art director Alex Wald, and walked out with 28 pages of Bill Reinhold art—to letter. Ironically, she was lettering Baron's deathless prose on an early issue of Badger. Eventually, she made the switch and is currently one of the best full time colorists in the business.

Linda is also a talented sculptress, and the mother of her child, Leanna, who as yet has not exhibited evidence of paranormal powers. Bill Reinhold is the father. ∎

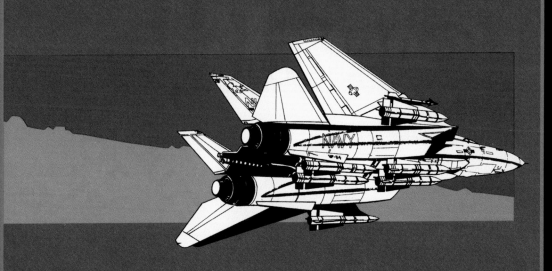

THE PUNISHER—an obsessed killing machine—the personification of revenge. The soul of **FRANK CASTLE** died when he and his family stumbled onto a mob rubout and fell under a rain of lead. **CASTLE**'s body alone survived, possessed by a desire to visit retribution on all those who flout the law and threaten the innocent.

In **INTRUDER**, a secret society with government connections uses murder to further their political ends. The well-equipped assassins begin a chain of events that bring them into hard-hitting conflict with **THE PUNISHER** when they target the wrong house and slaughter an innocent family. The action ranges from brutal hand-to-hand combat to soaring high-tech dogfights as both sides fight to the death.

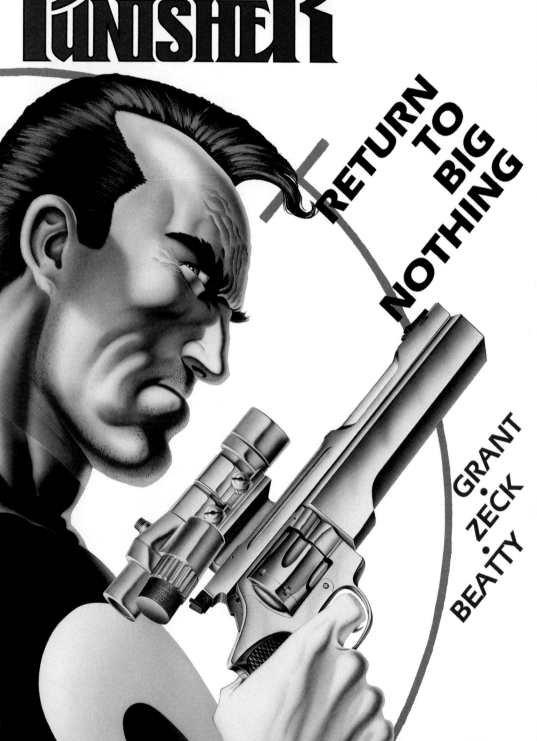

THE PUNISHER

RETURN TO BIG NOTHING

GRANT
·
ZECK
·
BEATTY

EPIC GRAPHIC NOVEL: PUNISHER — RETURN TO BIG NOTHING GN
SOFTCOVER 2ND-PRINTING (1990) COVER ART BY MIKE ZECK & PHIL ZIMELMAN

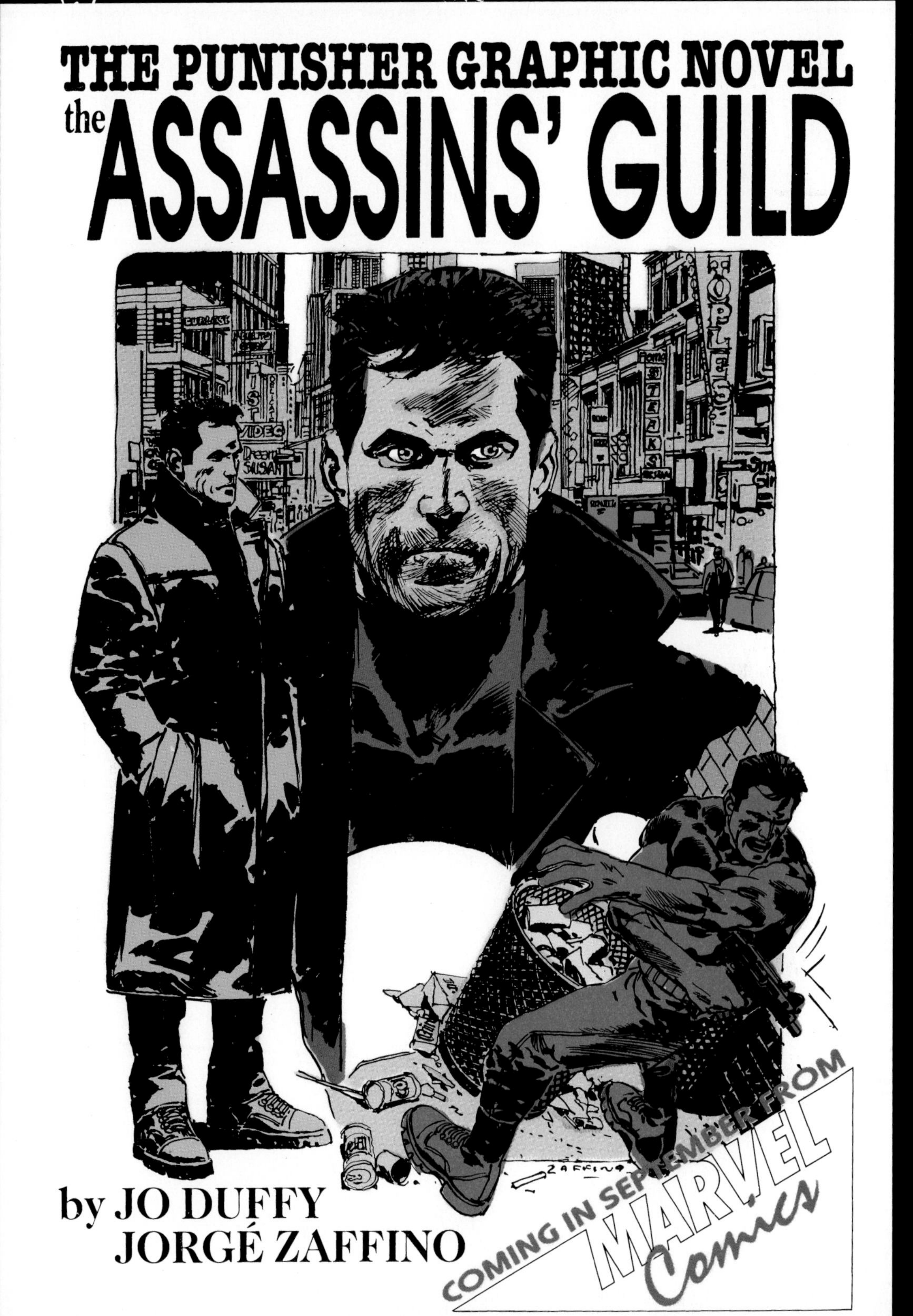

THE PUNISHER GRAPHIC NOVEL
the ASSASSINS' GUILD
by JO DUFFY
JORGÉ ZAFFINO
COMING IN SEPTEMBER FROM
MARVEL Comics
ZAFFINO

SPRING 1988 HOUSE AD BY JORGE ZAFFINO & JULIE MICHEL

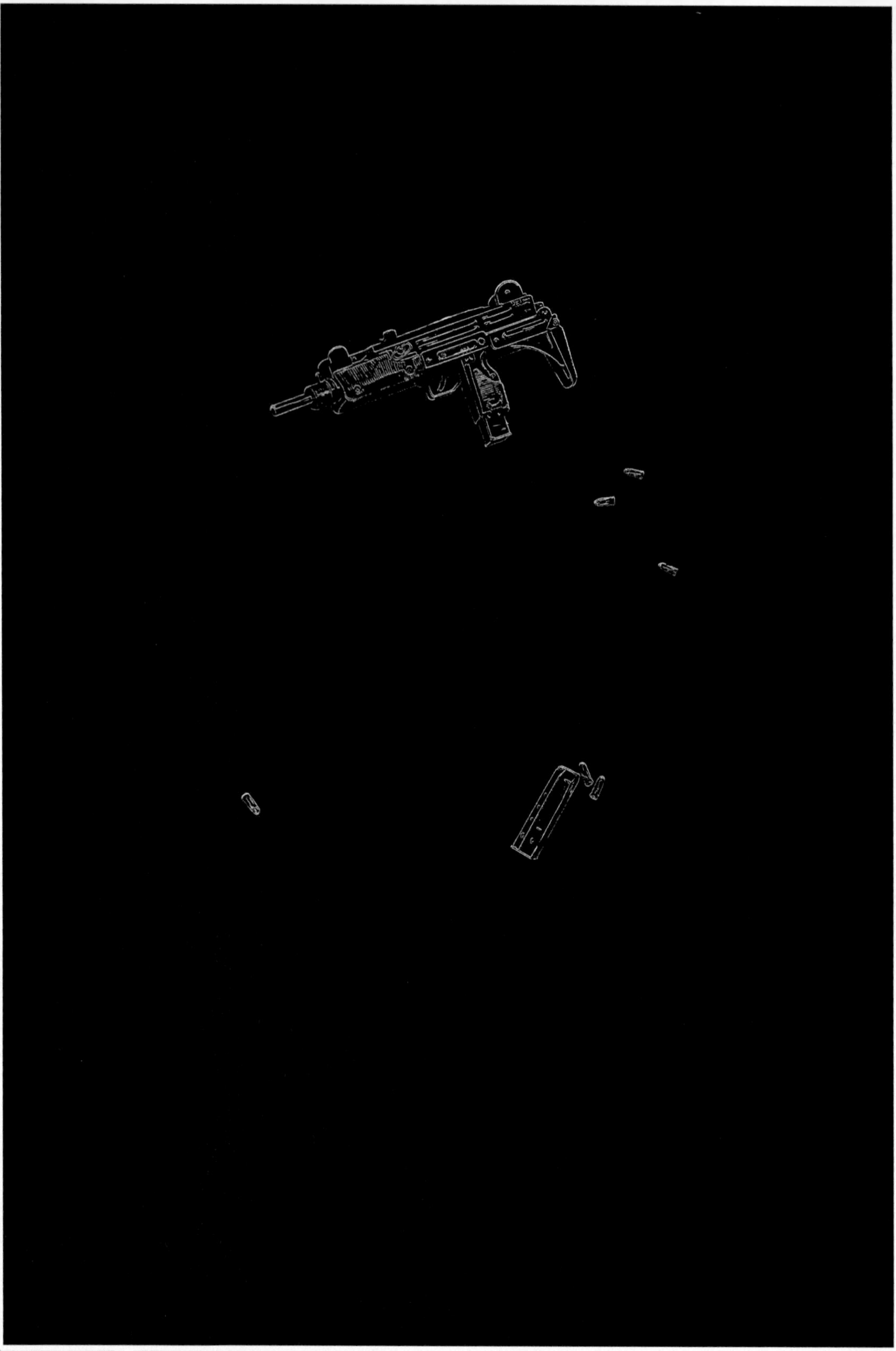

MARVEL GRAPHIC NOVEL: PUNISHER — INTRUDER GN FOIL-STAMPED HARDCOVER CASE ART

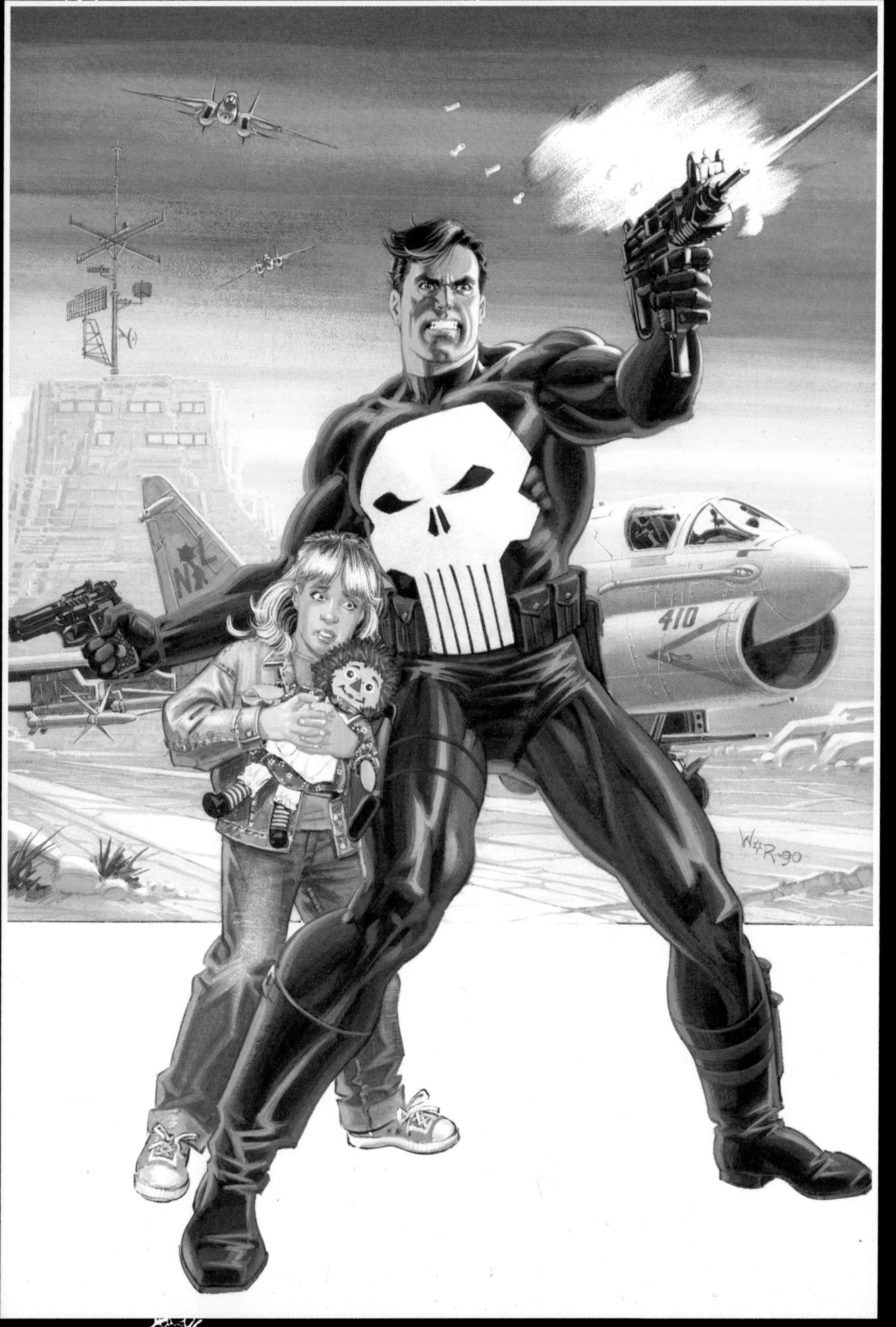
410
W★R-90

MARVEL GRAPHIC NOVEL: PUNISHER — INTRUDER GN
SOFTCOVER 2ND-PRINTING (1991) COVER ART BY **BILL REINHOLD**

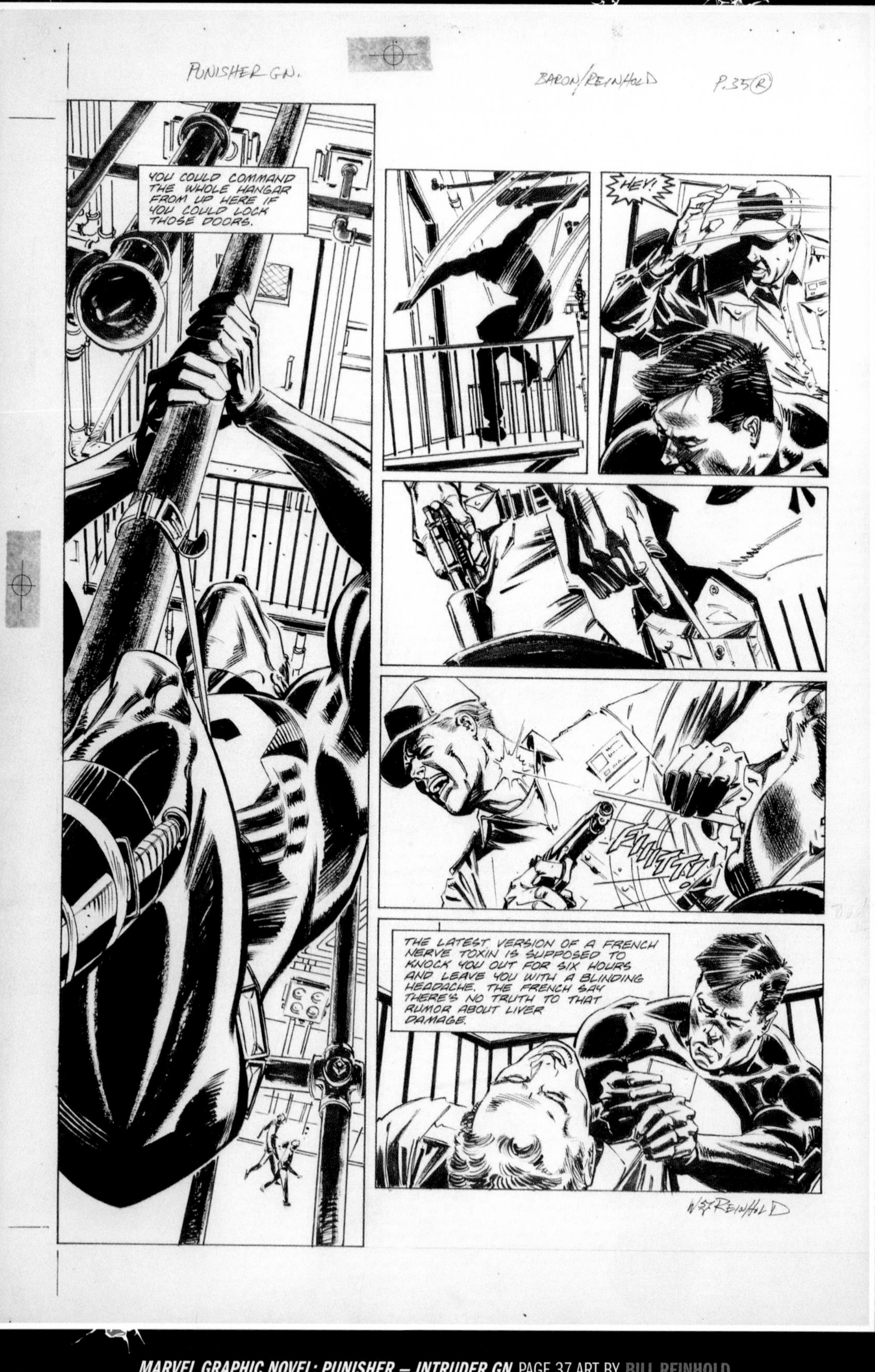
PUNISHER GN.
BARON/REINHOLD
P.35(R)
YOU COULD COMMAND THE WHOLE HANGAR FROM UP HERE IF YOU COULD LOCK THOSE DOORS.
HEY!
THE LATEST VERSION OF A FRENCH NERVE TOXIN IS SUPPOSED TO KNOCK YOU OUT FOR SIX HOURS AND LEAVE YOU WITH A BLINDING HEADACHE. THE FRENCH SAY THERE'S NO TRUTH TO THAT RUMOR ABOUT LIVER DAMAGE.

MARVEL GRAPHIC NOVEL: PUNISHER – INTRUDER GN, PAGE 37 ART BY **BILL REINHOLD**

COURTESY OF HERITAGEAUCTIONS.COM

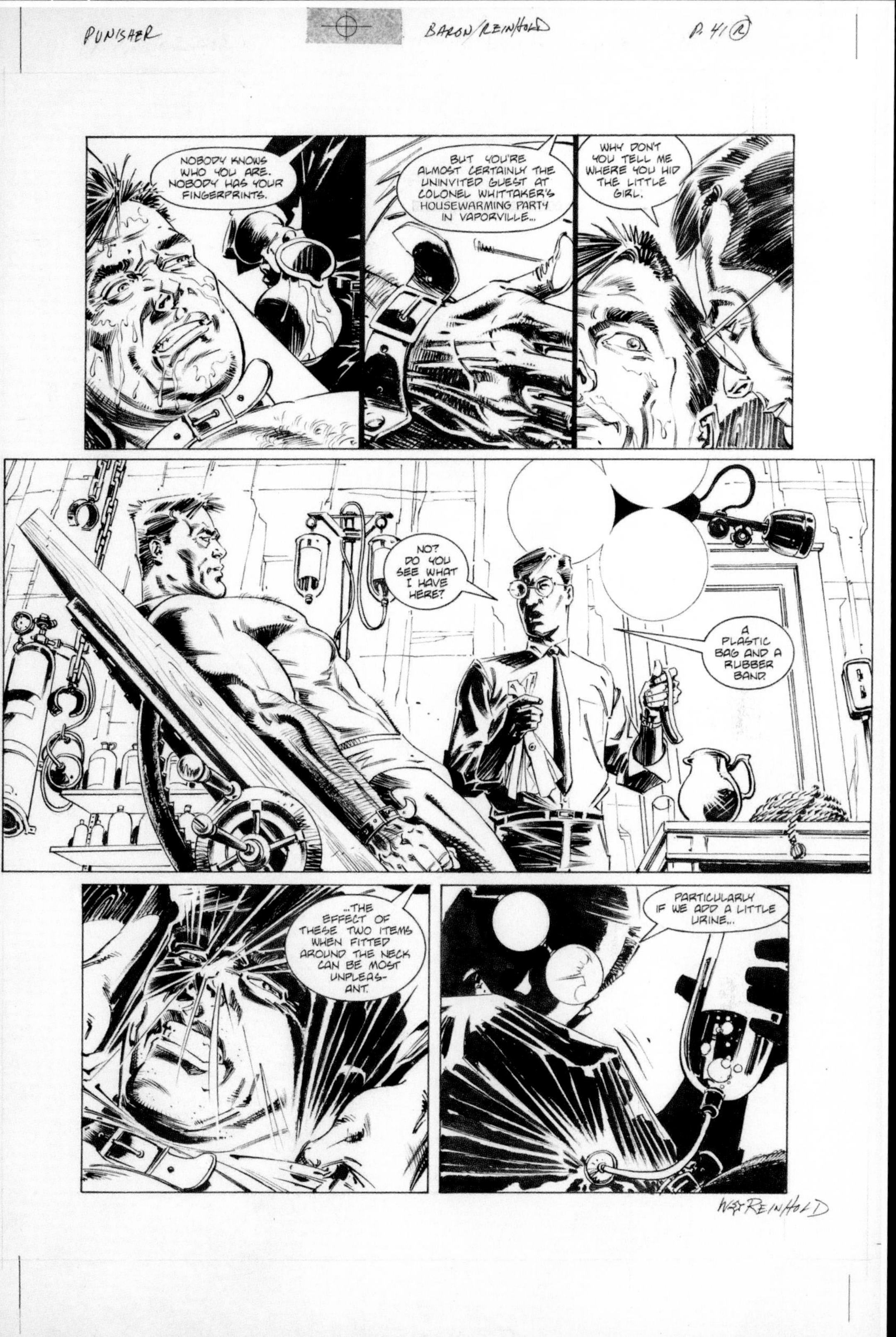
PUNISHER
BARON/REINHOLD
P. 41 R
NOBODY KNOWS WHO YOU ARE. NOBODY HAS YOUR FINGERPRINTS.
BUT YOU'RE ALMOST CERTAINLY THE UNINVITED GUEST AT COLONEL WHITTAKER'S HOUSEWARMING PARTY IN VAPORVILLE...
WHY DON'T YOU TELL ME WHERE YOU HID THE LITTLE GIRL.
NO? DO YOU SEE WHAT I HAVE HERE?
A PLASTIC BAG AND A RUBBER BAND.
...THE EFFECT OF THESE TWO ITEMS WHEN FITTED AROUND THE NECK CAN BE MOST UNPLEAS-ANT.
PARTICULARLY IF WE ADD A LITTLE URINE...
W. REINHOLD

MARVEL GRAPHIC NOVEL: PUNISHER — INTRUDER GN, PAGE 43 ART BY **BILL REINHOLD**

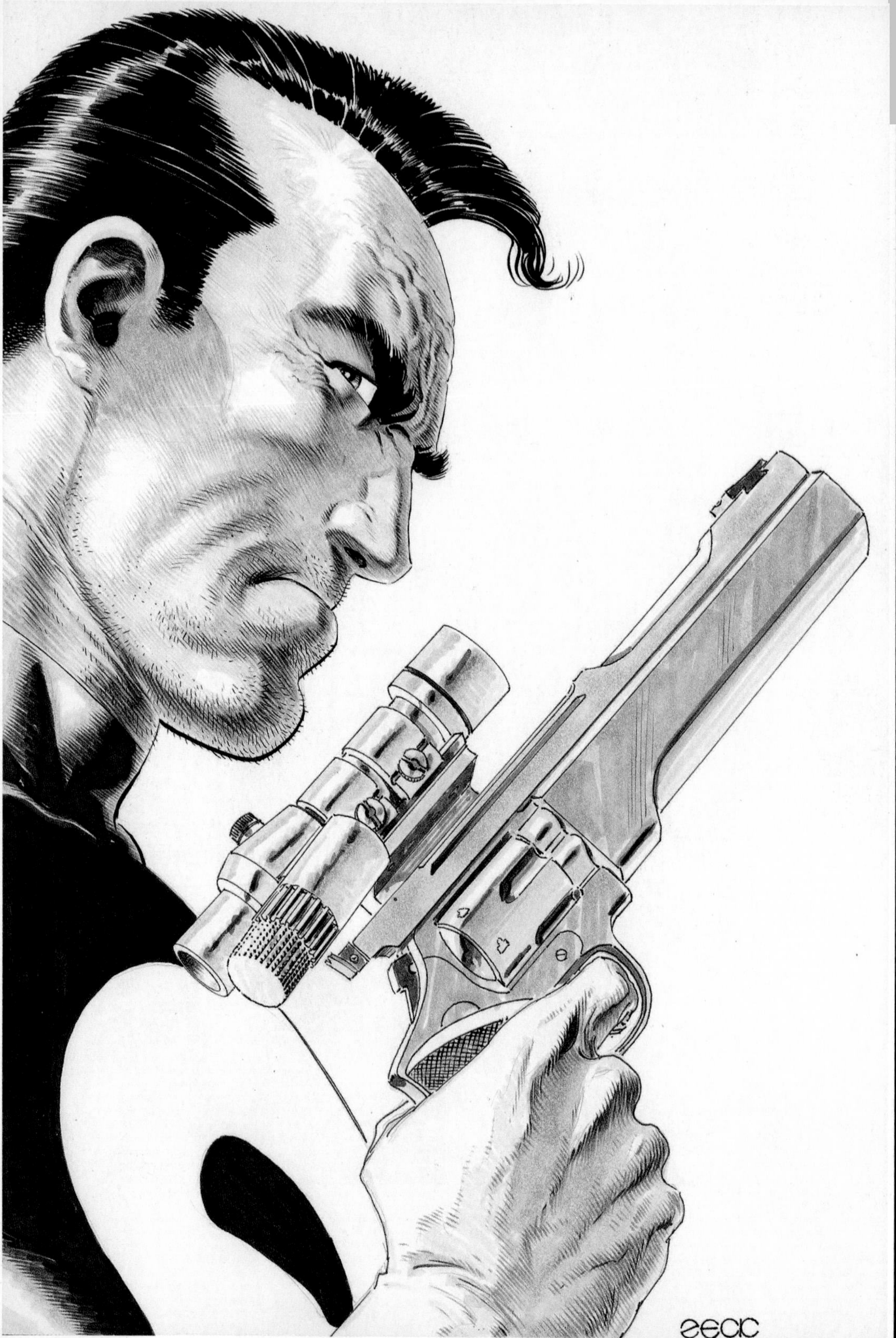